Colección Támesis
SERIE A: MONOGRAFÍAS, 407

FOES TO FRIENDS.
SPAIN, THE UNITED STATES AND THE
UNITED KINGDOM FROM THE CIVIL
WAR TO THE COLD WAR

Tamesis Books

Founding Editors
†J. E. Varey
†Alan Deyermond

General Editor
Stephen M. Hart

Advisory Board
Andrew M. Beresford
Zoltán Biedermann
Celia Cussen
Jo Labanyi
María E. López
Thea Pitman
Julius Ruiz
Alison Sinclair
Jonathan Thacker
Isabel Torres
Noël Valis

MONOGRAFÍAS
ISSN: 0587–9914 (print)
ISSN 2633–7061 (online)

Monografías publishes critical studies covering a wide range of topics in the literature, culture and history of the Iberian Peninsula and Latin America from the Middle Ages to the present day. It aims to promote intellectually stimulating and innovative scholarship that will make a major contribution to the fields of Hispanic and Lusophone studies. Work on un- or under-explored sources and themes or utilising new methodological and theoretical approaches, as well as interdisciplinary studies, are particularly encouraged.

Previously published books in the series may be viewed on our website.

FOES TO FRIENDS.
SPAIN, THE UNITED STATES AND THE UNITED KINGDOM FROM THE CIVIL WAR TO THE COLD WAR

Edited by
Emilio Sáenz-Francés

MONOGRAFÍAS
TAMESIS BOOKS

Originally published as *Franco, Estados Unidos, y Gran Bretaña durante la Primera Guerra Fría: Diplomacia, lobbies, intereses estratégicos y anticomunismo*
by Universidad Pontificia Comillas

© 2022 Emilio Sáenz-Francés, José Antonio Montero Jiménez, Pablo León Aguinaga, Joan Maria Thomàs, Wayne H. Bowen, and Universidad Pontificia Comillas

All Rights Reserved. Except as permitted under current legislation no part of this work may be photocopied, stored in a retrieval system, published, performed in public, adapted, broadcast, transmitted, recorded or reproduced in any form or by any means, without the prior permission of the copyright owner

First published 2025
Tamesis Books, Woodbridge

ISBN 978 1 85566 404 3

Tamesis Books is an imprint of Boydell & Brewer Ltd
PO Box 9, Woodbridge, Suffolk IP12 3DF, UK
and of Boydell & Brewer Inc.
668 Mt. Hope Avenue, Rochester, NY 14620–2731, USA
website: www.boydellandbrewer.com

Our Authorised Representative for product safety in the EU is Easy Access System Europe – Mustamäe tee 50, 10621 Tallinn, Estonia, gpsr.requests@easproject.com

The publisher has no responsibility for the continued existence or accuracy of URLs for external or third-party internet websites referred to in this book, and does not guarantee that any content on such websites is, or will remain, accurate or appropriate

A CIP record for this title is available from the British Library

CONTENTS

List of Illustrations	vi
Contributors	vii
Preface	ix
Introduction: A New (and Significant) Twist in Studies of Francoist Foreign Policy EMILIO SÁENZ-FRANCÉS	1
1 The United States and the Second Spanish Republic (1931–1936). An Overview from a Monetary Policy Perspective JOSÉ ANTONIO MONTERO JIMÉNEZ	6
2 The Chase, the World Commerce Corporation, and the Early Cold War Rehabilitation of Franco's Spain PABLO LEÓN AGUINAGA	38
3 The Struggle to Change U.S. Policy toward Franco's Spain 1948–1950: José Félix de Lequerica, Paid Lobbyists, "Friendly" Senators, the Spanish Lobby and the Spanish Bloc JOAN MARIA THOMÀS	74
4 "In Support of Our Prestige and Our Values": The Spanish Lobby and Local Politics in the United States, 1945–1955 WAYNE H. BOWEN	240
5 Toppling Franco? Great Britain, Spain, and the New World Order 1945–1951 EMILIO SÁENZ-FRANCÉS	265
Index	303

ILLUSTRATIONS

FIGURES

2.1. Alfred Barth greets Francisco Franco in the company of Charles Cain Jr and Winthrop Aldrich (behind the dictator), Madrid, 5 June 1950. Source: Winthrop W. Aldrich Papers, Box 238. Baker Library Special Collections, Harvard Business School, Boston, Massachusetts.   63

3.1 Lunch offered at the U.S. Senate in honor of the Spanish Ambassador, José Félix de Lequerica, and his wife. Attended by U.S. Secretary of State Dean Acheson and Senator Chávez, 19 January 1951. Source: Archivo ABC. Madrid.   79

3.2 Tribute from the Chamber of Commerce, Industry, and Navigation to the Spanish Ambassador in Washington, José Félix de Lequerica, 14 January 1954. Source: Archivo ABC. Madrid.   100

TABLES

1. American banks participating in the August 1939 EIB loan to Spain   44

2. Status of credits made available to Spain under the General Appropriations Act of 1951   67

The editor, contributors and publisher are grateful to all the institutions and persons listed for permission to reproduce the materials in which they hold copyright. Every effort has been made to trace the copyright holders; apologies are offered for any omission, and the publisher will be pleased to add any necessary acknowledgement in subsequent editions.

CONTRIBUTORS

Emilio Sáenz-Francés is Professor of History and International Relations at the Comillas Pontifical University in Madrid, where he has been head of the Department of International Relations (2016–2025). Additionally, he directs the Winston Churchill Observatory at the same university, which focuses on analyzing the relations between Spain and the United Kingdom. He has twice been a Visiting Fellow at Churchill College, University of Cambridge. He has also served as a visiting researcher at the Centre for the Study of the Two World Wars at the University of Edinburgh. He has published articles and specialized chapters in both Spanish and international journals and books, primarily centered on Spanish foreign policy during the Second World War, with a particular emphasis on Spanish–British relations. He collaborates with various media outlets and has a regular segment on history on Cadena Cope Radio. He published his third book, *Loyola de Palacio. Por España y por Europa* in 2017, and his earlier works include *¿Micronesia Españoña?* (2015) and *Entre la Antorcha y la Esvástica* (2009).

Pablo León Aguinaga is Tenured Researcher at the Department of International & Global History at the Instituto de Historia of the Spanish Council for Scientific Research (CSIC). His research has covered several aspects of the history of the United States in the world after 1939, including propaganda and public diplomacy, military assistance, economic diplomacy, and financial agents. His work has been published in journals such as *Cold War History*, *International History Review*, and *Ayer*. He co-published *Los Estados Unidos y el mundo: la metamorfosis del poder americano* (1890–1952) with his colleague José A. Montero (2019). His next book, *Philip W. Bonsal, Diario de un diplomático americano en España, 1944-1947. Estados Unidos ante la dictadura franquista* is forthcoming.

Wayne H. Bowen is Professor of History, Director of Interdisciplinary Studies, and Associate Dean for the College of Undergraduate Studies at the University of Central Florida. He received a B.A. in History from the University of Southern California, a M.A. and Ph.D. in European History from Northwestern University, and an M.A. in Strategic Studies from the U.S. Army War College. He is a specialist on modern Spain, focused on the era of the Franco dictatorship. Bowen is the author of nine books, six of them on Spanish history, from the early modern era to the Cold War. He has also published more than two dozen articles in academic journals, with subjects including the Middle East, the Mediterranean, and Great Power relations since 1800. His articles have been published in ten countries and translated into Spanish, Polish, French, and Turkish. Bowen is currently finishing a contracted book on Spanish workers in Nazi Germany and conducting research for a subsequent monograph on relations between the Spanish and Ottoman empires from the seventeenth to the twentieth centuries. Bowen is also a retired colonel in the U.S. Army Reserve, with service as a soldier in Iraq and with NATO in Bosnia-Herzegovina. He lives in Oviedo, Florida, named after the original Spanish city.

José Antonio Montero is Associate Professor of Contemporary History at Complutense University of Madrid. He holds a Ph.D. from the same university and was Prince of Asturias Distinguished Visiting Scholar at Georgetown University between 2007 and 2009. He is a specialist in the history of U.S. foreign policy, with a focus on the first half of the twentieth century, and has worked extensively on relations between Spain and the United States from multiple perspectives – political, economic, cultural, and intellectual – and on U.S. public diplomacy in Mexico in the early Cold War. He is currently working on Spanish–American financial relations between 1930 and 1960, while writing a book on U.S. policies towards the Second Spanish Republic (1930–1936). In 2019, he co-published *Los Estados Unidos y El mundo: La Metamorfosis del Poder Americano (1890–1952)* with his colleague Pablo León. They are working on a subsequent volume, which will take in the international history of the United States to the present day.

Joan Maria Thomàs is Professor of Contemporary History at the Rovira i Virgili University, Tarragona. He is the sole author of twelve books, three of which have been translated into English. His scholarly work focuses on Spanish fascism, the Franco regime, the United States's relations with Spain during the Second World War, and the struggle for strategic materials during the same conflict, and he has authored biographies of significant figures such as José Antonio Primo de Rivera, the founder of Spain's main fascist movement; Minister Ramón Serrano Suñer; and fascist leaders like José María Fontana. Thomàs has been honored with the City of Barcelona History Award, the Serra d'Or Critics Award, the ICREA Academia Prize, and the Narcís Monturiol Medal for scientific and technological merit by the Government of Catalonia. He is a Corresponding Academic of the Royal Academy of History and has served as a researcher, lecturer, or professor at universities in the United States, Australia, New Zealand, the People's Republic of China, India, the United Kingdom, the Federal Republic of Germany, the Dominican Republic, and Israel.

PREFACE

The book is the culmination of a research project funded by the Ministry of Science, Innovation, and Universities of Spain entitled "American and British Pro-Francoism during the Early Cold War: Actors, Agendas, Influence Strategies, and Spanish Interlocutors (1945–1960)." The research for this book was undertaken between 2018 and 2021, and it was previously published in Spain in 2022. It is for the reader to decide whether the book's distinctive approach to the survival of the Franco regime during the first years of the Cold War is a convincing one.

While I have had the privilege of preparing the English edition of this book with the assistance of the excellent team at Tamesis led by Megan Millan, the ultimate credit for this work goes to Joan María Thomàs. He was the principal investigator of the research team that came together in 2017, and he was fundamental to the ultimate success of this project. Thomàs is an internationally renowned authority on Francoism, particularly in its early years, and his inspiration, support, and encouragement were instrumental in overcoming the challenges posed by COVID-19. I have had the good fortune of knowing Joan María for over ten years, having invited him to a seminar that I organized in Madrid in 2010 on Francoist foreign policy during the Second World War. His work had previously shaped key aspects of my doctoral research, but this seminar marked the beginning of an enduring friendship, accompanied in my case by deep admiration. We have since worked together on various projects, including the volume that he co-edited with Raanan Rein, *Spain 1936: Year Zero* (2019). The present book is certainly the most significant collaborative venture, but fortunately it will not be the last one.

These are dark times where polemic and fury have all too often replaced dispassionate debate. Sadly, the historical profession is not immune. While the authors of this volume did not always agree, our work together under the leadership of Joan María was characterized by a common desire to further our knowledge of a critical period in international relations. As Marc Bloch has written:

> Un mot, pour tout dire, domine et illumine nos études: «comprendre».
> Ne disons pas que le bon historien est étranger aux passions; il a du
> moins celle là. Mot, ne nous le dissimulons pas, lourd de difficultés;
> mais aussi d'espoirs. Mot surtout chargé d'amitié.

In this spirit, I wish to extend my gratitude to Joan María, to the rest of the contributors, and to our good friend and colleague at the University of Edinburgh, Julius Ruiz, whose advice has been crucial in preparing the English edition of this book.

Emilio Sáenz-Francés

Introduction:
A New (and Significant) Twist in Studies of Francoist Foreign Policy

EMILIO SÁENZ-FRANCÉS

Francisco Franco's authoritarian regime continues to be the main focus of Spanish historians and foreign Hispanists. The Spanish Civil War of 1936–1939 and subsequent dictatorship, which only came to end with the Caudillo's death in 1975, is rightly seen now as an anomaly in the history of twentieth-century Spain. The military uprising of July 1936 initiated a long parenthesis in Spanish political development that was characterized by liberal monarchy and a democratic republic, before the fratricidal conflict, and a parliamentary monarchy, following the transition to democracy and the promulgation of the 1978 Constitution.

Yet it is also true that Francoism is inseparable from the broader history of Spain and the international context in which the dictatorship emerged. The enormous and ever-growing historiography on the Spanish Civil War shows that it maintains an extraordinary presence in the imaginations of Spaniards and foreigners alike. While some prominent historians – Stanley Payne, Paul Preston, Edward Malefakis, Santos Juliá, and Hugh Thomas – have written about the war and the long dictatorship in general, others – for example, Joan María Thomàs, Enrique Moradiellos, Julius Ruiz, Fernando del Rey, Manuel Álvarez Tardío, and Mercedes Peñalba – have penned empirically based monographs on specific aspects of the sad story of the collapse of Spanish democracy in the 1930s. Unsurprisingly, there is no historiographical consensus on the subject, and these debates have resonated far beyond the ivory towers of academia as the meaning and legacy of the war remain high on the contemporary Spanish political agenda. Certainly, the recent, controversial Law of Democratic Memory has kept these difficult years firmly in the public eye.

The same holds true for Francoist policy during the Second World War. Much has been written about the dictator's public allegiance to Hitler and Mussolini, his fascist patrons who contributed so much to the defeat of the Republic. The fact that Franco's ideological sympathies towards the Axis did not preclude a pragmatic – if reluctant – accommodation with the Western Allies, when the latter turned the military tide from 1942 to 1943, has only increased public fascination within Spain, a fact evident with every anniversary related to the 1939–1945 war. In many respects, 1945 marks a caesura in the history of Francoism. That year brought an end to radical dreams of prominence within a new totalitarian European order. The defeat of fascism meant Francoist international isolation and an expectation among many observers – not least among vanquished Republicans – that the victors of the Spanish Civil War would soon be consigned to the dustbin of history. This book begins at this dangerous moment for the regime, focusing on Spain's complex relationships with the two powers whom many assumed held the fate of Franco in their hands: the United States and Britain.

The following pages analyze an extraordinary change in the fortunes of the regime between 1945 and 1953. These pages chart how an international pariah came back in from the cold, considering how a repressive dictatorship was able to become an ally of the leader of the "Free World": the United States. There are many fine studies on how Franco was transformed into the sentinel of the anti-communist West during the early years of the Cold War. Most are only available in Spanish, such as Florentino Portero's *Franco aislado: la cuestión española, 1945–1950* (1989) and the most recent monograph by Xavier Hualde, *El «cerco» aliado. Estados Unidos, Gran Bretaña y Francia frente a la Dictadura Franquista (1945–1953)* (2016). This book builds on the insights provided by these Spanish scholars and provides a detailed analysis of the factors that ultimately enabled the regime to survive until Franco's death in 1975. Such an outcome was not preordained. Immediately following the defeat of the Axis powers in 1945, the Western Allies explored alternatives to Franco. Yet the Caudillo was able to navigate the choppy international waters with considerable skill, although he was fortunate that the growing threat of the Soviet Union made this veteran anti-communist appear to be more a prophet than a has-been fascist. With Britain and the United States increasingly willing to play down – if not wholly forget – Franco's past sins, authoritarian Spain would be offered some of the fruits of the Pax Americana.

But while the contributors to this volume do not deny the significance of political and diplomatic factors, they go beyond familiar Cold War narratives. In this new interpretation of what Portero called the "Spanish Question," the following themes emerge:

- **The fundamental importance of preexisting economic and financial relationships**. The first two chapters of this volume, by José Antonio Montero Jiménez and Pablo León Aguinaga, stress the significant conti-nuities in economic relations between the United States and Spain that went back to at least the 1920s and the Primo de Rivera dictatorship. These contacts – as much between private companies and individuals as governments – would endure despite the radically changing political contexts of the 1930s and underpin the emerging political and diplomatic rapprochement of the late 1940s.

INTRODUCTION

- **The limited capacity of Francoist activities within the United States to change policy**. In his exhaustive examination of the so-called "Spanish Lobby," Joan María Thomàs challenges the traditional emphasis on the Spanish embassy in Washington and its enigmatic ambassador, José Félix de Lequerica, when considering the shift in U.S. policy. The significance of their lobbying in altering American perceptions of the regime, he argues, has been exaggerated and suggests that pro-Francoist Americans acted in a less cohesive manner than the concept of "Lobby" suggests.
- **The geographical breadth of the Francoist charm offensive in the United States**. Spanish activities in Washington and New York – the traditional centers of political power – may not have been as effective as some historians have suggested but, in his chapter, Wayne H. Bowen demonstrates that Francoist consular efforts in California to stress the common Hispanic heritage between local Catholics and Spain did much to weaken public hostility to the Franco regime in that increasingly significant state, anticipating a change in attitudes at the national level.
- **The subordination to the United States of British policy towards Spain**. In the final chapter, I discuss how the post-war British Labour government struggled to come to terms with their much-diminished status in international affairs after 1945. Although Spain had traditionally been within the British sphere of interest, the failure of Ernest Bevin, the foreign secretary, to articulate a distinctive socialist policy on Francoist Spain reflected the dominance of the United States within the so-called "Special Relationship."

In sum, these chapters provide English-language readers with access both to the ground-breaking work being carried out by Spanish historians on this crucial period in their country's history and new perspectives on changing U.S. attitudes towards Franco by a leading American scholar in this field.

***

The first chapter of this book, titled "The United States and the Second Spanish Republic (1931–1936): An Overview from a Monetary Policy Perspective," by José Antonio Montero Jiménez, delves into the aforementioned antecedents during the Primo de Rivera dictatorship and, more importantly, during the era of the Second Republic. This chapter focuses particularly on Spain's pursuit of private and public loans in the United States. Montero's exploration has allowed him to establish notable and unusual continuities at different levels and practices, even within Spanish political and bureaucratic circles. Simultaneously, Montero challenges interpretations that have overly biased the relations between the United States and Republican Spain towards an ideological, particularly anti-communist, perspective.

Following on, the second chapter, "The Chase, the World Commerce Corporation, and the Early Cold War Rehabilitation of Franco's Spain," by Pablo León Aguinaga, addresses the pivotal role played by certain American financial and business sectors in the bilateral rapprochement between the United States and Spain. León Aguinaga's research focuses on institutions such as the Chase National Bank and entities like the World Commerce Corporation, analyzing the trajectory and actions of two key executives, Alfred W. Barth and Frank T. Ryan, respectively. These influential figures utilized contacts, networks, and financial mechanisms established during the Second World War in neutral Spain, where they played essential roles in designing and executing the operations of the U.S. Commercial Corporation and the Office of Strategic Services. The two corporations they represented would become privileged partners of the Franco regime, proving essential in contributing to the "normalization" of financial relations between the two countries. This process included, no less, the Dollar–Peseta Program, in effect from 1952 to 1959.

Undoubtedly, the central and most extensive chapter of the book is Joan María Thomàs's "The Struggle to Change U.S. Policy toward Franco's Spain 1948–1950: José Félix de Lequerica, Paid Lobbyists, 'Friendly' Senators, the Spanish Lobby and the Spanish Bloc." As mentioned earlier, Thomàs delves into a topic extensively covered by the historiography: diplomatic relations between Spain and the United States – and between the United States and Spain – during the period 1945–1953. Until now, with few exceptions, a genuinely talismanic concept has not been questioned – the so-called "Spanish Lobby." This concept emerged in American historiography, generating development and controversy in the United States, but not in Spain.

Thomàs differentiates between the lobbyists actually hired by Lequerica (who effectively managed the embassy in Washington in early 1949): lawyer Charles P. Clark, Father Joseph F. Thorning, and the Cummings, Stanley, Truitt & Cross law firm. In doing so, he challenges both the existence of an organized and hierarchical lobby and its presumed control, whether direct or indirect, by the embassy.

Thomàs has also identified pro-Franco congressmen who did not always act in concert with the embassy but often pursued their own interests and those of the states the politicians represented. On a third level, he distinguishes the realm of Congress from what he terms the "Spanish Bloc" – the diverse group of actively pro-Franco individuals who, since the Civil War and especially during the early Cold War, had been working to increase favorable opinions of Spain in the United States. His conclusion is that the change in U.S. policy towards the Francoist regime was not so much a result of Lequerica's actions – something he tended to attribute to himself during that period and for a long time afterward – but rather a change in U.S. policy adopted in 1950 following the outbreak of the Korean War.

INTRODUCTION

On the other hand, Wayne H. Bowen addresses an aspect, as previously indicated, that has been largely unexplored. In the chapter titled "'In Support of Our Prestige and Our Values': The Spanish Lobby and Local Politics in the United States, 1945–1955," he examines the actions of Francoist consular authorities in San Francisco and Los Angeles. The local–regional sphere is often overlooked in studies focused on foreign policy and bilateral relations, yet is crucial for a country as complex as the United States.

Bowen departs from the dominant spatial focus in historiography, which is often based on the Washington D.C.–New York axis, and reveals different local impulses, as well as their management by Francoist authorities. The consulate in San Francisco had to operate in an anti-Franco environment, in contrast to Los Angeles, where Spanish representatives could focus their efforts on cultural, religious, and historical initiatives tied to Hispanic heritage, working closely with the hierarchy, clergy, universities, and sectors of the Catholic population, with considerable success. This melting pot of influences leads Bowen to conclude that the American West perhaps preceded the East in the "normalization" of Spain in the United States.

As the author of the concluding chapter, "Toppling Franco? Great Britain, Spain, and the New World Order 1945–1951," I delve into the transformative impact of the Labour party's ascent to Downing Street in 1945 and the policies pursued by Prime Minister Clement Attlee and Foreign Office Secretary Ernest Bevin. In the ensuing years, Britain faced a dual dynamic: one driven by ideological hostility towards Franco and his regime, theoretically prompting unwavering support for regime change in Spain, and the other structural, reflecting the inherent nature of British foreign policy, which aimed to maintain a preeminent and autonomous global position befitting a major power destined to act as a moderating and guiding force in shaping the fledgling worldview of the United States.

The intricate nature of British–Spanish relations allows for an assessment of the challenging adjustments that the realities of the Cold War and the swift consolidation of American foreign action posed for the leaders of the Foreign Office. The conclusion drawn is that London's initial hostility towards Francoism after Attlee came to power (aligned with Labour's ideological foundations) and later acceptance of a shift in these relations were both primarily motivated by an inevitable alignment with the rhythms dictated from Washington rather than the British government's own political impulses.

1

The United States and the Second Spanish Republic (1931–1936). An Overview from a Monetary Policy Perspective

JOSÉ ANTONIO MONTERO JIMÉNEZ

Introduction

Existing studies of U.S.–Spanish relations in the years of the Second Spanish Republic (1931–1936) have been unduly influenced by two later events: the Cold War and the Spanish Civil War. The prevailing narrative is that the eyes of administration officials in Washington were tainted by an excessive zeal, leading them to see Communist agents where there were only leftist reformists. In turn, these suspicions paved the way for the policy of neutrality, parallel to European non-intervention, which the United States practised after 1936.[1] This interpretation is, to a degree, a somewhat ahistorical outlook, because both American and Spanish decision-makers were totally ignorant of events that lay only in the future. In fact, it is impossible to separate the Spanish policy of the Great Powers from the situation then existing in Europe. As Scott Ramsay has recently stated with respect to the United Kingdom:

> By considering Foreign Office perceptions of political developments in Spain between 1931 and 1936, British responses to the outbreak of the civil war came into focus not as an ideologically-driven attempt to facilitate the overthrow of the Republic, but as responses to what the British government perceived as a major threat to its foreign policy objectives.[2]

---

[1] D. J. Little, *Malevolent Neutrality: the United States, Great Britain, and the Origins of the Spanish Civil War*, Ithaca, Cornell University Press, 1985; A. Bosch, *Miedo a la democracia. Estados Unidos ante la Segunda República y la guerra civil española*, Barcelona, Crítica, 2012; Á. Viñas: *La soledad de la República*, Barcelona, Crítica, 2006, 18.

[2] S. Ramsay, "Ideological Foundations of British Non-Intervention in the Spanish Civil War: Foreign Office Perceptions of Political Polarisation in Spain, 1931–1936," *Diplomacy & Statecraft*, vol. 31 (2012), 44–64. Citation on p. 58.

There is ample evidence to say something of the same kind about the United States. The uncertainties that arose in official U.S. circles when the new regime was proclaimed in April 1931 soon vanished. On 18 April, Ambassador Irwin Laughlin marveled at the apparent absence of disturbances, which "speaks well not only for the Government which from the outset has appeared to have absolute control of the situation, but for the Spanish people in general."[3] When the first burning of churches took place in May, he attributed it to "irresponsible agents provocateurs" who had "inflamed the extremist elements of disorder," and not to the government.[4] Two years later, on the occasion of the formation of the third Azaña cabinet, the *chargé d'affaires*, Hugh Millard, praised both President Niceto Alcalá-Zamora's efforts "to consolidate the Republic," by supporting the reforms enacted in the so-called First Biennium, and Azaña's skill as head of the government, "who continues to be by far the outstanding figure in Spain."[5] With the arrival in Madrid, as U.S. ambassador, of journalist and historian Claude G. Bowers, the Republic gained a sympathetic foreign representative, who became a prominent admirer of Azaña and his reforms.[6] There is, thus, not so solid a foundation for blaming U.S. neutrality on so much mutual antipathy between Madrid and Washington as on American domestic affairs, which turned any direct support for the loyalist side in the Civil War into a kind of political suicide for President Franklin Roosevelt.[7] It was the *neutrality* policy enacted by Congress that determined the U.S. diplomatic stance towards wartime Spain.

When analyzing the policies of the Great Powers in general, and the United States in particular, towards the Second Spanish Republic, it is essential to look beyond the Iberian Peninsula. The troublesome trade relations between the United States and Spain – on the verge of being broken off several times

[3] Dispatch 339, Laughlin to Stimson, 18 April 1931, National Archives and Records Administration (NARA), Record Group (RG) 59, 1930–1939, 852.00/1834.

[4] Telegram 39, Laughlin to Stimson, 12 May 1931, NARA, RG 59, 1930–1939, 852.00/1839.

[5] Dispatch 34, Millard to Hull, 21 June 1933, NARA, RG 59, 1930–1939, 852.001-ZAMORA/19.

[6] C. G. Bowers, *My Mission to Spain. Watching the Rehearsal for World War II*, New York, Simon and Schuster, 1954; D. J. Little, "Claude Bowers and His Mission to Spain: The Diplomacy of a Jeffersonian Democrat," in K. P. Jones (ed.), *U.S. Diplomats in Europe, 1919–1941*, Santa Barbara, ABC-Clio, 1981, 129–46; A. Bosch, "Entre México y la Unión Soviética: La visión estadounidense sobre los conflictos sociales en la Segunda República Española (1931–1936)," *Historia Contemporánea*, vol. 15 (1996), 315–42.

[7] See R. Dallek, *Franklin D. Roosevelt and American Foreign Policy, 1932–1945*, New York, Oxford University Press, 1995, 127–8; D. Tierney, *FDR and the Spanish Civil War. Neutrality and Commitment in the Struggle That Divided America*, Durham, Duke University Press, 2007, 28–9. This idea was initially advanced by R. P. Traina, *American Diplomacy and the Spanish Civil War*, Bloomington, Indiana University Press, 1968, 227.

between 1930 and 1936 – as well the difficulties faced by some American investors who saw their profits blocked or their operations threatened – for instance, the International Telephone and Telegraph Corporation (IT&T), owner of the Spanish Telephone Company (CTNE)[8] at the time – were neither exceptional nor new situations in the European context. Trade tensions were not unique to U.S.–Spanish relations, nor the long talks necessary to negotiate an agreement under the aegis of the U.S. Reciprocal Trade Agreements Act (RTAA). The few treaties concluded with European countries before the Second World War – with Belgium, Sweden, the Netherlands, Switzerland, France, Finland, Czechoslovakia, and the United Kingdom – were not, for the most part, ready until 1936.[9] From a business perspective, while U.S. investments in Europe as a whole went down from $1,353 million to $1,245 million between 1929 and 1936, they grew in Spain from $72.23 million to $80.53 million.[10] In November 1932, when the dispute over CTNE had just subsided, the American commercial attaché fueled the impression that "conditions [in Spain] are relatively not so bad as in the majority of countries and – barring the unpredictable course of social legislation – that a rather firm basis exists on which to build future improvement when world conditions are more favorable."[11] The obstacles Madrid raised to prevent foreign firms from sending profits back to their mother countries were softer than those existing, say, in Nazi Germany.[12] In July 1935, Horace Merle Cochran, an American diplomat stationed in Paris, who would rise to serve as technical assistant to the secretary of the treasury, visited Spain on the orders of Henry Morgenthau Jr., concluding that politically and economically Spain could be considered a stable country.[13] This is but one instance of American tendencies to contrast Spanish affairs with the general European context.[14]

---

[8] D. J. Little, "Twenty Years of Turmoil: ITT, the State Department and Spain, 1924–1944," *Business History Review,* vol. 53, n. 4 (1979), 449–72. A. Martínez Ovejero, "Azaña versus Telefónica, los límites del poder," *Espacio, Tiempo y Forma. Serie V,* 16 (2004), 121–48.

[9] H. J. Tasca, *The Reciprocal Trade Policy of the United States*, Philadelphia, University of Pennsylvania Press, 1938, 312–13.

[10] A. Álvaro Moya, "Inversión directa extranjera y formación de capacidades organizativas locales: un análisis del impacto de Estados Unidos en la empresa española (1918–1975)," Ph.D. dissertation, Universidad Complutense de Madrid, 2011, 423–41.

[11] Charles A. Livengood, "Economic Conditions in Spain – October 1932," 8 November 1932, NARA, RG 151, entry 14, box 449, folder "November 1932."

[12] M. Wilkins, *The Maturing of Multinational Enterprise: American Business Abroad from 1914 to 1970*, Cambridge, Harvard University Press, 1974, 186.

[13] Tel. 596, from Strauss to Hull, 17 July 1935, NARA, RG 59, 1930–1939, 852.5151/131.

[14] Two examples in J. R. Jones, jr., *Tariff Retaliation: Repercussions of the Hawley–Smoot Tariff*, Philadelphia, University of Pennsylvania Press, 1934, 34–67. H. J. Tasca, *The Reciprocal Trade....*

We cannot study the interactions between the most important nations of the international system and Republican Spain as if they were marked *a priori* by internal strife and the subsequent dictatorship. Otherwise, we would risk losing sight of several important continuities between the republican period on one side, and the regimes that preceded and followed it, on the other. Confrontations with foreign investors were not rare in an atmosphere impregnated with a growing economic nationalism, to which Primo de Rivera, the Republic, and the Francoist dictatorship adhered. The final nationalization of CTNE did not take place under the Republic, but under early Francoism, and it was the authoritarianism of Primo de Rivera that had propelled the expropriation of assets of foreign oil companies. The authors of a pioneering history of Spanish trade policy were right when pointing out in 1979 that republican governments ended up being more orthodox and timid in their economic actions than their counterparts in France or Germany.[15] The persistence of economic policies was accompanied by a continuity of persons and institutions occupying key positions in U.S.–Spanish relations: National City Bank or IT&T had consolidated their assets in the country during the 1920s and remained important actors all through the 1940s. Some personalities filled important positions in Spain both in Republican and Francoist institutions. Such were the cases of Blas Huete, head of the Centro Oficial de Contratación de Moneda (Official Center for Monetary Transactions or COCM) and its Francoist equivalent Instituto Español de Moneda Extranjera (Spanish Institute of Foreign Currencies), or Pedro Pan Gómez, second vice-governor of the Bank of Spain between 1931 and 1936 and one of the managers of the same corporation in rebel territory between 1936 and 1938.[16] On the U.S. side, historian and economist Herbert Feis was the State Department's economic advisor under F. D. Roosevelt from 1933 until the end of the Second World War, while the ambassador who put his signature to the 1953 agreements between the United States and Spain, James C. Dunn, was in the months preceding the Civil War chief of the State Department's Division of Western European Affairs (DWEA), charged with conducting Spanish–American relations.

A reconsideration of U.S.–Spanish relations might also help us look with new eyes at the foreign policies of the Second Republic. Most experts have up to now focused excessively on political and strategic affairs, sometimes with the Civil War looming over their heads. In 1935–1936, Spanish diplomacy was indeed seriously concerned with the delicate balance of power in Europe – and it unsuccessfully sought a guarantee of its neutrality in case of a continental

---

[15] Á. Viñas, J. Viñuela, F. Eguidazu, C. Fernández Pulgar and S. Florensa, *Política Comercial Exterior en España, 1931–1975*, Madrid, Banco Exterior de España, 1979, 90–1.

[16] T. Tortella Casares, "Pedro Pan Gómez," in *Diccionario Biográfico Español*, Real Academia de la Historia, http://dbe.rah.es/biografias/21992/pedro-pan-gomez, accessed 19 August 2020.

conflict – not with reinforcing itself in the face of domestic strife.[17] Salvador de Madariaga's hint that the visit of French Prime Minister Édouard Herriot to Azaña in 1932 was a lost opportunity represents another instance of backward-looking wisdom, which ignores the conditions then prevailing.[18] As historian Santos Juliá pointed out more than ten years ago: the "fatalism [of the Civil War] was a prominent example of the hermetic principle *post hoc ergo ante hoc*, by which the consequence becomes the cause of the cause itself."[19] Though some dared to predict war, Spanish governments never acted as if it was either unavoidable or foreseeable. Spain's room for maneuver was strictly reduced amid the whirlwind that had hovered over Europe from the very same moment the Republic was proclaimed, which coincided with the Mukden incident in Manchuria. But this did not mean that the new regime remained inactive in other areas, such as the economy. As with most of its European counterparts, Spain's trade and finances depended on foreign sources and, given the situation that arose in 1929, it did not spare any efforts to preserve its monetary and commercial structures. Economic diplomacy consequently helps us assess the degree of either continuity or novelty, as well as the professionalism, of Republican foreign policy, and in this area interactions with the United States were as important as those with France or the United Kingdom.

This chapter aims to study Spanish–American relations between 1930 and 1936 from the point of view of monetary policy, a focus of international activity during the Great Depression. We intend to measure the intensity and tone of those interactions, paying special attention to the general attitudes of American decision-makers. We likewise try to determine the degree to which American policies with respect to Spain reflected U.S. general objectives for Western Europe. In this way, we assess whether Spain played a role in some of the timid internationalist endeavors that germinated in the Roosevelt administration, still deeply divided over the course that dealings with the Old

---

[17] On the foreign policy of the Second Spanish Republic, see M. Á. Egido León, *La concepción de la política exterior española durante la Segunda República*, Madrid, UNED, 1987; "La dimensión internacional de la Segunda República: un proyecto en el crisol," in J. Tusell, J. Avilés and R. Pardo (eds.), *La política exterior de España en el Siglo XX*, Madrid, Biblioteca Nueva, 2000, 189–220; "La proyección exterior de España en los años treinta," in M. Á. Egido León (ed.), *La Segunda República y su proyección internacional*, Madrid, Catarata, 2017, 9–28.; J. F. Berdah, *La democracia asesinada. La República Española y las grandes potencias, 1931–1939*, Barcelona, Crítica, 2002, 5–11; Denéchère, *La politique espagnole de la France. De 1931 à 1936*, Paris, L'Harmattan, 1999, 43–4; F. Quintana Navarro, *España en Europa, 1931–1936. Del compromiso por la paz a la huida de la Guerra*, Madrid, Nerea, 1993; J. L. Neila Hernández, *La 2ª República y el Mediterráneo*, Madrid, Dilema, 2006.

[18] S. de Madariaga, *Memorias (1921–1936). Amanecer sin mediodía*, Madrid, Espasa-Calpe, 1981, 373.

[19] S. Juliá, *Elogio de Historia en tiempo de memoria*, Madrid, Marcial Pons, 2011, 110.

THE UNITED STATES AND THE SECOND SPANISH REPUBLIC (1931–1936)   11

Continent should take. Finally, we attempt to explore if – and how – American interactions with 1930s Spain influenced the way U.S.–Spanish relations were managed in the early years of the Francoist regime.

From the Fall of Primo de Rivera's Dictatorship to the Proclamation of the Second Spanish Republic. The Morgan credit (1930–1931)

The monetary system inherited by the Second Spanish Republic was defined by the downward spiral of the peseta. The abrupt cessation of the extraordinary benefits Spain had reaped during the First World War had given way, once more, to permanent deficits in the balance of payments. Official figures show that the balance of trade went from a surplus of 239 million pesetas in 1919 to a record loss of 1,643 million pesetas in 1922. By the late 1920s, deficits ranged between 822 million pesetas in 1928 and 624 million pesetas in 1929. A highly protectionist tariff and a series of reciprocity agreements corrected the negative trade balances with France and the United Kingdom, but not with Spain's most important supplier: the United States. Trade deficits with America amounted to around 300 million pesetas in 1927 and 1928, falling to 178 million in 1929.[20] The substantial remittances from Spanish migrants to the Western Hemisphere did not make up the gap, so Spain was condemned to permanent indebtedness.

The influx of foreign capital depended as much on the evolution of domestic political affairs as on the international situation, both marked, in the early 1930s, by permanent instability. It seriously affected the value of the peseta, which fell from 22.40 pesetas/£ and 5.06 pesetas/$ in 1919 to 33.66 pesetas/£ and 6.97 pesetas/$ in 1925.[21] Primo de Rivera's success against the Moroccan rebels and the apparent stability that followed the reinvigoration of the gold standard in the second half of the 1920s put the peseta back on track in 1927, when it reached 28.51 pesetas/£ and 5.86 pesetas/$. Spanish Finance Minister José Calvo Sotelo was so elated that he dared predict that the peseta would enter the same standard. But he soon saw his hopes dashed. Between 1927 and 1929, the peseta/£ rate dropped again from 28.51 to 33.17, and the peseta/$ rate from 5.82 to 6.82. Calvo had hastened in 1928 to contact J. P. Morgan & Co., which on 6 August 1928 formed a syndicate of banks to grant Spain a revolving credit of $20 million, with an interest rate of 1 percent over the rate of discount of the Federal Reserve. The loan, which was renewed for another year, opened the first chapter in the interdepartmental divisions that would become typical in the following decade.[22] The Treasury Department supported

---

[20] Data gathered from different editions of the *Anuario Estadístico de España*.

[21] P. Martín Aceña and M. Á. Pons, "Sistema monetario y financiero," in A. Carreras and X. Tafunell (eds.), *Estadísticas Históricas de España*, Bilbao, Fundación BBVA, 2005, 705.

[22] Tel. 75, Hammond to Kellogg, 7 August 1928; and Letter, from Leffingwell to Castle, 29 July 1929, NARA, RG 59, 1910–1929, 852.51 BANK OF SPAIN/1 and 7.

the operation, while the State Department unsuccessfully attempted to make it conditional to concessions on the part of Spain.[23] The country's liquidity relied on the substantial gold reserves in the Bank of Spain, which between 1920 and 1936 permanently ranked fourth in the world, just behind those of the United States, France, and the United Kingdom. In late 1935, after the ups and downs of the post-Depression era, Spain held $737.7 million in gold for $10,125.2 million in the United States, $4,395.4 million in France and $1,648.4 million in the United Kingdom.[24] But for the Spanish authorities that gold was more a symbol of prestige than an asset to be mobilized to stabilize the peseta. Instead of using it, in December 1929 Calvo Sotelo issued 305 million pesetas in treasury bonds at a rate of 6 percent, of which the international market absorbed about 40 million. In June 1928, the minister had established the Comité Interventor de los Cambios (Committee for Exchange Intervention or CIC) to intervene in the currency market by buying pesetas to keep their value up. None of these actions stopped the depreciation of the peseta, which accelerated in 1930.[25]

When Primo de Rivera resigned on 28 January 1930, buying $1 cost 7.67 pesetas. Manuel Argüelles, the finance minister of the new government headed by General Dámaso Berenguer, decided to apply to monetary policy the liberalizing trend introduced in commercial affairs two years earlier with the adoption of the most-favored nation system. In early February, he stopped all exchange interventions, leading one of the American consuls in Barcelona to assert: "It remains to be seen what course foreign exchange will take under the new system and the trend of the peseta will probably be an index of the public's confidence in the new regime."[26] Argüelles seemed to be of the same opinion, because in July, shortly before leaving his post, with the peseta at 8.50 to the dollar, he was forced to create a new Consejo Regulador de Operaciones del Cambio (Council for the Regulation of Exchange Operations or CROC). His successor, Julio Wais, carried over to his new post the same regulatory tendencies he had exhibited as minister of national economy. On 27 July

[23] J. A. Montero Jiménez, *El despertar de la gran potencia. Las relaciones entre España y los Estados Unidos (1898–1930)*, Madrid, Biblioteca Nueva, 2011, 348–9.

[24] B. Eichengreen, *Golden Fetters. The Gold Standard and the Great Depression, 1919–1939*, New York, Oxford University Press, 1992, 352–3. The evolution of gold reserves from different countries in the monthly edition of the *Federal Reserve Bulletin*, https://fraser.stlouisfed.org/title/federal-reserve-bulletin-62?browse=1910s, accessed 20 August 2020.

[25] The monetary policy in the final years of the dictatorship in E. González Calleja, *La España de Primo de Rivera. La modernización autoritaria*, Madrid, Alianza, 2005, 250–5. A. Carreras y X. Tafunell, *Historia Económica de la España Contemporánea*, Barcelona, Crítica, 2006, 249–51.

[26] Report from the American Consul in Barcelona, 12 February 1930, NARA, RG 59, 1930–1939, 852.5151/43.

1930, he enacted a rise in tariffs, which affected 20 percent of all imports from the United States – unexposed cinematographic films, razors, sewing machines … – and most of all cars, whose duties were doubled. The Spanish cabinet justified the measure on the grounds of the urgent need to reduce trade deficits and halt the depreciation of the peseta. But both American officials and historians have interpreted it as a retaliation against the Smoot–Hawley tariff, similar to the responses that it provoked in nations such as Switzerland or Germany. Another of the consuls in Barcelona wrote:

> While it is probably true that the present tariff increases have been largely made with the idea of reducing imports and further cutting down the unfavorable trade balance as well as protecting certain local industries, the fact that imports from the United States have been particularly affected has probably not been entirely lost sight of in the preparation of this list of changes.[27]

In September, Wais established the Centro Oficial de Contratación de Moneda (Official Centre for Monetary Transactions or COCM), operated jointly by the ministry and the Bank of Spain, and charged with supervising all exchange transactions.[28]

These restrictive measures formed part of a more ambitious plan to attain, in the long term, the long-expected stabilization of the peseta, as a preliminary step to its entry into a gold standard that was soon to founder on a global scale. With this in mind, Wais resorted to the Bank of International Settlements (BIS), established in February 1930, to prevent the execution of the Young Plan from altering the currency market and to coordinate the monetary policies of the principal central banks.[29] The bank provided Spain with another revolving credit of $15 million, against the transfer of £3 million in gold to London, and with the professed objective of stabilizing the peseta.[30] The initiative seemed to work, because between late October and late November, the peseta/$ rate rose from 10.23 to 8.72. But in late November it was again at 9.5, something the U.S. *chargé d'affaires* in Madrid blamed on the political instability following the revolt of the garrison in Jaca: "An unfortunate result of the sedition will be […] the effect on the country's financial standing, shown by the immediate decline in the peseta."[31] Neither he nor Wise foresaw the extent to which the

---

[27] Report from the American Consul in Barcelona, 26 July 1930, NARA, ibid., 652.113 AUTO/23. The historians' opinion in D. A. Irwin, *Peddling Protectionism. Smoot–Hawley and the Great Depression*, Princeton, Princeton University Press, 2011, 167–8.

[28] Á. Viñas et al., *Política comercial…*, 35.

[29] B. Eichengreen, *Golden Fetters…*, 263.

[30] Á. Viñas et al., *Política comercial…*, 35–6.

[31] Dis. 237, Crosby to Stimson, 16 December 1930, NARA, RG 59, 1930–1939, 852.00/1799.

14 JOSÉ ANTONIO MONTERO JIMÉNEZ

crisis of the monarchy would be intertwined with the efforts to salvage Spain's financial standing.

On Saturday, 21 March 1930, Russell C. Leffingwell, one of the managers of J. P. Morgan & Co. and former undersecretary of the Treasury during the First World War,[32] phoned Wilbur J. Carr, assistant secretary of state, to announce that his bank had just formed a syndicate to open a $38 million line of credit to the Spanish government.[33] Wais and his replacement in the cabinet of Admiral Juan Bautista Aznar, the Catalan Juan Ventosa – who had already occupied the same portfolio in 1917–1918 – thought the transaction with the BIS had been successful enough to warrant using the existing ties with Morgan to look for a more ambitious loan. At the same time, another syndicate of European banks, led by the Banque de Paris et des Pays-Bas, provided another $22 million. The Morgan syndicate included, among others, the Chase National Bank, the First National Bank, the National City Bank, the Guaranty Trust Co., the Bankers Trust Co., the Bank of America, the National Association, the New York Trust Co., Dillon Read & Co., the International Acceptance Bank, the Irving Trust Co., Kuhn, Loeb & Co., Lee Higginson & Co., and Kiddy, Peabody & Co.[34] The Banque de Paris participated along with Credit Suisse, Stockholm's Euskilda Bank, Amsterdam's Hoppe Bank, the Banca Commerciale Italiana, and the Credito Italiano.[35] A total of $60 million would be at the Spanish government's disposal for eighteen months, "for the purpose of regulating the quotation of the peseta during the period of *de facto* stabilisation contemplated by the Spanish government preliminary to the definitive adoption of the gold standard."[36] The consortium earned a commission of 1.25 percent a year, while all withdrawn amounts would bear a yearly interest of 1 percent over the rate of the Federal Reserve, with a minimum of 4.5 percent.[37] The operation had been negotiated by the Bank of Spain, with the guarantee of the government, which authorized it through a royal decree of 14 March.[38]

[32] On Leffingwell, see the information provided in R. Chernow, *The House of Morgan. An American Banking Dynasty and the Rise of Modern Finance*, New York, Grove Press, 2010.

[33] The conversation is mentioned in a letter, Leffingwell to Carr, 27 March 1931, NARA, RG 59, 1930–1939, 852.51/202.

[34] F. L. Kluckhohn, "Morgan Group Lends $60,000,000 to Spain," *The New York Times*, 27 March 1931, 1 and 7.

[35] "Una extensa declaración del Ministro de Hacienda," *El Sol*, 28 March 1931, 4.

[36] Press report by J. P. Morgan on the Spanish loan, NARA, RG 59, 1930–1939, 852.51/202.

[37] "El ministro reúne a los directores de los periódicos de Madrid. Una nota de Hacienda," *El Imparcial*, 28 March 1931, 3.

[38] "Real decreto autorizando la apertura de un crédito por la cantidad de 60 millones de dólares, que se concertará por el Banco de España con la garantía del Estado," *Gaceta de Madrid*, 27 March 1931, 1,668.

THE UNITED STATES AND THE SECOND SPANISH REPUBLIC (1931–1936) 15

The so-called 'Morgan credit' came out of the ephemeral recovery of international credit that characterized the year 1930, when worn-out recipes were applied to a Depression that was unprecedented in scope and nature.[39] In any case, Spain's substantial gold reserves, its relative isolation from international financial currents, and its government's promise to stabilize the peseta, turned it into an apparently reliable customer. Frank L. Kluckhohn, the *New York Times* correspondent in Madrid, marveled at the operation, which he deemed "a tremendous victory for the government, since it is taken to imply that, after careful investigation of the situation here, a most important foreign banking group has decided that King Alfonso's regime is fundamentally sound."[40] The journalist was right to be amazed because the political furor the loan caused in Spain contributed to the *coup de grace* against the monarchy, coming as it did two weeks before the municipal elections that would signify its end. When, on 27 March, Minister Ventosa held a press conference in the ministry with the editors of the most important Madrid newspapers, the uproar against the loan seemed unanimous. The *Heraldo de Madrid* said: "Neither revolutionary skirmishes, nor street brawls, nor the rejection all through the nation of absolute power seem enough to hold the people in our government back."[41] Most of the opposition agreed with the *El Liberal* headline of 31 March, which clamored: "An Obvious Illegality."[42] They all interpreted the recent call for elections as the first step towards the resurrection of the 1876 Constitution, whose article 86 stated: "The government needs authorization for […] obtaining money on loan against the credit of the nation."[43] Some late-hour constitutionalist politicians – among them Santiago Alba, Joaquín Chapaprieta, and Santiago Alba – met at the home of former liberal minister Miguel Villanueva to label Ventonsa's announcement as "an outrageous abuse."[44] The Radical Republicans of Alejandro Lerroux recalled that "the rule of all constitutional and parliamentary peoples being that all legal rules must be dictated by the legislative powers," they wanted to express their "most vigorous protest." The socialists pointed to the apparently serious political and economic consequences of the loan, while the future president, Niceto Alcalá-Zamora, said that he had contacted Felipe Sánchez Román, who was rumored to have used

---

[39] Ch. P. Kindleberger, *The World in Depression, 1929–1939*, Berkeley, University of California Press, 1986, 117–23.

[40] F. K. Kluckhohn, "Morgan…".

[41] "El gobierno da oficialmente la noticia de que concierta un empréstito de sesenta millones de pesetas con la banca Morgan," *Heraldo de Madrid*, 27 March 1931, 7.

[42] "La ilegalidad es notoria. El sofisma que defiende la legalidad del crédito. Contra el empréstito en dólares," *El Liberal*, 31 March 1931, 1.

[43] J. Montero (ed.), *Constituciones y códigos políticos españoles, 1808–1978*, Barcelona, Ariel, 1998, 153.

[44] "Una extensa declaración del Ministro de Hacienda," *El Sol*, 28 March 1931, 4.

the operation to sue the government.[45] In a later conference with editors of economic journals, Ventosa repeated that Spain's credit relied on the absence of political turmoil, to which the count of Pedroso sharply replied that it was impossible to have any conflict when there was no parliament to discuss decisions. Another person in the audience took the opportunity to attack some of the credit's clauses.[46] A desperate minister admitted, to no avail, that "the sole objection that might be raised is that the current budget has not been voted for by the Cortes," but that:

> the same could be said with respect to all allocations in the expenditure budget which find themselves in the same situation. Should those allocations be thought illegal or impossible, we could not pay the debt back, nor the salary of public officials, line operators, or similar services. That is to say, all national life would be paralyzed.[47]

The protests of the opposition were in vain, but the Morgan credit never materialized. The proclamation of the Second Republic on 14 April 1931 provoked a commotion in diplomatic circles, especially because they had to decide whether to recommend official recognition of the new regime by their governments.[48] The American ambassador, Irwin Laughlin, communicated with alarm on 16 April that, "The resulting conditions have elements of the gravest nature. The 17th century minded Spanish people, captivated by Communist falsities, suddenly see a promised land that does not exist."[49] The day before, a memorandum written in the DWEA recalled that the new president of the provisional government, Alcalá-Zamora, "Immediately after his release [from jail] made a bitter attack on the Morgan credit for the stabilization of the peseta."[50] Doubts quickly vanished on 17 April, once Laughlin had his first encounter with the president, who had received him "most cordially."[51]

---

[45] "El Ministro de Hacienda expide otra nota oficiosa. Se acentúa la protesta contra el crédito extranjero," *El Sol*, 29 March 1931, 7.

[46] "El empréstito realizado por el Sr. Ventosa, con el asentimiento del gobierno, ha producido indignación general," *El Liberal*, 28 March 1931, 1.

[47] "El Ministro de Hacienda expide otra nota oficiosa. Se acentúa la protesta contra el crédito extranjero," *El Sol*, 29 March 1931, 7.

[48] D. J. Little, *Malevolent...*, 58–68. J.-F. Berdah, *La democracia...*, 5–7.

[49] Tel. 21, Laughlin to Stimson, 16 April 1931, NARA, RG 59, 1930–1939, 852.00/1818.

[50] Memo, DWEA, 15 April 1931, NARA, RG 51, 1930–1939, 852.00/1825.

[51] Tel. 24, Laughlin to Stimson, 17 April 1931, NARA, RG 51, 1930–1939, 852.01/19. In the case of telegrams, such as this one, which have been published on the series *Foreign Relations of the United States*, prepared by the State Department, we have reproduced the archival version, because the published one was paraphrased and, therefore, changed in its wording.

THE UNITED STATES AND THE SECOND SPANISH REPUBLIC (1931–1936)   17

In an analysis he penned the following day, the ambassador had switched course, referring again to the Spanish people,

> whose one desire seems to have been to help make the transfer of government as quiet and orderly as possible. The absence also of all signs of rancour on the part of the new Government toward the Monarchists in general has gone a long way toward lessening the tension and fearful participation which might well have been expected to follow such a radical political change.[52]

Loyal to the policy of not exerting any influence on the European political cauldron, the United States decided to wait for the reactions of the other Great Powers: "I consider," wrote the secretary of state, "the Spanish situation as primarily of European concern and feel therefore that their motives for their positions on recognition may not necessarily be applicable to ours."[53] Like Great Britain, Washington worried that Alfonso XIII's abdication had not been legal and that a prompt recognition of the new Republic might lead to an embarrassing situation.[54] France finally extended recognition on the night of 17 April, when the United Kingdom announced its intention to follow suit, as soon as the dominions' opinions were heard. At that moment, Laughlin telegraphed the secretary of state that "Nothing here delay immediate action on your part if you decide it desirable."[55] His European colleagues urged him "that early recognition in the interest of world order is highly important."[56] The ambassador insisted that the new authorities had preserved public order, enjoyed wide popular support, and seemed ready to respect foreign interests – the managers of IT&T thought likewise.[57] Laughlin finally extended recognition on 22 April, along with the United Kingdom and Germany – Italy waited until the following day.[58]

The guarantee over foreign interests the new authorities promised seemed to apply to the Morgan credit, but the bank's officials did not think the same. On the afternoon of 17 April, Parker Gilbert, another former undersecretary of the Treasury who had just lost his job as agent for reparations after the

---

[52] Dis. 339, Laughlin to Stimson, 18 April 1931, NARA, RG 51, 1930–1939, 852.00/1834. The telegram Laughling sent to his superiors that day was somewhat less optimistic. Tel. 26, Laughlin to Stimson, 18 April 1930, ibid., 852.01/30.

[53] Tel. 11, Stimson to Laughlin, 19 April 1931, NARA, RG 51, 1930–1939, 852.01/30.

[54] Tel. 12, Stimson to Laughlin, 21 April 1931, NARA, RG 59, 1930–1939, 852.01/33.

[55] Tel. 113, Laughlin to Stimson, 18 April 1931, NARA, RG 59, 1930–1939, 852.01/25.

[56] Tel. 27, Laughlin to Stimson, 20 April 1931, NARA, RG 59, 1930–1939, 852.01/33.

[57] Ibid.

[58] Tel. 30, Laughlin to Stimson, 22 April 1931, NARA, RG 59, 1930–1939, 852.00/41.

18   JOSÉ ANTONIO MONTERO JIMÉNEZ

establishment of the BIS, only to become partner at J. P. Morgan,[59] phoned Wilbur Carr, to tell him that,

> there had been delivered in Madrid today a letter jointly with the Bank of Paris and Pays-Bas, saying that the credit is no longer in operation, the reason being that under the terms of the contract it could only be drawn upon by presenting notes guaranteed by the *Government of the Kingdom of Spain*.[60]

Arriving in the midst of the recognition *imbroglio*, the news created alarm in Washington. On 25 April, Carr talked to Leffingwell to make him aware of the department's concerns and to express hope that "because of the implications arising from the reason given for the cancellation of the contract, no further publicity would be given to it." The banker downplayed the matter, explaining that he had merely stated that, as "the whole situation had changed [...] the credit has been terminated by mutual consent."[61]

Carr's fears were unsubstantiated. Regardless of whether the cancellation had taken place by mutual consent, it was certainly welcomed in Madrid, because it suited the opinion the new republican leaders had expressed just two weeks before. In a news conference at 2pm on 21 April, the new finance minister, the socialist Indalecio Prieto, declared that "the Morgan credit [...] had been totally cancelled," because that "absurd credit was not needed to stabilize the peseta."[62] Prieto stressed that the cancellation had been made at no cost to the government, which had been refunded the $1,120,000 commission without having to pay for any legal expenses.[63] The Spanish press looked at the termination with some relief, though it put the weakness of the peseta again at the forefront of the economic agenda. An op-ed in *El Sol* on 21 April warned:

> We must comprehend how difficult it was to solemnly ratify in power what had been violently attacked when in the opposition [...]. It is the first of the deplorable episodes we may witness in the immediate future should the lefts persist on transforming a passionate stance into government policy [...]. This reality unavoidably requires a policy of

---

[59] R. Chernow, *The House of Morgan....*

[60] Memo by Carr, 17 April 1931, NARA, RG 59, 1930–1939, 852.51/205. Italics are mine.

[61] Memo by Carr, 25 April 1931, NARA, RG 59, 1930–1939, 852.51/209.

[62] "Llevarse el dinero al extranjero – declaró ayer el ministro de Hacienda – será un negocio ruinoso," *El Liberal*, 22 April 1931, 3.

[63] "Se ha restringido, sin el menor quebranto para el Tesoro, el absurdo empréstito que negoció Ventosa para estabilizar la moneda," *Heraldo de Madrid*, 20 April 1931, 8. The detail is confirmed in tel. 596, Strauss to Hull, 17 July 1935, NARA, RG 59, 1930–1939, 851.5151/547.

direct intervention in the exchange market and of planning a quick stabilization more or less appreciative [of the peseta], to which the last governments had to submit.[64]

Stability With Feet of Clay

The situation Prieto faced was not easy. In its first month, the new regime saw the price of the dollar rise from 9.14 to 10.29 pesetas. The situation deteriorated even more with the flight of capital after 14 April. Under those conditions, even more onerous due to the financial orthodoxy influencing both the experts and the authorities, it was difficult to face with peace of mind the implementation of a new economic policy. The crux of the matter relied still on the balance of payments deficit, provoked in part by an excess of imports. To reduce them, officials could resort to the classic rise in tariffs, but the League of Nations had referred to the Spanish Cambó tariff of 1922 as the highest in the Western world. So, resorting to elevations in particular items, as the government had done in 1930, could just be an occasional measure. Thus, Spain decided to substitute a new series of reciprocal trade agreements for the most-favored nation system. They would be based on mutual concessions looking towards the equalization of exports and imports with each partner. This could be especially harmful for the United States, which in 1931 was responsible for 68 percent of the Spanish trade deficit. The signing of the first agreements with its European competitors made matters worse, both because Americans could not benefit from the advantages Spain gave to third countries and because those treaties aggravated the deficit, as they tended to level trade with countries, such as the United Kingdom or France, with which Spain had a positive balance – the surplus with France dropped from 194 million pesetas in 1931 to just 63 million in 1935.

After the signing of the commercial treaty between Spain and France in November 1931, the State Department did everything it could to reach some kind of agreement – albeit provisional – that prevented American exporters from being at a disadvantage. The task was a daunting one, if only because trade legislation in Spain, based on exclusive and mutual reductions in particular tariffs, and the United States, based on the most-favored nation clause, were clearly incompatible. Resisting the pressures of many exporters, and even the opposition of some government offices, the State Department was ready to use all administrative and legal levers to comply with some of Spain's unusual demands, while it resisted wielding some of the retaliatory measures contemplated in the Smoot–Hawley tariff against the Spaniards. Between 1929 and 1932, when global imports fell 29 percent, Spanish imports from the

---

[64] "La rescisión del crédito Morgan," *El Sol*, 21 April 1931, 1.

United States fell 49 percent.[65] In those years, the rate of exports with respect to GDP in the United States dropped from 5 to 3.8 percent.[66] Under those conditions, U.S. State Department officials charged with conducting trade negotiations with Spain thought it best to preserve whatever commerce they already had, no matter how depressed, than to risk a trade war that would tear it to pieces. Those attitudes encouraged the typical time-wasting strategies of the Spanish government, internally divided as to the best course to follow. Spain still depended on the goodwill of the United States to source primary resources – mostly cotton – but at the same time wished to reduce the trade deficit. The Ministry of State opted for accommodating the State Department demands, while the Ministry of Agriculture strove to punish the Americans for the sanitary restrictions they had imposed on some Spanish products, like grapes and onions. That strategy forced the Spaniards to use dilatory tactics, sustained on vague promises, never fulfilled, to improve the conditions of U.S. imports. Meanwhile, bilateral trade continued to flounder, though with the benefit of reducing the deficit for Spain, from 178 million pesetas in 1929 to 127 million pesetas in 1932. Trade talks extended throughout 1931 and 1932 but did not yield any practical results and were finally interrupted by Franklin Roosevelt's spectacular presidential election victory in November 1932.[67]

The results of Spain's quest for a better balance in trade were limited. The trade deficit went down from 624 million pesetas in 1929 to 233 million pesetas in 1932, but that was more a consequence of world economic conditions than of the efforts by the Spanish government. World exports had plummeted from $2,737 million to $936 million in the same period. Spain had but two options: either to impose further trade restrictions or to control the currency market. Spain only reluctantly followed the first course, designing a policy of contingents authorized in December 1931 but never seriously applied until 1935.[68] The exchange market offered several possibilities, but just one suited the economic thinking then prevailing. One choice was to mobilize part of the gold stored in the vaults of the Bank of Spain to stop the drainage of money, but both experts and politicians discarded this option because they did not want to risk so important an asset for the country's financial standing. Devaluation was fearfully mentioned. Even though the United Kingdom would soon follow that line in order to, among other things, boost exports, that would mean to officially renounce the cherished though unrealistic revaluation of the peseta. The remaining possibility was to toughen up exchange controls,

---

[65] D. A. Irwin, *Peddling...*, 181–2.

[66] D. A. Irwin, *Clahsing Over Commerce. A History of U.S. Trade Policy*, Chicago, University of Chicago Press, 2017, 394.

[67] Most of the information contained in this paragraph comes from NARA, RG 59, 1930–1939, 652.11 and in the old Archive of the Spanish Ministry of Foreign Affairs (AMAE), R513/70 and 72.

[68] Á. Viñas et al., *Política Comercial...*, 81.

THE UNITED STATES AND THE SECOND SPANISH REPUBLIC (1931–1936)   21

which Germany did in the summer 1931 to counter the series of bank failures that followed the bankruptcy of the Austrian Creditanstadlt.

Accordingly, one of Prieto's first moves as finance minister was to merge the CROC and the COCM. A decree of 29 May 1931 created the new COCM, also operated jointly by the Bank of Spain and the ministry, and charged with supervising all commercial transactions that had to be paid in foreign currency. It banned the exportation of capital for speculative purposes, while no traveler could take more than 5,000 pesetas abroad. All persons wishing to buy foreign items had to apply for authorization to the centre, which granted the corresponding license to buy foreign currencies. It studied all applications and arranged them according to the nature of the product to be imported, prioritizing national needs. All requests believed to be urgent were authorized promptly, while the rest had to wait until there were enough reserves of the required currency to cover the transaction. The system was bound to cause two kinds of difficulties. Firstly, it depended on the availability of foreign money, which could cause delays of several weeks, because some of the more important Spanish exports had a seasonal character. The situation was especially serious in the case of countries with which Spain had a trade deficit. At the same time, delays put an extra burden on the shoulders of Spanish importers, who had to cover price variations between the moment they applied for a license and the time they obtained it.[69] To offer some liquidity to the COCM and to try to contain the depreciation of the peseta, the provisional government saw no other option than to look again for foreign credit, but this time a public one. As soon as the Morgan credit was cancelled, Prieto opened talks with the French commercial attaché, which culminated in May in a revolving credit of 1,000 million francs from the Bank of France, at a 3.5 percent interest rate, against the dispatching of £6 million in gold to the lender's office in Mont-de-Marsan, where the £3 million previously sent to London against the BIS loan also ended up.[70] As a result, by late 1931 Spain's gold reserves amounted to only $434 million; the year before they had reached $478 million.[71]

The French loan produced long-term consequences, as did the exchange-control policy. It made Spanish monetary policy dependent on France. It is also likely – as American officials suspected – that Spain was forced to accept, in return for the loan, a commercial treaty that was somewhat harmful to Spanish

---

[69] Ibid., 55–6. Also Special Circular 31, Bureau of Foreign and Domestic Commerce, 20 May 1931; dis. 391, Crosby to Stimson, 8 June 1931 and dis. 397, Crosby to Stimson, 15 June 1941, NARA, RG 59, 1930–1939, 852.5151/64, 50½ and 51½.

[70] Credit negotiations in Y. Denéchère, *La politique...*, 151–6. More details in Á. Viñas et al., *Política Comercial...*, 57–8.

[71] Federal Reserve Board, *Federal Reserve Bulletin. December 1931*, Washington, Government Printing Office, 1931, 675.

interests.[72] The Madrid government saw the shackles of its monetary orthodoxy reinforced, because it was now in debt to the country that, up to 1936, led the so-called gold bloc, the last bastion of the ancient and dying standard that had sustained international convertibility for decades. Meanwhile, the United Kingdom let sterling float on 21 September 1931, and the United States would temporarily do the same with the dollar on 19 April 1933. International economic instability played into the hands of Spain because some of the capital that had fled the country returned, while migrants' remittances soared, stimulated by the ever-increasing regulations sprouting all over the world. In 1932 and 1933, Spain counted enough foreign currency to operate the COCM without any major inconvenience, while the peseta stopped its slide in 1932. The exchange rate with the franc stabilized between 37 and 42 pesetas until 1936, while that with the dollar did at 12 to 13 pesetas, until the 1933 devaluation left it at around 7.5 pesetas.

Under the Shadow of a Public Loan (1934–1936)

The year 1934 witnessed a series of events that brought monetary policy back to the center of U.S.–Spanish relations. On the American side, the delicate political balance that sustained the Roosevelt administration tilted timidly to the side of the internationalists. If one of the defining moments of 1933 was the sudden closure, after America's defection, of the London Economic Conference, 1934 saw the passing of two acts that opened a reluctant door to international cooperation at the height of the Depression. The first one, in February, established the Export-Import Bank (ExImBank), a public agency charged with funding trade operations that helped dispose of U.S. agricultural surpluses. In June, Congress approved the Reciprocal Trade Agreements Act (RTAA), which for the first time gave power to the president to negotiate commercial treaties offering possible reductions of up to 50 percent of the existing tariff, later extended to all trade partners through the most-favored nation system. The full consequences of both measures were not felt until after the Second World War, but at the time they gave some respite to those in the administration who nurtured hopes of a more ambitious economic policy. Secretary of the Treasury Henry J. Morgenthau Jr. was increasingly concerned with the amount of gold accumulating in the United States and thought the time had come to play all available cards to avoid the harmful effects of unilateral devaluations on international trade. The only benefit he reaped was the limited and belated Tripartite Stabilization Agreement of July 1936, which consisted of a joint declaration on the part of the United Kingdom, France, and the United States, advocating for concerted devaluations and supporting the depreciation of the French franc, which dealt the final blow to the gold

---

[72] Letter, Johnson to Castle, 1 July 1931, NARA, RG 59, 1930–1939, 652.113 AUTO/28.

THE UNITED STATES AND THE SECOND SPANISH REPUBLIC (1931–1936) 23

bloc.[73] Those plans, even the failed ones, are important because they served as a rehearsal for the kind of economic policies that would characterize the post-war international order;[74] one of them was conceived with Republican Spain in mind.

The respite the COCM had enjoyed ended in early 1934. On 15 March, the Fox Film Co. sought the help of the American embassy in repatriating between $60,000 and $70,000 in benefits. When studying the issue, the commercial attaché, John C. Greenup, found out that Fox was not the only U.S. firm whose request to send money back had been delayed. IT&T had 100 million pesetas in blocked benefits, while other companies, such as the Vacuum Oil Co., Ford, and General Motors accumulated another $4 million. The submanager of the International Banking Corporation – the Spanish subsidiary of National City Bank, the only American banking institution operating in Spain – said to Greenup that, up to then, commercial operations had not been affected by the delays.[75] Despite that, on 19 March, acting on the orders of Ambassador Claude G. Bowers, the attaché visited the directors of the COCM, Alfonso Ara – representing the Bank of Spain – and Blas Huete – representing the Finance Ministry – who surprised the American with an unexpected proposal. Though they promised that Fox would soon be authorized to take its funds out of the country, they also warned that dollars were scarce in Spain, and they did not know for how long commercial operations in that currency would continue to be approved:

> The United States must buy more in Spain, but it is understood that the channels of trade may not be changed overnight, so that this solution must come later, and cannot be of assistance in the immediate future. The other [solution] is to obtain a loan in the United States.

They did not specify any conditions, but Ara and Huete advanced a general outline of what they had in mind:

> [I]t would have to be for a large sum and for a long period; [...] it could be from the government or from a group of bankers; [...] of course it would be guaranteed by the Spanish government; and [...] with such a loan, there would be no difficulty in granting permits for American interests to remit [funds] to the United States.

---

[73] B. Eichengreen, *Golden Fetters...*, 378–80; Ch. P. Kindleberger, *The World...*, 246–60; Patricia Clavin, *The Failure of Economic Diplomacy. Britain, Germany, France and the United States, 1931–36*, London, Macmillan, 1996, 185–90.

[74] P. Clavin, *Securing the World Economy. The Reinvention of the League of Nations, 1920–1946*, Oxford, Oxford University Press, 2013, 1–10.

[75] J. C. Greenup, "Increasing difficulty in obtaining authorization for remittances to the United States," NARA, RG 151, entry 2, box 451, folder "March 1934."

The heads of the COCM had, nonetheless, a preferred prospective lender in mind, as shown when Ara asked if Greenup "thought the United States government would consider making such a loan to Spain." The attaché looked at the proposal with suspicion, judging that the Spanish situation was not as desperate as his interlocutors depicted it: "I am wondering if this could be a plan, another plan, for paying the United States with United States money."[76] From then on, Spain's withholding of exchange permits was always suspected by U.S. officials to be a planned move for the United States to make further concessions in such areas as trade relations.[77]

Back in Washington, the National Foreign Trade Council – a U.S. business association interested in the promotion of foreign trade – complained to Assistant Secretary of State Francis B. Sayre in March about the COCM delays.[78] In August, John L. Hickerson of the DWEA, thought the issue was relevant enough to be brought to the attention of the Spanish ambassador, Luis Calderón, who repeated that the deferrals responded to seasonal trends and that the situation would improve in the fall.[79] Soon after, one of Hickerson's subordinates came to believe that the Spanish practices were discriminatory, because Americans suffered longer delays than, for instance, the French or the British.[80] After the *New York Times* echoed these complaints,[81] Blas Huete saw himself forced to remind the Ministry of State:

> [T]here is no such thing as frozen credit, but only a delay in the granting of currency to pay for goods and services from North America, due to the scarcity of currency coming from there. That is to say, we do not stop attending to our obligations, but do so with longer delays [...] as a result of the aforementioned scarcity.[82]

The coming of the fall paid little heed to Ara's and Huete's predictions. While in November the COCM released 5 million pesetas for transactions with the United States, delays were affecting not only business remittances, but also trade operations.[83]

---

[76] Memo, Greenup to Bowers, 19 March 1934, ibid. Also dis. 314, Bowers to Hull, 20 March 1934, NARA, RG 59, 1930–1939, 852.5151/76.

[77] An example in dis. 432, Bowers to Hull, 11 July 1934, NARA, RG 59, 1930–1939, 852.5151/81.

[78] Cross-reference slips of the correspondence between Sayre and the Special Adviser to the President on Foreign Trade, NARA, RG 20, entry 6, box 3.

[79] Memo, Hickerson to Morgan and Culbertson, 16 August 1934, NARA, RG 59, 1930–1939, 852.5151/86.

[80] Memo by Morgan, 21 August 1934, ibid., 852.5151/81.

[81] "Trade with Spain Shows Big Jump," *The New York Times*, 5 August 1934, 56. See also dis. 348, Calderón to Ministry of State, 6 August 1934. AMAE, R706/3.

[82] Letter, Huete to Undersecretary of State, 22 September 1934, ibid.

[83] Letter, Jones to Martin, 17 December 1934, NARA, RG 20, entry 6, box 3, folder "Spain."

From 1934, despite efforts to the contrary on both sides, it became harder to distinguish between commercial and monetary issues. Since trade negotiations came to an end in late 1932, the only advance had been the overturning of Prohibition in December 1933. In February 1934, Spain was given a wine quota of 1.1 million gallons, in exchange for agreeing to buy 600,000 pounds of American tobacco for the Spanish Tobacco Monopoly, thanks to the help of an ExImBank credit of $1.3 million in favor of the S. B. Smith Co., approved in August 1934.[84] At the same time, congressional debates on the RTAA brought trade relations with Spain back into the spotlight. The Senate Tariff Commission asked in February 1934 for a report on Spain, along with several other countries.[85] In May 1934, one of the main obstacles to bilateral trade relations since the mid-1920s was removed with the reauthorization to import Spanish grapes, under certain sanitary conditions, into the United States. Meanwhile, the State Department resisted any compromise to open negotiations with Spanish officials as soon as the RTAA was passed. Initially, the Roosevelt administration was not as trustful of Spain as its predecessors and was not willing to take any real steps without obtaining more concessions from the Spaniards. Perhaps this impelled the Madrid government to announce that its policy on contingents would not affect the most important U.S. imports. Finally, in September 1934, a new round of trade talks began, which lasted until late 1935. As in the previous ones, difficulties arose from disagreements over trade legislation – Spain kept refusing to grant America most-favored nation status – from internecine divisions within both administrations between protectionist and liberal agencies, and from the Spanish government's dilatory tactics – which had worked well up until that very moment. The currency problem would soon add one more difficulty.[86]

In late 1934, U.S. imports had to wait about seventy days before being granted the required exchange permit. In February 1935, the waiting period had increased to eighty-five days, and then to 125 in May and 191 in September. By then, there were about 185 million francs in blocked funds for trade operations with America, apart from the 100 million pesetas in IT&T gains. Similar difficulties affected most of the other Great Powers, but the United States had the worst share: in the fall of 1935, delays with the United Kingdom were 132 days and amounted to 144 million francs in commercial operations and 27.5 million francs in blocked funds, and with France to 108 million francs

[84] The details of the loan in NARA, RG 275, entry 1, box 1, folder 11 "S. B. Smith & Co."

[85] "An Analysis of the Trade Between Spain and the United States," February 1934, NARA, RG 20, entry 14, box 3.

[86] The information of this round of negotiations comes from D. J. Little, *Malevolent...*, 164–183. When contrasting this work with archival sources, I have discovered some discrepancies in minor details, such as the amount of the Export-Import Bank credit, which Little says was of $675,000.

and 49.5 million francs respectively, with similar delays.[87] The sole exception was Germany, which on 1 January 1935 had signed an exchange treaty with Spain following the Third Reich's monetary policy. It was based on double payments and the complete elimination of deferrals.[88] In the State Department, officials thought again of a possible charge of discrimination against Spain, heeding the opinions of several businessmen involved in trans-Atlantic trade.[89] Always willing to see things from a Spanish perspective, Ambassador Bowers[90] dispelled such notions, saying that there was no ill-will on the part of Spain and that remittances to the United States took longer because of the scarcity of dollars in the Iberian Peninsula; the COCM was actually using some of the pounds obtained from the United Kingdom to buy dollars with which to cover operations with the United States. Therefore, Bowers underlined, if a nation had a right to complain of discrimination, it was Great Britain, which was subjected to postponements, despite having a negative balance of trade with Spain.[91] The ambassador insisted on the need to accelerate trade negotiations, because "more Spanish exports to the United States [...] will fundamentally improve the situation by making more dollars available."[92]

Not all interests involved were willing to wait for so long. In January 1935, one of the founders of IT&T, Sosthenes Behn, visited Washington with Logan Rock, one of his top managers, to resurrect the idea of a foreign loan that Ara and Huete had advanced months before. On the 21 January they met Ambassador Luis Calderón and Jay P. Moffat, chief of the DWEA. Before traveling, they had floated their idea to Pedro Pan, vice-governor of the Bank of Spain, and Huete himself.[93] Rock indicated that a good way to ease trade negotiations would be through granting a line of credit to Spain. When Moffat asked, "if this was to be a private loan," the IT&T men answered that "the bankers were unwilling to touch it and it would have to be a government loan." The proposal fell on deaf ears, because the authorities in Washington thought

---

[87] Data from letter, Jones to Martin, 17 December 1934; tel. 30, Bowers to Hull, 10 May 1935; dis. 755, Bowers to Hull, 13 May 1935; tel. 59, Bowers to Hull, 16 September 1935; tel. 65, Bowers to Hull, 27 September 1935; and dis. 903, Bowers to Hull, 1 October 1935, NARA, RG 59, 1930–1939, 852.5151/109, 113, 140, 141 and 144.

[88] Julian C. Greenup, "New Commercial and Exchange Agreement Between Spain and Germany," 28 January 1935, NARA, RG 151, entry 2, box 452, folder "Jan 1935."

[89] Tel. 25, Phillips to Bowers, 10 May 1935; letter, Celebrity Productions to Sayre, 31 May 1935, NARA, RG 59, 1930–1939, 852.5151/109 and 115.

[90] Two examples in letter, Bowers to Moffat, 23 April 1934, NARA, RG 59, 1930–1939, 611.5231/799½; and letter, Bowers to Roosevelt, 10 January 1934, FDR Library, FDR Papers, PSF, Series 3, box 50, folder "Spain."

[91] Tel. 59, Bowers to Hull... Also letter, Moffat to Celebrity Productions, 17 May 1935, NARA, RG 59, 1930–1939, 852.5151/115.

[92] Desp. 775, Bowers to Hull.

[93] Tel. 13, Calderón to Rocha, 21 January 1935, AMAE, R704/7.

THE UNITED STATES AND THE SECOND SPANISH REPUBLIC (1931–1936) 27

that "it would merely substitute the Government for the private American companies as the *holder of the bag*," in the form of blocked money.[94] It was also not the practice of the American government, since the fateful days of the First World War, to lend money to European countries, and the perennially controversial New Deal had not gone so far as to justify a change of precedent. On the Spanish side things did not turn out any better: the minister of state, Juan José Rocha, believed that a prospective loan would only obstruct the already protracted trade negotiations.[95]

The following months brought about a change of mind. In February, Bowers heard rumors that Spain had unsuccessfully approached the United Kingdom and France to obtain a new loan.[96] U.S. misgivings increased when George L. Harrison, the president of the Federal Reserve Bank of New York, talked with the secretary of the treasury to tell him that the Bank of France was trying to find out whether Spain was negotiating a loan with a consortium of American banks. The banker asked if the Treasury had been consulted to that effect, to which Morgenthau drily replied that, should France desire any information, it would do better to approach his department directly.[97] Morgenthau, who was then pondering the best way to use the government's resources to alleviate the financial situation in Europe, knew that, in the event Spain obtained a loan from any other country, it would be at the expense of liquidating the arrears of that nation, therefore worsening the situation of U.S. exporters. They were unwilling to lose any of their market share, which had decreased from 41 percent in 1931 to 21 percent in 1932, only to improve to around 25 percent in 1933 and 1934.[98] To make matters worse, between February and April 1935, panic spread among U.S. tobacco exporters that Spain would levy an exchange tax that would turn American cigarettes into a luxury item, beyond the means of the average Spaniard.[99]

[94] Memo by Moffat, 21 January 1935, NARA, RG 59, 1930–1939, 852.51/271.

[95] Tel. 10, Rocha to Calderón, 23 January 1935, AMAE, R704/7.

[96] Disp. 973, Bowers to Hull, 4 February 1935, NARA, RG 59, 1930–1939, 852.51/159.

[97] Henry Morgenthau, jr., Diary, 21 June 1935, FDR Presidential Library, Morgenthau Papers, Series 1, vol. 7, 142.

[98] Data deduced from Office of the Special Adviser to the President on Foreign Trade, *United States–Spain Economic Relations, February 1935*, NARA, RG 20, entry 11, box 2; and also from U.S. Department of Commerce, Bureau of Foreign and Domestic Commerce, *Foreign Commerce and Navigation of the United States*, 1934, 1935.

[99] Letter, Walker to Hull, 5 February 1935; tel. 12, Bowers to Hull, 7 February 1935; letter, Walker to Hull, 30 March 1935; memo by Greenup, 3 April 1935; disp. 729, Bowers to Hull, 9 April 1935, NARA, RG 59, 1930–1939, 852.5151/101, 100, 105, 106 and 107.

Nerves in Washington ran high when Joaquín Chapaprieta arrived in May at the Finance Ministry, a portfolio he combined with the premiership between September and December. He was a right-wing republican who knew how to appear as a capable financier before foreign diplomats and was determined to solve the exchange controversy. To back his image up, he immediately attempted to attract foreign capital by promising that any new investor would be allowed to repatriate his funds whenever he wished. The weakening of both sterling and the gold bloc, with rumors of a devaluation of the French franc, created the illusion that Spain could obtain money with which to alleviate the COCM.[100] Chapaprieta tried as well to buy some time, authorizing the center to issue promissory notes that exporters could discount abroad before being granted the corresponding exchange permit, thus assuming price differences between the time of application and the moment the goods were delivered.[101] In July, trade relations between Spain and France were broken off, giving U.S. exporters a comparative advantage for the first time since 1931. In a telephone call, Harrison said to Morgenthau that "As long as they're broken down it might be a good chance for [secretary of state Cordell Hull] to push his Spanish Treaty."[102]

Morgenthau had already made a move. On 22 June he ordered the financial secretary of the American embassy in Paris, Horace Merle Cochran, to travel to Spain to write a report on its monetary situation.[103] Bowers was not informed of the mission, which was meant to assess the country's creditworthiness, with a prospective loan in view. Before he returned to France, on 17 July, Cochran had visited Madrid, Barcelona, Toledo, and Seville and held interviews with Vice-Governor Pedro Pan and with representatives of, among others, the Banco Hispano-Americano, the Banco Urquijo, the IT&T, and the International Banking Corporation. His findings were encouraging: the consequences of the 1934 revolution aside, he considered the country had finally entered onto the path of political stabilization. Spain had weathered the Great Depression with a certain ease, there was room for further improvements, and unemployment figures were likewise stable. The banking system had not experienced any appreciable failure for some years, the budget deficit was covered with long-term bonds, the peseta was pegged to the franc, avoiding fluctuations, and the Bank of Spain held important gold reserves. The only problem was the persistent deficit in the balance of payments, which changes in trade policy had not solved and which had led to the collapse of the COCM.

---

[100] Disp. 790, Johnson to Hull, 15 June 1935, NARA, RG 59, 1930–1939, 852.5151/123.

[101] Á. Viñas et al., *Política Comercial...*, 110–17.

[102] Morgenthau's Diary, 2 July 1935, FDR Library, Morgenthau Papers, Series 1, vol. 8, 10–11.

[103] Tel. 39, 22 June 1935, NARA, RG 59, 1930–1939, 851.5151/526b.

THE UNITED STATES AND THE SECOND SPANISH REPUBLIC (1931–1936)   29

The defining moment of the trip was the meeting with Pedro Pan, who talked again of a public U.S. loan. He proposed the amount of around $130 million, for five years; it could be renewed, guaranteed by the government, as with the failed Morgan credit. Pan would later increase the figure to $250 million, with gold and silver bonds as collateral, along with specific quantities of both metals, which would remain in Spain.[104] Cochran seemed in favor of the proposal:

> American bankers evidently not disposed to endeavour to attempt Spanish bond issue in the United States and oppose short- or medium-term credit operation except against gold displaced to London. If any American Government agency is interested or could consider the proposition without requiring displacement of gold the help would be most welcome to Spain and trade advantages certainly could be procured. This credit alone would not solve Spain's exchange problem permanently. On the other hand, Spain's non-default record, general situation, gold and natural resources, lack of foreign indebtedness and potentialities as a field for American exports, commend this country as perhaps the best borrower risk in Europe if we are interested in lending abroad as our creditor position warrants.[105]

Morgenthau and Cochran were in full accord. The secretary of the treasury had decided to try his hand with the Spanish situation, with a view to advance the liberalizing agenda premiered in 1934. But the complex dynamics of the Roosevelt administration induced him to keep his intentions secret, and the scheme ended up dying among internecine fights on both sides of the Atlantic. The first doubts came from the European shore: Chapaprieta had told Sosthenes Behn on 10 July that he was not, at that moment, interested in a U.S. loan, because he hoped to obtain one in France.[106] Yet a few days later Pedro Pan spoke of it once again in an interview with the commercial attaché, discovering Cochran's mission to Bowers, who strongly protested to his superiors.[107] Though the State Department did its best to calm the ambassador down, officials at the Office of the Economic Advisor, headed by Herbert Feis, seemed worried. They began to compile information about blocked funds in Spain, while trying not to influence trade talks, which were then proceeding smoothly, but with emotions running high on both sides. The department tried to gain some time, and, after consulting with the Treasury, Secretary Hull finally sent Bowers some vague instructions: the ambassador

[104] Dis. 913, Bowers to Hull, 8 October 1935, NARA, RG 59, 1930–1939, 851.51/308.
[105] Cochran's report was sent via Paris in several sections. Tel. 596, Strauss to Hull, 17 July 1935, NARA, RG 59, 1930–1939, 852.5151/547.
[106] Letter, Page to Phillips, 16 July 1935, NARA, RG 59, 1930–1939, 852.5151/132.
[107] Letter, Bowers to Hull, 7 August 1935, NARA, RG 59, 1930–1939, 852.51/300.

was told to "endeavour to have discussion of all possibilities of financial arrangement deferred until the trade agreement negotiations were complete," but also "not to be too conclusive in any statement at this time, as to the possibility of credit arrangements helpful to the Spanish Government, but certain limitations on the possibilities are plain and serious [...]. Any such possibility [...] would require very deliberate consideration and much inter-departmental consultation."[108]

That was exactly what took place in the following weeks. When consulted by the State Department, the ExImBank opined that, instead of procuring a loan, Spain would do better to use its substantial gold reserves.[109] It was not until 1 November that Morgenthau finally disclosed his ideas to his colleagues at the State Department, during a visit the chief of the DWEA, James C. Dunn, paid to him to discuss the general situation in Europe. When Dunn was about to leave, the secretary assured him that the time had come to make a loan to some European country, "as we are rapidly accumulating all the gold and silver in the world, and it was up to us to do something about it." Morgenthau thought the ExImBank was too timid and should be controlled by both the State and the Treasury Departments, to pursue more ambitious schemes. Dunn answered that he did not want "to hook the loan up" with the trade negotiations, and Morgenthau then proposed to wait until they were concluded. The DWEA's chief agreed, not knowing that he was playing into Morgenthau's hand. The secretary confided in his diary that he "would much rather make the loan purely as a financial matter and entirely independent of any trade treaties." He was adhering to the practice inaugurated in 1928, when the Treasury had refused to tie the first Morgan loan to the State Department's needs. Morgenthau was not sure whether Henry Wallace, the secretary of agriculture, would be supportive; he was "in favour of our making loans abroad, but wants to tie it up very closely with the tariff. The Treasury chief promised to 'take up the idea of a loan to Spain with the President'."[110]

If the proposal ever went to Roosevelt's desk, the result was contrary to Morgenthau's wishes. Meanwhile, differences of opinion arose in Spain among officials in the Ministry of State. In July, Ambassador Calderón had written a personal letter to the undersecretary, José María Aguinaga – the highest-ranking non-political officer in the ministry – casting doubts on any loan, especially if it was conditional to the signature of a commercial agreement. He was worried about "the credit creating a precedent for other countries, so that

[108] Tel. 60, Hull to Bowers, 19 September 1935, NARA, RG 59, 1930–1939, 852.51/299A.

[109] Memo, Hansen to Grady, 16 September 1935, NARA, RG 59, 1930–1939, 852.5151/145.

[110] Morgenthau's Diary, 1 November 1935, FDR Library, Morgenthau Papers, Series 1, vol. 11, 1. Memo by Dunn, 1 November 1935, NARA, RG 59, 1930–1939, 852.51/314.

THE UNITED STATES AND THE SECOND SPANISH REPUBLIC (1931–1936)   31

it became a lever or a precondition for the signing of new trade agreements with us." It was also not clear to him if the loan should be of a public or a private nature, and he requested to be heard personally in Madrid before any final decision was made.[111]

The demise of Morgenthau's project was staged on 17 January 1936, when the secretary received Sosthenes Behn and Frank Page – also of IT&T – in the Treasury building. They had gone there to show their interest in the matter, only to see the secretary picking up his phone to call Dunn and make him a witness to their conversation. With the DWEA's head on the other end of the line, Morgenthau declared to Behn that the issue of the loan had been abandoned until the trade negotiations had come to an end. In any case, the Treasury had nothing against private citizens advancing their money for that very same end.[112]

In Search of a Private Loan (1936)

The managers of both the Bank of Spain and the COCM did not wait for the failure of the public loan option to approach private institutions with the same goal in mind. To guarantee it they banked on the success of an operation that was also part of Chapaprieta's reforms: the restructuring of the gold bonds Calvo Sotelo had issued in 1929. A total of 280 million gold pesetas were paid off in silver pesetas, while the 20 million pesetas held by foreign investors were exchanged with gold bonds at 4 percent. The recovered bonds were also converted to the new paper, to use them as collateral for new loans.[113] Pedro Pan went to Paris to approach representatives of different banking houses, among them the subsidiaries of Morgan and National City Bank. He had in mind a credit of $40 million – though through an intermediary he ventured a much higher figure: $150 million. His interlocutors were ready to study the proposal, but only if it was backed with gold sent to London. After conferring with U.S. businessmen, Pan thought he should try his chances directly in the United States, but the trip never materialized. He did contact French and British bankers, also to no avail.[114]

The situation deteriorated in early 1936. The COCM delays provoked more and more irate protests from Great Britain and France, which still did not understand why their goods were detained when Spain enjoyed substantial

[111] Letter, Calderón to Aguinaga, 10 July 1935. The same suspicions in disp. 417, Calderón to Rocha, 9 August 1935, AMAE, R704/9.

[112] Memo by Dunn, 17 January 1936, NARA, RG 59, 1930–1939, 852.51/321.

[113] Á, Viñas et al., *Política Comercial...*, 107–8. Also tel. 618, Marriner to Hull, 20 July 1935, NARA, RG 59, 1930–1939, 851.5151/550.

[114] Tel. 822, Marriner to Hull, 26 September 1935, NARA, RG 59, 1930–1939, 851.5151/613.

trade surpluses with them. The government of Manuel Portela Valladares, with Chapaprieta still at the Finance Ministry, was thus forced to negotiate exchange treaties with both countries, which in the case of France served to end the tariff war initiated the previous summer. The French agreement was signed on 21 December 1935 and was the more onerous because Spain promised to liquidate all arrears in a period of three months. The British treaty of 6 January 1936 envisaged that Spain would use all sterling obtained from exports to the United Kingdom to pay back those arrears, without any possibility of using it, as was common, to pay for U.S. imports.[115] The clock started ticking for the Madrid government to find the funds necessary to fulfil its newly acquired obligations to France. Back in Washington, the completion of a draft trade treaty had nurtured the hopes of the State Department, which saw with dismay that Spain was not making any move to ratify it, while the exchange situation kept aggravating. With British pounds blocked to pay U.K. exporters, licenses for importing American goods suffered delays of 331 days in March 1936.[116] All this happened in the midst of a political whirlwind provoked by the ineffectiveness of the Portela cabinet, the call for a new general election on 16 February and the ensuing victory of the Popular Front – a broad left-wing coalition. Three days later Manuel Azaña formed its fourth government.

The last attempts to find a new loan abroad failed with the new cabinet. In December 1935 Chapaprieta had finally found an institution – the Mendelssohn Bank of Amsterdam – willing to make Spain a loan of $10 million, but his successor at the Finance Ministry decided not to proceed with it. On 3 March 1936, Blas Huete had an interview with Georges de Castellane, who represented the interests of the U.S. Bankers Trust. Spain had by then been forced to send 150 million francs in gold to France to make good on its promise of liquidating the exchange arrears, and more shipments of gold would soon follow, so the Bank of Spain's reserves went down from $735 million to $718 million. De Castellane offered a low-interest credit of $80–100 million for two years against gold. Huete tried unsuccessfully to convince him to accept the new gold bonds, and then proposed to ship gold but only after the loan's termination. Huete's suggestion probably indicated that Spain could not maintain its refusal to use gold to cover the operations of the COCM for long. After consulting with his superiors, de Castellane indicated that his bank "would be definitely interested in the proposition." The U.S. commercial attaché was enthusiastic: "The whole matter is of exceptional interest and in the problematical event that it should prove possible to carry the negotiations

---

[115] The contents of the agreements in Á, Viñas et al., *Política Comercial...*, 110–11. Also in letters, Behn to Sayre, 8 and 13 January 1936, NARA, RG 59, 1930–1939, 852.5151/167 and 211.

[116] Disp. 1,062, Johnson to Hull, 4 March 1936, NARA, RG 59, 1930–1939, 852.5151/193.

THE UNITED STATES AND THE SECOND SPANISH REPUBLIC (1931–1936)   33

to a successful conclusion, would appear to provide an at least temporary solution of Spain's exchange problem."[117]

Azaña could not find even a provisional solution to the deadlock of the COCM. Officials in Washington wanted now to make the ratification of the trade agreement conditional on the limitation of delays in exchange permits.[118] When on 15 April 1936 the new prime minister presented his program before parliament, he admitted that the situation was extremely delicate, and seemed open to every option.[119] Hallett Johnson, the American *chargé d'affaires*, was rather doubtful: "the Prime Minister's views are well-known and thus there is not a better prospect for an improvement in the exchange situation."[120] But none of the alternatives seemed good enough for the government: financial orthodoxy showed its limitations once more, making a devaluation appear hideous. Gold was still considered a source of prestige, to be preserved at any cost. The political groups supporting the new cabinet looked at foreign loans with extreme reluctance, in line with their opposition against the Morgan credit five years before. In the aftermath of the February election, the daily *El Sol* had made a good assessment of the deadlock in the monetary situation:

> With good intentions, with the wishful hope tradition and custom dictate to us –that time will with some contingencies solve all economic difficulties – the exchange problem has been put aside on the table by all those whose obligation it was to solve it. For no apparent reason, the last one who stumbled upon it tried to put together some solutions, to weigh up some way out. He was not given enough time to develop a complete plan. The moment comes when no subterfuge or dilatory tactic will be enough. The problem is presented before us in all its integrity and will admit of no delay. We must pay. That is the only truth. And while we pay, we face the terrible complication that we must pay in gold. The line of resistance that had at all times prevented us from using the classical system is now broken; and it does so late and painfully. This is not the worst, but that nothing is now solved with this solution, which will drain, greatly or lightly, our gold reserves. France must be paid its arrears in exchange and so must the other nations. But even liquidating all the arrears, the exchange problem will not be solved, as we have said one and a thousand times. There will remain as a final task that of providing a solution to the main cause, which surely will not be pleasing to anybody, and

[117] Disp. 1,069, Johnson to Hull, 9 March 1936, NARA, RG 59, 1930–1939, 852.5151/195.

[118] Memo, Morgan to Phillips, 14 March 1936, NARA, RG 59, 1930–1939, 852.5151/195½.

[119] "La declaración ministerial. Discurso del Presidente del Gobierno," *El Sol*, 16 April 1936, 7.

[120] Desp. 1,062…

which task will have in itself the germ of greatest unpopularity. We shall insist on our unalterable point of view. Even if we have recourse to a readjustment of the peseta, we shall not have found a solution, because the anaesthesia of a lowering of exchange will avoid some difficulties, but it will not cure the sickness that exists, nor will it do away with the necessity of producing a readjustment in our complex economic system. Before taking any action, before giving solutions of the simplest kind and headed in only one direction, let us not forget this warning. It is necessary to find various connected solutions, linked and combined, which united give the most efficient result. The problem of exchange in Spain is not only a financial problem, but very much of an economic one.[121]

Though the coming of winter made it more plausible that, out of sheer necessity, the government would implement a radical solution, it is not strange that in the increasingly rarefied political atmosphere of 1936, both Azaña and his successor, Casares Quiroga, opted to delay any solution. The uprising of 17 July 1936 became a turning point leading to a completely different scenario. There had not been either an American loan or a U.S.–Spanish commercial treaty.

Coda

On 11 February 1935 Sosthenes Behn received an interesting piece of information from a Spanish importer in Madrid. The man had bought $300,000 worth of American tobacco and was experiencing the usual delays when asking for the mandatory COCM license. He had then come up with an idea that he shared with the centre: he "applied for a permit to use the peseta in the purchase of merchandise here to be exported and to apply the proceeds in payment of the tobacco previously purchased." This system of double payments, which avoided the export of currency on both sides, had a long history in U.S.–Spanish relations, dating back to at least 1918, and was widely used to overcome some of the financial effects of the Great Depression. It was probably for the latter reason that the merchant thought the Bank of Spain would not have any problem in accepting the deal. But it responded that "it had not previously allowed compensation transactions and were reluctant to do so."[122] The COCM suspected, with good reason, that should the method expand more widely, it would end up losing control of monetary operations. Exporters and importers would likely come to a private agreement before applying for permits, reducing the amount of currency at the disposal of the center and therefore its ability to prioritize the importation of vital supplies.

---

[121] "¿Se le va a pagar el oro a España? El problema del cambio," *El Sol*, 21 February 1936, 7.

[122] Tel. in letter, Page to Phillips, 16 July 1935, NARA, RG 59, 1930–1939, 852.5151/132.

THE UNITED STATES AND THE SECOND SPANISH REPUBLIC (1931–1936)   35

Despite being rejected, the proposal left its imprint and was taken up by the very same American embassy to fund some of its operations during the Second World War. Americans could then count on the experience they had accumulated in the 1930s and on their contacts among important official and private Spanish circles.[123] Therefore, it is not far-fetched to venture that, beyond the changes in Spanish domestic and international conditions provoked by the events unleashed on 18 July 1936, there were also meaningful continuities. A new regime came into being and, with the fall of the Republic, many of the protagonists of U.S.–Spanish relations moved away from the scene. But others, public and private, individual and collective alike, remained in their positions, allowing the know-how acquired before the Civil War to be kept alive on both sides of the Atlantic, ready to be recalled should the opportunity arise.

Sources

Archives, newspapers and journals

Old Archives of the Ministry of Foreign Affairs (Madrid, Spain)
Franklin Roosevelt Presidential Library (Hyde Park, NY, Estados Unidos)
National Archives & Records Administration (Estados Unidos) (College Park, MD)
The New York Times
El Sol
El Imparcial
Gaceta de Madrid
Heraldo de Madrid
El Liberal
Federal Reserve Bulletin

Bibliography

Álvaro Moya, A., *Inversión directa extranjera y formación de capacidades organizativas locales: un análisis del impacto de Estados Unidos en la empresa española (1918–1975)*, Unpublished doctoral thesis, Universidad Complutense de Madrid, 2011.
Berdah, J.-F., *La democracia asesinada. La República Española y las grandes potencias, 1931–1939*, Barcelona, Crítica, 2002.
Bosch, A., "Entre México y la Unión Soviética: La visión estadounidense sobre los conflictos sociales en la Segunda República Española (1931–1936)," *Historia Contemporánea*, 15 (1996), 315–342.
Bosch, A., *Miedo a la democracia. Estados Unidos ante la Segunda República y la guerra civil española*, Barcelona, Crítica, 2012.

---

[123] See Pablo León Aguinaga, *Sospechosos habituales. El cine norteamericano, Estados Unidos y la España franquista*, Madrid, CSIC, 2010; Joan María Thomàs, *Roosevelt y Franco. De la Guerra Civil española a Pearl Harbor*, Barcelona, Edhasa, 2007.

Bowers, C. G., *My Mission to Spain. Watching the Rehearsal for World War II*, New York, Simon and Schuster, 1954.

Carreras, A. and Tafunell, X., *Historia Económica de la España Contemporánea*, Barcelona, Crítica, 2006.

Chernow, R., *The House of Morgan. An American Banking Dynasty and the Rise of Modern Finance*, New York, Grove Press, 2010.

Clavin, P., *Securing the World Economy. The Reinvention of the League of Nations, 1920–1946*, Oxford, Oxford University Press, 2013.

Clavin, P., *The Failure of Economic Diplomacy. Britain, Germany, France and the United States, 1931–36*, London, MacMillan, 1996.

Dallek, R., *Franklin D. Roosevelt and American Foreign Policy, 1932–1945*, New York, Oxford University Press, 1995.

Denéchère, Y., *La politique espagnole de la France. De 1931 à 1936*, Paris, L'Harmattan, 1999.

Egido León, M. Á., *La concepción de la política exterior española durante la Segunda República*, Madrid, UNED, 1987.

Egido León, M. Á., "La dimensión internacional de la Segunda República: un proyecto en el crisol," in J. Tusell, J. Avilés and R. Pardo (eds.), *La política exterior de España en el Siglo XX*, Madrid, Biblioteca Nueva, 2000, 189–220.

Egido León, M. Á., "La proyección exterior de España en los años treinta," in M. Á. Egido León (ed.), *La Segunda República y su proyección internacional*, Madrid, Catarata, 2017, 9–28.

Eichengreen, B., *Golden Fetters. The Gold Standard and the Great Depression, 1919–1939*, New York, Oxford University Press, 1992.

Federal Reserve Board, *Federal Reserve Bulletin. December 1931*, Washington, Government Printing Office, 1931.

González Calleja, E., *La España de Primo de Rivera. La modernización autoritaria*, Madrid, Alianza, 2005.

Irwin, D. A., *Clashing Over Commerce. A History of U.S. Trade Policy*, Chicago, Amunárriz, Chicago Press, 2017.

Irwin, D. A., *Peddling Protectionism. Smoot-Hawley and the Great Depression*, Princeton, Princeton University Press, 2011.

Jones, J. R. jr., *Tariff Retaliation: Repercussions of the Hawley–Smoot Tariff*, Philadelphia, University of Pennsylvania Press, 1934.

Juliá, S., *Elogio de Historia en tiempo de memoria*, Madrid, Marcial Pons, 2011.

Kindleberger, Ch. P., *The World in Depression, 1929–1939*, Berkeley, University of California Press, 1986.

León Aguinaga, P., *Sospechosos habituales. El cine norteamericano, Estados Unidos y la España franquista*, Madrid, CSIC, 2010.

Little, D. J., "Claude Bowers and His Mission to Spain: The Diplomacy of a Jeffersonian Democrat," in K. P. Jones (ed.), *U.S. Diplomats in Europe, 1919–1941*, Santa Barbara, ABC-Clio, 1981, 129–46.

Little, D. J., "Twenty Years of Turmoil: ITT, the State Department and Spain, 1924–1944," *Business History Review*, vol. 53, n. 4 (1979), 449–72.

Little, D. J., *Malevolent Neutrality: the United States, Great Britain, and the Origins of the Spanish Civil War*, Ithaca, Cornell University Press, 1985.

THE UNITED STATES AND THE SECOND SPANISH REPUBLIC (1931–1936) 37

Madariaga, S., *Memorias (1921–1936). Amanecer sin mediodía*, Madrid, Espasa-Calpe, 1981.

Martín Aceña, P. and Pons, M. Á., "Sistema monetario y financiero," in A. Carreras and X. Tafunell (eds.), *Estadísticas Históricas de España*, Bilbao, Fundación BBVA, 2005, 645–706.

Martínez Ovejero, A., "Azaña versus Telefónica, los límites del poder," *Espacio, Tiempo y Forma. Serie V*, 16 (2004), 121–48.

Montero, J. (ed.), *Constituciones y códigos políticos españoles, 1808–1978*, Barcelona, Ariel, 1998.

Montero Jiménez, J. A., *El despertar de la gran potencia. Las relaciones entre España y los Estados Unidos (1898–1930)*, Madrid, Biblioteca Nueva, 2011.

Neila Hernández, J. L., *La 2ª República y el Mediterráneo*, Madrid, Dilema, 2006.

Quintana Navarro, F., *España en Europa, 1931–1936. Del compromiso por la paz a la huida de la Guerra*, Madrid, Nerea, 1993.

Ramsay, S., "Ideological Foundations of British Non-Intervention in the Spanish Civil War: Foreign Office Perceptions of Political Polarisation in Spain, 1931–1936," *Diplomacy & Statecraft*, vol. 31 (2012), 44–64.

Tasca, H. J., *The Reciprocal Trade Policy of the Unites States*, Philadelphia, University of Pennsylvania Press, 1938.

Thomàs, J. M., *Roosevelt y Franco. De la Guerra Civil española a Pearl Harbor*, Barcelona, Edhasa, 2007.

Tierney, D., *FDR and the Spanish Civil War. Neutrality and Commitment in the Struggle That Divided America*, Durham, Duke University Press, 2007.

Traina, R. P., *American Diplomacy and the Spanish Civil War*, Bloomington, Indiana University Press, 1968.

Viñas, Á., *La soledad de la República*, Barcelona, Crítica, 2006.

Viñas, Á., Viñuela, J., Eguidazu, F., Fernández Pulgar, C. and Florensa, S., *Política Comercial Exterior en España, 1931–1975*, Madrid, Banco Exterior de España, 1979.

Wilkins, M., *The Maturing of Multinational Enterprise: American Business Abroad from 1914 to 1970*, Cambridge, Harvard University Press, 1974.

2

The Chase, the World Commerce Corporation, and the Early Cold War Rehabilitation of Franco's Spain

PABLO LEÓN AGUINAGA

Introduction

Who benefited from the rapprochement between the United States and Spain at the beginning of the Cold War?[1] This basic question has not yet been satisfactorily answered in the historiography, especially as one moves from the macro to the micro level and from the political to the economic dimension. The fact that the Spanish dictatorship was reinforced internally and internationally is not disputed, since the marriage of convenience between Madrid and Washington effectively put an end to the quarantine that the United Nations had imposed on Franco's Spain; nor is it in doubt that U.S. security strategy was underpinned as a result of the rapprochement, albeit at the cost of eroding the image of the North American giant as *the* champion of democracy in the post-war world. Specialists also seem to agree that Spain gained little if at all in the way of security, since the national territory and some of its major cities became a target of potential Soviet attacks and were exposed to accidents with U.S. nuclear weapons (such as the one in Palomares in 1966), all without the Spanish government obtaining a guarantee of security from Washington and given that the scale of modernization of the Spanish armed forces was far from what was intended.[2] In economic terms, there seems to be a growing consensus that the bilateral rapprochement, although far from having effects comparable to the benefits derived from the Marshall Plan for countries such as Italy, did have positive effects for the Iberian country. American aid per se was most important for Spain for its intangible consequences, as Washington's

---

[1]   This chapter was made possible thanks to support from Projects HAR2017–82194-P and CUD2023–11.

[2]   L. Delgado, and P. León Aguinaga, "De la primacía estratégica a la difusión del modelo americano: Estados Unidos y la España del franquismo," in *Nuevos horizontes del pasado. Culturas políticas, identidades y formas de representación*, Santander, Publican, 2011, 171–185.

political support contributed to generating confidence in the viability of the country and was also instrumental in the training of human capital and the reorientation of macroeconomic policies that allowed the country to belatedly join the post-war cycle of Western prosperity.[3] But the more one descends in the analysis of these economic effects in search of the sectors and corporate agents most benefited by the bilateral rapprochement, the more unanswered questions pop up. To be sure, previous research has identified some key milestones, issues, and actors, but many of the latter's motives and roles are yet to be explored.[4] This chapter aims to partially correct the lack of information on the motivations of two of the most relevant corporate agents in the Spanish–U.S. early Cold War rapprochement: the Chase National Bank[5] and the American cotton sector.

The studies that have paid attention to the so-called "Spanish lobby" in the United States have repeatedly alluded to the importance of cotton interests in understanding the growing support for the normalization of bilateral relations in the U.S. Congress. However, no monographs have yet been written about it.[6] What companies made it up? Who were the key agents and supporters in Spain? Even more striking is the absence of work on Wall Street, especially given the importance of the loans made by Chase and National City Bank (NCB)[7] in 1949 and 1950 respectively. Existing studies have also revealed that the Chase was already involved in talks on upgrading the country's main airports in 1948, that the Spanish diplomatic mission in the United States courted the favor of Chase's President Winthrop W. Aldrich throughout that same year, and that the bank was involved in financial talks with several important Spanish companies since at least 1949.[8] But, as we shall see, the

---

[3] A summary of interpretations of the global and macroeconomic effects in A. Carreras and X. Tafunell, *Historia económica de la España contemporánea (1789–2009)*, Barcelona, Crítica, 2016, 304.

[4] A good overview in A. Álvaro Moya, *Inversión directa extranjera y formación de capacidades organizativas locales: un análisis del impacto de Estados Unidos en la empresa española (1918–1975)*, Unpublished doctoral thesis, Universidad Complutense de Madrid, 2011.

[5] The Chase, established in 1877, became the Chase Manhattan Bank in 1955.

[6] For the literature on cotton interests and the "Spanish Lobby" in the early Cold War, see the chapter by Joan María Thomàs. On the unique influence of the cotton lobby in the design of tariff and trade policies in the United States, see D. A. Irwin, *Clashing Over Commerce. A History of U.S. Trade Policy*, Chicago, University of Chicago Press, 2017.

[7] Established in 1867, NCB was renamed First National City Bank in 1955.

[8] B. Liedtke, *Embracing a Dictatorship. US Relations with Spain, 1945–53*, London, MacMillan, 1998, 55; X. Hualde Amunárriz, *El "cerco aliado". Estados Unidos, Gran Bretaña y Francia frente a la dictadura franquista (1945–1953)*, Bilbao, UPV/EHU, 2016, 215–226; M. J. Cava Mesa, *Los diplomáticos de Franco. J. F. de Lequerica, temple y tenacidad (1890–1963)*, Bilbao, Deusto, 1989, 268, 298; and A. Álvaro Moya, *Direct investment...*, 138–143.

historiography has not yet delved into that, nor has it dug deeper, leaving the most important questions to be answered: why did a corporation of the importance of Chase bet on working with a regime whose autarkic policy was hostile to foreign investment? How does such an attitude fit in with the Truman administration's policy towards the Franco regime? And with that of Wall Street in post-war Europe? What role did the new transatlantic capitalism that was rising from the ashes of war, the Bretton Woods conference, and the Marshall Plan play in this story?

Another gap in post-war U.S.–Spanish economic relations has to do with the lack of knowledge about the agents of the small yet revealing bilateral trade flow. Their identity, interests, and networks deserve greater attention, especially given the peculiarity and opacity of the operations necessary to finance exchanges between the great capitalist superpower and a country with an overvalued currency and an exchange and commercial regime as intricate as corrupt.[9] Filling in this gap is pressing, since some of these agents played a prominent role in bilateral economic relations until at least the late 1950s. This is the case with the World Commerce Corporation (WCC), a company based in New York but incorporated in Panama, one of the "islands" of the "offshore archipelago" of tax havens that emerged in the shadow of the expansion of the Bretton Woods system; another of these enclaves, Tangier, also played an important but mostly unexplored role in Spanish–American economic relations of the time.[10] Both the WCC and Chase – together with NCB and the Manufacturers Trust Company – were chosen as strategic partners of the Spanish Institute of Foreign Currency (IEME) in the very important Dollar–Peseta Program which, among other things, sought to stabilize the value of the peseta in Tangier between 1952 and 1959, which reaffirms the need to

---

[9] Scholarly attention to corruption in Spanish foreign economic relations has yet to take off. For a few exceptions see G. Sánchez Recio and J. Tascón (eds.), *Los empresarios de Franco. Política y economía en España, 1936–1957*, Barcelona, Crítica, 2003; B. de Riquer, J. L. Pérez Francesch, G. Rubí, L. Ferrán Toledano and O. Luján (dirs.), *La corrupción política en la España contemporánea. Un enfoque interdisciplinar*, Barcelona, Marcial Pons, 2018; C. Barciela López and M. A. del Arco (coords.), "Dossier. La corrupción en la España contemporánea," *Hispania Nova: Revista de Historia Contemporánea*, vol. 16 (2018), 473–734.

[10] V. Ogle, "Archipelago Capitalism: Tax Havens, Offshore Money, and the State, 1950s–1970s," *American Historical Review*, vol. 122, n. 5 (2017), 1431–1458. On Tangier, see V. Ogle, "'Funk Money': The End of Empire, the Expansion of Tax Havens, and Decolonization as an Economic and Financial Event," *Past & Present*, vol. 249, n. 1 (2020), 221–223. The importance of Tangier for the Spanish economy of the 1940s and 1950s is implicitly but tangentially addressed in most of the works on the economic history of Francoism, especially in connection with the price of the peseta in her free market. See for example: A. Carreras and X. Tafunell, *Historia económica de la España contemporánea (1789–2009)*, Barcelona, Crítica, 2016, 298–301.

THE CHASE, WORLD COMMERCE AND COLD WAR REHABILITATION   41

investigate the roots of their Spanish connections.[11] That is even more the case considering that Chase, NCB, and Manufacturers Trust were awarded the right to pre-finance most of the U.S. economic aid that began to flow to Spain in 1951, and that WCC also benefited from that flow of American taxpayers' dollars. That the Dollar–Peseta Program was a victim of Spain's belated access to the International Monetary Fund and the International Bank for Reconstruction and Development, that the Spanish entry quotas to both organizations were covered in part thanks to a loan from Chase, NCB, and Manufacturers Trust, and that again these three banks were the leading force behind a Wall Street syndicated loan in support of the Stabilization Plan of 1959 explains the importance of shedding light on the origins of their interests and operations in Spain.

In order to elucidate the relationship between the WCC, Chase, and the Franco dictatorship, this chapter will first look at the initial contacts between Wall Street and the Rebel or Nationalist side in the midst of the Spanish Civil War, as well as the loan that the government of the United States made to the new Spanish authorities via the Export-Import Bank (EIB) in August 1939, and to the subsequent attempts of the former to obtain financing from New York banks. The next section will focus on the effects of the Second World War on bilateral transactions, with special emphasis on the footprint left by U.S. economic warfare and covert operations in the Iberian Peninsula. The following section will focus on documenting the commitment of Chase and the WCC to operate in Spain during the most intense years of the isolation of the Franco regime by the United Nations. The fourth and last section will connect the intensification of these two corporate players' bet on the bilateral rapprochement that led to the granting of American economic aid and the normalization of diplomatic relations.

Throughout the chapter, the focus will be on the leading roles of Alfred W. Barth (Chase) and Frank T. Ryan (WCC) especially. Although both individuals had links with the U.S. espionage community, which had an ever-increasing influence on U.S. foreign policy after Pearl Harbor, this chapter proposes that the motivation behind the WCC's and Chase's bet on the survival of the Franco regime was predominantly monetary. The chapter will also focus attention on the role of the intermediaries and interlocutors of both companies in Spain, among whom figure individuals well-known in the historiography of bilateral

---

[11] For partial approaches to the program see: A. Viñas, J. Viñuela, F. Eguidazu, C. Fernández Pulgar, and S. Florensa, *Política Comercial Exterior en España, 1931–1975*, Madrid, Banco Exterior de España, 1979; E. Martínez Ruiz, *El sector exterior durante la autarquía. Una reconstrucción de las balanzas de pagos en España (1940–1958) (Edición Revisada), Estudios de Historia Económica n° 43*, Madrid, Banco de España, 2003 and J. de la Torre and M.M. Rubio Varas, *La financiación exterior del desarrollo industrial español. Estudios de Historia Económica n° 69*, Madrid, Banco de España, 2015.

PABLO LEÓN AGUINAGA

relations, for example lawyer Antonio Garrigues, as well as others who have been ignored to date, such as the Swiss-born merchant Victor Oswald and Spanish senior foreign trade and exchange officials including Blas Huete, Manuel Vila, Alejandro Bermúdez, and Manuel Arburúa.[12] The guiding hypothesis behind this research is that their behavior must be explored from a series of angles including their own interpretation of what constituted the national interest and the search for business opportunities.

Wall Street and the Coming of Dictatorship in Spain

During the Spanish Civil War the rebel side found a great deal of sympathy on Wall Street. Apart from ideological considerations, preexisting personal and professional connections played a role too. After all, as Montero's chapter points out, many of the Spaniards who had run bilateral economic and financial relations between the two nations before the internecine conflict – private and public bankers, merchants, diplomats, and trade representatives – held similar positions under the dictatorship that took control of Spain in 1936–1939. Sympathy, however, did not necessarily translate into cooperation, especially given the uncertainty created by the international situation and the political-economic dogma – autarkic pseudo fascism – adopted by the early Franco regime; in that sense, the wait-and-see attitude of the most relevant American banking institutions – including those with longer histories in Spain like the NCB – contrasted with the very tangible support for the rebel side from certain American companies in the automobile and oil sectors.[13]

For the duration of the hostilities and under the initiative of Vice-President G. Butler Sherwell, Manufacturers Trust was the most active Wall Street institution servicing the self-defined "National" rebels, for instance, in matters of "deposits in American banks from Spanish banks located in the National zone." The banker – and Hispanic Art collector – was likely guided in this

---

[12] The first three of them, the director and two vice presidents at IEME, played a key role during the Second World War and the immediate post-war period in the negotiations with the United States concerning Preventive Procurement and the Safehaven Program. See P. Martín Aceña, *El oro de Moscú y el oro de Berlín,* Madrid, Taurus, 2001. In the 1930s, M. Arburúa de la Miyar worked at the Bank of Spain and the Centro de Contratación de Moneda (IEME's precursor). During the dictatorship he was part of the Consejo de Economía Nacional and was one of IEME's founders, from where he joined the Subsecretaría de Comercio at the Ministry of Industry and Commerce in October 1940; in 1942 he was named director at the semi-official Banco Exterior: in 1951 he became minister of commerce; in 1957 he rejoined Banco Exterior as executive president, a position he held for two decades. See https://dbe. rah.es/biografias/7666/manuel-arburua-de-la-miyar.

[13] See J. M. Thomàs, *Roosevelt and Franco during the Second World War. From the Spanish Civil War to Pearl Harbor*, New York, Palgrave MacMillan, 2008, 28–31.

proactive approach by the same blend of sincere ideological sympathy and profit calculus that explained the behavior of other companies. There was little doubt that he intended to make his bank a strategic partner of the new Spanish regime, and that is exactly what Ricardo Pastor, one of the most important managers of the rebel force's finances, promised him: "this Spanish problem will be solved in a few days and then the time will have come to settle the score with people and entities depending how they treated us during the past two long years," adding that he "would support your bank receiving a good part of the Spanish banking business," while he criticized NCB's passive attitude.[14] In fact, when the war ended Manufacturers Trust was rewarded by becoming one of the three Wall Street correspondents of the IEME – the other two were NCB and Chase. Taking over the Comisión Nacional de Moneda Extranjera (1929–1936) and the Rebel's Comité de Moneda Extranjera (1936–1939), IEME's strategic role included defending the international value of the Spanish currency – the peseta – and overseeing all the autarkic country's silver, gold, and foreign exchange operations. For this purpose, the IEME, nominally under the powerful Ministry of Industry and Commerce (MIC), was independent from the Bank of Spain.[15]

Another prominent Wall Street firm that did not take long to enter into a commercial relationship with the new Spanish regime was Sullivan & Cromwell. The Bank of Spain hired their legal counsel services in the spring of 1939 in a $15 million lawsuit against the Federal Reserve of New York and two other entities of the U.S. Government in relation to a 1938 transaction involving the acquisition of silver from the Spanish National Treasury – the new authorities in Madrid claimed that the operation was illegal and therefore that the silver should be returned, and the Bank of Spain compensated.[16]

---

[14] See the correspondence between Ricardo Pastor (Banco Pastor), G. Butler Sherwell (Manufacturers) and José Larraz (Comité de Moneda Extranjera de la Junta Técnica de Burgos) in January–March 1939, AHBE, IEME, Caja 19. For the dominant position of NCB in bilateral financial relations in the interwar period see J. A. Montero Jiménez, *El despertar de la gran potencia. Las relaciones entre España y los Estados Unidos (1898–1930)*, Madrid, Biblioteca Nueva, 2011.

[15] IEME's functions were codified into law in August 1939 and were to "centralize, in exclusivity all transactions concerning coined or bullion silver and gold, all transactions concerning foreign exchange in Spain, all transactions concerning Spanish or foreign internationally listed titles, the reception and constitution of deposits, the opening of accounts in foreign exchange, to get or open credit in foreign exchange, and to have funds and get credit and other operations needed for the realization of the previous." IEME's director was nominated by the MIC and was supposed to coordinate also with the ministries of Finance and Foreign Relations. See J. de la Torre and M. M. Rubio Varas, *La financiación...*, 13–14.

[16] See P. Martín Aceña, *El oro de Moscú...*, 149–151. Future U.S. Secretary of State John Foster Dulles was the firm's lawyer in charge of the affair. It has been argued that such experience haunted him politically a decade later, when his rival pointed

44 PABLO LEÓN AGUINAGA

Preexisting contacts and former bilateral economic relations also explain why the U.S. government authorized a $12 million EIB loan to Spain in August 1939, barely a few months after the conclusion of the Spanish Civil War. It was the second EIB loan awarded to the Iberian nation; the previous one being a $15 million loan for tobacco awarded to the Republican government in 1934. Unlike the latter, the 1939 loan caused quite a stir in American public opinion because of the incredulity of anti-Fascist circles and the coincidence with the above-mentioned lawsuit, which was rejected by the Federal Court just in time for the loan's signature.[17] The credit was very much welcomed, however, in financial circles, with nine U.S. banks participating in opening of letters of credit to Spanish importers (Table 1), as well as among American cotton and rayon exporters, forty-four of whom dominated a trade that helped put an end to the sector's dry spell in their hitherto significant business with Spain.[18] Francoist authorities, for their part, paid back the credit by converting the foreign exchange created by Spanish textile exports to pound-sterling-area countries in the Middle East into dollars.[19]

Table 1. American banks participating in the August 1939 EIB loan to Spain

Manufacturers Trust Co.	National City Bank Co.	Chase National Bank Co.
International Banking Co.	Bank of Manhattan Co.	Irving Trust Co.
Central H. B. & Trust Co.	Chemical Bank Co.	Guaranty B. & Trust. Co.

Source: NACP, RG 275, Records of the Export-Import Bank of the United States, Credit Files, Credit no. #241, Box 55.

---

out to Dulles's work for dictatorial Spain in the closely fought senatorial election in New York in 1949 that ended the lawyer's short tenure in the U.S. Congress. See R. W. Pruessen, *John Foster Dulles: The Road to Power, Vol. 1*, New York, Free Press, 1982, 122–123.

[17] See J. M. Thomàs, *Roosevelt...*, 61–70. S. A comparison between the 1934 and 1939 loans in S. Trundle Jr., *The ExportImport Bank of Washington. Its Origins, Operations and Relationships with other Government agencies, 1934–1950*, New Brunswick, Rutgers University, 1950. On the EIB and U.S. trade from the Great Depression see D. A. Irwin, *Clashing....*

[18] In 1935, the last year before civil war broke out, cotton represented 60 percent of Spain's imports from the United States. See A. Álvaro Moya, "Inversión directa...," 130. Such relevance explains the preponderance of the textile sector in the Barcelona based American Chamber of Commerce in Spain.

[19] On the loan's beneficiaries see NACP, RG 275, Records of the Export-Import Bank of the United States, Credit Files, Credit no. #241, box 5. On the repayment method see "Concesión créditos norteamericanos por ExImBank a España," 3 November 1949, SEPI-INI-JAS, box 6.

The outbreak of the Second World War did not prevent the new Spanish authorities from pursuing new loans in the also neutral United States, either from the EIB or on Wall Street. The Spanish ambassador in Washington, Juan Cárdenas, was promptly directed to curry the favor of high-ranking bureaucrats at the Treasury Department who had an established relationship with Spain, such as H. Merle Cochran.[20] In May 1940, the diplomat also met with Undersecretary Summer Welles at the Department of State to explore the Roosevelt administration's position on the matter. Welles replied that his government would not interfere in operations of this nature since the banks were "free to operate on their own account," adding that he was willing "to interpose his good offices" near the EIB. That same month, Jesús Rodríguez (IEME) traveled to Manhattan to explore "a possible major impulse to the limited banking support that we have hitherto obtained" in the form of "short-term commercial credits." In New York both Rodríguez and Cárdenas, either together or separately, were received at the headquarters of the Manufacturers Trust, Chase, NCB, and Morgan.[21] They were not very successful.

In the final report of his exploratory mission, Rodríguez explained that any attempt to divert the conversation to more concrete issues about trade and financial relations between Spain and the United States "ran into the wall of the new world war" – something unsurprising given that the Germans' spring offensive had just broken the Franco-British lines in France. At Chase the response was blunt: "If I now presented a proposal to the Board of the Bank to extend our operations with Spain, given the European situation, they would take me for a crazy person and throw me out of the Bank." A vice-president at NCB excused himself with a "if it weren't for the war a lot could be done but...," although at least Rodríguez was able to liquidate a sale of silver from the Spanish National Treasury worth $1.5 million (the next Spanish silver operation in Wall Street would have to await until 1948). At the better predisposed Manufacturers Trust, the specific plans presented by Rodríguez also fell on deaf ears. Faced with a proposal to explore credit operations guaranteed by Argentine securities deposited in the Buenos Aires branch of a U.S. bank, Manufacturers Trusts' response was that "we cannot venture or risk one more step." All four major banks had shown themselves open to dialogue and future collaboration with the Spanish authorities, but if the war raged on Rodríguez concluded that "little or nothing can be done." He also

---

[20] See Embajada de España en París, "Reglamento general del Export-Import Bank de Washington," 15 June 1938, Telegrama IEME a Sr. Cárdenas, embajador de España en los Estados Unidos, 11 November 1939 and Manuel Arburúa (IEME). A. H. Merle Cochran, Treasury Department, 18 October 1939. AHBE-IEME, box 19. Cochran's personal archive at the University of Arizona does not seem to contain information of his Spanish contacts.

[21] "Informe sobre mi viaje a los EE.UU." and annexes 1 to 5, no date [5/1940], AHBE, IEME, box 19.

pointed out in his report that in every single interview Wall Street executives expressed their discomfort with Spain's foreign exchange legislation, delayed transfers, and blocked funds, as well as with the absence of "statistics" and reliable information "on the financial panorama of his country," including the "balance sheet of the issuing bank," a thinly veiled reference to the lack of transparency of both the Bank of Spain and the IEME.[22]

At the end of 1940, when Nazi Germany was seemingly approaching total victory in Europe, a freshly re-elected Roosevelt was rallying his country's pro-Allied stand, and a brief British-American boycott of supplies to now "non-belligerent" Spain had just been lifted – it had been imposed after Spain's unilateral occupation of the International City of Tangier in June 1940 – a representative of NCB consulted the Treasury Department about a hypothetical private $10 million loan to the Spanish government.[23] The proposal did not materialize, but it is illustrative of the intentions of certain American financial institutions with respect to Spain at the time. The international events of 1941, a year in which the United States declared economic warfare against the Axis and ultimately became a belligerent, postponed such contacts until the post-war period. By then, the Chase had become Spain's main partner in Wall Street.

Total Warfare and Its Legacy for Bilateral (Economic) Relations

In wartime Washington, Franco's Spain represented an important theater in the economic, diplomatic, and intelligence spheres of the total war of the United Nations against the Axis. After Pearl Harbor, the size of the U.S. embassy in Madrid grew accordingly to accommodate a growing number of officers and emergency or wartime agencies. Their deployment, completed throughout 1942, coincided with the arrival of a new ambassador handpicked by Roosevelt: Carlton Hayes, who would stay in the country until January 1945.[24] Hayes and the diplomats on whom he relied during his mission in Madrid, especially his two senior advisers, William Beaulac and Walt Butterworth, went on to clash with many of the aforementioned emergency agencies, which had their own agendas and whose personnel was on many occasions new to the modes and

---

[22] Ibid.

[23] "The Proposed Loan to Spain," 16 December 1940 and "Letter Dictated over the Telephone by Mr. H.C. Sheperd, Vice President of the National City Bank of New York, 18 April 1940," NACP, RG 56, OASIA, Subject Files, 1934–1972, box 24. See also J. M. Thomàs, *Roosevelt...*, 93–100. On the first oil embargo to Spain in the context of U.S. economic warfare, see T. Mulder, *The Economic Weapon. The Rise of Sanctions as a Tool of Modern War*, New Haven and London, Yale University Press, 2022.

[24] J. M. Thomàs, *Roosevelt and Franco and the end of the Second World War*, New York, Palgrave MacMillan, 2011, 2–4.

THE CHASE, WORLD COMMERCE AND COLD WAR REHABILITATION   47

hierarchies of the diplomatic world. In the case of Spain, these differences were notable in terms of propaganda and in relation to the performance of the Office of Strategic Services (OSS), the precursor of the CIA.[25] The tension also ran high between the Washington agencies responsible for economic warfare and the legation in Madrid, specifically because of the divergences on how to exploit Spain's dependence on U.S. strategic exports such as oil, cereal, and cotton.[26]

Less controversial was the coordination between the embassy and the U.S. Commercial Company (USCC), the wartime branch of the Reconstruction Finance Corporation responsible for executing the Preventive Procurement Program on the ground and in coordination with its British counterpart (UKCC) and the U.S. mission in Lisbon. Day-to-day negotiations between the USCC and its Spanish interlocutors – the economic ministries and IEME – was in the hands of Butterworth and the commercial attaché Ralph Ackerman, but they depended on the technical specialists that the USCC assigned to Madrid.[27] Alfred Barth, an executive on leave from the Chase, stood out among them. His stay in the Spanish capital, which began in the autumn of 1942, would last until November 1944, coinciding with the liberation of the Pyrenean border and the termination of the USCC mission in Spain.

Alfred William Barth was born in 1903 in Zurich, a city that epitomized Switzerland's bid to become a hub of the international financial industry.[28] After completing his education in international trade at the Handelsschule des Kaufmännnischen Vereins, Barth moved to the United States in 1921, settling in Manhasset, Long Island, New York. Soon after, he landed a job at Equitable Trust, a prestigious Wall Street firm. After the merging of Equitable and Chase, Barth and his immediate superior, Charles Cain Jr., joined the giant

---

[25] For the case of propaganda, see P. León Aguinaga, "The Trouble with Propaganda. World War II, Franco Spain, and the Origins of U.S. Postwar Public Diplomacy," *International History Review*, vol. 37, n. 2 (2015), 342–365; for the general lines of the conflict between the embassy and the OSS, whose work is awaiting a monographic investigation, see J. M. Thomàs, *Roosevelt....*

[26] For the evolution of that tug of war, which had its climax in the tungsten crisis, J. M. Thomàs, *Roosevelt...*, chapters 2 and 3.

[27] The work of the USCC and the Preventive Procurement Program in Spain is still awaiting a case study. For partial approaches see E. K. Lindley and E. Weintal, "How We Dealt with Spain," *Harper's Magazine*, vol. 190 (1944), 23–33; H. Feis, *The Spanish Story: Franco and the Nations at War*, New York, Knopf, 1948; Viñas et al., *Política comercial...*; C. Leitz, *Economic Relations between Nazi Germany and Franco's Spain, 1936–1945*, Oxford, Clarendon Press, 1996 and P. León Aguinaga, *Sospechosos habituales. El cine norteamericano, Estados Unidos y la España franquista, 1939–1960*, Madrid, CSIC, 2010, chapter 2.

[28] C. Farquet, *Histoire du paradis fiscal Suisse*, Paris, Science Po, 2018.

led by Winthrop Aldrich.[29] In 1938, Barth was promoted to assistant cashier, the position he held when the United States declared economic warfare on the Axis powers: he oversaw the process of freezing all Axis-owned assets at the Chase Bank, which affected hundreds of accounts and deposits. In January 1942, Barth was rewarded with a promotion to the rank of vice-president of the International Department headed by Cain Jr.[30] The fact that the Chase was under federal investigation for possible violation of the *Trading With the Enemy Act of 1917* for a series of movements in the frozen assets Barth had dealt with did not seem to matter. The complex case would take long enough to be resolved to allow for the banker to serve his adoptive nation before a judgement could be made.[31]

Barth made an instant impact on the Spanish scene. He was key to the technical execution of the late 1942 agreement – signed in the footsteps of Operation Torch – between the U.S. embassy and the Spanish government that allowed USCC to tap into 796 frozen bank accounts of American companies in Spain, earned before the Spanish Civil War, to fund the Preclusive Program.[32] As U.S. needs for pesetas kept growing, Barth was also in charge of seeking a deal – sealed in October 1943 – by which USCC was authorized to acquire even more frozen assets of American companies, as well as to experiment with innovative trade operations by way of compensation for Spanish exports – mostly of sherry wine – inspired by one advanced in February 1943 by Stanton Griffis, a businessman on the executive board of Paramount Pictures – Hollywood companies held some of the largest frozen accounts in Spain.[33]

The U.S. embassy also asked Barth to go hunting for "free pesetas" – the euphemistic name for the illegally obtained local currency that was required to support covert operations in the country, which were carried out either by the offices of the military attaches or the mushrooming presence of OSS operatives in Spain. The banker came up with a system that exploited the rampant foreign-exchange black market that fed the illegal trade concerning import licenses and dubbing licenses of Hollywood movies in Spain. The

---

[29] See "Charles Cain Jr.," *The New York Times*, 25 January 1982. "Alfred Barth, Banker," *The New York Times*, 27 July 1988. I thank Prof. Matthieu Leimgruber (Zurich University) and Antonia S. Mattheou (History Center, Manhasset Public Library) for their cooperation in completing Alfred Barth's bio data.

[30] "Chase Bank Promotions," *The New York Times,* 15 January 1942.

[31] "Chase Bank Acquitted. Federal Jury Finds Verdict in Trading with Enemy Case," *The New York Times,* 7 May 1945.

[32] See Ralph H. Ackerman, U.S. Commercial Attache to a Blas Huete, Director, IEME, 5 and 25 October 1943, Huete to Ackerman, 7, 21 October 1943, 18 November 1943 and Manuel Vila, IEME to Ackerman, 3 November 1943, AHBE, IEME, box 19.

[33] S. Griffis was to become U.S ambassador to Spain in January 1951. See León Aguinaga, *Sospechosos...*, 150.

Madrid offices of the USCC became the center of an illegal trade that was no secret in the Spanish capital and that generated a constant flow of free pesetas – from then on also known as "film pesetas" – that funded U.S. covert operations in Spain well into 1947.[34] But Barth's financial engineering went further than that.

Although the banker arrived in Madrid as a financial expert for the USCC, he also worked covertly for the OSS. "Laurel" – his codename – had joined the organization on the recommendation of Frank Timothy Ryan – alias "Royal" – himself in charge of the Iberian operations of OSS's Secret Intelligence (SI) unit.[35] The personal intercession of William Donovan, the director of the OSS, had convinced Carlton Hayes to accept Ryan in Madrid. Royal arrived in the Spanish capital on 10 February 1943 with a twofold mission: to reorganize the SI and to establish a climate of cooperation between the OSS and the U.S. embassy. However, the secret agent collided head-on with Beaulac and Hayes.[36] Ryan's – and for that matter Donovan's – vision for the role of a spy agency had nothing to do with that of Hayes and the diplomatic corps. In fact, Donovan had given free rein to Ryan's real plans, which consisted in establishing an intelligence network independent of embassy control: SI intended to deploy a network of American agents whose members would not have contact with each other until they had perfected their covers in the world of bilateral trade – then expanding within the framework of the Preventive Procurement program. Laurel was to play a major role in the "Timothy only" network – as it was referred to within the OSS – because his work was to provide the free pesetas with which to fund their expenses, destined among other things to sustain a wide network of Spanish collaborators.[37]

Barth seemed to excel at his secret mission. Apart from the film pesetas scheme, he became proficient in the illegal trade in foreign exchange, securities and precious metals that went on in Madrid and was closely intertwined with the black markets of Lisbon and Tangier. His hyperactivity, however, soon

---

[34] Ibid., 138–168.

[35] Engagement Sheet, "Alfred W. Barth," no date, NACP, RG 226, Personnel Files of the Office of Strategic Services, 1942–1962, box 40 and F. L. Mayer to W. L. Mellon Jr., 22 February 1943, NACP, RG 226, Personnel Files of the Office of Strategic Services, 1942–1962, box 18.

[36] G. Howland Shaw (DoS) to the Director of the OSS, 1772/1943; and Shaw to Frank T. Ryan, 17 February 1943; Frank T. Ryan to William J. Donovan, 25 September 1943; and "Memorandum," 25 September 1943, NACP, RG 226, Personnel Files of the Office of Strategic Services, 1942–1962, box 18. On SI's inauspicious beginnings in Spain see D. Waller, *Wild William Donovan. The Spy Master Who Created the OSS and Modern American Espionage,* New York, Simon & Schuster, 2011, 159–63.

[37] F. L. Mayer to W. L. Mellon Jr., 22 February 1943, NACP, RG 226, Personnel Files of the Office of Strategic Services, 1942–1962, box 18.

caught the attention of OSS financial officers in London and New York, who in February 1943 demanded that Ryan terminate Laurel's employment. When Royal resisted, they insisted once again:

> Since your departure from Washington, reports have reached me that there were certain events in this man's [Barth] financial career which give raise to extremely serious suspicions regarding his former associations. Although I am not at liberty to communicate to you the exact nature of these qualms nor the personalities implicated, I am firmly convinced, as are others in this organization, that we are playing with dynamite, and that steps must be taken immediately to curtail this individual's operations, insofar as this organization is concerned at least, and ease him out of the picture as rapidly as possible. It is quite clear to me that this unfortunate situation may very well be embarrassing to you personally on account of the fact that, as far as I am able to determine, you recruited him and have worked with him closely on the various activities in which he is undoubtedly an expert of real ability. I realize, I think, how useful it has been to have someone who understands ins and outs of these particular problems, but circumstances at present make it necessary for us both to face the facts squarely and overlook his present usefulness in the light of what I am convinced is an extremely dangerous probability.[38]

Ryan, however, was able to navigate the internal waters of the OSS and keep Laurel in Madrid until the very end of the USCC mission in Spain.[39] Ironically, Royal had to leave the country much earlier, when his name and that of his SI deputy – Jack Pratt, alias "Silky" – were compromised as a result of the arrest of two Spaniards recruited by the "Timothy-only" network, caught in an illegal currency operation – which happened soon after the fall of two OSS networks in Bilbao and Barcelona and the so-called "Malaga incident."[40] Hayes took the opportunity to demand that Donovan recall Ryan and to request the support of the State Department and the military for dismantling the OSS in Spain. The ambassador achieved the first of his objectives, but not the second (although Donovan suffered a strong reprimand from the chiefs),

---

[38] #527 to Royal, 31 May 1943, NACP, RG 226, Personnel Files of the Office of Strategic Services, 1942–1962, box 18.

[39] W. Lane Rhem (OSS) to C. J. Lenninhan Jr. (OSS), 26 April 1944 and W. Lane Rhem (OSS) to Alfred W. Barth, 24 November 1944, NACP, RG 226, Personnel Files of the Office of Strategic Services, 1942–1962, box 40.

[40] The Malaga incident was OSS major debacle in Spain, having to do with the collapse of the so-called Operation Banana, which ended in the death and detention at the hands of local security forces of several Spaniards who, recruited by the OSS in exile and North Africa, had landed in southern Spain at the beginning of 1943. The incident appears frequently in OSS histories as an example of the mistakes made by the first U.S. spy agency.

because the information collected by SI on the other side of the Pyrenees was considered valuable, as well as the fact that the embassy did not have enough staff to take charge of surveilling American exports to Spain – a good part of SI personnel had as a cover their work in the petroleum products control program.[41] Donovan, who considered that Hayes had acted in bad faith, kept Ryan at the OSS headquarters in charge of SI for the Iberian Peninsula until the end of the war in Europe.

Who was Frank Timothy Ryan and where did his interest in Spain come from? Born in 1907, he had joined the OSS in August 1942 with the blessing of Donovan's deputy, G. Edward Buxton Jr., with whom he shared a professional background in the textile sector during the interwar period. In Ryan's case, this experience had been developed in the family business, John J. Ryan & Sons, based in his hometown of Troy, New York, and run jointly with his three brothers. Jack, the eldest, was in charge of the day-to-day operations, while Frank, for his part, had turned to the export side of the business after abandoning his studies at the University of Georgetown in 1927. Between 1935 and 1940, Ryan was resident in Third Reich Berlin, from where, according to the curriculum that the OSS reviewed when evaluating his recruitment, he had traveled frequently throughout the rest of Europe on behalf of his company. The itineraries for these trips included several commercial visits to Spain, during and immediately after the Spanish Civil War, in which he supposedly gained access to the Palacio del Pardo, which General Franco turned into his personal residence in 1939. In August of that year, John J. Ryan & Sons was one of the forty-four companies to benefit from the EIB's loan to Spain (see previous section). Not long after Ryan returned to the United States, and following the attack on Pearl Harbor, he joined the Office of Price Administration as head of its Waste Materials Unit (responsible for cotton and artificial silk), a responsibility he held until joining the OSS.[42]

It is very likely that Ryan's contacts in the Spanish textile sector and with the country's foreign trade authorities explain his suitability for SI Spain. The truth is that, during the seven intense months he stayed in Madrid in 1943, Ryan

---

[41] F. George Dyas to Whitney H. Shepardson, "Status of Frank Ryan," 2 September 1943, NACP, RG 226, Personnel Files of the Office of Strategic Services, 1942–1962, box 669. Frank T. Ryan to William J. Donovan, 25 September 1943 and "Memorandum," 25 September 1943 NACP, RG 226, Personnel Files of the Office of Strategic Services, 1942–1962, box 18.

[42] G. Edward Buxton to Major David Bruce, "Frank T. Ryan," 8 July 1942; R. G. D'Oench (OSS) to William A. Kimbel (OSS), "Frank T. Ryan," 17 November 1942; and "Personal History Statement of Frank T. Ryan," 26 September 1943, NACP, RG 226, Personnel Files of the Office of Strategic Services, 1942–1962, box 18. Engagement Sheet, "Frank T. Ryan," NACP, RG 226, Personnel Files of the Office of Strategic Services, 1942–1962, box 669.

did not hide his interest in textiles and the cotton trade in particular.[43] After all, it was not difficult for him to justify as an obligation of his intelligence work. The textile industry was one of the strategic sectors of the Spanish economy, being the largest employer and main engine of Catalonia, the most developed region of the country – and one of the bastions of the defeated side in the Spanish Civil War – which, in addition, shared an extensive border with occupied France. The sector's importance was such that the Franco dictatorship was forced to tolerate the highly opaque mechanisms that fueled the imports that kept Catalan factories open and had their epicenter in the black market in foreign currency in Tangier. Anyone interested in doing business in the Spanish textile sector had to internalize this double dimension: the industry was a transcendental sector for the economic viability and social peace of the country, so collaborating in the supply of imports could contribute to internal stability; and it was at the same time an exponent par excellence of the generalized corruption deriving from the autarkic legislation and peculiar international position of the Spanish government.[44]

As the end of the war approached, Ryan communicated to his superiors at OSS his decision to return to the corporate world. He even told them of an upcoming business trip to Europe to revive the operations of the family company, which would include a stop in his "beloved Peninsula."[45] In December 1945, *La Vanguardia Española* of Barcelona reported the arrival in Spain of an "important American industrialist" on behalf of John J. Ryan and Sons and Bache & Co. – a Wall Street company where he had again come into contact with Buxton Jr.[46] Thus Ryan joined the trickle of American businessmen – representing the likes of ITT, Standard Oil, TWA, General Electric, Armstrong Cork, United Press, Reader's Digest, Central Hanover Bank, etc. – who traveled to Spain from the end of the war and throughout the following year in order to assess their current position and sound out

[43] See some references in #527 to Royal, 24 March 1943, FMB to Royal, 12 April 1943, and #527 to Royal, Undated [May 1943], NACP, RG 226, Personnel Files of the Office of Strategic Services, 1942–1962, box 18.

[44] The American embassy was aware of this both during the war and in the post-war period. See, for example, the report by Hubert M. Curry (MSA Economic Group, Madrid) to Raymond L. Jones (Export-Import Bank) and Carter de Paul Jr. (MSA), "End-Use Check on Credit NO. ECA-X-52–1, $5,000,000 for Cotton, and Study of Economic Aspects of Spanish Cotton Textile Industry," 26 November 1953, NACP, RG 84, Administrative Records Pertaining to American Economic Assistance Loans to Spain, compiled 1950–1955, box 1. A rare confession of a black-market operator in Tangier – and future IEME director – in M. Ortínez i Mur, *Una vida entre burgesos. Mèmories*, Barcelona, Edicions 92, 1991.

[45] Tim [Ryan] to Argus, 6 May 1945; Frank T. Ryan to Whitney S. Shepardson, 6 May 1945; and Whitney S. Shepardson to Frank T. Ryan, 10 May 1945, NACP, RG 226, Personnel Files of the Office of Strategic Services, 1942–1962, box 18.

[46] "Mr. Frank T. Ryan en Barcelona," *La Vanguardia Española*, 4 December 1945.

THE CHASE, WORLD COMMERCE AND COLD WAR REHABILITATION   53

future business opportunities despite the uncertainty generated by the Truman administration's policy towards the Franco regime.[47] The local interlocutors of such visits tended to be of two types. At the official level, they included senior officials from the ministries responsible for their business areas, IEME, and the National Institute of Industry (INI), as well as influential lawyers with U.S. connections – such as Antonio Garrigues, who was then working with the U.S. embassy on German assets in Spain – and bankers and merchants with experience in bilateral economic relations – such as Manuel Arburúa of the semi-official Banco Exterior and his colleague Víctor Oswald.[48] If there was a constant in those visits, which on many occasions included personnel from the U.S. embassy, it was the moment when the conversation turned towards the possibility that Spain might obtain loans in the United States, either from the EIB or on Wall Street.[49] Frank Ryan and Alfred Barth, uniquely well versed in the intricacies of the Spanish economy and its leading players, were eager to exploit that precious information for their own advantage.

Eroding the Western Isolation of Spain (1945–1948)

The end of the Preventive Procurement Program, the cessation of hostilities, and the diplomatic quarantine to which the Franco regime was subjected by the United Nations left Spain in a precarious position, both politically and economically. The country, which had not been invited to the conference in Bretton Woods to restructure the world economy in the post-war period, nevertheless depended on foreign countries for the machinery and technologies necessary for its desired industrialization, for the grain and fertilizers that would avoid a food collapse, and for the raw materials that would maintain the

---

[47] That trickle was very well reflected in the diary of the U.S. *chargé d'affaires* in Madrid from the beginning of 1946 to mid-1947: Pablo León Aguinaga (ed.), *Philip W. Bonsal, Diario de un diplomático americano en España, 1944–1947. Estados Unidos ante a la dictadura franquista,* Zaragoza, Prensas de la Universidad de Zaragoza, forthcoming.

[48] On the role of Garrigues and his links with the U.S. embassy, see N. Puig Raposo and A. Álvaro Moya, "La Guerra Fría y los empresarios españoles: la articulación de los intereses económicas de Estados Unidos en España, 1950–1975," *Revista de Historia Económica*, vol. 22, n. 2 (2004), 410, as well as multiple entries in *Philip W. Bonsal....* This diary documents the Arburúa–Oswald friendship, as well as the peculiar nature of some of the commercial operations in which the latter specialized (see for example the entry of 7 April 1947). On the Safehaven program in Spain, see C. Collado Seidel, *España, refugio nazi*, Madrid, Temas de Hoy, 2005, M. Lorez-Meyer, *Safehaven, The Allied Pursuit of Nazi Assets Abroad*, Columbia, University of Missouri Press, 2007 and D. A. Messenger, *Hunting Nazis in Franco's Spain*, Baton Rouge, Louisiana State University, 2014.

[49] See for example the entries of 9 April and 13 December 1946 in *Philip W. Bonsal....*

activity of its factories. However, the political identity of the Franco regime made it unfeasible for the victors to grant public loans in the immediate future, and the autarkic orientation of its economic policy did not exactly invite foreign private investment. As if that were not enough, the means of payment available to the Spanish government were limited, dependent on seasonality (of the crops destined for export) and at the mercy of the country's irregular climate (a problem accentuated by the shortage of artificial fertilizers and irrigation). Discarding the possibility that the governments of the main democratic countries of Western Europe would offer a lifeline to the Franco regime in the short or medium term, the dictatorship and the economic elites placed their hopes of external financing in three specific points on the globe: Switzerland, whose banks had been providing services to Francoist Spain since the Spanish Civil War; Argentina, especially after Perón's triumphant return to power in February 1946; and, of course, the United States, then at the very apex of her geopolitical and financial power.

Swiss banks, with the approval of their government, opened credit lines to the Spanish government at the end of 1945 (Société de Banque Suisse, 9 million Swiss francs), in 1946 (Crédit Suisse, 8 million), and again in 1947 (Société, 7.5 million), but their size was insufficient to prevent the deterioration of the precarious Spanish economy.[50] More important was Argentina's decision to open new lines of credit to Spain in 1946 for the purchase of food, which allowed the situation to be alleviated temporarily but did not solve the country's structural problems.[51] Only the United States had the financial and industrial muscle to achieve something similar in the immediate post-war period. However, for political reasons, the Truman administration showed no signs of being willing to grant economic aid to Spain. On Wall Street, for its part, there were more than enough reservations about resuming lending operations to the Western European democracies to think of doing the same for Spain, a country that was also waiting for an agreement with the Allied Control Committee (ACC) to allow the use of the gold bullion reserves that the IEME had accumulated during the world war – 67.4 million tons – as collateral without fear of lawsuits from third parties.[52] At Chase, however, that did not seem to matter.

[50] S. Farré, *Franco's Switzerland and Spain. De la guerre civile à la mort du dictateur (1936–1975)*, Lausanne, Antipode, 2006, 321.

[51] On the Spanish–Argentine embrace in the first Franco regime, see M. Quijada, *Relaciones hispano-argentinas, 1938–1948. Coyunturas de crisis, Tesis doctoral inédita*, Universidad Complutense de Madrid, 1989, R. Rein, *La salvación de una dictadura. Alianza Franco-Perón 1946–1955*, Madrid, CSIC, 1995; M. González de Oleaga, *El doble juego de la hispanidad. Spain and Argentina during World War II*, Madrid, UNED, 2001.

[52] For the gold accumulated by the IEME during the war see J. P. Martín Aceña, *The Nazi Gold...*, 258. On 5 May 1945, Spain complied with article VI of the Bretton

In May 1945, Federal Judge Simon H. Rifkind exonerated the Chase National Bank from any wrongdoing in the pending process for violation of the Trade with the Enemy Act. By then, Alfred Barth, who had been a key witness for the defense, had rejoined the International Department of a banking corporation that was looking abroad for its ambitious post-war expansion plans.[53] Its president, Winthrop Aldrich, was betting on the recovery of Western Europe and the development of oil exploitation in the Persian Gulf as the major venues for the foreign expansion of Wall Street after the long trek through the desert of the Great Depression. Such a bet explains in part Aldrich's support for Truman's revolutionary foreign policy in the early Cold War years, of which the Chase became one of the most enthusiastic backers on Wall Street. The relevance of such support, strengthened by Aldrich's influence at the Chamber of International Commerce and selection by Truman to head the Committee for Financing Foreign Trade, could have been especially important in galvanizing the support of New York banks for the Marshall Plan and the activation (and reorientation) of Bretton Woods's major institutions.[54]

The closeness of the Chase with the foreign policy of the U.S. government in the early Cold War made itself obvious soon afterwards, when the corporation loaned to Tito's Yugoslavia even before Washington's official aid had started to flow toward the Socialist regime that first eroded the unity of Communism in Europe. And in 1950, when the European Recovery Program was yet to prove the right medicine for Western Europe, the Chase was at the head of a $225 million Wall Street loan to France. Alfred Barth, first vice-president at Chase since June 1946, was the lead negotiator in both cases – for his role he would be awarded the Légion d'Honneur by France's Fourth Republic.[55] By then, Barth's prolific European travels included frequent stops in Madrid, where the government led by Francisco Franco was already enjoying a credit–lender relationship with the Chase National Bank.

In November 1945, the government-controlled news agency CIFRA reported that the "Vice President of the Chase National Bank of New York,

---

Woods Final Act (which assumed the philosophy of the Declaration of Gold of February 1944), thus taking the first step for negotiations on this subject and that of German assets and nationals in Spain (Safehaven Program).

[53] "Chase Bank Official Testifies at Trial," *The New York Times,* 3 April 1945, "Declares Chases Bank Obeyed Freeze Order," *The New York Times*, 1 May 1945, and "Chase Bank Acquitted. Federal Jury Finds Verdict in Trading with Enemy Case," *The New York Times,* 5 May 1945.

[54] See N. Prins, *All the President's Bankers. The Hidden Alliances that Drive American Power*, New York, Nation Books, 2014, 14–16.

[55] D. Wilson, *The Chase. The Chase Manhattan Bank N.A.,* Boston, Harvard Business School, 1986; "Bank Notes," *The New York Times*, 29 June 1946 and "Alfred Barth, Banker," *The New York Times*, 27 July 1988.

Mr. Alfred Barth, will be coming to Spain shortly."[56] In March 1946, just after France had unilaterally announced the closure of the border with Spain (27 February), and coinciding with the Tripartite (British-French-American) Condemnation of Francoism (4 March 1946), the *chargé d'affaires* of the United States in Madrid received a report disclosing Barth's dealings with Isaac Jacob Salama, a well-known operator in the black markets of Tangier and the Spanish protectorate of Morocco and vice-president of the Spanish Chamber of Commerce in the international city.[57] But Barth was getting other Spanish-related businesses for his bank. For instance, on 3 September the minister of finance authorized IEME to sell 300 tons of coined silver in the United States. The Chase National Bank was picked to oversee the melting and commercialization processes in exchange for a very attractive fee. Alfred Barth informed IEME that the first such operation was completed on October 1946; two more followed in 1947.[58] The value generated by the aforementioned silver sales could be used to acquire gold for the IEME reserves, the same ones that would be necessary to mobilize as collateral in the event that Wall Street granted a loan to Spain. Unsurprisingly, at the same time, senior executives of the Chase consulted the State Department in Washington on the government's position concerning a hypothetical $10 million loan to Spain, backed in gold. The proposal collapsed when Chase was informed that the Treasury Department was not willing to accept the gold in the event of a Spanish default, since Madrid had not yet reached an agreement with the ACC.[59]

[56] See "El vicepresidente del Chase National Bank de Nueva York viene a España," *El Noticiero* de Zaragoza, 15 November 1945.

[57] E. Paul Tenney to Bonsal, 1 March 1946, NACP, RG 59, DF 952.4061, MP-3–146 and León Aguinaga, *Sospechosos habituales...*, 233. On Salam or Salama, see M. R. Madariaga: "El lucrativo negocio del protectorado español," *Hispania Nova*, vol. 16 (2018), 618. For an example of the Spanish authorities' knowledge about Salama's involvement on black market operations, see Minutes of the C.R.C.E of 21 February 1946, paragraph 5, "Bolsa Negra – Salam (Jacob) – Administración Económica Nacional – Harina, importaciones," AHBE, IEME, box 50. In 1948 Salama had legal problems due to a seizure carried out in Seville that ten years later was still to be resolved judicially. See Serrano Suñer a Ullastres, 18 January 1958, AGUN 093/312.

[58] The first shipments left Bilbao for New York on 11 October 1946 and 9 November 1946. See IEME, "Note to Mr. Navascués," undated; General Directorate of the Public Treasury of the Ministry of Finance to Mr. Directot General of IEME, 10 September 1946; IEME to The Chase National Bank, "Attn: Mr. Alfred Barth," 11 October 1946; Alfred Barth to IEME, 15 January 1947 and Alfred Barth to Alejandro Bermúdez (IEME), 28 January 1947, AHBE, IEME, box 91.

[59] Wood to Neter, 2 August 1946, NACP, RG 56, OASIA, Subject Files, 1934–1972, box 24 C. and R. McNeill, Memorandum, 30 September 1946, NACP, RG 56, OASIA, Subject Files, 1934–1972, box 24. See also P. Martín Aceña, *El oro de Moscú...*, 363–364.

THE CHASE, WORLD COMMERCE AND COLD WAR REHABILITATION 57

In parallel with the movements that sought to pave the way for private credit in the future, Alfred Barth and Victor Oswald, whom the banker was using as Chase's unofficial agent in Spain, had been placing their personal skills at the service of local authorities to secure cotton for Catalan factories, through very dubious arrangements that raised doubts even at the IEME.[60] These operations involved Anderson, Clayton & Co. and McFadden & Bro., two giant corporations prominent in the National Cotton Association – the American cotton lobby – that already in February 1947 was calling for a change in the policy of the United States towards Spain.[61]

Barth was not the only American businessman determined to keep bilateral trade afloat and, by doing so, support key sectors of the Spanish economy. Another was his former superior at OSS, Frank Ryan. In this his appointment as director of a company incorporated in 1945 in Panama, which focused on barter-like trade and which in September 1947 was renamed Word Commerce Corporation, was instrumental. WCC had been established by a handful of illustrious Wall Street representatives well-connected in Washington and London and with connections to their respective countries' wartime intelligence services. The founding shareholders of the British American Canadian Corporation – WCC's first name – included the likes of William Donovan (former director of the OSS), William Stephenson (former head of British intelligence in America), and Edward Stettinius (former Secretary of State). The company was born shortly after the dismantling of the OSS in October 1945 with the grandiloquent purpose of "breaking the chains that impede free trade among the nations of the world," as the "best way to oppose the expansion of communism."[62] Donovan's leading influence explains why veterans of the OSS proliferated within its ranks. Such was the case of Frank Ryan, whose appointment as director pushed WCC to set its sights on Spain, where he relied on the contacts he had established while at SI – like Ricardo Sicre.[63]

---

[60] Alfred Barth at IEME, 15 January 1947, AHBE, IEME, box 91. At the same time, Oswald had no qualms about confessing that he was "sending all the money he can to Switzerland" in the face of the deteriorating economic situation. See the entry of 4 February 1947 in *Philip W. Bonsal....*

[61] X. Hualde, *El "cerco"...*, 212.

[62] "World Trade Group Ready to Function," *The New York Times*, 24 September 1947; R. Dunlop, *Donovan: America's Master Spy*, New York, Skyhorse, 1982, chapter 36 and B. Hersh, *The Old Boys: The American Elite and the Origins of the CIA,* New York, Scribner's, 1992, 229. Also in V. Ogle, "Archipelago...," 1440–1441.

[63] Ryan trusted the opening of WCC office in Madrid to Aline Griffith, another veteran of SI Spain. See Aline, countess of Romanones, "The OSS in Spain during World War II," in G. C. Chalou, *The Secret War: The Office of Strategic Services*, College Park: U.S. National Archives, 1991, 126–127. In the second half of the 1950s, WCC hired Harris H. Williams, who had been vice-consul in Barcelona in the late 1940s. There exists a documentary on Sicre's interesting life that however sheds little

However, there is no evidence that WCC maintained active contacts with OSS successor agencies in Spain.[64]

WCC's first commercial operation in Spain did not involve the cotton sector, but the steel industry and its main representative in Spain: Altos Hornos de Vizcaya (AHV). The country's acute foreign exchange crisis of 1947 threatened to paralyze the output of this company, the main employer in the large urban center of Bilbao, where that same year the first general strike of the Franco dictatorship was organized clandestinely. Spanish coal was not sufficient to cover the needs of AHV, which relied on imports. American coal was especially prized, but getting the dollars needed to pay for it in 1947 was an almost impossible mission. It was at that time that Ryan offered the services of the WCC, no doubt taking advantage of his contacts in the country. The proposal that was finally accepted involved the import of 20,000 tons of North American coke, in return for the export of 6,000 tons of pig iron for sale in the United States; other similar operations followed in the succeeding years.[65] Ryan was so proud of the operation that he did not hesitate to use it as an example of his company's philosophy in an interview in *The New York Times*, in which he stated that, "on principle," his company "refused to admit that when a country lacked dollars it forced it to cease its commercial exchanges."[66]

Despite the hyperactivity of individuals such as Barth and Ryan, along with Swiss bank loans, Spain's economic outlook remained grim in 1948. The U.S. government still resisted the grant of public aid to the Iberian nation, as the failure of the O'Konsky Amendment to the Marshall Plan (30 March) made

---

light concerning his role in WCC. See Pablo Azorín and Marta Hierro, *Agente Sicre. El Amigo americano*, Dossoles, Burgos, 2014.

[64] On the work of the CIG and the SSU in Spain, see D. Alvarez, "American Clandestine Intelligence in Early Postwar Europe," *Journal of Intelligence History*, vol. 4, n. 1 (2004), 12–14; and D. Alvarez and E. Mark, *Spying through a Glass Darkly: American Espionage against the Soviet Union, 1945–1946*, Lawrence, University Press of Kansas, 2016. The first chief of station of the CIA – established in September 1947 – in Spain was another veteran of the OSS, Alfred Conrad Ulmer, who arrived in the country in 1948. See "Ulmer, Alfred Conrad, Jr. (1916–2000)," in W. T. Smith Jr., *Encyclopedia of the Central Intelligence Agency*, New York, Facts on File, 2003, 232. Ulmer, like other future station chiefs in Spain – such as Archibald Roosevelt in the late 1950s – was a specialist in the Arab world.

[65] For an apologetic account of the origins and evolution of the AHV–WCC relationship see Antonio Goyoaga (General Manager, Altos Hornos de Vizcaya) to Export-Import Bank through Central Siderúrgica S.A., 6 November 1951, NACP, RG 84, Project Files Pertaining to American Economic Assistance Loans to Spain, compiled 1950–1954, box 1; and Altos Hornos de Vizcaya and Central Siderúrgica S.A. to Export-Import Bank, "Segundo crédito Eximbank para carbones – coal para gas," 22 January 1954, NACP, RG 84, Project Files Pertaining to American Economic Assistance Loans to Spain, compiled 1950–1954, box 7.

[66] "Anglo-U.S. group called 'Little ECA,'" *The New York Times*, 2 January 1949.

evident. Washington's reluctance contrasted with Spain's apparent progress with Western European nations and Argentina. In the latter case, the Spanish press tried to hide the derailment of the Amendment by celebrating the Franco–Perón Protocol, which on 9 April increased the credit lines opened to Spain by the South American country. In the former case, Spain and France signed a trade and financial agreement in May after the full reopening of the border in February.[67]

The arrival of José Félix de Lequerica as *de facto* Spanish ambassador to Washington in mid-April was aimed at acquiring loans from the United States, either in the form of Marshall-Plan-like aid through the EIB or, at the very least, Wall Street loans.[68] To the latter end, Spain adopted a more accommodating position that helped conclude the negotiations over Nazi gold. The agreement between ACC and Spain, signed on 3 May 1948, foresaw the immediate unblocking of the 67.4 million tons of gold accumulated by the IEME during the war, which Spain could now use as collateral for private loans.[69]

By then it was clear that the Cold War had become the main driver for Spanish–American rapprochement. At the end of 1947, George Kennan's personal private secretary had put the need for a change of policy towards Spain on the table, one which would include a progressive normalization of relations with its government – renouncing the demand for an internal political evolution as a prerequisite for the normalization of the bilateral relationship; the purpose of the new direction was none other than to facilitate the integration of the Iberian Peninsula into the defensive strategy of the United States at a time of growing tension with the Soviet Union. That December, the United States and its allies voted against a Soviet resolution against Spain at the UN. And in the first half of 1948, formal and informal contacts between the two governments multiplied, including an interview between Franco and Truman's envoy to the Vatican, and the proliferation of contacts between U.S. naval and military attachés and the Spanish military leadership. During the latter, the Pentagon's interest in having airstrips capable of accommodating heavy planes in Spain came to light. When the Spanish requested financial aid for such construction projects, the U.S. government told Madrid to ask the Chase for help in the form of a $10 million loan.[70] Historians have not been

---

[67] This would be complemented by a new Trade and Payments Agreement in June 1949.

[68] See Joan M. Thomàs's chapter in this book.

[69] P. Martín Aceña, *El oro de Moscú...*, 323, 346–355 and A. Viñas, *En las garras del águila. Los pactos con Estados Unidos, de Francisco Franco a Felipe González (1945–1995),* Barcelona, Crítica, 2003, 51.

[70] X. Hualde, *El 'cerco...*, 215–226 and B. Liedke, *Embracing...*, 55. See also Tel. 401, Culbertson to Sec. of State, 19 June 1948, NACP, 852.51/6–1948 and Hickerson to Lovett, "Case of Chase Bank Loan for Equipment for Spanish Airfields," 22 June 1948, NACP, 852.51/6–2248.

able to uncover how Spain paid to update facilities at the major airports, but one way or another, Barajas (Madrid) inaugurated its new runway – suitable for heavy aircraft – in August 1948, and in 1949 it was the turn of San Pablo (Seville), Muntadas (Barcelona), Sondika (Bilbao), and Los Rodeos (Santa Cruz de Tenerife).[71]

The U.S. government's policy towards the Franco regime continued evolving with the approval of NSC 3 on 26 July 1948, which recognized the importance of the Spanish government to American strategic interests.[72] However, the unexpected re-election of Truman ensured that the rapprochement would follow the slower pace favored at the White House, whose occupant felt little affinity for the Spanish dictatorship and assumed that such a diplomatic maneuver would have political costs in Western Europe – at a time when Washington's priority on the continent was to make the Marshall Plan work and secure the Atlantic Alliance. Thus, while some kind of public aid for the country governed by General Franco began to be glimpsed on the horizon, Washington was in no hurry to move in that direction. However, after the ACC agreement, Washington would no longer block Wall Street loans. On 13 November 1948, the Spanish newspaper *ABC* reprinted statements by Frank Ryan requesting that Spain receive up to $300 million under the Marshall Plan.[73] Alfred Barth, for his part, traveled shortly after to Madrid to negotiate the first private loan from Wall Street to Francoist Spain.

Reaping the Harvest: Economic Aid and Business Opportunities (1949–1952)

On 8 February 1949, after two months of negotiations – in which Antonio Garrigues acted as legal counsel for Chase – and with the approval of the State Department, the Wall Street giant announced a $25 million loan to Spain backed by gold equivalent to 105 percent of the total amount. The loan was to be used to pay for the import of cotton and the construction of a chemical plant

---

[71] See its reflection in the magazine of the Air Force Ministry: "Una nueva pista en el aeropuerto de Barajas," *Revista de Aeronáutica*, vol. 93 (August 1948); "Un Globemaster en Barajas," *RdA*, 97, December 1948; "El Ministro del Aire habla a los periodistas de las actividades de su departamento" and "El Jefe norteamericano de ayuda aérea en Madrid," *RdA*, 98, January 1949; "Inauguration of the new facilities of Los Rodeos airport," *RdA*, vol. 99 (February 1949).

[72] *Foreign Relations of the United States 1948, Volume III, Western Europe,* Washington D.C, U.S. Printing Office, 1974, 1041–1045.

[73] "Farley returns to talk about relations with Spain," *ABC*, 13 November 1948.

THE CHASE, WORLD COMMERCE AND COLD WAR REHABILITATION   61

for fertilizers.[74] The relevance of the loan was not lost on anyone, especially since it coincided with the derailment of the Spanish–Argentinian special relationship.[75] Moreover, the internal situation in Spain remained grim. On 18 March, an alarmist CIA memo that reached the White House spoke openly of the likelihood of "economic collapse" unless a substantial alleviation of the country's economic plight occurred before the next winter.[76] A month later, President Truman greenlighted the EIB to hear proposals for loans from Spanish companies.[77]

On 18 April, the government of Spain announced that 100,000 titles in "Treasury Bonds for National Reconstruction" worth £1000 each – up to a maximum of $100 million– were now available to investors. The IEME received support for this commercialization from its foreign correspondents in the United States, which by that time were the Chase, NCB, Manufacturers Trust, Irving Trust Co., and Swiss Banking Co.[78] The treasury bonds were intended to channel funds for the country's industrialization plans through the hands of the INI, and specifically sought to attract funds from "Spaniards residing abroad," an undisguised attempt to facilitate the repatriation of some of the capital that had fled the country in the previous decades, a process reactivated during the crisis of 1947, as U.S. intelligence reported at the time.[79] By then, Barth and Ryan were working on a formula to facilitate this repatriation and turn it into a business opportunity: the future Dollar–Peseta Program.

As the Spanish government continued to search for foreign currency and dollars, in Washington, in 1949, José F. Lequerica set up a lobby in the pay of the Spanish embassy (led by lawyer Charles Patrick Clark and the law firm Cummings, Stanley, Truitt & Cross), which was focused on garnering support in Congress. For his part, Juan Antonio Suanzes, at the time minister of industry and commerce and president of the INI, sent some of his collaborators to Washington to try to accelerate the grant of EIB loans and disseminate Spain's willingness to accept that "some other mechanism or financial group" –

---

[74] "Chase Grants Spain Loan of $25,000,000," *The New York Times*, 9 February 1949. A. Álvaro Moya, "Inversión directa…," p. 130 and *Foreign Relations of the United States 1948…*, 1058.

[75] R. Rein, *La salvación…*, chapter 6.

[76] CIA, Intelligence Memorandum No. 145: "Political Repercussions of the Economic Situation in Spain," 18 March 1949. HSTL, Papers of Harry S. Truman, PSF, Subject File, 1940–1953, Foreign Affairs File, box 164.

[77] *Foreign Relations of the United States 1949, vol. IV, Western Europe,* Washington D.C., U.S. Printing Office, 1975, 735–737.

[78] Law of 17 July 1948 on the issue by the Spanish State of Treasury Bonds for national reconstruction, BOE, 18 July 1948, 3271. See also AHBE, IEME, Box 86.

[79] For an example in relation to the heritage of Francisco Cambó, see CIG, "Investment of Spanish Capital in Argentina," 15 September 1947, CIA-RPD82–00457R000900250002–7.

like the Chase – be brought in.[80] The fact that the latter coincided with the negotiations for short-term loans between Chase and large Spanish companies like Iberia and Renfe led Lequerica to criticize the predominance of the entity chaired by Aldrich in Spanish economic contacts on Wall Street.[81]

At the beginning of 1950, U.S. public loans were still not flowing to Spain, although Secretary of State Dean Acheson reiterated the president's willingness to assess granting loans to Spain through the EIB. Meanwhile, in January, the Chase decided to extend the line of credit granted a year earlier to $30 million, a decision certified with a visit to the Palacio del Pardo by the Barth–Oswald duo.[82] Shortly thereafter, a Decree Law of 23 February authorized the Bank of Spain to deliver 500 tons of coined silver to the IEME for sale in New York via Chase – and despite the fact that another American company, American Metal, had made a more advantageous offer.[83]

In February 1950, NCB announced that it had made a $10 million loan to Spain, also backed in gold, for the acquisition of cereal in the Western Hemisphere (mainly Canada). After a visit to the State Department in which NCB executives had shared the details of the operation, the diplomats highlighted how, "on this occasion," Barth had been "defeated" by his competitors, and underlined that the Spanish decision responded in part to their awareness of the need to expand its range of lenders on Wall Street.

[80] See J. M. Thomàs's chapter in this book.

[81] "Granting credits...," 3 November 1949, SEPI-INI-JAS, box 6; and Lequerica to Martín Artajo, 17 September 1949, Archive Ministry of Foreign Affairs, Renewed Fund R-20210–10. Document courtesy of J. M. Thomàs.

[82] "Chase Bank Urged to Fight Low Rate," *The New York Times*, 1 February 1950; "U.S. Banker Sees Franco," *The New York Times*, 8 February 1950; and "U.S. Banker Parleys with Franco Enlivens Spain's Hope for a Loan," *The New York Times*, 9 February 1950. Memo of Conversation: "Spain," Participants: Alfred Barth (VP, Chase National Bank), Dunham (WE), 6 January 1950, NACP, RG 59, 852.10/1–650; Tel, 3675, Amemb Madrid to State, 11 January 1950, NACP, RG 59, 852.10/1–1050; Alfred W. Barth (VP, Foreign Dept. Chase National Bank) to Willian B. Dunham (Spanish Section, State), 19 January 1950, NACP, RG 59, 852.10/1–1950. Theodore G. Achilles (Dir. Office of WEA) to Alfred W. Barth (VP, Foreign Dept. Chase National Bank), 24 January 1950, NACP, RG 59, 852.10/1–2450. See also the correspondence between Alfred Barth and Antonio Garrigues at SEPI-INI-JAS, box 6.

[83] Director General IEME to the Minister of Industry and Commerce, 17 February 1950, "Nota para el Excmo. Ministro de Industria y Comercio," 23 February 1950, Antonio Garrigues to Alejandro Bermúdez (IEME), 14 March 1950 and annexes and Alfred Barth to Antonio Garrigues, 26 January 1951. Alfred Ayrton to the Minister of Finance, 26 April 1950, Director General IEME, "Sale of plant to the United States," 3 May 1950, AHBE, IEME, box 91. In 1950, 92 percent of Spanish gold, silver and platinum exports went to the United States. N. Puig Raposo and A. Álvaro Moya, "Los empresarios...," p. 397.

Figure 2.1. Alfred Barth greets Francisco Franco in the company of Charles Cain Jr and Winthrop Aldrich (behind the dictator), Madrid, 5 June 1950.
Source: Winthrop W. Aldrich Papers, Box 238. Baker Library Special Collections, Harvard Business School, Boston, Massachusetts.

According to the same report, Chase and NCB were to be joined in the near future by Manufacturers Trust, an entity "which had been of great help to Franco's forces during the civil war."[84]

---

[84] Memo of Conversation, "National City Bank loan to Spain," Participants: Sheen (VP National City Bank) and Durham (WE), 2 February 1950, NACP, RG 59, 852.10/2–250 and Tel. 108, Ambemb Madrid to State, 28 February 1950 and Des. 204 Ambemb Madrid to State, "Negotiations for Credits to the Spanish Government," 26 February 1950, NACP, RG 59, 852.10/2–1650. See also Des. 371, Emb Madrid to State, "Status of Gold Holdings of the Bank of Spain," 20 March 1950, NACP, RG 59, 852.10/3–2050 and U.S. Consulate Valencia to State, "Shipment of Spanish Bullion to United States," 4 May 1950, NACP, RG 59, 852.10/5–450. For a personal account of the Chase–NCB banking duel in Spain in 1950, see "Interview to Charles Cain Jr., 25 May 1966," Folder 24, box 240, Winthrop W. Aldrich Papers, Baker Library Special Collections, Harvard Business School (HBS).

An opportunity to please Butler Sherwel's bank was not long in coming. At the beginning of June, he traveled to Madrid to negotiate with the authorities. But his visit there coincided with that of none other than the chairman of the board of directors of Chase National Bank, which triggered rumors of new loans for Spain in the New York press. Winthrop Aldrich was accompanied by Charles Cain Jr. Barth, who joined the Chase delegation in Madrid, persuaded the dictator to receive the trio of executives at his residence on 5 June 1950. That event, which received great media coverage, confirmed the unique position Barth had achieved for Chase in Spain just in time: diplomatic relations were about to be normalized, and therefore business opportunities – like those derived from American aid – were expected to grow.[85]

In August 1950, the U.S. Congress pushed through an amendment that linked the funding of foreign economic aid in Western Europe to the granting of a loan – eventually worth \$62.5 million– to Spain.[86] The business of pre-financing public loans via the opening of letters of credit had been one of the sweeteners with which Washington had secured Wall Street's support for the Marshall Plan, and Chase had exploited that like no other competitor, aware that, beyond the immediate economic returns, the letters of credit offered an ideal opportunity to establish contacts and synergies in key sectors of the economies of Western Europe.[87] The same door was now finally opening in Spain and Barth intended to be first in passing through, as he soon made known to his Spanish interlocutors.[88]

In January 1951, the Spanish embassy in the United States, the Ministry of Foreign Affairs, and the MIC discussed the best way to apportion the business of credit letters among Spain's friends on Wall Street. The consensus decision reached was to divide it as follows: 35 percent for Chase, 35 percent for NCB, 20 percent for Manufacturers Trust, and 10 percent for Bank of America.[89] This equitable distribution was not to the liking of Barth, who considered that the services provided by his entity deserved better. From the Spanish point of view, however, it made sense because, as the reports of the U.S. embassy

---

[85] "U.S. Bankers' Visits Encourage Madrid. Calls by Leaders of Chase and Bankers Trust Cause Lively Speculation in Madrid," *The New York Times*, 5 June 1950 and "More food output is urged on Spain," *The New York Times* 8 June 1950. A brief mention also in Aldrich's official bio by A. M. Johnson, *Winthrop W. Aldrich: Lawyer, Banker, Diplomat*, Cambridge, Harvard University Press, 1968, 363.

[86] See J. M. Thomàs's chapter.

[87] See A. Sampson, *The Money Lenders. Bankers in a Dangerous World*, London, Hodder & Stoughton, 1981, 73–74.

[88] Alfred Barth to Alejandro Bermúdez, 26 and 27 September 1950, SEPI-INI 765; Alfred Barth to Antonio Garriges, 1171/1951, annex to Antonio Garrigues to Manuel Vila (Director General of IEME), 13 January 1951, AHBE, IEME, box 89.

[89] Tel. Cif. 46, Suñer a Lequerica, 7 February 1952, Tel. Cif. 28, Lequerica a Suanzes, 24 February 1951, Tel 38. Cif. Suanzes to Lequerica, 26 January 1951, SEPI-INI-JAS, box 8.

THE CHASE, WORLD COMMERCE AND COLD WAR REHABILITATION   65

pointed out, the mere possibility of new public loans made Spain a more desirable destination for all Wall Street entities. Not surprisingly, these four banks were the ones that between the end of 1950 and the beginning of 1951 granted short-term loans without collateral to INI companies (for example, to the newly created SEAT automobile company in the case of Chase), a risk that they were willing to assume, anticipating that American aid to Spain would increase and that the Spanish authorities "would favor those entities that had demonstrated a liberal credit policy towards Spain."[90]

Barth did convince Suanzes that the commercial office of the Spanish embassy in the United States should hire a Chase-connected lobbyist – Walter Sterling Surrey[91] – to act as their key consultant in matters of foreign aid. Chase thus ensured it had privileged access to information when it came to applying for the loans under the $62.5 million package.[92] In fact, Surrey went on to secure most of the letters of credits he was seeking for Chase.[93] For instance, he acquired those directed towards the textile sector. Aware that the main constant in the objectives of the U.S. government towards Spain since 1945 was to favor the progressive liberalization of the country's economy, Barth did

[90] Des. 1051. AmEmb Madrid to State, "Spain's International Financial Position of the Eve of Negotiations with the United States," 15 April 1952, NACP, RG 59, 852.10/4–1552. A loan to SEAT worth $2 million would have to be renegotiated due to the company's inability to meet the deadlines of its repayment. See Barth to Suanzes, 23 January 1952 and Suanzes to Barth, 772/1952, SEPI-INI-JAS, box 87.

[91] Surrey, born in 1916 and a graduate of the University of Virginia and the prestigious Yale Law School, was a specialist in international law, serving his government between 1941 and 1950, first in the Department of Justice and then in the State Department. During the war he worked on the strategy of economic warfare in Sweden (1943–1945), and in the immediate post-war period in relation to the claim of Nazi gold to neutrals such as Spain (1945–1947) and the implementation of the Marshall Plan and NATO (1947–1950). In 1953 he was one of the founding partners of the law firm Surrey, Karasik, Gould & Efron, specialized in advising nations receiving aid from the American government and, in particular, that related to the PL 480 programs. See "Obituaries," *The Washington Post*, 1 February 1989. Surrey maintained his interest in Spain at least until 1957, when he proposed to the Spanish embassy in Washington a trilateral operation with France and the PL 480 Program. See AGUN 093/58/8. On the role of Surrey in relation to the post-war question of Nazi gold and neutrals, see P. Martín Aceña, *El oro de Moscú...*, 246–247.

[92] Suanzes to Luis García Llera (Commercial Counselor of the Embassy of Spain in Washington), 4 May 1951, Suanzes to Lequerica, "Technical advice of Chase Bank," 4 May 1951, SEPI-INI-JAS, box 7 and Secret Office Memo, Jack C. Corbett to Thorp: "Application of Spain for $5million wheat Loan," 9 February 1951, NACP, RG 59, 852.10/2–851.

[93] He did not always get away with it, such as the loan for Hidro Nitro (see Table 2), which motivated his protest to the Spanish authorities See Tel 52. CIF, Minister AAEE to the Foreign Economy Counselor of the Embassy in Washington, 14 February 1951, SEPI-INI-JAS, box 7.

not hesitate to link the loans for the importation of cotton with that objective. In the meetings he had at the State Department for this purpose, the banker did not shy away from classifying as "inappropriate" the fact that the EIB required "gold backing" for that credit (see X-52–1, Table 2) or that it put obstacles in the way of the recipient being the Consortium of Cotton Textile Industrialists (CITA), whose notorious lack of transparency and dependence on the Spanish government was especially uncomfortable for Washington. Barth also did not hesitate to recommend to the EIB that it "go as far as possible in complying with the request of the Spanish government," as it would be "a show of real support for [Manuel] Arburúa," minister of commerce since February 1951, who, according to Barth, "was trying to bring order to many of the issues to which the government of the United States has objected in the past." The appointment of Arburúa, coupled with the departure of Suanzes from the MIC, was effectively interpreted in the American embassy as a step in the right direction.[94]

Another sector for which Barth showed a special predilection was the steel industry. Chase initially secured the three loans for the sector under the $62.5 million package, one destined exclusively to AHV, and another two for CESA – an AHV-dominated consortium.[95] The steel industry was one of the privileged sectors in the industrialization plans promoted by the INI – of which Suanzes remained president after his departure from the council of ministers. For its part, Frank Ryan's WCC secured a good portion of the North American coke-import contracts financed with U.S taxpayer's money.[96]

The proactive work of Alfred Barth and Frank Ryan in favor of the rapprochement between Spain and the United States by stimulating commercial and financial relations was duly rewarded by the Franco regime, which turned their companies into privileged partners of the Spanish post-war economy. The culmination of this process was the adoption by the IEME, with the backing of Manuel Arburúa, of the Peseta–Dollar Program, in operation from October 1952 – although it had been run on an experimental basis for the

[94] Memo of conversation: "Spanish Cotton," Luis García de Llera (Economic Counselor, Spanish Emb.), Ricardo Giménez-Arnau (Commercial Attaché), and Corbertt (OFD), 3 December 1951, NACP, RG 59, 852.10/12–351; Memo of conversation: "Spanish Cotton," Alfred Barth (Chase), Walter Surrey (Attorney), and Thorp, Dunham and Colbert, 29 November 1951, NACP, RG 59, 852.10/11–2951.

[95] The loan to CESA stirred tensions within the Spanish government, since Lequerica was a shareholder of Basconia and considered that AHV had been unduly benefited. See Lequerica to Suanzes, 17 June 1953, SEPI-INI-JAS, box 105.

[96] Memo to Files, "Status of Credits Made Available to Spain under the General Appropiations Act of 1951," 15 May 1952, NACP, RG 84, Administrative Records Pertaining to American Economic Assistance Loans to Spain, compiled 1950–1955, box 1 y Central Siderúrgica S.A., "Importación de carbón norteamericano con cargo a crédito ECA X-6–52. Informe de la Ejecución de esta operación," 10/1952, NACP, RG 84, Project Files Pertaining to American Economic Assistance Loans to Spain, compiled 1950–1954, box 1.

Table 2. Status of credits made available to Spain under the General
Appropriations Act of 1951

Credit No.	Amount ($)	Loan Beneficiary	Letters of Credit
X-51–11	6,000,000	Altos Hornos de Vizcaya	Chase
X-52–1	5,000,000	Consorcio Ind. Textiles Algodón (CITA)	Chase
X-52–6	3,500,000	Central Siderúrgica S. A. (CESA)	Chase
X-52–16	2,400,000	Unión Eléctrica Madrileña	Chase
X-52–19	2,000,000	Various (tin sector)	Chase
X-52–36	1,800,000	CESA	Chase
X-52–15A	1,500,000	Various (potashes)	Chase
X-52–9B	1,200,000	Río Tinto Co.	Chase
X-52–4	700,000	Sociedad Ibérica del Nitrógeno	Chase
X-52–22	375,000	CEPSA	Chase
X-52–5(7)	7,250,000	Comis. Gen. Abastec. y Transp.	NCB
X-52–3	3500000	Dir. General de Agricultura	NCB
X-52–24	1,840,000	Hidro Nitro Española	NCB
X-52–14	973,000	ENESA	NCB
X-52–13	728,000	ENESA	NCB
X-52–9D	164,000	Agromán	NCB
X-52–8	7,500,000	RENFE	Manufacturers Trust
X-52–3(12)	3,450,000	Dir. General de Agricultura	Manufacturers Trust
x-52–9A	200,000	Cía Española Minas del Rif	Manufacturers Trust
9 credits	8,175,000	Various	Unknown

Source: Memo to Files: "Status of Credits Made Available to Spain under the
General Appropriations Act of 1951," 15 May 1952, NACP, RG 84, Administrative
Records Pertaining to American Economic Assistance Loans to Spain, compiled
1950–1955, Box 1.

past two years – to 21 July 1959.[97] Devised by the Barth–Ryan duo, and with the participation of the WCC, Chase, NCB, and Manufacturers Trust, the program had ambitious objectives, which included ending the black market for foreign currency based in Tangier and facilitating the repatriation of funds from abroad. To this end, it granted the participating North American entities the business of making the invisible transactions of U.S. dollars to Spain, which until then had been frequently diverted to Tangier, and which corresponded mainly to the purchase of pesetas for American tourism to Spain –which began to take off at that time – the remittances of "family assistance" from Spanish migrants in the Western Hemisphere, and the repatriation of Spaniards' benefits and goods, also mainly from Latin America. Up to 31 December 1956, the program channeled $350 million to the coffers of the IEME, paying valuable fees to the participating North American entities.[98]

Conclusion: Rethinking the Spanish–American Cold War Rapprochement

On 18 July 1967, the foreign minister of Spain informed Alfred William Barth of the receipt of the Order of Isabel la Católica, the highest civil honor awarded by the dictatorial government of Francisco Franco's Spain.[99] After four decades in the world of international finance, Barth, then about to retire due to statutory limits, was at the very apex of a banking career that had taken him to the executive vice-presidency of the Chase Manhattan Bank, the quintessential financial corporation of global capitalism in the Bretton Woods era. In the 1960s, the banker had combined his responsibilities at Chase with service on the Foreign Exchange Committee of the New York Money Market and the executive board of the National Foreign Trade Council, which led to the kind of public and media exposure that he had hitherto avoided.[100]

---

[97] See Tel. 2135, State to Emb Madrid, 8 August 1950, NACP, RG 59, 852.131/8–850 and Alfred W. Barth, Vice-President, The Chase Manhattan Bank to José A. Montes, Deputy Director, I.E.M.E., 4 August 1959 and José A. Montes, I.E.M.E. to Alfred W. Barth, Vice-President, The Chase Manhattan Bank, 11 August 1959, AHBE, IEME, box 113Bis.

[98] The data in Des. 793. Amembassy to SecState, "New Exchange Rate for Tourism and Invisibles," 2 May 1958, NACP, RG 59, 852.131/5–258.

[99] 18 July was a national holiday in Franco's Spain commemorating the "uprising" (the coup) that gave way to the Spanish Civil War (1936–1939) and the subsequent dictatorship (1936/1939–1976/1977).

[100] "Chase Manhattan Bank Promotes an Officer," *The New York Times*, 21 December 1961; "Worldly Banker Is a Symbol of Trade Revolution," *The New York Times*, 2 February 1962; "Barth, Alfred William," in *Marquis Who's Who in Commerce and Industry, Volume 14*, St. Louis, The Von Hoffman Press, 1965, 66; "Three are named to currency unit," *The New York Times*, 18 February 1964, "Banker gives plan on overseas funds," *The New York Times*, 10 August 1966, 22; "Bankers Protest

When Alfred Barth received the news of the Spanish award, he soon identified his old friend Antonio Garrigues as the likeliest instigator. In his letter of thanks to those who played the role of private partner par excellence of American investment in the years of the so-called Spanish economic miracle – Chase and Garrigues's law firm partnered in Liga Financiera, one of the most important vehicles for channeling FDI in Spain in the 1960s[101] – the banker wrote with false modesty that he was "surprised" by the fact that

> my modest efforts to be helpful to Spain should be rewarded in this manner is not only surprising but quite overwhelming –particularly so that it represents one of the highlights of my professional career as an international banker and reached me, so to say, on the eve of my retirement from the bank.

To showcase his satisfaction, Barth did not refer to the important business the Chase was doing in 1960s Spain – like making loans to the country's ambitious civil nuclear program[102] – but to the operations he had led in autarkic Spain, when the country was subjected to a diplomatic quarantine due to its government's original sin of cooperation with the defeated Axis nations:

> Do you remember the first gold loan agreement when Minister Suanzes asked 'What do all these words mean?' – when I had to explain to him in two sentences 'if you meet your obligations the collateral will be returned; if you do not meet your obligations, the collateral will be sold'. Also I remember –and here I would like to refresh your memory – our first meeting with another Minister of Commerce, namely Ullastres, when we had to explain to him the dollar-peseta program, although the documents lacked legal powers; nevertheless it produced over 350 million dollars for the Instituto [IEME] and killed the black market in Tangiers.

In his reply to Barth, Antonio Garrigues told him that the idea of the award had been enthusiastically received by "every person" in the higher

---

foreign funds tax," *The New York Times*, 10 August 1966, 73; "Chase shuffles senior officers," *The New York Times*, 16 September 1967; "Statement of Alfred W. Barth, Executive Vice President, the Chase Manhattan Bank, Accompanied by Stuart E. Keebler, Counsel," in *Legislative History of H.R. 13103, 89th Congress: Foreign Investors Tax Act. Public Law 89–809. Committee on Ways and Means. U.S. House of Representatives. Nineteenth Congress. First Session. Part I.*, U.S. Government Printing Office, Washington D.C., 1967, 113–133.

[101] A. Alvaro Moya, *Inversión directa...*, 138–143. Garrigues remains today one of Spain's most important and internationally oriented law offices.

[102] See J. De la Torre and M. M. Rubio, La financiación exterior del desarrollo industrial despañol, *Estudios de Historia Económica*, 69, Madrid, Banco de España, 2015, 116–120.

echelons of government and society who desires to "show you in some way the recognition of the Spanish people for what you did for our nation in the hardest and most difficult times above all concerning the lack of [foreign] understanding and [international] isolation."[103] Antonio Garrigues, who by then had been ambassador to the United States (1961–1963) and together with his son Joaquín was about to become an important player in the country's transition to democracy, was very much aware of Chase's significance in the rehabilitation of Spain in the eyes of the American superpower and the Western financial community in the early Cold War years. Garrigues had little doubt that the banking corporation, under the initiative of Alfredo – as he familiarly referred to Barth – had played a tangible role in championing Spain's interests, which the likes of Antonio Garrigues equated to the survival of the political regime headed by general Franco after the end of the Second World War.

The historiography on U.S.–Spain relations, however, has so far been content to point to the Cold War and the lobby organized by Lequerica as the structural and human architects, respectively, of the bilateral rapprochement.[104] This chapter demonstrates the need to re-evaluate that history and broaden the analytical focus to take into account the role of Wall Street and, in particular, Chase National Bank and the WCC in that process, and, therefore, to integrate into this historical narrative the legacy of U.S. total warfare in Spain as well as the expansion of the American financial industry – including its offshore operations – in the immediate post-war period. Likewise, the prevalence of the black market for foreign exchange in Tangier, the intricate nature of Spain's foreign trade operations, and the nature of the competition for the opening of letters of credit for economic aid loans, remind us of the need to have crony capitalism in mind when studying and understanding this phase of bilateral relations.

Sources

Archives

Archivo General de la Universidad de Navarra, Pamplona, Spain
Archivo Histórico del Banco de España, Madrid, Spain.
Archivo de la Sociedad Española de Participaciones Industriales, Madrid, Spain
Harry S. Truman Library, Independence, Missouri, United States
Harvard Business School, Boston, Massachusetts, United States
U.S. National Archives at College Park, Maryland, United States

[103] Barth to Garrigues, 7 August 1967 and Garrigues to Barth, 29 August 1967, AGUN 010/014/002–11.

[104] Garrigues himself had serious doubts about the real relevance of Clark's very well-paid lobbying. See correspondence with Castiella in AGUN 010/01 and 010/06.

Bibliography

Aandahl, F., et al., *Foreign Relations of the United* States *1949, Volume IV, Western Europe,* Washington D.C., U.S. Printing Office, 1975.

Alvarez, D. "American Clandestine Intelligence in Early Postwar Europe," *Journal of Intelligence History*, vol. 4, n. 1 (2004), 7–24.

Alvarez, D. and Mark, E., *Spying through a Glass Darkly: American Espionage against the Soviet Union, 1945–1946*, Lawrence, University Press of Kansas, 2016.

Álvaro Moya, A., *Inversión directa extranjera y formación de capacidades organizativas locales: un análisis del impacto de Estados Unidos en la empresa española (1918–1975)*, Ph.D. dissertation, Universidad Complutense de Madrid, 2011.

Barciela López, C. y del Arco, M. A., "Dossier. La corrupción en la España contemporánea," *Hispania Nova: Revista de Historia Contemporánea*, vol. 16 (2018), 473–734.

Carreras, A. y Tafunell, X., *Historia económica de la España contemporánea (1789–2009)*, Barcelona, Crítica, 2016.

Cava Mesa, M. J., *Los diplomáticos de Franco. J. F. de Lequerica. Temple y tenacidad (1890–1963)*, Bilbao, Deusto, 1989.

Chalou, G. C., *The Secret War: The Office of Strategic Services*, College Park, U.S. National Archives, 1991.

Chernow, R., *The House of Morgan. An American Banking Dynasty and the Rise of Modern Finance*, New York, Grove Press, 2010.

Collado Seidel, C., *España, refugio nazi*, Madrid, Temas de Hoy, 2005.

Delgado, L. and León Aguinaga, P., "De la primacía estratégica a la difusión del modelo americano: Estados Unidos y la España del franquismo," in *Nuevos horizontes del pasado. Culturas políticas, identidades y formas de representación*, Santander, Publican, 2011, 171–185.

De la Torre. J. y Rubio Varas, M. M., *La financiación exterior del desarrollo industrial español. Estudios de Historia Económica n° 69*, Madrid, Banco de España, 2015.

Dunlop, R., *Donovan: America's Master Spy*, New York, Skyhorse, 1982.

Escobedo, R., "La embajada en Washington de Antonio Garrigues Díaz Cañabate (1962–1964): ¿Una diplomacia para el aperturismo?," *Historia y Política*, vol. 23 (2010), 243–273.

Farquet, C., *Histoire du paradis fiscal Suisse*, Paris, Science Po, 2018.

Farré, S., *La Suisse et l'Espagne de Franco. De la guerre civile à la mort du dictateur (1936–1975)*, Lausanne, Antipode, 2006.

Feis, H., *The Spanish Story: Franco and the Nations at War*, New York, Knopf, 1948.

González de Oleaga, M., *El doble juego de la hispanidad. España y la Argentina durante la Segunda Guerra Mundial*, Madrid, UNED, 2001.

Goodwin, Ralph R., et al, *Foreign Relations of the United States 1948, Volume III, Western Europe,* Washington D.C., U.S. Printing Office, 1974.

Hersh, B., *The Old Boys: The American Elite and the Origins of the CIA,* New York, Scribner's, 1992.

Hualde Amunárriz, X., *El "cerco aliado". Estados Unidos, Gran Bretaña y Francia frente a la dictadura franquista (1945–1953)*, Bilbao, UPV/EHU, 2016.

Irwin, D. A., *Clashing Over Commerce. A History of U.S. Trade Policy*, Chicago, University of Chicago Press, 2017.

Johnson, A. M., *Winthrop W. Aldrich: Lawyer, Banker, Diplomat*, Cambridge, Harvard University Press, 1968.

Leitz, C., *Economic Relations between Nazi Germany and Franco's Spain, 1936–1945*, Oxford, Clarendon Press, 1996.

León Aguinaga, P., *Sospechosos habituales. El cine norteamericano, Estados Unidos y la España franquista*, Madrid, CSIC, 2010.

León Aguinaga, P., "The Trouble with Propaganda. World War II, Franco Spain, and the Origins of U.S. Postwar Public Diplomacy," *International History Review*, vol. 37, n. 2 (2015), 342–365.

León Aguinaga, P. (ed.) *Philip W. Bonsal, Diario de un diplomático americano en España, 1944–1947. Estados Unidos ante a la dictadura franquista*, Zaragoza, Prensas de la Universidad de Zaragoza, forthcoming.

Liedtke, B., *Embracing a Dictatorship. US Relations with Spain, 1945–53*, London, MacMillan, 1998.

Lindley, E. K. and Weintal, E., "How We Dealt with Spain," *Harper's Magazine*, vol. 190 (1944), 23–33.

Lorenz-Meyer, M., *Safehaven, The Allied Pursuit of Nazi Assets Abroad*, Columbia, University of Missouri Press, 2007.

Madariaga, M. R., "El lucrativo "negocio" del protectorado español," *Hispania Nova*, vol. 16 (2018), 590–619.

Marquis Who's Who in Commerce and Industry, Volume 14, St. Louis, The Von Hoffman Press, 1965.

Martín Aceña, P. *El oro de Moscú y el oro de Berlín*, Madrid, Taurus, 2001.

Martínez Ruiz, E. *El sector exterior durante la autarquía. Una reconstrucción de las balanzas de pagos en España (1940–1958) (Edición Revisada), Estudios de Historia Económica n° 43*, Madrid, Banco de España, 2003.

Messenger, D. A., *Hunting Nazis in Franco's Spain*, Baton Rouge, Louisiana State University, 2014.

Montero Jiménez, J. A., *El despertar de la gran potencia. Las relaciones entre España y los Estados Unidos (1898–1930)*, Madrid, Biblioteca Nueva, 2011.

Montero Jiménez, J. A., y León Aguinaga, P., *Los Estados Unidos y el mundo. La metamorfosis del poder americano (1890–1952)*, Madrid, Biblioteca Nueva, 2019.

Mulder, T., *The Economic Weapon. The Rise of Sanctions as a Tool of Modern War*, New Haven & London, Yale University Press, 2022.

Muñoz, J., Roldan. S. y Serrano, A., *La internacionalización del capital en España, 1959–1977*, Madrid, Edicusa, 1978, 422–424.

Ogle, V., "Archipelago Capitalism: Tax Havens, Offshore Money, and the State, 1950s-1970s," *American Historical Review*, vol. 122, n. 5 (2017), 1431–1458.

Ogle, V.: "'Funk Money': The End of Empire, the Expansion of Tax Havens, and Decolonization as an Economic and Financial Event," *Past & Present*, vol. 249, n. 1 (2020), 213–249.

Ortínez i Mur, M., *Una vida entre burgesos. Mèmories*, Barcelona, Edicions 92, 1991.

Prins, N., *All the President's Bankers. The Hidden Alliances that Drive American Power*, New York, Nation Books 2014.

Pruessen. R. W., *John Foster Dulles: The Road to Power, Vol. 1*, New York: Free Press, 1982.

Puig Raposo, N. y Álvaro Moya, A., "La Guerra Fría y los empresarios españoles: la articulación de los intereses económicos de Estados Unidos en España, 1950–1975," *Revista de Historia Económica*, vol. 22, n. 2 (2004), 387–424.

Quijada, M., *Relaciones hispano-argentinas, 1938–1948. Coyunturas de crisis, Tesis doctoral inédita*, Madrid, Universidad Complutense de Madrid, 1989.

Rein, R., *La salvación de una dictadura. Alianza Franco–Perón 1946–1955*, Madrid, CSIC, 1995.

Riquer, B. de, Pérez Francesch, J. L., Rubí, G. Ferrán Toledano, L. y Luján, O. (dirs.), *La corrupción política en la España contemporánea. Un enfoque interdisciplinar*, Barcelona, Marcial Pons, 2018.

Rosendorf, N., *Franco Sells Spain to America. Hollywood, Tourism and Public Relations as Postwar Spanish Soft Power*, Madrid, Palgrave MacMillan, 2014.

Sampson, A., *The Money Lenders. Bankers in a Dangerous World*, London, Hodder & Stoughton, 1981.

Sánchez Recio, G. y Tascón, J. (eds.), *Los empresarios de Franco. Política y economía en España, 1936–1957*, Barcelona, Crítica, 2003.

Smith Jr., W. T., *Encyclopedia of the Central Intelligence Agency*, New York, Facts on File, 2003.

Thomàs, J. M., *Roosevelt and Franco during the Second World War. From the Spanish Civil War to Pearl Harbor*, New York, Palgrave MacMillan, 2008.

Thomàs, J. M., *Roosevelt and Franco and the end of the Second World War*, New York, Palgrave MacMillan, 2011.

Trundle, S., *The ExportImport Bank of Washington. Its Origins, Operations and Relationships with other Government agencies, 1934–1950*, New Brunswick, Rutgers University, 1950.

US Congress. *Legislative History of H. R. 13103, 89th Congress: Foreign Investors Tax Act. Public Law 89–809. Committee on Ways and Means. U.S. House of Representatives. Nineteenth Congress. First Session. Part I.*, Washington D.C., U.S. Government Printing Office, 1967.

Viñas, Á., *En las garras del águila. Los pactos con Estados Unidos, de Francisco Franco a Felipe González (1945–1995)*, Barcelona, Crítica, 2003.

Viñas, Á., Viñuela, J., Eguidazu, F., Fernández Pulgar, C. y Florensa, S., *Política Comercial Exterior en España, 1931–1975*, Madrid, Banco Exterior de España, 1979.

Waller, W. *Wild William Donovan. The Spy Master Who Created the OSS and Modern American Espionage*, New York, Simon & Schuster, 2011.

Wilson, D. *The Chase. The Chase Manhattan Bank N. A. 1945–1985*, Boston: Harvard Business School, 1986.

3

The Struggle to Change U.S. Policy toward Franco's Spain 1948–1950: José Félix de Lequerica, Paid Lobbyists, "Friendly" Senators, the Spanish Lobby and the Spanish Bloc

JOAN MARIA THOMÀS

This chapter deals with one aspect of the relations between the United States and Franco's Spain – and vice versa – during the years in which the policy implemented by President Harry S. Truman and Secretary of State Dean Acheson required the Franco regime to make liberalizing reforms. The policy was opposed by some sectors of Congress, the armed forces, various economic interests, personalities from the world of culture and the press, and a part of public opinion, who pressed for a change that would take Spain out of diplomatic "quarantine" and no longer exclude it from the strategic and economic alliances struck by the United States in Western Europe.

Paradoxically, the president and Acheson implemented the policy at the same time as their administration was doing its utmost to contain communism. Of course, Franco was at the head of one of the most doctrinally anti-communist regimes in Europe, so they clearly gave more weight to the fascist nature of the regime and Spain's friendship with the powers defeated in 1945 than to its undeniable anti-communism. This raises various issues such as the singularity of Spain's position in the immediate post-war period; the struggle between the executive and legislative powers in the United States to direct foreign policy; the increasing influence of the armed forces on the design of this foreign policy; the relations between the Allies in the years of transition from anti-fascism to anti-communism as the fundamental paradigm of international relations, with Spain being a surviving case that aroused anti-fascist feeling; and the influence of personal factors – beliefs, feelings, emotions, prejudices – on politics, in particular those of Truman and his anti-Franco sentiments. Truman was an anti-Francoist for religious reasons but also because he was an anti-totalitarian and so also adopted a policy of confrontation with the Soviet Union. In this latter respect, some diplomats who had been stationed in Moscow had considerable influence over President Truman, who was initially

THE STRUGGLE TO CHANGE U.S. POLICY TOWARD FRANCO'S SPAIN   75

insecure and eager to free himself from the long shadow of his predecessor, Franklin D. Roosevelt.[1]

Truman's anti-Francoism was based as much on his anti-fascism and anti-totalitarianism as on his Baptist faith. And he also refused to accept the lack of freedom (and sometimes harassment) of Protestants in Spain and General Franco's systematic persecution of freemasonry because he was a prominent freemason himself. For his part, Dean Acheson, appointed secretary of state on 21 January, 1949, was also a convinced anti-Francoist,[2] although less personally involved than the president. Like Truman and the previous secretary of state, General Marshall, his fundamental concern was to maintain the alliance with the United Kingdom and France, whose coalition governments and general public could not conceive of any political rapprochement with a regime such as the Spanish one that had come into being with the help of the fascist powers. This explains why Spain was kept in diplomatic quarantine – when the UN decided to withdraw all ambassadors in December 1946, and not to accept Spain as a member – and why it was excluded from the economic benefits of the Marshall Plan and the North Atlantic Treaty, the new military alliance. Both of these initiatives were promoted by the United States, were clearly anti-communist in nature and, as we have said, should theoretically have been able to accommodate Spain.

On the other hand, some sectors in the United States were pulling in the opposite direction and fighting to change the prevailing policy. Among them were major economic interests, the armed forces – led by the U.S. navy and the recently created U.S. air force – and members of Congress who represented these economic interests, the specific interests of their states or their own ideological convictions. Historiography has very imprecisely referred to this group as the "Spanish Lobby" – a concept that we will question throughout this chapter. In an effort to influence these sectors and also for other propaganda purposes, the Franco regime sent a former minister of foreign affairs to Washington with a considerable amount of funding at his disposal that he

---

[1] See F. Costigliola, "After Roosevelt's Death: Dangerous Emotions, Divisive Discourses, and the Abandoned Alliance," *Diplomatic History*, vol. 34, n. 1 (January 2010), 1–23; and by the same author, *Roosevelt's Lost Alliances: How Personal Politics Helped Start the Cold War*, Princeton, Princeton University Press, 2012.

[2] In April 1946, when he was under secretary of state, he had described Franco as "a Nazi-Fascist of the worst kind [...] who cooperated with the Germans and the Italians during the War" and he also said that he was "a character who we whole-heartedly wish to see removed": Memorandum of Conversation, "Spanish Problem," 8 April 1946, Decimal File Box 6338 RG 59 Decimal File Box, National Archives and Records Administration (NARA-2) cited in A. Ferrary, "Los Estados Unidos y el régimen de Franco, 1945–1973. De la 'kick-Franco-out-now-policy' al 'solving the 'Spanish Problem': modernización y apertura exterior," *Memoria y civilización. Anuario de Historia*, vol. 21 (2018), 288.

76   JOAN MARIA THOMÀS

could use as "grants" for hiring professional lobbyists. The pro-Franco sectors that we refer to as the "Spanish Bloc" assisted in these efforts.

This chapter focuses on the period between the decision to change the policy on Spain in late 1947 – reluctantly approved by Truman in January 1948 – and the effective implementation of this change in late 1950. In these three years, and in opposition to the sectors that wanted to end Franco's diplomatic isolation and bring Spain into the U.S.-backed strategic and economic alliances, the president and Acheson refused to put the change into practice unless Franco undertook a series of liberalizing reforms in social, political, and economic matters. But Franco did not buckle to U.S. pressure, and the policy was not changed until three years after the decision had been taken. When President Truman finally consented, he did so more because of the international situation and the spiraling Cold War than because of the "Spanish debate." So, to some extent, we can speak of a twofold failure: Truman and Acheson did not achieve any significant liberalization of the Franco regime, and Franco only achieved a belated and minor change in U.S. policy.

This does not mean that, during the three years we discuss below the Francoists in Washington, their paid lobbyists and their "friends" in Congress did not have any success. In fact, on one memorable occasion in 1950, Senator McCarran managed to raise a loan for Spain and, as a group, they did create a more favorable environment for changing the policy on Spain and improving the image of the country in some sectors of American public opinion.

The sections below contain a new approach to a stage in United States–Spain/Spain–United States relations that has already been closely examined by historiography.[3] It is an approach from within that analyzes José Félix de

---

3   See F. Portero, *Franco aislado. La cuestión española (1945–1950)*, Madrid, Aguilar, 1989; A. Viñas, *Los pactos secretos de Franco con Estados Unidos. Bases, ayuda económica, recortes de soberanía*, Barcelona, Grijalbo, 1981, and by the same author *En las garras del águila. Los pactos con Estados Unidos, de Francisco Franco a Felipe González (1945–1995)*, Barcelona, Crítica, 2003; P. Martín Aceña, *El oro de Moscú y el oro de Berlín*, Madrid, Taurus, 2001, R. R. Rubottom-J. C. Murphy, *Spain and the United States since World War II*, New York, Praeger, 1984; B. N. Liedke *Embracing a Dictatorship. US Relations with Spain, 1945–1953*, London, Macmillan Press, 1998, A. Jarque Iñíguez – *"Queremos esas bases" El acercamiento de Estados Unidos a la España de Franco*, Alcalá de Henares, Universidad de Alcalá, 1998; M. J. Cava Mesa *Los diplomáticos de Franco. J.F. de Lequerica. Temple y tenacidad (1890–1963)*, Bilbao, Universidad de Deusto, 1989; W. H. Bowen, *Truman, Franco's Spain, and the Cold War*, Columbia, University of Missouri Press, 2017; J. Edwards, *Anglo-American Relations and the Franco Question 1945–1955*, New York, Oxford University Press, 1999; F. Termis Soto, *Renunciando a todo: el régimen franquista y Estados Unidos desde 1945 hasta 1963*, Madrid, Biblioteca Nueva, 2005; P. León Aguinaga, *Sospechosos habituales. El cine norteamericano, Estados Unidos y la España franquista, 1939–1960*, Madrid, CSIC, 2010; I. Sánchez González, *Diez años de soledad. España, la ONU y la dictadura franquista 1945–1955*, Seville, Universidad

THE STRUGGLE TO CHANGE U.S. POLICY TOWARD FRANCO'S SPAIN   77

Lequerica y Erquiza (Bilbao, 1890–1963) and his time at the Spanish embassy in Washington, the U.S. lobbyists hired by the embassy and the "friends" in Congress – some of whom were undoubtedly paid (that is to say, bribed) – who were working with the legislative chambers, the administration, the press and other sectors to change policy on Spain. The analysis also focuses on U.S. citizens who were in favor of the Franco regime for ideological, religious, or economic reasons.

This study has had to overcome a variety of obstacles: the unavailability of the main protagonist's personal archive;[4] the deletion of material from archives such as Senator Pat McCarran's ("cleansed" by his daughters) or Carlton J. H. Hayes's ("cleansed" by his wife); the sparseness of other archives (for example, Robert Owen Brewster's); the lack of information about Spain (for example, Alvin O'Konski's); or the total lack of documentary evidence (for example, Charles Patrick Clark's, some of whose affirmations could only be checked in the occasional letter or through third parties,[5] or Father Joseph F. Thorning's). Neither has it been easy to make any significant progress in identifying the "subsidies," bonuses, payments, or pure bribes that were handed out by the Francoists, sometimes with considerable reluctance by the government in Madrid, but with great eagerness by their main proponent, none other than Lequerica himself.

The chapter is structured in three main chronological sections, each of which deals with one of the years studied, and is further divided into subthemes.

---

de Sevilla, 2015; F. Costigliola, *Roosevelt's Lost Alliances...*; M. Weil, *A Pretty Good Club. The Founding Fathers of the US Foreign Service*, New York, Norton, 1978; J. M. Thomàs, *La batalla del wolframio. Estados Unidos y España de Pearl Harbor a la Guerra Fría (1941–1947)*, Madrid, Cátedra, 2010 (English version, *Roosevelt, Franco, and the End of the Second World War*, New York, Palgrave-Macmillan, 2011); C. Collado Seidel, *El telegrama que salvó a Franco. Londres, Washington y la cuestión del Régimen (1942–1945)*, Barcelona, Crítica, 2016; P. J. Briggs, *Making American Foreign Policy: President–Congress Relations from the Second World War to the post-Cold War Era*, Lanham, Rowman & Littlefield, 1994; and X. Hualde Amunarriz – *El "Cerco" aliado. Estados Unidos, Gran Bretaña y Francia frente a la dictadura franquista (1945–1953)*, Universidad del País Vasco, 2016.

4 If such an archive still exists today, it is just one of a long list of personal archives of leading figures of the Franco regime that needs to be retrieved despite the advances that have been made recently. It was made available, however, to his biographer María Jesús Cava Mesa so that she could write her book, cited in the previous footnote.

5 For example, between 1959 and 1961, the ambassador in Madrid (1955–1961) John Davis Lodge (John D. Lodge Papers. Hoover Institution Archives. Stanford University), a little more recently (1963–1964) the ambassador in Washington between 1962 and 1964, Antonio Garrigues y Díaz Cañabate (Fondo Antonio Garrigues y Díaz Cañabate. Archivo General de la Universidad de Navarra). I am grateful to Pablo León Aguinaga for providing me with documentation from both their collections of papers.

1948

José Félix de Lequerica was the Spanish minister of foreign affairs at the end of the Second World War (from August 1944 to July 1945) and ambassador in France, first in Paris (from March 1939 to June 1940) and then in Vichy (from July 1940 to August 1944). He arrived in Washington as an inspector of embassies and legations on 19 April 1948 entrusted with leading the embassy and working from the U.S. capital to fully normalize relations between the United States and Spain. Because it was unthinkable that they should enter into any formal agreements in the midst of the highly irregular diplomatic situation, this normalization involved exchanging ambassadors whose main aim was to negotiate loans and subsidies in both the public and private spheres in the United States, so that the Spanish economy could extricate itself from the crisis in which it was immersed. But "normalization" also required lifting of the UN resolution from December 1946 concerning Franco's regime – a follow-up to the Tripartite Note condemning the regime on the previous 4 March – which called for the withdrawal of ambassadors from Spain.[6] In turn, this required him to work with the delegations of those countries whose interests were potentially similar. At the time, the UN's provisional headquarters was in Lake Success (New York), and meetings were held in different countries. If Lequerica was successful in his attempt to have the restrictions lifted, he would be appointed ambassador.

In other words, Lequerica was sent to Washington to increase the presence and image of Franco's Spain in U.S. political, economic, military, and press circles, and bring about a change in policy that would give the country much-needed economic assistance in the process of modernization. At the same time, he would counteract the Spanish Republican exiles and the U.S. anti-Franco sectors who had been giving the regime such a bad name. Lequerica was also going to show the United States the "reality" of Spain by exploiting the support of a group of sympathizers who had been making themselves heard in the country since the Spanish Civil War and whose support was likely to grow amid the increasing fear of communism that was becoming more and more dominant in politics and society.

This was the situation when Lequerica arrived in what was also an election year. The Republican candidate, Thomas E. Dewey, was expected to defeat President Truman, an assumption on which the Spanish representation in Washington had been working for some time. What is more, the (short-lived) O'Konski Amendment had just revealed the existence of pro-Franco sectors in the U.S. Congress, and it had also become known that the armed forces – led by the navy and the air force – were interested in Spain's joining the Western defense effort just when there seemed to be a very real possibility of another

---

6   This withdrawal was respected with only four exceptions: the Vatican, Portugal, Switzerland and El Salvador. All the other representations were left in the hands of *chargé d'affaires* ad interim.

Figure 3.1. January 19, 1951. Lunch offered at the U.S. Senate in honor of the Spanish Ambassador, José Félix de Lequerica, and his wife. Attended by U.S. Secretary of State Dean Acheson and Senator Chávez. Archivo ABC.

world war breaking out in Europe with the Soviet Union and its satellites as enemies. So the time was right. There had also been a change in U.S. policy on Spain, the first signs of the beginning of the end to what was known within the State Department as the kick-Franco-out-now policy. And dominating everything else was the growing tension between the Western Allies and the Soviet Union and its satellites, which the Franco regime rightly believed could work in its favor. Things, however, would prove to be much more complex than Franco thought, and they would not get any clearer for another three years.

The title of inspector with which Lequerica arrived in the United States was little more than a subterfuge to cover up his real mission. Spain's official representative was Baráibar, the *chargé d'affaires ad interim*, so Lequerica could not have formal meetings with the president just as the U.S. *chargé d'affaires* in Madrid since May 1947, Paul Trauger Culbertson, could not meet with the Spanish head of state. However, Lequerica aspired to become ambassador. In fact, as far back as 1945 the Spanish Ministry of Foreign Affairs had attempted to obtain the *agrément* but to no avail.[7] They had not wanted to appoint him

---

[7] In October 1945: Entry 521 1 November 1945. P. León Aguinaga (ed.), *Philip W. Bonsal. Diario de un diplomático americano en España, 1944–1947. Estados Unidos ante la dictadura franquista*, Zaragoza, Prensas de la Universidad de Zaragoza, forthcoming.

80 JOAN MARIA THOMÀS

chargé d'affaires either, probably because they would have come up against the same problem that had prevented the *agrément* from being accepted and because he was unwilling to accept a rank that was below that of his previous post as foreign minister or his status as career ambassador.

The Change in U.S. Policy on the Franco Regime in January 1948

At the General Assembly of the UN, in November 1947, the United States and Great Britain had taken up the Soviet Union's proposal and prevented more radical measures against Spain. This was the first result of the policy on Spain being reworked by the head of the Policy Planning Staff[8] of the State Department, George F. Kennan, at the request of Norman Armour, the former ambassador to Spain in 1945 and at that time under secretary for political affairs. This reworking, which had now become a directive of the National Security Council (NSC 3),[9] was reluctantly approved[10] by President Truman[11] on 21 January 1948. In the National Security Council, the opinion of the military played a decisive role in the final approval.[12]

NSC 3 recognized that the policy to isolate Spain diplomatically had not only failed but had actually reinforced Franco at home. In addition, the restriction on imports and exports between the two countries had interfered with Spain's recovery and given the United States a bad name there, which could have consequences if a new war broke out in Europe. It was now

---

[8] Set up by the new secretary of state in January 1947, General George C. Marshall and placed under the leadership of George F. Kennan, author of the famous *Long Telegram* who had laid the foundations of the Containment Doctrine or the Truman Doctrine in his speech to Congress on 12 March 1947. See Costigliola, "After Roosevelt's Death... and *Roosevelt's Lost...*; J. Lewis Gaddis, *Estados Unidos y los orígenes de la Guerra Fría 1941–1947*, Buenos Aires, Latinoamericano, 1989; ibid., *The Cold War. A New History*, London, Penguin, 2005; R. L. Messer, *The End of an Alliance: James F. Byrnes, Roosevelt, Truman, and the Origins of the Cold War*, Chapel Hill, University of North Carolina Press, 1982; A. A. Offner, *Another such Victory: President Truman and the Cold War 1945–1953*, Stanford, Stanford University Press, 2002; G. F. Kennan, *Memoirs 1925–1950*, New York, Pantheon Books, 1983; R. H. Ferrell, *Harry S. Truman and the Cold War Revisionists*, University of Missouri, 2006.

[9] Set up as a result of the National Security Act of July 1947. The CIA was also set up.

[10] On 21 January 1948 Truman passed the NSC 3 with the expression "concurred in" instead of the more habitual "approved by": Edwards, *Anglo-American Relations* ..., 97.

[11] Although it had been applied previously, as had been seen in the UN: Hualde, *El "cerco"* ..., 204; Edwards, *Anglo-American Relations* ..., 97.

[12] On the influence of the Pentagon in the adoption of this change in policy, See P. Whitaker, *Spain and Defense of the West: Ally and Liability*, New York, Council of Foreign Relations/Harper & Brothers, 1961, 32.

advocated that there should be no new UN sanctions and that a new resolution should lift the restrictions imposed in December 1946 and relax the economic policy applied up to that moment.[13] So the aim now was not to bring the Franco regime down – the aforementioned kick-Franco-out-now policy – but to adopt a policy of greater openness and rapprochement.

However, when the time came, the State Department decided to adopt the policy advocated by John Hickerson (director of the Office of European Affairs), Theodore C. Achilles (head of the Division of Western European Affairs), William B. Dunham (head of the Spanish desk) and, at the highest level, Norman Armour;[14] that is to say, they insisted on the regime implementing political and economic reforms as a condition for rapprochement and aid. In fact, the department was divided into two camps on the issue of changing relations with Spain and the conditions for doing so. Those who were least in favor of any change (mentioned above) were in line with the clear anti-Franco attitudes of Under Secretary Acheson and President Truman. In one of their first meetings in Washington, Armour told Lequerica that he found it annoying that Franco was constantly and publicly bragging that he had been the first to defeat the threat of communism and that he had warned the Western Allies of the problem they were now facing "as if they [the Franco supporters] were the only ones to have made the right predictions and wanted to show the world how things should be done [...] We also have our pride."[15]

On Armour's orders, Hickerson explained the new directives to Culbertson – a former assistant of his at the division between 1945 and 1948[16] – so that the Spanish government could be informed. He made it clear that, although "we want to bring about the gradual normalization of relations between Spain and the United States [...], complete normalization would be difficult, if not impossible, without some democratization in Spain."[17] He believed that this process of democratization was now in the hands of the Franco regime since the previous U.S. policy had failed and was no longer going to be pursued. But he was not prepared to make his new position public until Franco began to make reforms. Neither was he prepared to take any steps to change the 1946 resolution or the ban on Spain's sending ambassadors and being granted access to the UN's specialized agencies. And, in terms of finance, Spain would be given authorization for private loans only if they could be guaranteed with

---

[13] Hualde, *El "cerco"* ..., 197.

[14] On Armour's demands for reforms in Spain, see Cava Mesa, *Los diplomáticos de Franco* ..., 422.

[15] Ibid., 296.

[16] Martín Aceña, *El oro de Moscú* ..., 321.

[17] The Chief of the Division of Western European Affairs (Achilles) to the Chargé in Spain (Culbertson), 5 January 1948, *Foreign Relations Of The United States*, 1948, Western Europe, vol. III, 1019–1020.

gold. In this regard, he told him that "one private $25,000,000 cotton deal is currently hung up on the question of a 40% gold coverage and similar loans might well follow" and that "satisfactory conclusion of the current gold negotiations would make this possible." As we shall see, this was very soon to be a reality. But he would not accept the Export-Import Bank awarding official loans until Franco gave "concrete signs that it [Spain] has the intention of moving toward greater democratic and economic efficiency and that it has begun to do so." This was quite unlike the immediate post-Spanish Civil War period when, in August 1939 the Export-Import Bank had awarded a loan of $11 million for the purchase of U.S. cotton.[18]

The decision on whether to include Spain in the European Recovery Program (which was to be responsible for implementing the Marshall Plan) was left up to the sixteen countries affected, but the general feeling was that it would not be possible "in the absence of substantial political and economic changes within Spain." In other words, the aim was to persuade "Franco to inaugurate gradual and orderly liberalization rather than trying to force him out."[19] This was how those in charge of the Spanish question in the State Department envisaged the new policy.[20]

Of course, when these directives were rejected outright when they were communicated by Culbertson to the Minister of Foreign Affairs, Alberto Martín Artajo, in a tense meeting during which José Sebastián de Erice, Director General of Foreign Affairs, acted as interpreter.[21] Apparently exasperated by the

[18] To forty-four U.S. exporting companies. See P. León Aguinaga, "The Chase Bank, the WCC and the (Financial) Rehabilitation of Spain in the Early Cold War," *SAHFR – Themed session on CAPITALISM. Panel: "International Bankers, Offshore Merchants, and Foreign Diplomats: Change and Continuity in U.S. Foreign (Spanish–American) Relations from the Great Depression to the Bretton Woods Age,"* 2021, 13–14, 19.

[19] He concluded by saying that: "Assuming that you get anything short of a complete rebuff from Franco (which would make us look again at our whole policy), I think you should take substantially the same line with all other elements in Spain – Army, Church, Monarchists and the moderate left. The extreme left is seeking disorder and communism rather than democracy in Spain and we do not care what they think. Other leftist elements may well react unfavorably, possibly bitterly, but we believe with complete sincerity that there is no chance whatever of achieving a really democratic regime in Spain through the former policy of attempting international coercion and that there is a reasonable possibility of bringing it about through the new one."

[20] Hualde, *El "cerco"* ..., 203.

[21] *(1177) May 28 [1947].* "Paul and María Culbertson and their two young daughters arrived from Bilbao at 8 pm. I had the leading Embassy people and their wives to meet them. Paul is looping well and sounding delighted to be here. He told M and me that Ambassador Baruch had asked particularly for us to be assigned to his Embassy in The Hague – I wonder if this is a cover-up for a slightly guilty conscience on Paul's part! Neither Paul nor his wife speak a word of Spanish." León, *Philip W. Bonsal*....

THE STRUGGLE TO CHANGE U.S. POLICY TOWARD FRANCO'S SPAIN   83

Spaniard's refusal to cooperate, Culbertson blurted out that Spain was a "police State, where there was considerable political repression, practically everything was considered a crime against the State"[22] and the Spanish National Institute of Industry (INI) and the Regime's general policy of autarky and intervention were making things very difficult for free trade. In this respect, he insisted, there was an urgent need for economic and political liberalization. To this the minister responded by saying that

> if the Regime were to liberalize in a manner such as I [Culbertson] apparently had in mind, revolution and civil strife would break out here and the credits received by reason of their liberalizing action would have to be used to restore order.

At the end of the meeting, Erice told the *chargé d'affaires* that he would send him a list of the liberalizing changes adopted by the Spanish government since 1945 to which Culbertson responded that he was more interested "in a statement of what was going to be done in the future and when."

A few days later there had been another meeting, this one more informal – a lunch – between Culbertson himself, now accompanied by William Dunham of the Spanish desk, who had traveled to Spain, and Randall, an economic adviser, with the head of the Foreign Ministry's Undersecretariat for Foreign Economy and Trade, Emilio de Navasqüés Ruiz de Velasco, accompanied by the latter's director general for economic policy, Mariano de Yturralde. They discussed the subject of U.S. loans to Spain. During the meeting, Culbertson had stated that "the US government considers that the discussion surrounding the Spanish presidency, on which it had hitherto maintained a critical position, is no longer topical and is an internal Spanish matter."[23] And on the issue of loans he maintained what he had said on previous occasions:

> At the present time only private negotiations between American and Spanish interests who wish to find mutually convenient formulas for financial or industrial cooperation are possible. The Department of State, which has hitherto been opposed to encouraging negotiations of this kind, withdraws all objection to them if there are American interests intent on carrying them out. On the other hand, this is not the time to extend the formula by involving the Export-Import Bank, much less to include it in the Marshall Plan or other similar bodies.[24]

---

[22] Memorandum of Conversation by the Chargé in Spain (Culbertson), 2 February 1948, *Foreign Relations of the United States*, 1948, Western Europe, vol. III, 1021–1022.

[23] Under-Secretary of Foreign Economy and Trade to Minister, 12 February 1948, Ministry of Foreign Affairs. I am grateful to Pacho Fernández Larrondo for obtaining this memorandum.

[24] Ibid.

He also warned Navasqüés not to make any attempt to travel to the United States for this purpose, and was

> so explicit on this point that he even went so far as to echo rumours that the Government was planning to send the undersigned on a special mission to the United States with a view to arranging a loan or credit for the economic reconstruction of Spain. Mr. Culbertson, in terms of the highest consideration for me, made it quite clear that if this were to be the case he would have no chance of entering into useful talks.

He was also keeping an eye on the end of the negotiations on the Nazi gold issue. The fact that the Franco regime may have been in possession of reserves of this origin was hindering the possibility of obtaining private loans, because the U.S. Treasury Department had been sending warnings to the banks. Martín Artajo and Franco himself reacted to the news of this change in U.S. policy on Spain by reasserting their own policy and readying themselves to play their new card: sending Lequerica to Washington as a catalyst and organizer of the U.S. support they knew they already had and the support they believed they could acquire, particularly in Congress from among such friendly senators as the highly influential Republican for Maine Ralph Owen Brewster. Meanwhile, in Madrid, they continued to work closely with friendly diplomatic missions and seek other channels to bring isolation to an end and have access to loans. They refused to accept Culbertson's demands and were hopeful that the international climate would deteriorate even though they realized that they were regarded as political outcasts by the vast majority of Western European countries. At this point in February 1948, the situation in Europe was increasingly strained and the outbreak of another war was a real possibility for a variety of reasons: the Greek Civil War had flared up again, the Soviet Union was pressuring Turkey, Italy was about to hold elections (in April) and the communists looked likely to become a major political force or even win, and in Czechoslovakia the communists had seized power. In the light of all this, Franco believed that the Spanish mainland, coast and islands had a much greater strategic value. In all events, the situation would continue to deteriorate as a result of the Berlin crisis in the following June.

The U.S. Armed Forces and Spain

Franco and Martín Artajo were also very aware that they had the support of the sectors of the U.S. armed forces – the navy and air force – interested in using bases on Spanish territory. They had been informed of this support by

THE STRUGGLE TO CHANGE U.S. POLICY TOWARD FRANCO'S SPAIN   85

the naval attaché at the U.S. embassy, Captain Preston Virginius Mercer,[25] and a U.S. informant based in Madrid and/or Paris who signed his communications with the initial M and who was in close contact with the U.S. military. Thanks to this informant they knew that Secretary of the Navy James V. Forrestal had visited Secretary of State General Marshall in 1947 before the UN November vote to recommend that the U.S. delegation abstain from voting on the Soviet proposals about Spain. And, through Mercer, they had learned of the U.S. armed forces' intention to engage in a secret military mission in Spain without the State Department's knowledge. The aim of the mission was to assess the state of the Spanish armies, equip them, and use them as part of the Western defense system, because they were convinced that, in the event of an attack, Soviet troops would reach the Pyrenees in three weeks.[26] On 10 January, 1948, Mercer himself had met with the undersecretary of the Presidency of the Government and naval captain, Luis Carrero Blanco, Franco's closest collaborator, who was known to be against the policy of the State Department. Asked if Spain would be prepared to receive "a small, secret North American [military] commission" like the one that had been sent to Great Britain to make plans for military aid four years before the outbreak

---

[25] Some sources link Mercer to the CIA and suggest he was its head in Spain, which seems highly unlikely: its head between 1948 and 1950 was Alfred Conrad Ulmer, a veteran of the Office of Strategic Services, which was dismantled and replaced by the CIA. On Ulmer see. W. T. Smith Jr., *Encyclopaedia of the Central Intelligence Agency*, New York, Facts and File, 2003, 232.

[26] "Conversation between the Undersecretary of the Presidency Mr. Luis Carrero and the American Captain Preston Virginius on 10 January at half past six in the evening, in the presence of W. Middleton and Commander Sobredo," 10 January 1948, Presidency of the Government Record Group, Head of State, file number 72–07660 General Administrative Archive (AGA). During the Second World War, Mercer had been assistant to chief of the United States Pacific Fleet, Admiral Nimitz, and had recently been sent to Europe to work on the defense of Italy and Spain, working in liaison with the Operations Section of the U.S. Navy's General Staff. Between February and June 1944 he had served as assistant chief of staff and flag secretary of the staff commander-in-chief Pacific. When he left his position as attaché in Madrid, he was awarded the Cross of Naval Merit Third Class with white decoration by the Spanish Ministry of the Navy. *Diario Oficial de la Marina*, 5 January 1950, 26.

Mercer was the first American naval attaché to establish contacts at the highest level, but a few months earlier, on 16 July 1947, his predecessor, Captain Rutt, had visited the military commander of the navy in Malaga, to ask about the state of the beaches for a possible landing in the event of a new war with "Russia" after arriving in London. There he had taken part in a meeting where American aid against Communism had been discussed and it had been concluded that Spain was of the utmost importance: Chief of the Naval Staff to Undersecretary of the Ministry of Foreign Affairs, 31 July 1947, Ministry of Foreign Affairs. I am grateful to Pacho Fernández Larrondo for providing me with a copy of this letter.

of the world war – also without the knowledge of the State Department – he had replied that he would have to consult Franco.

Carrero had taken the opportunity to argue in favor of Spain's need for U.S. economic aid. He understood that

> for tactical reasons the State Department would never agree to giving public economic aid to Spain; but, just as [according to Mercer] there were ways to prepare militarily, the military could also find a way, a subterfuge, that would allow us to receive the financial aid we needed to solve our economic problem, which was so closely connected to the military problem.[27]

Mercer had responded that he "would bring this up with the military establishment, but that the possibility of financial aid always met with the opposition of the State Department." For his part, M informed that the *chargé d'affaires*, Culbertson, was hindering Mercer's work whereas "the US military is willing to do everything possible to make the State Department understand how necessary Spain is for our security."[28]

During another interview a few days later, Carrero informed Mercer that Spain had agreed to the secret commission, which he would put in touch with General Juan Vigón, chief of the Defense Staff. Mercer promised to relay the response to Washington. Then Carrero, undoubtedly on Franco's instructions, lectured him on the probable failure of the Marshall Plan in countries with a communist presence, predicting that it would be sabotaged. But above all else he had insisted on the possibility of establishing bilateral economic aid. Mercer's response was that "they too had problems and political commitments that prevented a sudden change in policy on Spain, although they hoped to change it little by little."[29] He also announced that on 2 February 1948 Admiral Forrest P. Sherman, recently appointed chief of the Mediterranean Fleet, would be arriving in Spain despite the obstacles put in his way by the State Department.[30]

These obstacles must have been greater than expected because Admiral Sherman never actually arrived, and no secret military commission was ever

---

[27] Ibid.

[28] Ibid.

[29] Interview held on 19 January 1948 at 8 pm between the Undersecretary of the Presidency Mr. Luis Carrero and the American Naval Attaché, Captain Preston Virginius [Mercer] in the presence of W. Middleton and Commander Sobredo, Presidency of the Government Record Group, Head of State, file number 72–07660 AGA

[30] "He smilingly told me that the State Department had not made his passage through Spain easy; but he claimed that his daughter was here and that he wanted to see her. He added that he suspected that the Admiral had sent his daughter to Madrid earlier precisely so as to have a pretext for stopping in Spain." Ibid.

sent. All this meant that the attempt to get round the State Department and Culbertson[31] had not been a success. What had been a success, however, was the initiative to gather information on Spanish military needs, which the military attaché, Colonel Charles Dasher, requested from General Vigón in June. This had prompted Culbertson[32] to protest to Undersecretary of State Robert A. Lovett, who in turn spoke with Forrestal, by that time secretary of defense, who managed to modify the orders given to the military attachés so that they could continue collecting information but also make it clear to their Francoist interlocutors that official U.S. policy had not changed.[33]

Meanwhile, in Washington, the air attaché in Madrid, Colonel Miller, and General Anderson, head of the USAF, went to discuss the pressing need for three airfields in Spain with Hickerson, the director of the Office of European Affairs, and Outerbridge Horsey, assistant chief of the Division of Western European Affairs. In particular, they were thinking of Madrid, Barcelona, and Seville, the only ones capable of withstanding the traffic of heavy American bombers, although their facilities and equipment would have to be modernized urgently with U.S. funding. This modernization had been agreed upon, albeit on the condition that the funding came from private and unofficial sources. Moreover, a few days later, Secretary Forrestal urged Assistant Secretary of State Armour to unfreeze the funds Spain had in the United States for the Safehaven program and the Nazi gold, and at the same time sent two military emissaries to negotiate a loan for the airfields with the Chase National Bank.[34]

In any case, according to Franco's direct U.S. sources of military information, there was no shortage of leading military figures, fervent anti-communists and admirers of what Franco had done in Spain, who spontaneously approached Minister Martín Artajo to offer their help to normalize relations between the two countries, assist Lequerica in Washington, and leak information to Franco's diplomats about the attitude of the armed forces to Spain. One such figure was Major General Charles A. Willoughby, chief of General MacArthur's intelligence services in the Pacific theater of operations until 1945 and subsequently in Japan until 1951. He is a good example of a member of the Spanish Bloc. He was driven by ideological motives and, at that time, he was already in contact with such influential senators in Congress as Harry P. Cain – Republican for Washington – and Arthur H. Vandenberg – Republican for Michigan and chairman of the Foreign Relations Committee in 1947. And in 1949 he made contact with Senator Patrick A. McCarran – a Catholic

[31] Letter from "M" on 31 March 1948, Presidency of the Government Record Group, Head of State, file number 72–07660, AGA.

[32] Culbertson to Secstate, 25 August 1948, U.S. Embassy Madrid Classified General Records 1940–1963, RG 84, box 2, NARA-2.

[33] Edwards, *Anglo-American Relations* ..., 222–223.

[34] Hualde, *El "cerco"* ..., 215–216.

88 JOAN MARIA THOMÀS

Democrat from Nevada[35] – who would soon prove to be a staunch and effective pro-Francoist, and with the retired colonel, Robert R. MacCormick, director of the *Chicago Tribune*,[36] one of the most influential Midwest newspapers.

To sum up, the U.S. military was clearly concerned, but the policy of the State Department prevailed. And, as we have said, it would take a lot more time and the international situation would have to deteriorate much more before the possibility of military collaboration between the two countries would be officially entertained.

The Marshall Plan, the O'Konski Amendment and Spain (March 1948)

The problem for Franco and his supporters in 1948 was the lack of time. The catastrophic situation of the economy meant that Spain was unable to pay for essential imports, and the regime urgently needed foreign aid. At that time Franco was negotiating with the Argentine Republic to import wheat but, more importantly, he also wanted to be included in the Marshall Plan, the U.S. economic aid plan for Europe, from which Spain had been the only country explicitly excluded by the Paris Conference of July 1947 when work on the plan had begun. The plan had first been announced by Secretary of State Marshall the previous June in a speech delivered at Harvard University, then turned into a bill and, since March 1948, was being debated in Congress. It would finally be implemented through the so-called Economic Cooperation Administration after it had been legally ratified by the House of Representatives, the Senate, and President Truman on 3 April.

The leaders of the Franco regime knew that France and Great Britain[37] were at the heart of the opposition to Spain being included in the Marshall Plan. They were accompanied by the vast majority of the other countries,

[35] See letters between General C. A. Willoughby, Major General, G.S.C. Ass't Chief of Staff G-2 (General Headquarters Far East Command Military Intelligence Section) and Eva Adams, Administrative Assistant to Senator McCarran, 31 October and 29 November 1949, Eva B[ertrand], Adams Papers, University of Nevada, Reno.

[36] Author, among other works and articles, of *Bailén and the Spanish Bridgehead, 1808–1948* (1947): On the character, see the excellent paper by N. Sesma Landrín, *Un yanqui en la corte del general Franco. Charles A. Willoughby y la larga marcha hacia los Pactos de Madrid (1947–1953)*, Working Paper 2013/5, History Seminar, Department of Social History and Political Thinking UNED/Department of the History of Thought and of Social and Political Movements UCM/Ortega y Gasset University Research Institute, 2013. He was born Karl von Tscheppe und Weidenbach in Germany and, after retiring from the army on 31 August 1951, he went to live in Madrid, where he became involved in pro-Franco circles: I. Buruma, *Año Cero. Historia de 1945*, Barcelona, Pasado y Presente, 2014, 188.

[37] Viñas, *En las garras...*, 42 and 46.

THE STRUGGLE TO CHANGE U.S. POLICY TOWARD FRANCO'S SPAIN   89

particularly the United States,[38] which also feared that including Spain could increase the chances of the left wing in the Italian elections on 18 April. Despite this situation, Spain's leaders had worked until the last minute to be admitted, although they never actually made a formal application. First, they asked the other dictatorship from the Iberian Peninsula (Portugal, with whom they had friendly relations) to intercede on their behalf. Prime Minister Oliveira Salazar had done so, but with little success.[39] And then they focused on the U.S. Congress, where they believed they had the support of some of its members, and tried to exploit the growing anti-communist feeling, largely stimulated by the Catholic Republican senator from Wisconsin Joseph (Joe) McCarthy.

Franco and Foreign Minister Martín Artajo believed they could take advantage of the opposition of the Republican majority in the House of Representatives and the Senate, the support of the armed forces, and the pressure exerted by the lobbies of some economic interests (cotton and cereals, banking, mining, industry, and trade). These sectors were interested in unblocking United States–Spain relations so that they could dispose of their surpluses. This was particularly the case with the National Cotton Council, which since the previous year had been working closely with the legislature to recover its volume of pre-war trade with Spain. During its meeting of March 1948 it had submitted a petition to the government[40] and was constantly pressuring the congressmen – both Democrats and Republicans – of the states where cotton was a major crop, as it was in most of the southern states.

As a result of all this activity, the *chargé d'affaires* in Washington, Germán de Baráibar, set to work. Just a few weeks before Lequerica arrived in Washington, on 30 March 1948, he had asked the Republican representative for Wisconsin, Alvin O'Konski, to submit an amendment to the European Recovery Program bill, which proposed that Spain be included in the Marshall Plan. A Catholic, an anti-communist, a Franco supporter, and the representative of a state with a

---

[38] As the acting secretary of state, Robert A. Lovett telegraphed at the time to the *chargé d'affaires* in Madrid, Culbertson, on 2 April: "The view of this Government has been and continues to be that initiative on Spain's inclusion lies with original CEEC countries. They have made it crystal clear that it is politically impossible for them to cooperate with Spain along lines ERP under present conditions there. Immediate and violent reaction in West European countries and here against proposed inclusion Spain underlines views this Government." He also pointed out that "notwithstanding Franco's anti-Communist record, inclusion Spain under present conditions would be manifestly contrary to purposes of ERP. Bill declares it 'to be policy of people of US to sustain and strengthen principles of individual liberty, free institutions and genuine independence in Europe through assistance to those countries in Europe which participate in joint recovery program based upon self-help and mutual cooperation.'" Acting Secretary of State to Embassy in Madrid, 2 April 1948, FRUS 1948, 1.035–1.036.

[39] Viñas, *En las garras...*, 46–47.

[40] Cited in Amunárriz, *El "cerco"...*, 212.

surplus of wheat,[41] O'Konski agreed[42] to play along and based his amendment on the arguments and materials Baráibar provided him with.[43] And, incredibly, the amendment was passed by 149 votes in favor to 52 against. It was Spain's last chance because in the Senate the law had been passed with four favorable mentions of Spain but no specific amendment of this type.[44]

The O'Konski amendment argued that the two countries that most benefited from the Marshall Plan – Great Britain and France – engaged in intense commercial activity with Franco's Spain, and pointed out that Spain could also make a contribution to European recovery. It also stressed a major contradiction of the Plan itself: it invited the Eastern European countries in the orbit of Moscow to adhere to it but not Spain. It was even open to the two countries that had sparked the previous war – Germany and Italy – but refused to accept Spain, which had remained neutral. But the heart of the amendment was anti-communism, and O'Konski used it to accuse the State Department and the Truman administration in general of having been infiltrated by the Soviet Union. In his words:

> By what rule of logic should Spain be excluded? Is it because the pinkos [Communist sympathizers] still control our State Department? Is it because our State Department fears Russia may not come in if Spain does? To eliminate Spain from this bill is nothing but shameful and stupid appeasement of the pinkos in Moscow and the pinkos in our State Department and Department of Commerce.[45]

During the debate, this had elicited a response from the representative for New York and the American Labor Party, Leo Isacson, who had left-wing leanings:

> Does the gentleman forget that the Government of Spain is a Fascist government which was imposed on an unwilling people by mercenary

---

[41] Edwards, *Anglo-American Relations* ...., 114.

[42] O'Konski, educated by the Jesuits and owner of a radio station in his home state, was married to Veronica Hemming, a teacher with Irish roots at the Normal School and an enthusiastic Hispanist. He was a Catholic of Polish origin, radically anti-communist and, of course, he advocated a non-communist Poland.

[43] O'Konski had apparently "inserted [...] almost all of Baráibar's text" into his amendment, as Baráibar himself wrote to Madrid: Letter from Baráibar to Martín Artajo on 10 April 1948, Presidency of the Government Record Group, Head of State, file number 72–07660, AGA.

[44] B. Scowcroft, *Congress and Foreign Policy: An Examination of Congressional Attitudes Toward the Foreign Aid Programs to Spain and Yugoslavia*, Ph.D. dissertation, Columbia University, 1967, 18. This author, a career military officer in the U.S. air force, was stationed in Yugoslavia and served as Secretary of State Henry Kissinger's number two and then as national security advisor under President Gerald Ford from 1975 to 1977 and again under George W. Bush from 1989 to 1993.

[45] U.S. Congressional Record, 80th Cong., 2nd session, 1948, XCIV Part 3, 3428.

THE STRUGGLE TO CHANGE U.S. POLICY TOWARD FRANCO'S SPAIN   91

Moors imported from Africa, by Italian Fascists imported from the legions of Mussolini, and by Nazi soldiers brought over from Germany? Does the gentleman forget that there is a Spanish Republic in exile voted by secret ballot, by democratic processes, in the best American traditions? Does he forget that the Spanish Government was born in blood and that it continued to exist at the cost of the blood of Spanish people. Does he forget all these things?[46]

O'Konski had given a "hard-hitting speech" with references to the "large Communist blocs within Italy and France that were slated to receive Marshall Plan aid." He had finished by saying that "if war broke out within a week, you would find that the fighting front would be Spain, the only country which would offer effective resistance,"[47] and referring to the recent crisis in Czechoslovakia, which had definitively converted the country into a Moscow-controlled regime.[48]

The amendment approved by the House of Representatives – which had been passed with the help of the votes of the southern cotton states – was a success for the Francoists and had an impact on the administration and on some sectors of American opinion public. It was also a stumbling block for the official policy, which had to be overcome at once. But the most important thing was that it demonstrated for the first time that there were a considerable number of representatives who supported a change in policy on Spain and who aimed to move more quickly than the State Department, the government, and the president, and in a different direction. Truman was now forced to take decisive action to counteract the amendment in question.

Likewise, the approval of the amendment had rattled the governments of Great Britain and France and forced Secretary Marshall to assure the foreign ministers of both countries that it would not prosper. But, to make sure that it did not, the president himself had to enter the fray: he threatened a veto and argued that the decision to make a country a beneficiary of the plan could only

---

[46] Ibid, 3429.

[47] P. J. Briggs, *Making American Foreign Policy: President-Congress relations from the Second World War to the post-Cold War era*, Lanham (MD), Rowman & Littlefield, 1994, 54.

[48] Cellar, Douglas, Holifield and Javits, all Democrats, had also responded. Of the latter two, Baráibar pointed out their Jewish ancestry and influence over President Truman, whose opposition to the amendment he explained in terms of "his duties as a 33rd degree freemason, and of his eagerness not to further offend the susceptibility of the considerable Jewish contingent in the ranks of his party. The President had already greatly upset this contingent because, on Forrestal's recommendation, he had changed the policy of partitioning Palestine, and the inclusion of Spain was regarded in UN circles as a further rectification of the measures previously taken by this international body." Letter from Baráibar to Martín Artajo on 10 April 1948, Presidency of the Government Record Group, Head of State, file number 72–07660, AGA, file number 72–07660, AGA.

be taken by all the other beneficiaries, not just the United States. Eventually, the law was passed by the Conference Committee for reconciliation of the differences between the House and Senate Versions by 318 votes to 75[49] without the O'Konski Amendment. But once again the vote showed that there was a group of congressmen from both houses in favor of the change in policy on Spain, who were independently following an alternative path to the State Department and working more quickly.

Subsequently, O'Konski advised Baráibar to arrange for Franco's parliament to extend an official invitation for a representation of the U.S. Congress to visit Spain. It would be a trip for study and documentation, paid for by the United States, which would help them to better understand Spain and be able to work together more efficiently in the future. The advice was duly noted, and the following year Lequerica and the lobbyists hired by the embassy decided to act on it and organized a trip for congressmen (but paid for by Spain). However, Congress also organized other trips of its own. So many, in fact, that by the second half of 1949 it seemed that the congressmen were suffering from "Spanish fever." Another lesson the embassy learned from the O'Konski affair was that the American public was no longer as adverse to Spain as before and that they were now more in favor of intervention.

In Madrid, the final failure of the amendment had dashed Franco's hopes of Spain being included in the Marshall Plan and, in response, Minister Martín Artajo ordered the ambassador in Buenos Aires, José María de Areilza, to announce the Franco–Perón Protocol (signed on 9 April 1948), which extended the loan granted by Argentina in 1946 so that Spain could purchase Argentine wheat, corn, and edible oils.[50] In this way he tried to compensate for the disappointment. But in January 1949 the supply of Argentine products began to dry up, and it ceased altogether in the following August, as a result of disagreements over how to apply the agreement and the difficulties Spain had in making payments and providing the guarantees required by Argentina.[51]

Lequerica in Washington

Lequerica's arrival in Washington on 19 April, 1948 heralded a real shake-up at the embassy. This was not only because of his status as former minister and inspector, his internal rank of ambassador, and the mission with which he had been entrusted, but also because he had been extremely active with his

---

[49] Scowcroft, *Congress and Foreign Policy* ..., 21–22.

[50] On the propagandistic use of the protocol, see the doctoral thesis by P. Herrero García *La labor como embajador de José María de Areilza en Argentina, los Estados Unidos y Francia*, Universidad San Pablo-CEU, 2018; R. Rein, *La salvación de una dictadura. Alianza Franco–Perón 1946–1955*, Madrid, CSIC, 1995, 92.

[51] Rein, *La salvación de una dictadura* ..., 205.

contacts even before he arrived. On a personal level, his interest in going to the United States as a diplomat came from afar. His personal relationship with the American ambassador in Madrid, Carlton J. H. Hayes (1942–1945), when he had worked with him in his capacity as minister of foreign affairs, must have had some influence. From the very beginning Hayes was one of Lequerica's supporters in the United States. He started to make his brazen pro-Franco stance public and, in so doing, ruined much of his academic prestige. In his memoirs, *Misión de guerra en España*, he described this period and made it clear that he was in favor of normalizing the relations between the two countries. In fact, before his return to the United States, Hayes had agreed with Lequerica that he would write the book.[52]

It is also likely that Lequerica's interest in representing Spain in the United States was more general, related to his desire to travel, to reside abroad again, and to get to know American politics and the country that had become the center of the Western world during the war. He must have felt that he was more than prepared for the challenge given his background and excellent command of English.[53] His appointment as ambassador meant that he was back in the

---

[52] His memoirs were also published in English under the title *Wartime Mission in Spain, 1942–1945*, New York, The Macmillan Company, 1945. The last edition in Spanish of this work, with an introduction by J. M. Thomàs, was *Misión de guerra en España*, Zaragoza, Prensas de la Universidad de Zaragoza, 2018.

[53] After graduating in Law and in Philosophy and Arts from the University of Deusto, he completed a doctorate in Law at the Central University (with a thesis on Georges Sorel and revolutionary syndicalism) and was awarded a scholarship to study for two semesters – without obtaining a degree – at the London School of Economics and Political Science. See Cava Mesa for information: (1) on his political career prior to the stage we are studying (a Maurista, member of parliament for the Conservative party for Illescas, Toledo, between 1916 and 1923; undersecretary of the Presidency of the Council of Ministers under Antonio Maura; financier of Ramiro Ledesma's publications "La Conquista del Estado" and "JONS" and others; signatory of the manifesto of Calvo Sotelo's National Bloc in 1934, mayor of Bilbao 1938–1939); (2) on his fortune and shares in family companies – Compañía Anónima la Basconia – and others – Vidrieras Españolas, Banco Urquijo, La Basauri, Tubos Forjados, Alambres del Cadagua; (3) and on his intellectual activity in Bilbao – Grupo Hermes/Literary group of the café "Lyon d'Or" together with Pedro Eguillor, Ramón Basterra, Rafael Sánchez Mazas, Joaquín Zuazagoitia and Pedro Mourlane Michelena – and in Madrid, as well as in journalism and publishing. By the same author, the most up-to-date text on Lequerica can be found in the *Diccionario de la Real Academia de la Historia*, http://dbe.rah.es/biografias/12004/jose-felix-de-lequerica-y-erquicia. On his time as foreign minister and his relationship with the United States and Ambassador Hayes, see J. M. Thomàs, *La batalla del wolframio. Estados Unidos y España de Pearl Harbor a la Guerra Fría (1941–1947)*, Madrid, Cátedra, 2010. On his role as ambassador to France and his relationship with Franco's attempts to extradite Republican exiles from Vichy and the handing over to the Spanish police of the former president of the Catalan

94   JOAN MARIA THOMÀS

sphere of foreign policy, something he had been longing for since his traumatic and unwanted dismissal in 1945. In fact, even in his last year as minister, shortly before he had been replaced, his name had come up as a possible candidate for the post of ambassador in Washington, against the wishes of his successor, Alberto Martín Artajo, but with the support of Franco.[54] This difference of opinion would be a constant feature of the following years, although Franco and Martín Artajo also often had the same private misgivings about Lequerica's performance in Washington. His aspirations to become ambassador had been temporarily thwarted when the State Department had refused to give its *agrément* to the nomination by the Ministry of Foreign Affairs in October 1945.[55] For his part, Franco had not accepted Martín Artajo's candidate for the position, José Larraz, a former fellow member of Popular Action–CEDA and former minister of finance (1939–1941), whose differences of opinion with the Caudillo had led to his resignation, a highly unusual occurrence in the regime. This impasse meant that the occupant of the post since 1939, Ambassador Juan Francisco de Cárdenas, had to remain in Washington for a further two years, until 31 March 1947.[56]

Relations between Lequerica and Cárdenas had never been easy, but they deteriorated after the United States refused to give the *agrément*, because Lequerica suspected that the Spanish embassy had manipulated the State

---

government, Lluís Companys, and the former PSOE deputy Luis Zugazagoitia – the subjects for which Lequerica is most often cited – see J. Benet, *Lluís Companys, afusellat*, Barcelona, Edicions 62, 2005; and J. Guixé Corominas, *La República perseguida. Exilio y represión en la Francia de Franco (1937–1951)*, València, PUV, 2012. Ramón Serrano himself provides a cynical self-exculpation and a version of Lequerica's actions in France in *Entre el silencio y la propaganda. La Historia como fue*, Barcelona, Planeta, 1977. And this self-exculpation is criticized in J. M. Thomàs, "Ramón Serrano Suñer. El personaje real y el personaje inventado," en Adrián Gómez Molina y Joan Maria Thomàs (coords.), *Ramón Serrano Suñer*, Barcelona, Ediciones B, 2003.

A man of personal wealth, he married his long-time partner, Josefa Ramírez San Román, in Paris in 1942. Twelve years his junior, their relationship had not been formalized until then, apparently because she was from a lower social background. His wife accompanied him to Washington: Cava Mesa, *Los diplomáticos de Franco ...*, 36.

54 Portero, *Franco aislado ...*, 112. He was dismissed as minister on 20 July: Letters from Lequerica to Franco on 20 July 1945 Legajo 1489, Archive of the Francisco Franco National Foundation (ANFF). In the second letter, he thanked him for the award of de ellas le agradecía la concesión de la Grand Cross of the Order of Charles III.

55 Portero, *Franco aislado ...*, 132; León, *Philip W. Bonsal....*

56 M. Arturo López Zapico, "Against all odds. El diplomático Juan Francisco de Cárdenas durante la Guerra Civil española y el primer franquismo," in A.C. Moreno Cantano, *Propagandistas y diplomáticos al servicio de Franco (1936–1945)*, Gijón, Trea, 2012, 303–328.

THE STRUGGLE TO CHANGE U.S. POLICY TOWARD FRANCO'S SPAIN   95

Department.[57] In fact, in his time as minister, Lequerica had sought to dismiss Cárdenas and move him to Brussels, because he believed him to be incapable of putting the necessary policy into practise in the United States in the new phase after the Allied victory in 1945.[58] He had even found a replacement: his Basque friend, the businessman and journalist Víctor Urrutia Usasola,[59] although in the end he had not been able to make the change as he himself was dismissed. But he had managed to appoint a new press attaché, another Basque friend, Manuel Aznar Zubigaray, former director of *El Sol* and other newspapers, to launch a pro-Spanish propaganda plan.[60] According to Lequerica, this appointment had not gone down at all well with Cardenas, who had tried to "prevent the change at all costs."[61] Moreover, as we shall see below, Lequerica always firmly believed that Cárdenas, after his return and affiliation to the ministry, had worked hand in hand with the U.S. *chargé d'affaires* in Madrid, Culbertson, to deny him his first visa application in 1948, as we shall see below. And, subsequently, in 1949–1950, he had again worked with Culbertson and also with Hickerson, Achilles, and Dunham of the State Department in an attempt to force him to leave the United States.

Lequerica was appointed ambassador by the Spanish cabinet on 18 April 1947, less than a month after Cárdenas's resignation, which suggests that plans had already been in place to send him to Washington, and he was immediately appointed inspector of diplomatic and consular missions, created with him in mind.[62] How did he do it? His biographer Cava Mesa mentions the

[57] (906) 24 October. [1946] "Lequerica [is] certainly is down on Cárdenas, the Spanish Ambassador in Washington – whom I like and respect." León, *Philip W. Bonsal*....

[58] An example of his opinion of Cárdenas is the paragraph he wrote about him in a note to the head of state in March 1945: "As Ambassador Hayes said, the inferiority complex, is still there in full measure. The Ambassador, a very kindly man, must be tired and at the same time an impassive public official, maybe unconvinced. He has his limitations but is always decorous with the competence of expertise. Nevertheless, he does not have the slightest influence on the political elements of the country." Dated 6 March 1945, Lequerica Archive, cited in Cava Mesa, *Los diplomáticos de Franco* ..., 216.

[59] Civil engineer, businessman, son of Juan de Urrutia (the founder of Hidroeléctrica Ibérica, the main Spanish electricity company in the 1920), former director of the newspapers *El Sol* and *La Voz*. He would later become vice-chairman of CAMPSA and Butano and a director of Banco de Vizcaya and Banco de Crédito Industrial.

[60] Perhaps based on an old plan, dated 2 April 1945, "Project for the organization of a Spanish institute for cultural relations in the United States" by the Vice-secretariat of Political Studies, 1945, Legajo 1368, AFNFF.

[61] Letter from Lequerica to Martín Artajo, 5 December 1947, file 14443, AFNFF.

[62] Ambassador assigned to the Ministry as head of section, "without prejudice to the freedom of movement that the nature of the post [of inspector] required." Cava Mesa, *Los diplomáticos de Franco* ..., 250.

involvement of two close friends, fellow party members and Basques like himself, Fernando María de Castiella and José María de Areilza.[63] He had never hidden, nor would he hide in the future, his desire to hold office[64] after the setback of his dismissal in 1945,[65] and he had even thought of returning to his previous position of minister of foreign affairs,[66] which did little to improve his relationship with Martín Artajo. It seems clear that in 1947 he was still eager to go to the capital of the United States, and that he had the consent of Franco – with whom he had a direct relationship – and of the somewhat more reluctant foreign minister.[67]

Whatever the case may have been, after being given permission by the minister, he moved heaven and earth to get his wish. Through friends of his living in Washington, he looked into the possibility of being accepted by the

---

[63] Ibid.

[64] (906) 24 October (1946) "Lequerica came to lunch – very diverting still as comically doleful as ever about his absence from public office. He does really miss it. And there is no doubt that if one places emphasis on the possession of executive talent and grace in wearing the official mantle rather than on high principle that he makes a magnificent public servant." León, *Philip W. Bonsal*....

[65] (418) aust 12 [1945] "He began by describing his surprise and chagrin at finding himself out of the Foreign Office. He said it was only after insistent rumor that he approached the Caudillo on the subject – and the latter then told him he was making a reshuffle in the course of which he would require the *cartera* of Foreign Affairs. Franco was very cordial – gave him the Grand Cross of the Order of Carlos III, an autographed letter and a promise of employment either at home or abroad in the very near future. Lequerica stressed his regret at leaving the Ministry and his hope of again becoming active soon. He is hanging on the phone awaiting a call from the Caudillo and any thought that he is in 'opposition' must be dismissed. Only post he mentioned was Buenos Aires – not Washington." León, *Philip W. Bonsal*....

[66] This was an aspiration of his for many years: See Lieutenant General F. Franco Salgado-Araujo, *Mis conversaciones privadas con Franco,* Madrid, Planeta, 2005, 357 ff.

[67] (1173) My 25 [1947] "M and I went to the Prado where we found Lequerica standing in front of Greco's great portrait El Caballero con la Mano al Pecho. He was very cordial and voluble as usual. Said he was getting to have Republican sentiments as his father had had. He says he is planning to start on his Ambassadorial functions – he has been made Inspector of Spanish Embassies with the rank of Ambassador – in Switzerland and the Scandinavian countries and that along about October he hopes to go to the States. Fact is that I have intentionally avoided congratulating him on this appointment." León, *Philip W. Bonsal*.... For his part, Cava points out that the report he wrote after an inspection in London – on Britain's attitude towards Spain and recommending specific diplomatic action towards the Anglo-Saxon powers – might have prompted the minister to send him there as a test before agreeing to send him to the United States. For between his appointment as ambassador-inspector and his being posted to the United States he had been commissioned to make inspection trips to the United Kingdom, Switzerland and the Netherlands: Cava Mesa, *Los diplomáticos de Franco ...*, 253.

State Department, in an attempt to anticipate whether a new rejection was likely. The fact that he did all the work himself instead of entrusting it to the Spanish diplomatic representation in the United States is surely a sign of his special situation within the Palacio de Santa Cruz (home to the Spanish Ministry of Foreign Affairs). He was helped in his investigations by Teotónio Pereira, Portuguese ambassador to the United States and former ambassador in Madrid, who he commissioned to sound out Norman Armour, the assistant secretary for political affairs.[68] The American's response, relayed by Pereira in September 1947, was to fob him off (albeit amicably) and to suggest that the situation might improve in the near future: "You should not come with a visa for 'inspectors' but wait a few more weeks and see if the problem clears up."[69] Not content with the answer, Lequerica asked another friend, William Macy Brewster, a senior executive of the oil company TEXACO and twice decorated by Franco (in 1939 with the Encomienda and in 1945 with the Grand Cross of the Order of Charles III,[70] for the help the company had given the Nationals during the Civil War[71]) to requestion Armour. This time his response was that "there is no objection to your visiting Washington as long as you come in March [1948] or later."[72] Between the first and the second contact with Armour, in the UN on 17 November 1947, the United States had changed its attitude towards Spain and the resolution of December 1946. Armour himself had been involved in this change, which made Lequerica think he was free to go ahead. As he wrote to Martín Artajo: "This is the first time that my friend N.[orman] A.[rmour] has said yes [...] This positive response is a great step forward."[73]

However, he forgot – or conveniently chose to forget so that he would be granted permission to travel – that Armour had referred to a possible "visit," that he had warned against coming in the capacity of inspector, and that he had only mentioned the possibility of changes without going into detail. On the other hand, he correctly interpreted

> the evolution of United States policy and adopted the reasonable intention to take things calmly and avoid the clashes and problems that might arise as the result of any action regarded as premature by our enemies in a country enjoying full political freedom.

[68] Although he had arrived in Madrid on 24 March 1945.

[69] Letter from Lequerica to Martín Artajo, 5 December 1947.

[70] A nominal list of the Ministry of Foreign Affairs' records on the award of decorations. Box 82/012241 (R-4751), files 60 and 61, AGA. I am grateful to Mr Daniel Gozalbo Gimeno, of AGA, for his information on this point.

[71] As head of the TEXACO office in Paris and on the orders of Rieber, he passed on information to Franco about Republican oil tankers sailing from foreign ports, which made it possible for the "pirate" (Italian) submarines and the Francoists to sink them, or for the Francoist Navy to seize them.

[72] Letter from Lequerica to Martín Artajo, 5 December 1947.

[73] Ibid.

JOAN MARIA THOMÀS

And he believed that in the future he would be there, a stimulating participant in this evolution.[74]

This, however, was not to be, probably because he feared his appointment would not be approved. When Lequerica applied for his one- or two-month inspector's visa in January 1948,[75] it was rejected by Culbertson in Madrid. In fact, by that time the Division of Western European Affairs of the State Department had known of his possible arrival in Washington for several months (at least since June 1947) and suspected that Baráibar would be replaced by Aznar as *chargé d'affaires*. His "first job will doubtless be to try to smooth the way for the visit of his crony, Lequerica,"[76] and Culbertson was entrusted with the task of stopping him. In fact, the visa was only finally granted after the general director of foreign policy, the undersecretary of the ministry, and the minister himself had intervened. Culbertson stuck to his guns and, in early March 1948, in an interview with Martín Artajo, he argued that Lequerica's arrival there would be interpreted as a maneuver to have Spain included in the Marshall Plan. Which of course it was.[77]

After overcoming all these obstacles, Lequerica set off to the United States as an inspector, a position that everything suggested would only be temporary, although it was hoped that he would make a decisive contribution to normalizing relations between the two countries and eventually be appointed ambassador. However, the contradiction between the declared objective – his supposed inspection – and the real objective – to act as ambassador – was clear and would generate a good deal of tension with the State Department. As early as June 1948, Culbertson reported to William Dunham, from the Iberian desk, that there were rumors in Madrid that "Lequerica has sent for all his clothes, linens, etc., etc., and his French chef," which were signs of a long stay. And he asked the department how they would respond if "he tries to settle down as an undesignated ambassador or the Spanish should ask for his agreement."[78]

---

[74] Moreover, he could not contain his ambition when he repeated to the minister the words that Manuel Aznar had written to him from Washington on 29 October: "If I could choose, I would like you to come with a *chargé d'affaires* visa by hook or by crook." Ibid.

[75] Lequerica to Martín Artajo, 7 December 1949, Ministry of Foreign Affairs, file number 82–7487, AGA.

[76] Outerbridge Horsey – Assistant Chief of the Division of Western European Affairs – to Culbertson, 30 June 1947, U.S. Embassy Madrid, Classified General Records 1940, 1963, RG 84, NARA-2.

[77] Conversation between Culbertson and Martín Artajo, 8 March 1948 in L. Suárez Fernández, *Francisco Franco y su tiempo*, vol. IV, Madrid, Azor, 1984, 238.

[78] Culbertson to Dunham, 11 June 1948, U.S. Embassy Madrid, Classified General Records 1940, 1963, RG 84, NARA-2.

Meanwhile, on 31 October 1948, the Ministry of Foreign Affairs changed his mission and made him "the head of the embassy" in Washington,[79] of course without informing the State Department. Also, to keep up the appearance that he was indeed an inspector, Lequerica made several trips to other consulates in the United States, as well as to the Spanish embassies in Ottawa and Havana. He never introduced himself as *chargé d'affaires*, and the formal diplomatic relations with the U.S. administration were always the responsibility of the officially appointed and recognized Baráibar. But, behind closed doors, it was Lequerica who was giving the orders in Washington.

However, six months into his stay, he tried – somewhat crudely it must be said – to get his permanent status in the capital recognized by having the embassy ask the State Department about how he should figure on the official U.S. diplomatic list. The option of simply including his name was immediately rejected, and the Department reminded the embassy that this list could contain only "permanent members of the staff of embassies and legations [...] [and] that the names of persons admitted to the United States for brief visits, such as inspectors, were not eligible."[80]

If any further proof were required that he was the real number one, after staying for a short time at the Hotel Ritz, he moved into the embassy building with his wife and niece while the *chargé d'affaires* went to live in a flat.[81] He immediately began to order works of art to decorate the building and requested funds from the ministry and pieces of value from the Spanish agency National Heritage and the Prado Museum. As far as his staff was concerned, he managed to surround himself with a group of collaborators specially selected from the acquaintances he had known during his time in France and leading cultural personalities, thus setting up a permanent and powerful system of cultural relations in the United States.

In particular, he tried to recruit his former number two from Vichy, Cristóbal del Castillo, and his former military attaché, Colonel Barroso, by that time a general. In both cases, his attempts were unsuccessful because they were already occupying other posts. However, he did manage to attract another military attaché[82] from that period, Colonel Mendoza, which immediately provoked Culbertson's protest in Madrid, and another former employee, his private secretary, Mr. Rafael.[83] Subsequently, in 1949, he would replace Baráibar with Eduardo Propper de Callejón, also a former colleague from his

---

[79] Cava Mesa, *Los diplomáticos de Franco ...*, 255.

[80] Question on 20 October 1948. Answered by the State Department on 3 November 1948, Ministry of Foreign Affairs Record Group, file number 82–5987, AGA.

[81] Cava Mesa, *Los diplomáticos de Franco ...*, 266.

[82] H. Ickes, "The State Department's Siesta," *The New Republic*, 23 May 1949.

[83] Ibid.

Figure 3.2. January 14, 1954. Tribute from the Chamber of Commerce, Industry, and Navigation to the Spanish Ambassador in Washington, José Félix de Lequerica. Archivo ABC.

time in France, in Paris and Vichy[84], who in 1945 the government of liberated France had refused to accept as counselor of the Paris embassy because he had been accused of helping the Germans while consul general in Casablanca during the Allied landing of November 1942.[85] Lequerica also proposed that diplomats and economic experts such as Ángel Sanz Briz, Otero, Elorza, who was later appointed as commercial attaché, Bermejo, and Aguilar should be assigned to Washington. He also tried to bring into the fold the then director of the Institute of Hispanic Culture and former international president of Pax Romana, Joaquín Ruiz Jiménez – future minister of national education – and Alfredo Sánchez Bella, at that time a young employee at the institute. In neither case was he successful. And, again, he showed his animosity towards Cárdenas by refusing to include him on his staff because – as he said in a letter to the minister – he was a "stateless cosmopolitan, equally open to all contacts."[86]

---

[84] M. Séguela, *Franco-Pétain. Los secretos de una alianza*, Barcelona, Prensa Ibérica, 1994, 49.

[85] On Propper's time in Morocco and France, see R. H. Lane to J. W. Jones, Madrid Embassy, 2 March 1950, U.S. Embassy Madrid, Classified General Records 1940, 1963, RG 84, NARA-2.

[86] Cava Mesa, *Los diplomáticos de Franco* ..., 265. The comment may have had something to do with the fact that Cárdenas was married to a Romanian woman.

But it soon became clear that Lequerica was just the right person to be entrusted with building up the Spanish representation in Washington and, as soon as he arrived, he was instantly involved in a hectic social program. It was fortunate that he was still in touch with the U.S. contacts he had made as minister of foreign affairs and during his time in France. Among the former were diplomats, companies, and banking institutions that had previously had interests in Spain.[87] He immediately arranged meetings with such leading figures as the former ambassador to Paris William Bullitt; the former ambassador to Vichy, Admiral William D. Leahy; the former ambassador to Madrid Hayes; the former U.S. military attaché in Madrid Colonel Hoffman; the deputy director of the Chase National Bank Alfred Barth – former senior official of the United States Commercial Corporation in Madrid during the Second World War and responsible for setting up the financing system for many of its transactions;[88] the former CEO of the National Telephone Company of Spain and executive of the International Telephone and Telegraph, Fred Caldwell; the president of International Telephone and Telegraph, Colonel Sosthenes Behn; and Captain Thorkild Rieber from TEXACO, the major supplier of gasoline to the Nationals during the Civil War.

In the month of April, a meal was organized in his honor by the diplomat Bullitt, an ardent anti-communist who had just left the Democratic Party to join the Republicans[89]and who, in 1940, had been suddenly dismissed from his post in Paris for not wanting to leave and follow the French government to Bordeaux. It was attended by none other than Under Secretary of State Robert A. Lovett; Admiral Roscoe H. Hillenkoetter, first director of the CIA; State Department Director of Near Eastern and African Affairs Loy W. Henderson; and President Theodore Roosevelt's daughter, Mrs. Longworth. The meal was also attended by *chargé d'affaires* Baráibar and commercial attaché Elorza representing the embassy.[90] He also met with Norman Armour and, thanks to the former *chargé d'affaires ad interim* in Madrid, William Walter Butterworth, with the head of the Division of Western European Affairs, Theodore C. Achilles. And his friend Bradford, European head of United Press, set up a

---

[87] Cava Mesa, *Los diplomáticos de Franco ...,* 274.

[88] León Aguinaga, *Sospechosos...,* 144 ff.

[89] Bullitt had been the first U.S. ambassador and a close associate of President Roosevelt's on European affairs until his fall from grace in 1940. Convinced that his dismissal was due to Undersecretary of State Sumner Welles, who was in turn pitted against Secretary Cordell Hull, he had conspired against him by spreading information of a sexual nature that the president refused to use until 1943, when Hull decided to get rid of his subordinate and Senator Robert Owen Brewster threatened to take the matter to the Senate. On this issue, see Weil, *A Pretty...,* 140–141 ff; Thomàs, *La batalla del wolframio ....,* 79–83.

[90] Letter from Lequerica to Martín Artajo, 27 April 1948 in Cava Mesa, *Los diplomáticos de Franco ...,* 268.

meeting with Secretary of State General George Marshall himself at the beginning of June. In New York, the economic capital of the country, Hayes put him in touch with a wide range of bankers: Aldrich, president of the Chase National Bank, with whom he was to become good friends;[91] the Catholic Blair, vice president of the National City Bank; and Barth, also from the Chase National Bank. Also in New York, he met Rieber, Behn, and Caldwell.

At the same time, he began to work on his relations with the members of the press, both those that were sympathetic to the Franco regime, such as the United Press agency, and those that were not, such as the *New York Times*, to whose general manager, Julius Ochs Adler, he was introduced by Caldwell. He also met the editor of the newspaper, Adler's brother-in-law Arthur H. Sulzberger,[92] the avowed anti-Francoist Edward Weintal, editor of *Newsweek*, whom he already knew from Madrid, and whose close relationship with Culbertson was of particular concern, and probably the most influential journalist specializing in international relations in the country, Walter Lippman,[93] who coined the term "Cold War." His aim with all this was to become familiar with the arguments of those who may have been against Franco, but who he thought he could bring round to his way of thinking in one way or another. In his letters to Martín Artajo, Lequerica was careful to highlight not only the anti-Francoism of Adler, Sulzberger and others but also their Judaism, which he believed lay behind it (the regime had a pro-Arab policy). One of his main objects of desire was soon to become one of the most influential U.S. "Israelites" (as he called them), the millionaire, philanthropist, and former adviser to President Franklin D. Roosevelt, Bernard Baruch. Senator Brewster also introduced him to the owner and editor of the *New York Herald Tribune*, Whitelaw Reid. However, he hoped to be able to use the banking institutions to seduce the press, because he was aware of their decisive influence.

But Lequerica went further than just meeting with these major figures. Although he was a rich man and a *bon vivant* in his own right, he used their influence as a quick route into the most elite clubs. In New York he became a member of the Knickerbocker on the recommendation of Colonel Hoffman and the University Club thanks to friends from the United Press. And in Washington, also thanks to Hoffman, he was accepted by the Metropolitan, a favorite among diplomats. During this initial period in the United States, he was also given a helping hand by the embassy lawyer, William Smith Culbertson, a former diplomat (ambassador to Romania and Chile), member of the military (army colonel), and brother of the *chargé d'affaires* in Madrid.

---

[91] Such good friends that he even spent whole weekends at his home: ibid., 298.
[92] Ibid, 273.
[93] Ibid., 281.

As well as all this, some Catholic clergymen were also fundamental to his being accepted into the political and economic elites of the capital. As a former student of the Society of Jesus and the University of Deusto, he immediately contacted the Jesuit Father Robert S. Lloyd, rector of the Manresa-On-Severn retreat in Annapolis (Maryland), who enlightened him about the anti-Spanish prejudices of many sectors of society. And in July, in New York, he visited Cardinal and Archbishop Francis Spellman, a professed Franco supporter, who introduced him to Thomas E. Dewey, the Republican candidate for the presidential elections that were to be held in November, and John Foster Dulles, a member of the U.S. delegation to the UN, who seemed to be set to become secretary of state. Both were Protestants, but the cardinal had already discussed the "Spanish question" with both of them, and the need for a change in relations between the two countries. Dewey had worked as a lawyer for Francoist interests in the United States during the Civil War.

The Spanish Bloc

Even before Lequerica arrived in the country, there was a wide range of active pro-Francoists in the United States, some of whom had been working since the Civil War and the Second World War, and others in the period that we are studying, to encourage a more favorable opinion of Spain in their country. Their objective was largely to "normalize" relations of all kinds between the United States and Spain, which had been disturbed for the first time in 1936 and, again, more significantly, in 1945. In many cases they were motivated by ideology: anti-communism; Catholicism, in particular some hierarchies within the church; and/or cultural or personal preferences. And many also recognized the contribution made by Franco and Catholic Spain to the fight against communism in the war from 1936 to 1939, his (alleged) neutrality during the Second World War, and his (also alleged) favorable attitude to the Allies during the conflict. In general, they were seeking a broad and permanent collaboration between the two countries in all areas, not only diplomatic, political, economic, and military relations, but also technology, culture, education, etc. They felt that since the end of the Second World War the United States had been treating Spain "unfairly" and "wrongly." This group also contained executives, managers, and businessmen, who largely shared these opinions, but they were more interested in their own business expectations with Spain or the interests of the companies or banks they represented.

The leading figures in the Spanish Bloc were the following: Cardinal Spellman of New York; the Jesuit priest Joseph F. Thorning who in 1949 put Lequerica in touch with Patrick Francis Clark, both of whom were employed as lobbyists by the embassy; Hayes, former ambassador, professor of History at Columbia University, and former president of the American Historical Association, who in 1951 published a new, blatantly pro-Franco book on

Spain; the Jesuit Francis X. Talbot, editor of the magazine *America*,[94] who in late 1938 had helped set up the American Union for Nationalist Spain with Merwin K. Hart, Ogden Hammond, Hildreth Meière, and John Eogan Kelly;[95] Colonel Hoffman; bankers and businessmen like Alfred W. Barth, of the Chase National Bank; James A. Farley, from Coca-Cola, a Catholic and former chairman of the Democratic National Committee between 1932 and 1940, who had masterminded Roosevelt's victories in 1932 and 1936 until he resigned in 1940 and was appointed to the board of Coca-Cola, which he was to make a household name the world over; Eric A. Johnston, president of the Motion Picture Association of America; and Frank Timothy Ryan, former head of the Iberian desk of the Office of Strategic Services (OSS), the predecessor of the CIA and co-owner of the New York cotton export firm John J. Ryan and Sons, one of forty-four that had exported raw cotton to Spain in August 1939 thanks to a loan from the Export-Import Bank.[96] The last names in this list were Americans who had much more material reasons for acting in the way they did. They negotiated with the administration or Congress in favor of normalizing the relations between the United States and Spain so that their companies and they themselves could benefit. To achieve their goals, they took advantage of the contacts most of them had made in Madrid during the Second World War. In Farley's case, in particular, his Catholicism also played an important role because, as a man close to Pope Pius XII in the 1930s, he had been responsible for the diplomatic rapprochement between the United States and the Holy See.[97]

---

[94] D. Mota Zurdo, "Un sueño americano: el gobierno vasco en el exilio y Estados Unidos (1937–1979)", Doctoral thesis, Department of Contemporary History, Universidad del País Vasco, 2015, 47.

[95] In which Elly Sedgwick, Ignatius M. Wilkinson, General Henry Joseph Reilly, Anne Morgan, John Pierpont Morgan, Anne Tracy Morgan, Lucrezia Bori, and Clare Singer Dawes, among others, would also take part: M. E. Chapman, *Arguing Americanism: Franco Lobbyists, Roosevelt's Foreign Policy and the Spanish Civil War*, Kent, Kent State University Press, 2011, 108 ff.

[96] On Ryan, see León Aguinaga, "The Chase Bank, the WCC…". On his activity in the OSS and the WCC in Spain during the Second World War and early post-war period, see also Aline, countess of Romanones, *El fin de una era*, Barcelona, Ediciones B, 2010, 70–72. On Ryan's presence in Galicia in the post-war period, see J. R. Rodríguez Lago, "'Aliados pola forza. Redes para unha victoria'. Os Aliados e os Estados Unidos na Galicia da II Guerra Mundial," *Xornadas Galicia e a II Guerra mundial*, Consello da Cultura Galega, 13–14 April 2021.

[97] Letters from Farley to the Architetto dei Sacri Palazzi Apostolici on 23 November 1950 and Pius XII on 18 July 1952, Farley Papers, box 21, Manuscript Division, Library of Congress.

The Main Aims of Lequerica and the Spanish Embassy in Washington in 1948

The policy implemented by Lequerica and the Spanish embassy in Washington in 1948 had four main aims: to support the Republican candidate in the November elections; to seek out loans ("long-term loans for particular reconstruction work of ours"[98]), attract U.S. investment and put investors in touch with the Franco government; to improve the perception of the Franco regime in the United States, particularly in the press; and to work within the UN to annul the 1946 resolution on Spain.

As far as the first of these aims was concerned, everything seemed to suggest that President Truman would be defeated in the elections, and the Spanish government,[99] Lequerica, and the embassy were convinced that the Republican victory would pave the way for the much-needed loans and subsidies and herald the end of diplomatic isolation. In fact, ever since the National Republican Convention in Philadelphia, the "inspector" had been invited by Ralph Owen Brewster to attend meals with Republicans, both members of Congress and of the public, who were against Truman's foreign policy. One such event had been held on 26 May in Washington, and was also attended by Reece, the president of the party's national committee, and Brewster himself. On that occasion Carlton Hayes had other obligations elsewhere, but he sent Brewster a letter for him to read on his behalf. In it, he described Lequerica as "a personal friend and true friend of the United States" and denounced that the propaganda

> of the Soviet Union, and its conscious or unconscious apologists in this country, has served, especially during the last three years, to conceal from the American people the signal services which Spain rendered us in the critical war years of 1942 to 1945, and to induce our Government to adopt toward Spain a policy which I can only regard as contrary to American interests and derogatory to American honor.

He ended by arguing that

> whatever may be the outcome of our presidential election this year, I sincerely trust that then, if not earlier, we will reverse our Spanish policy [...] We should resume full and friendly diplomatic relations

[98] Ibid.

[99] According to Cava Mesa, Lequerica had been told by Madrid that "only a Republican victory was considered favourable to Spain. It was a party without fanatical passions, highly administrative and economic, with a candidate along the same lines, supported by the deep-seated economic interests desirous of a deal with Spain": Cava Mesa, *Los diplomáticos de Franco ...*, 299.

with Spain [...] counsel our other friends in Western Europe to do likewise [...] [and] to secure Spain's admission to the United Nations or to any other world or regional organization which may supplant or supplement it.[100]

The Republicans did not immediately opt to nominate Thomas E. Dewey as their candidate.[101] Lequerica and the embassy's initial preference had been for Senator Robert A. Taft, who was very close to Brewster, largely because "he was in favor of the agreement with Spain against Communism."[102] The other candidates were Vandenberg, Stassen, and Dewey himself, governor of the state of New York, who had the support of Aldrich, the president of the Chase National Bank, a Republican who got on well with President Truman and who must have had some influence on Lequerica on this question.[103] In fact, Lequerica put in an appearance at the Republican National Convention, which was publicly denounced in the press by the former secretary of the interior and anti-Francoist Harold Ickes,[104] and he may even have made a donation.[105] After Dewey had been nominated, Cardinal Spellman put Lequerica in touch with him, as noted above. Three months later, in September, Lequerica was convinced that there would be a future Republican government, and everybody

[100] Letter from Hayes to Brewster, 21 May 1948, Ralph Owen Brewster Papers, Bowdoin College Library, Brunswick In any case, the option of the G.O.P. by Thomas E. Dewey – that is, his nomination as a candidate – was not immediate, initially Lequerica and the embassy leaning towards Senator Robert A. Taft, to whom Brewster was very close. This one, in addition, had been [...] in favor of the agreement with Spain against communism. The others were Vandenberg, Stassen and the aforementioned Dewey, governor of the State of New York, who was supported, among many others, by Aldrich, the president of Chase, a Republican in very good relations with President Truman and who must have influenced Lequerica in this matter. In fact, Lequerica appeared at the Republican National Convention, something that the former secretary of the interior and anti-Franco Harold Ickes would publicly denounce in the press. And he probably made a donation. Upon his nomination, Cardinal Spellman would facilitate personal contact with Dewey, as noted above. Three months later, in September, Lequerica took for granted a future Republican administration, with a Dewey in whose triumph everyone discounted. And he promised them happy for Spain. Frustration would come soon.

[101] Letter from Carlos de Goyeneche y Silvela, Marquis of Balbueno to Minister Martín Artajo, 19 July 1949, Ministry of Foreign Affairs Record Group, file number 82–5987, AGA.

[102] Telegram from Lequerica to Martín Artajo, 14 May 1948, file 14252, AFNFF.

[103] Cava Mesa, *Los diplomáticos de Franco* ..., 298.

[104] Harold Ickes, "The State Department's...".

[105] This could be deduced from Cava Mesa's mention of "electoral expenses": ava Mesa, *Los diplomáticos de Franco* ..., 308.

took for granted that Dewey would be victorious.[106] Things were looking up for Spain. But not for long.

As far as the objective of negotiating loans was concerned, one of the first things Lequerica had done on his arrival in Washington had been to complain to the State Department that the O'Konski Amendment had been blocked. He had been keeping track of events before he set off for the United States, he had discussed it with Culbertson, and he was outraged that Congress had done a U-turn. Nevertheless, he had taken advantage to request another sort of public funding – Export-Import Bank loans – but with no success. In view of this, he told Martín Artajo that he would begin to look into private banking options, the only path left open to them, beginning in New York with his friend Barth's Chase National Bank.[107] At that time he was not considering using a gold guarantee because a decision on the issue of Nazi gold in Spain was still pending, albeit imminent.

In terms of the second objective – attracting U.S. investment – both Baráibar and Lequerica channeled requests from U.S. executives to meet with Minister of Foreign Affairs and the Minister of Trade and Industry Juan Antonio Suanzes. The oil company Standard Oil, which was tendering to construct the CAMPSA refinery in Cartagena, and the electrical corporation Westinghouse even requested an interview with Franco himself. However, the executives of Standard Oil were slow off the mark and, by the time their tender reached Madrid, the minister of trade and industry had already awarded the contract to build the refinery to a consortium made up of INI, the Californian company Caltex, and CEPSA, one of whose owners was former Minister of Trade and Industry Demetrio Carceller Segura. All this and the modernization of the three aerodromes mentioned above was proof that there was growing interest in investing in Spain despite the fact that the question of the Spanish loan guarantees still had to be resolved.

In this respect, on 3 May 1948 there was an important change. Spain and the Allied Control Commission signed an agreement on the so-called Nazi gold, such important news that Lequerica immediately passed it on to the U.S. bankers. The possibility that the Franco regime was in possession of Nazi gold was a Sword of Damocles preventing Spain from being granted loans because the private banks were being advised by the Department of the Treasury not to accept looted gold as collateral. The removal of this threat was a major step forward. In fact, just three years previously, on 5 May 1945, Lequerica himself, as minister for foreign affairs had been forced by Ambassador Armour and his British counterpart Mallet into complying with resolution VI of the Bretton Woods Agreement and the Gold Declaration of 1944 and applying the Safehaven program in Spain. All these instruments had been created by the

---

[106] Letter from Lequerica to Martín Artajo, 29 September 1948, Leg 8849, AFNFF.
[107] Letter from Lequerica to Martín Artajo, 14 May 1948, Leg 14252, AFNFF.

Allies to prevent German assets from being transferred, to confiscate German property – which in Spain included SOFINDUS and its companies and such banks and multinationals as IG Farben, Osram, Siemens, and Bosch – and, in general, to restore the land seized by Germany in the occupied countries to its legitimate owners. In particular, they were designed to recover the gold robbed from central banks, institutions, and citizens by the occupying Nazis, and to imprison and then hand over to the Allies all German personnel resident in Spain.[108] Since May 1945 the Allies and the Spanish Institute of Foreign Currency – the institution responsible for buying gold – had been trying to negotiate a deal on German assets and gold, and over the three-year period the U.S. negotiators had been constantly changing. The initial team was headed by the *chargé d'affaires* who had replaced Ambassador Armour, Philip W. Bonsal, and agents from the Foreign Economic Administration, and the last by Paul T. Culbertson, the *chargé d'affaires* since June 1947, alongside the trade attaché, Harold Randall, and other civil servants. Finally, on 3 May 1948 they reached an agreement with the Allied Control Commission to return 101.62 kilos of gold,[109] an amount below that initially demanded by the United States. The decision to settle for less had been affected by the change in policy of the State Department at the end of 1947, which had prevailed over the greater demands of the Department of the Treasury and its head, John Snyder.[110] In other words, from this point on Spain was free to use the rest of the gold that had been stockpiled during the war as a guarantee to obtain loans in the private sphere in the United States. Indeed, over the next two years, the regime was granted private loans by the Chase National Bank and the City National Bank[111] as the result of negotiations initiated at this time and helped by the fact that on 28 May the United States finally unfroze $60 million of Spanish assets in the country.[112] The first loan for $25 million was granted on 8 February 1949 by the Chase National Bank.[113]

---

[108] Martín Aceña, *El oro de Moscú ...,* 323–324; 329; C. Collado Seidel, *España, refugio nazi*, Madrid, Temas de hoy, 2005, 155 ff; D. A. Messenger, *Hunting Nazis in Franco's Spain*, Baton Rouge, Louisiana State University Press, 2014, 75. Between 3 May and 5 June, while the Act of Surrender was being signed, the Spanish authorities had officially sealed off all official Nazi premises in the country, but allowed German officials to surreptitiously remove all kinds of belongings, documents, works of art, etc. See M. Martorell Linares, "Cualquier obra de tipo medio alcanza aquí precios extraordinariamente buenos: España en la dispersión del expolio artístico nazi," in L. Pérez-Part Durbán and G. Fernández Arribas (eds.), *Holocausto y bienes culturales*, Huelva, Universidad de Huelva, 2019, 97; also Collado Seidel, *España, refugio nazi ...,* 166 ff.

[109] Martín Aceña, *El oro de Moscú ...,* 350.

[110] Ibid., 348.

[111] Ibid., 366.

[112] A. Viñas, *En las garras...,* 51.

[113] Hualde, *El "cerco" ...,* 255.

Lequerica and the embassy regarded the third objective – improving the perception of the Franco regime in the United States and responding to anti-Franco news and opinions via the press – as a prerequisite if they were to overcome the obstacles to their mission. However, their success in this respect was only modest. First of all they tried to procure a press outlet that would serve their interests by financing the leading New York newspaper in Spanish, *La Prensa*. They would have had to send the funds to the newspaper itself and also to the director, Julio Garzón, in person, and this would have involved a considerable amount in dollars. However, when Lequerica's proposal was submitted by Martín Artajo, who was in favor, the expenditure was not approved by the cabinet in Madrid.[114] As an alternative, Lequerica suggested setting up a publicity agency, with Garzón and others at the helm. It was to be called IBI and would operate out of New York and Washington with the press attaché, Antonio Cacho Zabalza, and the counselor for cultural relations, Pablo Merry del Val, acting as liaisons with the embassy.[115] They even got so far as to discuss which correspondents would be appointed, possible candidates being such leading journalists as Carlos Sentís, Casares, or Massip. But once again the project was not approved by Madrid. Lack of funding was also the reason for the failure of other cultural-propaganda projects. One such project, devised by Father Thorning, was to set up an association of friends of Spain headed jointly by Hayes and Hoffman, with Lieutenant Colonel Hinkel, former Civil War correspondent, as secretary. Apparently, the reason so many proposals never got off the drawing board was that Minister Suanzes refused to free up funds that he had earmarked for other purposes.[116] So, not having a press outlet at the embassy's disposal, Lequerica would spend the first months attempting to iron out the problems caused by his contract between the official Spanish agency EFE and the United Press. Exactly how the propaganda drive should be structured was still unresolved but, after the dismal Republican showing at the presidential elections, it was more successful and better funded. And as from 1949, the "subsidies" came into play.

In their attempts to make headway on the fourth objective – to annul the UN's resolution of December 1946 – during the summer of 1948 both Lequerica and the *chargé d'affaires* were in close contact with the State Department. The first approach was made by Baráibar[117] because, by virtue of his position, he was officially capacitated to do so. He met with Achilles and Dunham to inform them that the Spanish government was going to call municipal elections in October and November, thus proving that the Franco

[114] Cava Mesa, *Los diplomáticos de Franco ...*, 279–280.

[115] M. Douglas, "Remembering Julian Pitt-Rivers. A personal note," in Honorio M. Velasco (coord.), *La Antropología como pasión y como práctica. Ensayos in honorem Julian Pitt-Rivers*, Madrid, CSIC, 2004, 50.

[116] Cava Mesa, *Los diplomáticos de Franco ...*, 281–284.

[117] https://history.state.gov/historicaldocuments/frus1948v03/d655.

regime was, or was about to become, a democratic one. In fact, it was little more than the implementation – more than three years after it had been passed – of the Law Regulating Local Government of 17 July 1945, which enabled families, unions and institutions to elect town councilors. Of course, the only political party that was allowed to compete was the official, fascist FET y de las JONS (the Traditionalist Spanish Phalanx of the Councils of the National Syndicalist Offensive, hereinafter referred to as the Falange). Achilles gave a general response in line with the spirit of the official policy that any initiative taken by Spain for purposes of greater democracy was positive in the eyes of the department, particularly if it was before the UN General Assembly in Paris.

But a few days later, on 25 August,[118] when Lequerica went to see Achilles and Dunham's immediate superior, Hickerson, the attitude was much less accommodating. He was received by both Hickerson and Achilles, and, to start with, after introducing himself as inspector, he had to put up with their comments that his inspection must be a very long one because he had already been there for four months. And they went on to reproach him that Spain was not really making the liberal changes it had been asked to make in either the political system or the economy. Lequerica replied that there was no need to make any political changes, but he was in favor of changes of an economic nature, which he believed were both necessary and possible. As far as the issue of the UN was concerned, Hickerson questioned the resolution of 1946 because it was based on the premise that Spain was a threat to peace. He admitted that it had been an interference in Spain's domestic affairs and that the United States did not believe that it would be effective, although he also made it clear that if Spain did not make the changes other nations had demanded it would be difficult to get the two-thirds of the vote required to annul it. Even so, he did say for the first time that Washington was prepared to support a modification to the resolution that would allow Spain to belong to specialized UN agencies and, more importantly, have ambassadors sent to Madrid. However, the U.S. delegation would not make the proposal.

When Hickerson had finished, Lequerica suggested a strategy: they could present a new resolution to the General Assembly, identical to the 1946 resolution, and, after the vote, which would not get the two-thirds majority required, it would be ruled out. Therefore, *de facto*, the previous resolution would have to be annulled. He also handed his surprised interlocutors a note with the text of his proposal, which argued that a vote in 1947 that had not yielded a two-thirds majority had prompted four countries – Bolivia, El Salvador, Santo Domingo, and Peru – to send their ambassadors to Madrid. He also advocated that a U.S. ambassador should be sent to Madrid, with the highly unusual argument that, once there, the Spanish government would achieve "miracles" in economic terms. He exemplified this by explaining how

---

[118] Memorandum of Conversation, 25 August 1948, FRUS 1948, 1047–1049.

much Ambassador Armour had achieved when he was minister of foreign affairs. Achilles replied that the United States had no intention of getting anything from Spain; on the contrary, Spain wanted to get readmitted to the international community. To this, Lequerica said that all future progress in the relations between the two countries depended on the United States. Hickerson and Achilles, however, claimed the exact opposite: everything was in the hands of the Spanish government.

In fact, between the two interviews, on 26 July 1948 the State Department passed an internal directive in response to the general policy laid down by the NSC 3. It stated that the aim of the policy on Spain was to "reintegrate" the country politically, economically, and militarily into the free Western world by means of a gradual normalization of diplomatic relations, although this would be impossible unless Spain made internal changes for political and economic liberalization. It claimed that there was no desire to destabilize the country or to spark off another civil war, but "the present conditions of oppression and corruption [...] can only lead to an explosive political situation unless relieved in a gradual and orderly manner."[119] Given that "a broadly free and democratic regime is both almost unknown in Spanish history and impossible of attainment at any time in the near future," they demanded that Franco adopt "some moderate evolutionary steps." This standpoint was in stark contrast to that of the Soviet Union, which demanded that the dictator be toppled.

The directive gave no advice on Spain's future form of government and whether it should be a republic or a monarchy, with or without Franco. This it left in the hands of the Spanish people, although it explicitly criticized several factors that were preventing progress: for example,

> the obstinacy of Franco and his close supporters, passions remaining from the Civil War, the inherent instability of Spanish politics, the complacency and support of the present regime by various rightist groups and the present repression of political expression in Spain.

Convinced that the United States could influence domestic matters in Spain, they wanted to show

> rightist elements, now supporting the regime, particularly the Army and the Church, that we do not want to favor foreign intervention in Spain and are not seeking to reverse the outcome of the Civil War, but we do hope to see orderly evolution toward a more broadly based government, under which their legitimate interests would not suffer and which would restore Spain to its full political and economic place in the international community. We hope the center and non-Communist

---

[119] Policy Statement by the Department of State on Spain, 26 July 1948, FRUS 1948 1041–1045.

112   JOAN MARIA THOMÀS

left will recognize that such evolution will afford a better chance for genuine attainment of their objectives than revolution.[120]

On the economic level, the directive pointed out that the Franco regime needed to do away with the obstacles to free trade, and that the lack of dollars and the corrupt and inefficient control of economic issues were the main obstacles to private trade between the two countries. It also suggested that the recent solution to the gold problem was a possible way forward, but made it clear that the United States would use the granting of public loans as a weapon to ensure that the aforementioned changes were made. In particular,

> positive economic assistance from this Government should await, and serve as an inducement for the taking of concrete steps toward liberalization in Spain. We expect to coordinate our economic assistance with political developments in Spain and to utilize it to encourage evolution.

And with respect to the Marshall Plan, although the decision to include Spain would have to be taken by the beneficiaries of the plan, for many of them "the question of Spain is still a domestic political issue" and

> whether these nations do in fact eventually invite Spain to participate will undoubtedly depend upon steps which the Spanish Government is willing to take to improve its international reputation and thus make it politically possible for a majority of ERP countries to invite Spain to participate. If these nations should decide at some future time that conditions have changed and they wish to propose the inclusion of Spain, we have indicated publicly that we will consider that new situation on its merits.[121]

It also pointed out that the issue of relations with Spain was fundamentally political, not military. Great Britain and France were the main allies of the United States in Europe and, strategically speaking, they were both extremely interested in Spain's integration, although they felt that this was impossible on a political level. This was partly because the socialists in power in many European countries loathed Franco almost as much as communism, something they had demonstrated in their reaction to the vote in the House of Representatives on the O'Konski Amendment. For the United States, the issue was the strategic importance of Spain's geographical location and the need to prevent a future communist government there. This was why they took such an interest in Spain's economic and political rehabilitation. Now, they saw that domestic support for Franco had increased as a result of the

[120] Ibid.
[121] Ibid.

UN's policy of international isolation and that Franco himself was convinced that he would eventually receive economic and military aid from the United States because of the country's strategic position. However, the more stable situation in Italy and in Europe was weakening Franco's resolve and may have prompted him to accept some sort of political and economic liberalization, particularly if it meant that Spain would be included in the Marshall Plan. But, for the moment, the recent economic agreements Franco had signed with Argentina, Great Britain, and France meant that inclusion in the plan was not quite so pressing. For all these reasons, the directive concluded, the regime should not be pressured with international measures, but should be required to adopt measures of political and economic liberalization.[122]

A few days later, Secretary of State Marshall himself addressed all the U.S. ambassadors in Latin America to explain the action to be taken. He also announced that the Brazilian government had complained that, in view of the trickle of ambassadors being sent to Madrid, there was a need to adopt a common stand on Spain. He reasserted his previous position and made it clear that the U.S. vote would be in Spain's favor if Franco took liberalizing measures.[123]

In this state of affairs, the United States began to work towards the partial lifting of the 1946 UN resolution, as suggested by Baráibar and Lequerica. It did so during the first session of the third General Assembly, which began in Paris on 21September 1948, and in which Poland presented a proposal to denounce what it considered to be non-compliance with the 1946 resolution by the Western Allies. According to Poland, they had signed trade agreements with Franco – which was true in the cases of the United Kingdom and France – as had Argentina and other countries, although this was not prohibited by the resolution. In fact, Poland and the communist bloc led by the Soviet Union used the case of Spain to counter the accusations of anti-democracy leveled against them, and argued that Westerners were supporting a regime set up with the help of the Nazis and fascists.

Hickerson and Achilles called Baráibar to the Department on 27 September to explain that they were planning to have the 1946 resolution partially lifted – without seeming to be the proponents – so that Spain could engage in full diplomatic relations with other countries and take part in UN agencies and commissions. In fact, U.S. ambassador to the UN, Warren Austin, was working in Paris on a proposal made by a Latin American country in an effort to get the two-thirds majority required. He had already agreed with twenty-seven countries that they would vote in favor of the ambassador issue and predicted that the votes against would be those of the Soviet bloc plus Guatemala, Venezuela, Mexico, and some other countries. Great Britain, France, and

[122] Ibid.
[123] The Secretary of State to Diplomatic and Consular Offices in the American Republics, 28 July 1948, FRUS 1948, 1045–1047.

Belgium had said they would abstain, but would vote in favor if necessary. On the issue of the specialized agencies, the votes in favor were the same plus, probably, France. After Baráibar had been informed, he was asked to keep the information in the strictest confidence.

Nevertheless, Lequerica – who referred to the *chargé d'affaires* as his "second-in-command"[124] – was quick to give the good news to Minister Artajo, who had also been notified by Culbertson.[125] But as a sign of the level of information that "he" was capable of obtaining from the State Department, he also told him the news leaked to him by a high-ranking U.S. citizen in the Department with the code name "Número 50"[126]: namely, that in a meeting with Hickerson and Achilles on the previous 29 September they had discussed who would next be sent to Madrid as ambassador. They had admitted that Truman was having difficulties in appointing "a friend of Dewey's," which shows how confident they were at that time that he would win the election. Another option they had discussed had been to send not an ambassador but a high-ranking representative such as Assistant to the Under Secretary for Transportation and Communications Garrison Norton, a man who was very well disposed to Spain and whom "Número 50" claimed had overcome Hickerson's opposition. They had also spoken of the need to assess the state of North American public opinion on Spain, which they believed to be less hostile at that point in time, and they planned a set of questions that could become the embryo of a Gallup poll in support of the department's policy of greater acceptance of Spain. In fact, "Número 50" had leaked the poll questions to Lequerica. They were:

What percentage of the American people:

1. Have any interest in Spain (or Franco). Pro or Con.

2. Believe that in the present international situation the US should seek improved relations with Spain?

3. Have any interest in or objection to inclusion of Spain in the European Recovery Program?

4. Believe US Government should otherwise extend financial assistance to Spain?[127]

Meanwhile, in Madrid, aware that Brazil was interested in appointing an ambassador to Spain and had been negotiating with the UN to annul the

---

[124] Letter from Lequerica to Martín Artajo, 28 September 1948, Leg 8852, AFNFF.
[125] Ibid.: Handwritten note in the same document.
[126] Letter from Lequerica to Martín Artajo, 29 September 1948, Leg. 8849, AFNFF.
[127] Ibid.

THE STRUGGLE TO CHANGE U.S. POLICY TOWARD FRANCO'S SPAIN 115

1946 resolution, the Ministry of Foreign Affairs worked to ensure that Brazil would present a proposal to the General Assembly, which would also serve to counter the Polish proposal. To contribute to the cause and to bring in as many votes as possible, the Palacio de Santa Cruz sent a delegation to Paris, headed by the undersecretary of the ministry, Carlos de Miranda y Quartín, count of Casa Miranda.[128]

So things seemed to be looking up, particularly when Republican Senator John Chandler Gurney – president of the Armed Services Committee – returned from a visit to Spain where, on 30 September, he had met with Franco. He publicly expressed his opinion that full diplomatic relations between Spain and the leading Western powers, the United States included, should be restored. However, he had also had meetings with recently appointed Defense Secretary James V. Forrestal, with the secretaries of the army, navy, and the air force – subordinate to Forrestal – and with members of the Joint Chiefs of Staff. On all of this, the *New York Times* gave the opinion that:

> Mr Gurney obviously and openly represents the Pentagon point of view, or that formidable section of Washington opinion, dominated by the military, which holds that the United States frontier is in the Pyrenees, or, in any case, that the security of Western Europe never can be guaranteed without the utilization of Spanish, and German, manpower.[129]

In fact, the journalist responsible for the article believed that being able to count on Spain was crucial not only because the military wanted to draw up agreements with the country but also because of the effect it could have on the Western Allies since setting the defense of Europe in the Pyrenees meant, *de facto*, giving up on another line of defense centered on the banks of the Rhine or the Elba.[130]

In November, seven other senators from the same committee as Gurney traveled to Europe, made a flying visit to Spain and, on their return, also spoke out in favor of a change in policy.[131] And two months previously, in September, on his way back from a meeting of the Inter-parliamentary Union in Rome, Lequerica's friend and supporter Senator Ralph Owen Brewster had spent a week in Madrid, holding meetings with the U.S. embassy and Franco's representatives. Likewise, a whole sector of the press, represented by the "Hearst, Patterson, and Scripps-Howard newspaper chains and the

---

[128] Sánchez González, *Diez años....*, 105.
[129] H. W. Baldwin, "US 'Frontier' is Issue," *New York Times*, 10 October 1948, 11. Also R. W. Gilmore, *The American Foreign Policy-Making Process and the Development of a Post-World War II in Spanish policy, 1945–1953: A Case Study*, Ph.D. dissertation, University of Pittsburgh, 1967, 183.
[130] Ibid.
[131] Scowcroft, *Congress and Foreign Policy ...*, 27.

self-proclaimed 'realists' of the period," was pushing for a change in U.S. policy on the Franco regime. A good example of this standpoint was what one of Hearst's columnists, George Rothwell Brown,[132] wrote about Gurney's trip, pointing out that it

> may mark the beginning of the end of an intolerable situation with regard to Spain. American hostility to the Franco regime is a regrettable and dangerous hang-over, from the Roosevelt New Deal. The studied refusal of the United States to admit Spain into the society of European states, and the exclusion of Spain from the ERP is a continuing diplomatic blunder.[133]

But the members of the State Department responsible for Spain were not of the same opinion as Gurney. When the commercial attaché, Elorza, went to see Dunham at the Spanish desk, he was informed that the dpartment had known nothing about the visit to Spain, which was probably the result of a last-minute decision taken by General Marshall in Paris in response to the Berlin crisis, the deteriorating international situation, and the outcome of some meeting with the foreign ministers of the Western European Union. In fact, according to Dunham, war could break out at any moment, and, if Europe fell into the hands of the Soviet army, Spain would be able to defend itself only for two or three weeks in the Pyrenees because of its poor economy and transport system (railways, roads, ports, airfields, etc.). He assured him that this was what the War Department had communicated to the State Department, and it meant that the last line of defense would be set in Morocco. And he insisted that the United States was not prepared to unilaterally change its policy on Spain; if it did so, it would go through UN channels, in accordance with what had already been discussed with *Chargé d'Affaires* Baráibar. However, whether war broke out or not, and under one administration or another – an allusion to the imminent presidential elections – the United States was determined to change its policy in the immediate future.[134]

But this immediate future was not to be. In the first place, things went awry in Paris. While Undersecretary Carlos de Miranda was working closely with Brazilian Foreign Minister Raul Fernandez on his proposal,[135] Secretary Marshall met with the British and French foreign ministers – Ernest Bevin

---

[132] U. S. Department of State; American Opinion Report, 15 October 1948, in Gilmore, *American Foreign Policy-Making ...,* 209.

[133] Ibid.

[134] Interview between Francisco Javier Elorza and William Dunham, 30 September 1948, Ministry of Foreign Affairs Record Group, file number 54–08916, AGA. See also Baráibar to Martín Artajo, Presidency of the Government Record Group, file number 54–08916, AGA.

[135] Sánchez González, *Diez años....*, 106.

and Robert Schuman, respectively – who did not agree with voting in favor of Spain and against Poland. In fact, because of internal problems in their government coalitions (France) and public opinion (United Kingdom), they preferred not to discuss the Spanish issue. And that is exactly what they did. On 26 October 1948, the Consultative Council of the Brussels Treaty – consisting of the United Kingdom, France, and the Benelux countries – decided to avoid the debate and persuade Brazil not to present its proposal. And, although the Polish proposal was not removed from the agenda of the General Assembly, when the first session of the Third Assembly ended in December 1948, the Spanish issue had not been discussed.[136]

In other words, in its negotiations with the United Kingdom and France, the United States had played a double game. On the one hand, it had done what they asked; on the other, it had instructed its delegation that, if a proposal was finally presented in support of Spain's membership of the UN technical agencies and/or the exchange of ambassadors, it should vote in favor.[137] Of greater importance, however, is that the Spanish issue was not discussed at that time because there were much more pressing issues on the table, such as Greece, Palestine, and Korea. Even so, the Spanish cause was not helped by the fact that it was the constant focus of media attention due to Franco's insistence on propaganda and the (presumed) indispensability of Spain to the defense of the West. All of this was in stark contrast to Salazar, the much more discrete Portuguese dictator.[138] In the end, the discussion was scheduled for the second session, which was to begin in New York in April 1949.[139]

In short, Spain's hopes of even partially lifting the 1946 resolution had been frustrated. Despite this, it had made some progress compared to the previous year, given that it had gained support in Latin America and the Arab world. And, above all, the United States now seemed prepared to resolve the issue. After learning of the outcome in Paris, Lequerica had been satisfied with the offensive launched by the Spanish delegation and held out good hope for the future. But at the same time, he sent Baráibar to protest to the State Department that they had made promises that they had not kept. And to explain what had happened in Paris, he informed Martín Artajo of a conversation he had had with the American ambassador in Brazil, William D. Pawley, who had been involved in the negotiations. According to Pawley:

> [Secretary] Marshall was fully determined to bring the Spanish affair to a satisfactory conclusion in the last Assembly. It was the English Socialists who had insisted on the need to delay the solutions, strongly

---

[136] Ibid., 112–113.
[137] Hualde, El "cerco" ..., 252.
[138] Edwards, *Anglo-American Relations* ..., 113.
[139] Ibid., 253.

118 JOAN MARIA THOMÀS

supported by two or more influential State Department officials in Paris, whose attitude had been reinforced by the fact that they were no longer under the threat of the "new broom" announced by Dewey.[140]

That is to say, they were vengeful and relieved that they had not been dismissed, as Dewey had promised they would be if he had emerged victorious from the presidential elections. Even so, Lequerica was still quite optimistic, particularly because "at the April meeting we can count on the renewed promise of the State Department."[141] But he was in for another disappointment. In his conversation with Pawley, he had also been criticized for his attempts to put pressure on the department. Unmoved, when he informed the minister, he again insisted on the need to "wake up and push [the State Department] every now and again."[142] Very soon, however, he had first-hand experience of how the members of the department operated: they tried to throw him out of the country.[143]

1949

Professional Lobbyists (January–February 1949) and the So-called Spanish Lobby

The year 1949 began with the inauguration of Harry S. Truman's second term as president, an event that boded no good for the Franco regime. The first problem was that the president appointed Dean Acheson, a committed anti-Francoist like himself, as secretary of state, to replace the acting undersecretary,

---

[140] Lequerica to Martín Artajo, 31 December 1948, Ministry of Foreign Affairs Record group, file number 82–8869, AGA.

[141] Ibid.

[142] Letter from Lequerica to Martín Artajo, 14 December 1948, Ministry of Foreign Affairs Record Group, file number 82–5987, AGA.

[143] Lequerica had also been optimistic when he informed the minister that Truman had apparently ruled out Admiral Leahy as ambassador to Madrid on health grounds and was considering appointing Anthony J. D. Biddle to the post. Lequerica described him as a personal friend whom he had known since his time in Paris, where Biddle had arrived after leaving Poland as U.S. ambassador at the outbreak of the Second World War in September 1939 and before going to London to act as diplomatic representative to the governments of the German-occupied European countries that had sought asylum there. As Cardinal Spellman had leaked to Lequerica, Biddle's son was also to be posted to Madrid as embassy secretary and was married to the daughter of another friend (Bullitt). He asked Martín Artajo to be particularly attentive to him. Although he acknowledged that the situation was somewhat strange because of his low rank, he considered it important to the work he had been doing for his father and future ambassador. As things turned out, he was never appointed ambassador because the president reconsidered, but finally ruled out at the end of 1950, the option of Leahy, whose health had improved considerably.

THE STRUGGLE TO CHANGE U.S. POLICY TOWARD FRANCO'S SPAIN   119

General Marshall. Initially, this did not worry Lequerica or the embassy, at least with regard to the UN issue, which they believed was well on the way to being solved. Quite another thing, however, was the State Department's demands for economic and political changes in exchange for public loans. To get round these demands and finally become the beneficiaries of the long-awaited financial aid after the failures of 1948, they decided to follow the advice of their American friends and set up an organized structure to act in Congress in favor of Spanish interests. As we have seen, they already had some support there: the senators Robert Owen Brewster and Chan Gurney, the representative Alvin E. O'Konski and several others, among whom were Pat McCarran and Brewster, who would very soon be vying for prominence.[144]

In compliance with U.S. legislation, a legally registered professional structure was set up with the objective of working in the legislature to further Franco's interests. The professional lobbyists hired for this purpose were required to work hand-in-hand with congressmen and persuade them to favor Spain, to coordinate possible joint projects, to prepare legal initiatives that the congressmen could present for the benefit of Spain (particularly with regard to the granting of financial aid and loans), to advise and work with public and private banks to obtain credits for Spain, to feed the media, and to help organize trips for congressmen to Spain either as a reward for services rendered or as a way to win them over to "the cause." To start with, the team of lobbyists consisted of a single person – who would then subcontract another – and a law firm, which was paid monthly.

The individuals and the law firm encouraged congressmen to vote for legislative measures in Spain's interests both internationally (UN, Marshall Plan) and domestically (loans, bilateral agreements, military agreements, etc.). In this way, Lequerica and his team tried to build on the existing support in the legislature. This support consisted of sectors of the Pentagon in favor of improving relations between the two countries with a view to procuring air and naval bases on Spanish territory; congressmen with similar ideas and even activists, who were prepared to play a key role; and the group that we have called the Spanish Bloc, which would provide help and support. All this unfolded in the midst of the escalation of the Cold War and a climate of rampant anti-communism, which boded well for the Spanish cause.

The agents employed were given instructions by the embassy about how to proceed in Congress, but they were also required to make proposals. As part of their work with congressmen, the embassy and the agents were required to get the press on their side by giving money – euphemistically called "subsidies" – to journalists or newspapers so that they would write favorably about Spain, or about the initiatives proposed in Congress. This system of payment for services rendered replaced the previous idea of setting up their own unit and imitated

---

[144] With his two daughters, who were nuns.

JOAN MARIA THOMÀS

the system of electoral funding and subsidies to the Catholic Church.[145] As Lequerica wrote to the minister:

> Whether what we are doing works out or not, we need to continue spending [...] because otherwise it would be like hoping to win a lottery prize without buying a ticket [...] It is not a question of corrupting people. That is not possible. It is about helping companies. This is possible and decent. If it were not, we would not even propose it.[146]

And, afraid of possible leaks, he said to Martin Artajo "that if this could be kept between His Excellency [the head of state] and you, so much the better."[147]

At other times, Lequerica was more explicit. For example, in 1951, in a veiled reference to "subsidies" probably to McCarran himself or others, he wrote the following to the minister of foreign affairs:

> We also have the option of the Appropriations Committee [the chairman of which was Senator McCarran], which can with good reason adopt specific resolutions in the interests of Spain but we would have to resume our activities, which, as you are well aware, have come to a halt at the present time.[148]

In some cases, the law firm in the employ of the Spanish embassy, Cummings, Stanley, Truitt & Cross, was systematically handing out large sums of money [149] (for example, to the Dominican Republic and its dictator Leónidas Trujillo).[150] And it seems quite feasible that McCarran too was accepting payments. In fact, Truman had grown so weary of McCarran's pro-Franco stance and all the other issues on which they disagreed that in May 1949 he told those closest to him that "[McCarran] has been reached." One of his team responded that "a certain United States Senator said that McCarran was the only United States Senator whom he had positive proof he was a crook."[151] But whether or not he was accepting payments from the Francoists – and it

---

[145] Cava Mesa, *Los diplomáticos de Franco* ..., 308.

[146] Cited in Cava Mesa, *Los diplomáticos de Franco* ..., 308. She goes on to explain in her own words what Lequerica wrote: "So [Lequerica] avoided any mention of possible immorality concerning the economic aid provided for electoral, journalistic and religious influence which, of course, were a considerable expense."

[147] Ibid.

[148] Telegram sent by Lequerica to Martín Artajo, 7 September 1951, Ministry of Foreign Affairs, file R-3599 E-38, cited in Viñas, *En las garras...*, 130.

[149] R. D. Crassweller, *Trujillo. La trágica aventura del poder personal,* Barcelona, Bruguera, 1966, 334–335.

[150] The representation of Trujillo's law firm in Shannon, "The Franco Lobby"....

[151] Entry for 6 May 1949 in R. H. Ferrell (ed.), *Truman in the White House. The Diary of Eben A. Ayers*, Columbia, University of Missouri Press, 1991, 309.

THE STRUGGLE TO CHANGE U.S. POLICY TOWARD FRANCO'S SPAIN   121

seems that he was – what is beyond all doubt is that for several years he had been able to blackmail high-ranking members of the administration with his power in the Senate.[152]

The money to fund this whole scheme came from the Ministry of Foreign Affairs, after approval by the Council of Ministers, although some of the "subsidies" were probably only known to Martin Artajo and Franco. There are no conclusive figures for these operations. According to Viñas, in the first year Lequerica was not sent any money to pay the lobbyists, and he ran up a deficit of $44,000, which was corrected with $50,000 in 1950. And of the $740,000 he requested in 1950, he only received $100,000, including $30,000 for radio publicity. In 1951, it seems that he was sent $50,000 more.[153] However, there is proof that $140,000 was transferred in 1949 for the so-called "Plan Otoño" ("Fall Plan") – a trip to Spain for congressmen that we will discuss below.[154] As for 1950 and 1951 we have not found the total of the amounts that were undoubtedly paid.[155] And in 1952 Lequerica once again demanded that the money approved should be sent to him.[156]

In general, getting approval for the funds was not always a straightforward process for Martín Artajo. It required lengthy discussions in the cabinet because large amounts had to be transferred and, like other strong currencies, dollars were in short supply in the country and were needed to purchase the imports essential to keeping the impoverished Spanish economy afloat. According to Minister of Industry Juan Antonio Suanzes the economy was on the verge of

[152] Other mentions of corrupt behavior by the senator in the same entry: 6 May 1949: "The President said Senator McCarran had been trying to get this recognition for Franco and that the senator had gone to Secretary of State Acheson and threatened him with the loss of State Department appropriations unless an Ambassador is named [...] He said that Acheson had told him that in 1945, McCarran came to Acheson, then assistant secretary of State, and demanded that McCarran and his wife be sent to the United Nations Organization meeting in San Francisco and threatened then that if they weren't the Department's appropriations would suffer. The President said he told Acheson to tell McCarran to go to hell. However, the Department decided to pay the shot and he went. The president said blackmail worked then and McCarran was trying it now." Ferrell, *Truman...*, 309.

[153] Viñas, *En las garras...*, 59.

[154] "Today I urgently need the Ministries of Finance and Trade to issue the Consulate General New York with a money order for 140,000 dollars by virtue of the agreement of the Council of Ministers. Of this amount, 65,000 should remain in the Consular Fund as payment for advances already made to Your Excellency so that the New York Consulate can settle outstanding accounts with the Ministry of Finance. The remaining 75,000 will be given to Your Excellency to make payment of the 72,000 mentioned in your letter and to use the remainder for Merry's trip and additional expenses."

[155] Telegram from Martín Artajo to Lequerica, 1 September 1949, Ministry of Foreign Affairs Record Group, file number 82–5987, AGA.

[156] February 1952, file 815, AFNFF.

collapse because of the "prolonged drought resulting from the lack of foreign aid."[157] And, for some, approving funds to be sent to Lequerica even raised moral questions.

Historiography and political science have tended to use the term "Spanish Lobby" to refer to all those sectors that worked to change U.S. policy on the Franco regime from within Congress or from without. The first academic to formulate the concept – which had already been used in the press by the journalist William V. Shannon and the historian Arthur P. Whitaker[158] – was Theodore J. Lowi. He identified five different, albeit largely overlapping, sectors as components of the aforementioned lobby: (1) Catholic congressmen, (2) anti-Communists; (3) supporters of military bases in Spain, including members of the armed forces and military secretaries; (4) anti-Truman congressmen; and (5) congressmen who represented the cotton interests of the South. Among them were Republicans, Democrats, Protestants, and Catholics, all organized by the attorney Charles Patrick Clark[159] under Lequerica's supervision. Historiographically speaking, this division of the lobby into groups has enjoyed great success. However, in one respect it is far from enlightening because it does not distinguish the professional network set up and funded by the embassy from the group of congressmen, sectors, and other interests that fought for Spain in Congress. Particularly misleading is that it suggests a leadership and an organization that we do not believe existed. Neither does it seem that there was a stable coordination between the sectors Lowi lists as parts of the Spanish Lobby. And the analysis made here of the sectors of the Congress working to change the policy toward Spain does nothing to suggest that there may have been.

We believe that the congressmen who worked for Spain – particularly McCarran and Brewster – often followed instructions from Lequerica and the embassy or reached some sort of an understanding with them. On one of these occasions, in 1950 and 1951, McCarran managed to negotiate two loans because of his deeply rooted anti-communism and conservatism, his sympathies for the

---

[157] Culbertson to Acheson, 14 February 1949 cited in Hualde, *El "cerco"* ..., 255.

[158] Precisely to stress the need to study it: "The history of this lobby remains to be written, but it is said by those who knew them both to have been more effective than the more highly publicized China lobby of the period" (Whitaker, *Spain and Defense of the West* ..., 32). On the other hand, we believe that he is mistaken to go on to say that "From what we know of the congressional supporters of a softer policy towards the Franco regime, their motivations seem to have been religious, humanitarian, social, and economic, as well as military, but not political-ideological." In this respect, it seems to us that anti-communism also played a key role.

[159] T. J. Lowi, "US Bases in Spain," in Harold Stein (ed.), *American Civil-military Decisions. A Book of Case Studies,* Tuscaloosa, University of Alabama Press, 1963, 676.

Franco regime, and the fact that he had almost certainly been provided with some sort of "subsidy." They also proposed debates on the Spanish question. For their part, the paid lobbyists managed to sway representatives from both houses to more pro-Franco positions on particular issues, although others acted *de motu proprio*, for their own interests and/or for the economic interests of the states they represented. Yet others, particularly Republicans, took up the Spanish cause as part of their political opposition to the Truman administration and as a way to harm a president who bore Franco considerable ill will.[160]

Not all of the activity in Congress in favor of Spain can be attributed exclusively to the professional network set up by Lequerica. Some institutions worked directly with Congress. The Pentagon, for example, shared so many aims with the pro-Francoists that in 1950 a secret meeting was held with McCarran, at his insistence. And many representatives worked to protect the interests of the leading economic sectors of their states, the most important of which was the cotton sector in the South, with Walter George and Tom Connally, from Georgia and Texas, respectively, controlling the Senate Foreign Relations Committee and the Senate Finance Committee; Burnet Maybank, from South Carolina, chairman of the Banking Committee; and Kenneth McKellar, chairman of the Appropriations Committee. And among many other sectors that had pro-Franco sympathies were: silver mining, one of whose representatives was McCarran, born and bred in Nevada, a state that also produced cotton; companies importing cork, mercury, olives and luxury goods from Spain; industries interested in selling their machinery to Spain; oil companies; promoters of the expansion and modernization of airports in the United States and abroad, also involving McCarran and Brewster, who was hand in glove with Juan Trippe of Pan American Airlines; and banking interests.

As far as the paid lobbyists were concerned, the lawyer Patrick Francis Clark soon became their most visible member. He was brought into the team on the insistence of Father Thorning, who Clark went on to employ with

---

[160] "Another group in favor of sending aid to Spain is the militant Republican Party coalition, totally opposed to Acheson. Most of the 35 votes for Brewster's amendment came from this group, including its leaders, Taft, Wherry, Bridges and McCarthy. Their motives in this case are similar to their motives for supporting Nationalist China. Spain is a stick with which to beat the Administration and can be used to demonstrate the Department's 'weakness' vis-à-vis the Communists ('If we recognize the Russians, why not the Spanish?'). Following Clark's lead, this group claims that it was Alger Hiss who started the campaign against Franco. Finally, since the beginning of the Spanish Civil War these people looked on Franco's 'stable,' 'orderly' regime as preferable to the 'radical' Republican Government. The Spanish question fits neatly into the frame Roosevelt-Yalta-Hiss-Communism." Shannon, "The Franco Lobby"....

another "hefty monthly wage."[161] They worked together until 1953, when Clark stopped payments and Thorning, in a fit of anger, refused to work for the embassy anymore. According to Lequerica, this did not "cause too much trouble."[162] Officially, according to the register of the Department of Justice, Clark was employed as the representative of the embassy's cultural relations adviser Pablo Merry del Val.[163]

Clark was a Catholic of Irish origin. Born in New York in 1907, he studied at the Jesuit universities of Fordham and Georgetown, from which he graduated with honors. He started work at the embassy on 31 January 1949 with an annual salary of $50,000 plus expenses in the capacity of "special legal adviser in the Section of Cultural Relations of the Spanish Embassy," and his functions were to "promote and stimulate friendly relations and good will between the United States and Spain through discussions with members of the American press, Congress and the executive branch of the government." His appointment looked promising, given his previous close relationship with President Truman – at that time only Senator Truman – under whom he had worked in what was known as the Senate Truman Committee in the capacity of associate chief counsel to Chief Counsel Hugh Fulton. With the official name of the Senate Special Committee to Investigate Contracts Under the National Defense Program, this committee had been set up in March 1941 to oversee the contractors working for the armed forces and had very soon shown that it was highly efficient at correcting excesses and profiteering. It saved the country enormous amounts of money. After the United States had entered the war, it became the Special Committee to Investigate the National Defense Program and, once again, proved to be highly efficient. When it was first set up, it had ten investigators and ten members of the administrative staff but it gradually grew in both size and budget, although Truman himself stepped down from the leadership to concentrate on his electoral campaign as vice-president to President Roosevelt.[164] His work at the head of the committee had made him popular and well-respected and was largely the reason why Roosevelt had chosen him as his right-hand man. Another member, who joined the committee in 1943 after being wounded in combat, was General Harry Hawkins Vaughan, a friend of Truman's from Missouri and a fellow soldier during the First World War. He had been Truman's secretary when he was senator and his military aide once he became president. Vaughan was pro-Franco and by 1949 he was

---

[161] Lequerica to Martín Artajo, 14 May 1953, Ministry of Foreign Affairs Record Group, Head of State, file number 72–07661, AGA.

[162] Ibid.

[163] Cava Mesa, *Los diplomáticos de Franco* ..., 286.

[164] Subsequently, the leadership fell to the pro-Franco senator, Robert Owen Brewster, who was to lead a high-profile (and unsuccessful) attempt to frame Howard Hughes. The Committee was disbanded in 1948.

THE STRUGGLE TO CHANGE U.S. POLICY TOWARD FRANCO'S SPAIN   125

already a friend of Lequerica's and closer to Truman than Clark was. Even so, Clark was to remain in his job, paid by the embassy, until well into the 1960s.[165]

As for Thorning, who was subcontracted by Clark, he practiced in Maryland and had been fervently pro-Franco ever since the Spanish Civil War. A radical anti-communist,[166] he had tirelessly spread propaganda in favor of the so-called "national" side by organizing numerous events, writing articles, and taking part in campaigns, the most important of which had been to force President Roosevelt to lift his embargo on the sale of arms to Spain. As soon as the Second World War had ended, he had come out against Truman's policy on Spain, believing that it was based on an Allied proposal and, therefore, Soviet-inspired. In 1949, this interpretation was gaining ground because the pro-Franco U.S. media were attributing the intellectual authorship of the U.S. vote in the UN resolution of 1946 to Alger Hiss, a civil servant working for the State Department who was on trial on suspicion of being a communist spy. And since the resolution had been passed, Thorning had been campaigning to have it lifted, publishing letters in newspapers with a wide readership – particularly the *New York Times* – giving lectures or sending letters to congressmen (who had sometimes included favorable mentions of Spain in their speeches).[167]

Immediately after Clark was taken on, in February the second big contract was awarded by the embassy to the corporate lawyers Cummings, Stanley, Truitt & Cross, one of the most important law firms in Washington.[168] This firm was probably chosen because of its indirect institutional importance. One of its partners, Max O'Reill Truitt, was the son-in-law of Truman's recently appointed vice-president, Alben W. Barkley, while another, Homer Cummings – president of the firm – had been attorney general. Yet another partner, Albert J. Reeves Jr., was the son of a notorious federal judge who had been entrusted with the case against Judith Coplon, one of the three cases in the media spotlight against (real[169] or alleged) communist spies in the service of the Soviet Union who had been public employees or high-ranking officials. The

---

[165] Correspondence between Garrigues and Castiella dated 4 March, 2 April, 15 and 22 October 1963, and 24 February 1964. Also a letter from Castiella to Garrigues dated 16 March 1963 in the Antonio Garrigues and Díaz-Cañabate Collection, General Archive of the University of Navarre.

[166] Thorning also had a lot of connections in Chile, where he had been a lecturer at the Catholic University (Santiago).

[167] Personal interview on 28 October 1966. A. J. Dorley Jr., *The Role of Congress in the Establishment of Bases in Spain*, Ph.D. dissertation, St. John's University, 1969.

[168] Shannon, "The Franco Lobby"....

[169] Recent historiography points to Hiss as actually being a member of a Soviet espionage network in the United States. Cited in Montero-León, *Los Estados Unidos...*, 326.

126   JOAN MARIA THOMÀS

other two cases were against Alger Hiss (mentioned above) and Whittaker Chambers.

Like Clark, the law firm was registered in the Section of Foreign Agents of the Justice Department, and was contracted to provide services of consultancy on "normal relations" between the United States and Spain, to act as a liaison with the State Department "when necessary," and to work on "maintaining friendly relations" between the two countries.[170] At the beginning of the contract, the embassy paid the firm $4000 up front to cover initial expenses.[171] But before they did, they relieved William Smith Culbertson, the former ambassador, member of the military, and brother of the *chargé d'affaires ad interim* in Madrid, Paul Trauger Culbertson, of his duties of legal – not political – representation. According to Lequerica's account of events, which coincides with direct sources,[172] they decided on this course of action because the lawyer himself claimed that there were issues of incompatibility with his brother (although this is difficult to believe because at that time he did not hold a post in the department). Whatever the case may be, from this point on, the "inspector" believed him to be resentful and that the dismissal was one of the reasons why his brother, the *chargé* in Madrid, felt such animosity towards him.[173]

[170] E. A. Harris, "Ya no nos hace falta Franco, pero continúa el pasilleo en Washington a favor del dirigente español," *St. Louis Post Dispatch*, 4 June 1949.

[171] The contract was dated 31 January 1949 and was signed by Baráibar in accordance with Lequerica's instructions. He was to be paid $2000 a month plus expenses as counsel for the Spanish embassy. The rate was lowered on 22 May 1951 to $1000 per month: Letter from Cummings to Lequerica, 22 May 1951, Government Presidency Record Group, file number 54–08869, AGA.

[172] When asked to leave his post because he was the brother of the *chargé d'affaires* in Madrid, he had expressed his surprise and stated that, after being appointed during the Cárdenas period, he had been doing less work until Lequerica had called him back: Memorandum of Conversation Theodor C. Achilles-William S. Culbertson, 19 July 1948, U.S. Embassy Madrid, Classified General Records 1940–1963, RG 84, NARA-2.

[173] "One of the reasons for the hostility of the American C. [the code name he used in his correspondence with Martín Artajo Lequerica, the other C. being the former ambassador to Washington, Francisco de Cárdenas] was that his brother had been removed from the post of legal adviser to the Embassy. He resigned stubbornly and emphatically, saying that the Department had required him to do so because of incompatibility with his brother. Only then was a new appointment made, the Vice President's son-in-law [Truitt], and God knows that we should have been thankful for the replacement. But later, I think he found that he was out of his league. I heard that the brother lawyer had some misgivings about the new appointee, his political influences, etc., etc." Letter from Lequerica to Martín Artajo, 3 May 1949, file 12749, AFNFF.

THE STRUGGLE TO CHANGE U.S. POLICY TOWARD FRANCO'S SPAIN   127

According to the contract, the law firm Cummings, Stanley, Truitt & Cross would act as "general counselor for the Embassy of Spain" and they would be paid $30,000 per year.[174] The members of the firm entrusted with dealing with Spanish affairs were Truitt himself and one of the staff members, Albert Reeves Jr., a former Republican representative for Missouri.[175] Truitt was one of the best-paid lobbyist lawyers in Washington and, as mentioned above, he also represented General Trujillo's Dominican Republic, the major Argentine shipping companies, and several oil companies.[176]

The relations between the professional lobbyists in Spanish pay and the leading pro-Franco congressmen were not always harmonious and, in some cases, they never were. Clark, for example, was against McCarran going to Spain on his own and not as part of the congressional trip organized by the embassy in September–October 1949 (the so-called "Plan Otoño"). And McCarran distrusted Clark, for reasons we cannot be sure of, but probably because they were competing with each other in their dealings with the embassy.[177]

As far as the results obtained are concerned, there is some controversy in the scant American historiography on the issue about the role these paid lobbyists, especially Clark, actually played in the successes of the Franco regime in the U.S. Congress. For Albert Joseph Dorley Jr., Clark's involvement was fundamental. According to this author, "he worked particularly closely with Senator Pat McCarran, the powerful House member Eugene Keogh, Speaker McCormack, Senator Owen Brewster, and Senator Styles Bridges."[178] Riley William Gilmore, however, casts doubt on this and attributes the successes to McCarran or to pressure from the Pentagon. But he points out that Clark did manage to improve Franco's reputation in the United States, in an environment of Cold War escalation and rampant anti-communism, and he praised him for focusing on congressmen who were initially undecided or had no clear position on Spain.[179] Gilmore's assessment seems to be a good reflection of what really happened.

---

[174] "[The firm] is responsible for a lot of conventional legal work for the embassy and also handles the ongoing negotiations for a loan from the Export-Import Bank": Shannon, *The Reporter*, 20 June 1950.

[175] Ibid.

[176] According to Shannon, his "many clients and his delicate personal relationship with the vice-president" prevented him from "making all the congressional contacts he needed." So Clark had been hired for this purpose, although this did not prevent him from "discreetly" doing "his bit of lobbying at the highest levels as well.": Ibid.

[177] Letter from McCarran to Eva Adams, 26 October 1949, 82–11/IV/1, box 28, Eva B. Adams Papers, University of Nevada-Reno.

[178] Dorley Jr., *The Role of Congress* ..., 138.

[179] Gilmore, *American Foreign Policy-Making* ..., 202: "The work of the Spanish lobby (mainly of Charles Patrick Clark) was less significant than that of McCarran or the military. Still, Clark appeared to be successful in reconstructing the image of

The occasional "successes" of the Francoists in Congress can only be explained by factors such as the outstanding pro-Spanish operations led by senators McCarran and Brewster; the plotting and scheming of those working at the embassy or in the embassy's pay with Congress, the administration, and the press; the pressure of some sectors of the Pentagon, led by the U.S. navy and the U.S. air force; the pressure exerted on congressmen by economic and financial sectors with interests in Spain, or the personal crusade of the congressmen from southern or western states, where numerous economic sectors (particularly the cotton growers) were interested in trade with Spain; and the efforts of financiers and businessmen who made up what we have called the Spanish Bloc, and whose main interest was to do business with the Franco regime. Most notable among the latter were James A. Farley, of Coca-Cola, who continued to be a leading light in the Democratic party and in continuous contact with Franco,[180] but also Eric Johnston (Motion Picture Association of America), Alfred W. Barth (Chase National Bank), and the cotton grower Frank T. Ryan.

But, as we shall see later, and as we shall make clear now, the change in policy on Spain implemented by Truman and Acheson in 1950 was not motivated in the least by the occasional successes of friendly congressmen or lobbyists hired by the embassy. Rather, it came about for strategic reasons related to the escalation of the Cold War in Korea and to the possibility of the outbreak of new conflicts, in view of which it was of utmost importance to have bases on Spanish soil.

In reaction to all this, at the end of 1949 the Basque delegate in Washington, Jesús Galíndez, attempted to organize the Basques and Spanish republicans in exile in the United States into an anti-Franco Spanish lobby. His initiative was modified by the *lehendakari* (the president of the Basque government), José Antonio Aguirre. Instead of "attracting men well placed in the North-American administration in an attempt to influence it," as Galíndez had hoped to do – probably taking inspiration from Lequerica, also a Basque – Aguirre suggested setting up a commission that would represent all Spaniards in exile.

Franco Spain in the changing international environment. As the professional lobbyist, Clark avoided the attempt to convert the committed, but sought to persuade those who were on the borderline what American relations with Franco Spain should be in the context of a growing communist-anti-communist schism in the international environment. As such, he reenforced [sic] the strength of those individuals seeking to undermine current American policy towards Spain."

[180] See correspondence with Franco, with the head of the Civil Household Marquis of Huétor de Santillán and with General Secretary Francisco Franco Salgado-Araujo 1948–1955 in James A. Farley Papers, boxes 20, 21 and 22, Library of Congress Manuscript Division, Library of Congress. I am grateful to Pablo León Aguinaga for giving me access to this source.

THE STRUGGLE TO CHANGE U.S. POLICY TOWARD FRANCO'S SPAIN   129

This commission finally came into being in December 1949 and made contact with the unions AFL and CIO, with the association Americans for Democratic Action, with Michael Straight of *The New Republic,* with the journalist Charles Foltz and many others. But it was soon shut down because of lack of funds.[181]

Lequerica, the Embassy and the Second Session of the Third UN General Assembly in Spring 1949: Another Frustration

Although Lequerica was well aware that the new secretary of state, Acheson, had anti-Franco sentiments and left-wing views, he was not alarmed by his appointment in the slightest. On the contrary, he regarded it as a new possibility for Spain because his predecessor, Marshall, had been indecisive and lacking in conviction and was also afraid of Great Britain. He was confident that "the increasingly deceptive circumstances" – in a reference to the international political situation – would force Truman to adopt a "more reasonable" policy on Spain. His main source of information was the former first secretary of the embassy in Madrid and the head of the United States Commercial Corporation in Spain during the Second World War, William W. Butterworth. Some months later, he was appointed assistant secretary of state for far eastern affairs and he praised Acheson for his "extraordinary intelligence and rectitude."[182] Consequently, on 3 February 1949, Lequerica unofficially sent the State Department an aide-mémoire signed by the *chargé d'affaires* Baráibar – although it had in fact been drafted by the law firm Cummings, Stanley, Truitt & Cross[183] – demanding "the renewal of full diplomatic relations with Spain by the United States."[184] The aide merited no response from the department, however, because of the unofficial channel by which it was delivered.

In April and May, the second session of the UN's third General Assembly was to be held in Lake Success (New York), and the information the embassy had was encouraging. Culbertson, the *chargé d'affaires,* had told Pedro de Prat y Soutzo, marquess of Prat de Nantouillet and director general of America at the Ministry of Foreign Affairs, that

> ever since the Paris meeting, and also partly because of the evolution of the international political situation, it has been clear that our country

[181] I. Bernardo and I. Goiogana, *Galíndez: la tumba abierta. Guerra, exilio y frustración,* Bilbao, Sabino Arana Fundazioa, 2006, 182–184.

[182] Lequerica to Martín Artajo, 10 January 1949, Leg. 23596, AFNFF.

[183] "I will tell you 'off the record' that it was prepared by the legal firm of Cummings, Stanley, Truitt and Cross." Letter from Lequerica to Brewster, 29 April 1949, Ralph Owen Brewster Papers, Bowdoin College Library.

[184] Embassy of Spain, Aide-Mémoire to the State Department, 3 February 1949, Ralph Owen Brewster Papers, Bowdoin College Library.

130   JOAN MARIA THOMÀS

will come out victorious. Even the British Labour party now sees the Soviets as a real danger.[185]

Meanwhile, in the United States, the press attaché Cacho Zabalza had been called to New York by a member of the U.S. delegation of the UN, Ambassador Francis P. Corrigan, to give him detailed information about U.S. strategy on the Spanish question in an attempt to reverse the points of the 1946 resolution on full diplomatic representation in Spain and Spain's admittance to UN commissions and specialized agencies.[186]

In his explanation to Minister Martín Artajo, Lequerica said, according to Corrigan, that the United States was prepared

> for the 1946 recommendation not to appoint heads of mission in Spain to be done away because of the ineffectiveness of the measure, the lack of compliance by some members of the Organization and the fact that the Security Council has stated that Spain does not represent a danger to world peace.

However, the United States was not prepared

> to make any effort to put an end to the discourse against the Regime [...] so as not to hurt the feelings of the governments of the European block who fear it might have an effect on public opinion. The new agreement will only extend the procedure agreed to in Bogotá for continental [American] countries that governments can be recognized even though they are not approved.[187]

As far as Britain was concerned, he said that the country "has prepared and is preparing public opinion to approve the proposal to abolish the recommendation" because it is ineffective and because the presence of heads of mission in Madrid "may help the Spanish regime return to the community of democracies without focusing on time or person." On the other hand, France finally abstained after keeping its vote secret until the last minute. According to the ambassador, the policy of his country in the UN was to maintain the prestige of the organization and for this very reason the State Department had advised the Latin American countries who had expressed the desire to normalize their relations with Spain to wait until the General Assembly changed the 1946

[185] Marquis of Prat de Nantouillet to Martín Artajo, 21 March 1949, Ministry of Foreign Affairs Record Group, file number 82–05987, AGA.

[186] Lequerica to Martín Artajo, 23 March 1949, Ministry of Foreign Affairs Record Group, file number 82–05987, AGA.

[187] Attached document with no date or signature, Presidency of the Government Record Group, file number 82–05987, AGA.

THE STRUGGLE TO CHANGE U.S. POLICY TOWARD FRANCO'S SPAIN   131

resolution. And, given Brazil's very public desire to present a new proposal favoring Spanish interests, he immediately went on to recommend that the Spanish delegation should "work on" getting Chile's and Uruguay's vote. On the other hand, he assumed that Mexico would vote against any such proposal as would the "revolutionary juntas" (as he called them) that had popped up in several countries in Central America, afraid of being branded as "fascists" if they voted in favor. Likewise, he expected Venezuela to abstain, and Costa Rica and El Salvador to vote against.

On the basis of this information, Lequerica and the embassy designed what they called a "plan of attack" for the next General Assembly by which they hoped to sway the more friendly delegations and some of the others they believed could be brought round to their way of thinking. Their initial premise was the following:

> Bearing in mind the interest that the United States has in the United Nations Organization, we should avoid attacking it in any way and we should take advantage of any opportunity to show that Spain is not hostile to the Organization although we are clearly against the resolution (of 1946). Neither should we criticize the North Atlantic Treaty, although we should make it clear that we regret not having been invited to join. This elegant attitude will satisfy the United States.

They also argued that they needed to

> make the American States understand that the Spanish Republicans are no such thing; rather they are Russian agents who are trying to turn Spain into a Soviet bastion, as they had tried to do when they were in power, which is why the Civil War broke out.

And they went on:

> We have to show that the proposals and attacks against Spain have always been Soviet-inspired. We must show that all votes have been the result of Soviet pressure. We must show that the information in possession of the UN General Secretary against Spain has been provided by Spanish Republicans, constant satellites of theirs, and that under the guise of democracy they are the real Soviet wolf [...] Among other things, the Reds have proposed to make wide-ranging democratic changes in Spain, and they have entered into agreements with the Western bloc to do so.

They believed that the attacks on the regime in the General Assembly would be of a different nature:

132 JOAN MARIA THOMÀS

> Unlike other occasions, instead of focusing on acts of repression, [...]
> they are going to target political-economic issues: items on the state
> budget for funding a political party [the Falange], which is totali-
> tarianism; the financing of the armed wing of this same party [the
> militia]; the role of the political junta [of the Falange] and its funding;
> the role of the National Council [of the Falange] and its funding; the
> civil governors and how they are appointed; the National Institute
> for Industry and the distribution syndicates, which not only suffocate
> private industry but also cut off private initiative and subject it to
> possible political reprisals.[188]

On the other hand, the official position of the United States had been established in March in a memorandum submitted by Hickerson to Assistant Secretary of State Dean Rusk.[189] So everything seemed to be going well for Franco's Spain. In fact, even one of the delegates, Ray Atherton – Secretary Acheson's right-hand man – had publicly announced that he was in favor of supporting the Brazilian proposal.[190]

But things went awry. There was a rebellion in the ranks of the American delegation. The rebels were supported by both Acheson and President Truman because the Franco regime had not made any of the political or economic changes that had been demanded, because there was no support from the British and French governments, and because of their own anti-Francoism. To make matters worse, the "rebels" were not merely diplomatic officials. One of their number was none other than Eleanor Roosevelt, the president's widow and a reference for American anti-fascism. The "rebellion" had taken place during a meeting of the delegation on 17 April when some of its members had questioned the advisability of following Hickerson's memorandum and argued that it posed a problem of communication between them and the State Department since they were not willing simply to obey orders.

As ambassador to the UN and head of the delegation, Warren Austin, told Acheson that three members – out of a total of five – had refused to follow the State Department's directive. One of these was Mrs Roosevelt, who believed that the directive meant bowing down to "the opinions of military sectors" and because it was in fact "an indirect way of recognizing Franco by providing Spain with concrete assistance, albeit not through the European Recovery Program but though private channels." She also believed that public opinion in the United States could accept "a more indulgent policy on Germany and

---

[188] Ibid.

[189] Memorandum by the Director of the Office of European Affairs (Hickerson) to the Assistant Secretary of State (Rusk), Secret, Washington, 4 March 1949, FRUS 1949, Western Europe, vol. IV, 731–734.

[190] Harold Ickes, "A State Department Shell Game," *The New Republic*, 8 August 1949, 16.

Italy since Hitler and Mussolini are no longer in power but Franco is and the Spanish government has not changed in the slightest since the resolution of the General Assembly in 1946." If the guidelines laid down by the department were followed, she went on, they could create difficulties for the democratic governments in Western Europe "by giving solid arguments to the Communist opposition who would use any modification in the resolution against Franco for its own ends."[191] In other words, in her opinion, which was also Austin's, a favorable vote could be interpreted in Western Europe and in working-class sectors "as an ominous indication that the United States was forgetting how dangerous the right-wing dictatorship could be."[192]

The second of the "rebel" delegates was John Foster Dulles, the Republican who could have been secretary of state if Dewey had won the elections. He believed that "the position of the United States would be much more solid if it strongly opposed all forms of totalitarianism, both Fascist and Communist." He also felt that it would be unfortunate "to give the impression that we are joining forces with Fascist totalitarianism for purposes of military convenience, particularly in this situation and in light of the recent signing of the Atlantic Treaty." Nevertheless, he also believed that if "for military or security reasons it is necessary to change our attitude towards Spain, the delegation can do little more than agree." The third disobedient delegate, Benjamin V. Cohen, agreed with Mrs Roosevelt that "the moral position of the United States in Western Europe would be weakened by any change in the United States's attitude to Spain." He believed that other countries may draw the conclusion that "we were taking the initiative on this policy, particularly in light of the fact that opinion in Latin America was divided."

Apparently, the other members of the delegation were in favor of following the directives sent by the State Department, although we only know the reasons given by Dr Philip C. Jessup. He argued that "after examining the documents on our Spanish policy in the Department I did not agree that it was largely based on military factors [...] The Resolution of 1946 had not fulfilled its purpose; it had strengthened Franco not weakened him."[193] Another member, the president of the Senate Foreign Relations Committee, Tom Connally, agreed with him, and stated subsequently that he had been forced to back down.

---

[191] The U.S. Representative at the United Nations (Austin) to the Secretary of State, New York, 13 April 1949, 8:57 pm, FRUS 1949, vol. IV, 738.

[192] EFE Washington, 20 December. And he went on: "I have it on good authority that Mrs Roosevelt and Cohen have informed the State Department that they would now be in favor of setting aside the 1946 Resolution, as long as a new resolution makes it clear that the reintroduction of heads of mission in Madrid does not mean an endorsement of the Franco regime."

[193] The U.S. Representative at the United Nations (Austin) to the Secretary of State, New York, 13 April 1949, 8:57 pm, FRUS 1949, vol. IV, 738.

134   JOAN MARIA THOMÀS

As a result of the controversy, Austin suggested that the delegation should vote "for the Resolution's regulation on specialized bodies as well as for the repeal of the proposal on the heads of missions."[194] After consulting with President Truman, Secretary Acheson gave his approval. The president was particularly satisfied with this because it was a significant reduction in the delegation's initial intentions and would be detrimental to the Franco regime.[195] It was agreed, then, that the delegation would abstain from voting to amend the 1946 resolution in terms of the return of ambassadors but would vote in favor of Spain's participation in the UN's specialized agencies as long as the agencies in question believed that Spain could make a contribution to their specific objectives.[196]

It was in these circumstances that, between 4 and 7 May, the UN debated the issue of Spain in the First Committee, which deals with political and security issues. Plans for two resolutions were discussed. The first, put forward by Poland, reasserted the 1946 resolution and the fascist nature of the Franco regime, and accused the United States and the United Kingdom of reinforcing their political and economic ties with Spain and recommending all member states to abstain from selling arms or signing agreements or treaties with the country. The second, presented by Brazil with the support of Bolivia, Colombia, and Peru, argued that the 1946 resolution had failed in its primary purpose and proposed giving "member states full liberty of action as far as their relations with Spain were concerned."

In the ensuing debates, the United States was accused by the Polish, Soviet, Yugoslavian, and Belarusian representatives of supporting Franco militarily, economically and politically. These accusations were denied by the Assembly delegate, Ray Atherton. And when the time came to vote on 7 May, the committee rejected the Polish proposal and accepted the Brazilian one by twenty-five votes for, sixteen against and sixteen abstentions, among which were the United States, the United Kingdom, and France. This meant that the votes in favor did not reach the two-thirds majority required for the proposal to be adopted by the General Assembly, so things remained just as they were. Once again, the expectations of Spain, Lequerica, and the embassy had been frustrated.

Franco and his government were extremely irritated by the abstentions of the three Western Allies, particularly the United States, because of the expectations that had been created. In fact, they had found out how the United States was going to vote a few days before the session (on 2 May) when Culbertson had informed a high-ranking member of the Ministry of Foreign

[194] Ibid.

[195] Edwards, *Anglo-American Relations ...,* 142.

[196] The Secretary of State to the United States Mission at the United Nations, Secret, Washington, 20 April 1949, noon, FRUS 1949, vol. IV, 743.

THE STRUGGLE TO CHANGE U.S. POLICY TOWARD FRANCO'S SPAIN 135

Affairs of the latest intentions of his country's delegation.[197] The abstentions of Great Britain and France were equally irritating because at that time they were engaged in trade talks with Spain. And in hindsight Franco expressed the view that the draft resolution submitted by Brazil should have been withdrawn so as not to lose the vote (by not reaching the two-thirds majority) and the only result of the meeting would have been the rejection of the resolution submitted by Poland. Franco could have presented this as a success. While he was particularly irritated by the abstentions of Great Britain and France,[198] he was very careful when he referred to the United States during the opening of the Spanish parliament in Madrid on 18 May.[199] Lequerica subsequently explained that Dulles had refused to follow orders because of his professional relationship with the businessman Dannie Heineman, the administrator of the Belgian holding company Société Financière de Transports et Enterprises Industrielles-SOFINA, the majority shareholder in Barcelona Traction Light & Power, a company that since 1948 had been involved in lawsuits with the Spanish financier Juan March. He always referred to Heineman as the "Israelite."

The State Department's Change of Mind about the Export-Import Bank Granting Official Loans to Spain

In parallel to its position on the UN resolution of 1946, the State Department also decided to change its mind about not allowing Spain access to loans by the Export-Import Bank (that is to say, official economic aid).[200] This decision had been influenced by the reports sent by Culbertson from Madrid, which described the country's catastrophic economic and financial situation, which had been aggravated by a drought. For the third year in a row, harvests had been 40 per cent down, and factories in Catalonia had only six hours of electricity a day.[201] But, despite the change of mind, the department had also expressed doubts about the ability of Spain to make the repayments and pointed out that this ability would be assessed in the minutest of detail before

[197] Written communication dated 3 May 1949 about a conversation held the previous day at an after-dinner conversation between Culbertson, the Director General of America, the Marquis of Prat de Nantouillet, and Ambassador Domingo de las Bárcenas, Ministry of Foreign Affairs Record Group, file number 82–05987, AGA.

[198] The *Chargé* in Spain (Culbertson) to the Secretary of State, Confidential, Madrid, 23 May 1949, no. 267. Conversation with Ambassador Nicholas Franco, brother of the Chief of State, FRUS 1949, vol. IV, 747.

[199] *La Vanguardia*, 19 May 1949.

[200] Secretary of State to Culbertson, 13 April 1949, FRUS 1949, Western Europe, vol. IV, 736.

[201] Culbertson to Acheson 17 February 1949 FRUS 1949, Western Europe, vol. IV, 730.

any loans were granted. Spain would also be required to make economic reforms – although not necessarily beforehand – one of which was to do away with the cap on the foreign share in Spanish companies. As Acheson explained to Culbertson on 13 April, Spanish companies would be able to apply for loans from the Export-Import Bank, but in the same conditions as other countries and always as a function of their ability to repay the amounts borrowed. In return, he asked Culbertson to convince Franco of the need to make another change in the peseta/dollar exchange rate, reduce the influence of Spain's National Institute of Industry (INI) on the economy, and, as mentioned, to suppress the limit on the foreign share in Spanish companies.[202] Two days before, on 11 April, President Truman had agreed to lift the veto on U.S. public loans. This was an important step forward.

The "Spanish Question" in the Senate and the Reactions of Acheson and Truman (May–June 1949)

Now that the change in the policy of official loans, albeit restricted to companies, had opened a window of opportunity, Lequerica, the embassy, all those in the pay of Spain, and the congressmen with Spanish sympathies redoubled their efforts to persuade the Truman administration to make a general change in policy so that the Franco regime could become a part of the Western Bloc, which meant the Marshall Plan and the North Atlantic Treaty, the UN, and economic and military aid.

A few days after the UN vote, the two congressmen closest to Lequerica – McCarran and Brewster – set to work with a will for the first time in the Senate. And the Spanish Lobby did likewise in the House of Representatives. McCarran and Brewster's activities in the Senate prompted the secretary of state to issue a press release, which was responded to not only by the two senators in question but also by Madrid, in the form of a lengthy *note verbale* from the Ministry of Foreign Affairs delivered to Culbertson, and by a leading light in the Falange, the national delegate for syndicates Fermín Sanz-Orrio. And in the United States the two pro-Franco movements also prompted a public response from President Truman. As a result of all this, by the end of spring 1949 the "Spanish question" increasingly began to be a part of the political scene in the United States, which it had not been since the Spanish Civil War, albeit on a somewhat smaller scale.

Of the two reactions to the UN vote in Congress, the most forceful was that of senators McCarran and Brewster, apparently acting on their own initiative but in reality in connivance with Lequerica and the embassy. They were so openly indignant that they initiated a debate among the members of a commission who had no say in the matter at all. The debate that took place in the House

[202] The Secretary of State to the embassy in Spain, 13 April 1949, FRUS 1949, Western Europe, vol. IV, 735–737.

THE STRUGGLE TO CHANGE U.S. POLICY TOWARD FRANCO'S SPAIN   137

of Representatives was not so visible or important and it was instigated by the congressmen in the pay of the lobby. And there were more pro-Spanish pronouncements outside the House by congressmen who opposed the president, who had political and ideological agendas of their own, or who had simply agreed with the delegation's position before the change in policy. They were indignant and they expressed themselves with vehemence. Among the influential senators who spoke out were Robert A. Taft from Ohio, chairman of the Republican Political Committee; Arthur H. Vandenberg from Michigan, also a Republican and chairman of the Foreign Relations Committee in 1947; and the Democrat senator for Texas Tom Connally, chairman of the Foreign Relations Committee at that time. After Acheson and the president himself had responded to these pronouncements, battle lines were well and truly drawn.

However, Lequerica had to pay the price for his scheming. The State Department started to ask questions about exactly what he was doing in the United States and put pressure on the Spanish Ministry of Foreign Affairs to have him withdrawn and returned to Spain. And, incredibly, the department seemed to have support not only in the ministry but also, even more surprisingly, in the embassy in Washington. Lequerica had become a thorn in the flesh of the department and he was within an inch of being forced to leave.

Nonetheless, this tension merely indicated that his activism was working both inside and outside Congress, and always to the detriment of the Truman administration. Inside, the well-disposed congressmen and the lobbyists in his pay were working for the same cause and, outside, the businessmen, corporations, and economic sectors hoping to engage in business with Spain in the future and who shared Franco's anti-communism, Catholicism, strategic vision, and other interests were assisted by the activism of some of the media (for example, Hearst and much of the Catholic press). Also contributing to the cause were intellectuals of well-earned (but waning) prestige such as the former ambassador, Carlton Hayes, and some top-ranking Catholics such as Cardinal Spellman, who came out publicly against the government by attacking Eleanor Roosevelt (no less) for having supported the Spanish "Reds and Communists."[203]

It all began on 9 May, when Senator McCarran started the ball rolling in the Senate, in collusion with Brewster and in agreement with Lequerica and Baráibar.[204] In fact, by that time the inspector was already boasting to Minister Martín Artajo that he was engaged in the "fruitful task" of setting

---

[203] Jarque Iñiguez,*"Queremos esas bases" ...,* 251.

[204] As regards McCarran, a letter from General Charles A. Willoughby (apparently to Minister Martín Artajo, but not recorded on the document) dated 15 June 1949 is relevant. It reads: "I believe that Baráibar and Lequerica were somewhat misled by Senator McCarran's enthusiasm. I do not doubt the Senator's good faith, but American politicians are capable of being aggressive at times when patience is indicated. However,

up "a parliamentary movement to support our interests."[205] But before taking a stand McCarran and the president of the Appropriations Subcommittee had met with the secretary of state himself and his aides to ask them to change their policy towards Spain. To no avail. He had then decided to take the initiative, realizing that he was a link in a chain of events: the House of Representatives was soon to vote on U.S. membership of the North Atlantic Treaty Organization (NATO). Both he and Brewster were banking on Spain also being a member, inclusion in the Marshall Plan, and the appointment of an ambassador to Madrid. They did not achieve any of these goals, but they did achieve considerable propaganda success.

The setting chosen by McCarran to make his move was a meeting of the Senate Budget Committee that was scheduled to discuss the budgets proposed for the Treasury Department and the Postal Service. He initiated a debate there that can hardly be called a debate because all those present were in agreement. Senator Connally, in particular, stood out for his forcefulness and the revelations he made.

Specifically, McCarran requested that a newspaper article published that morning in the *New York Times*, entitled "Capitol Stuff" and authored by John O'Donnell,[206] be read and discussed as part of the proceedings of the session. The ploy was somewhat bizarre and, of course, quite unusual, but it worked. Moreover, the fact that he used this course of action shows how relevant it was. The article in question was highly critical of the administration and was published alongside a more measured editorial in the same newspaper – "The U.N. and Spain"[207] – which was also read during the session, in this case at Brewster's request.[208]

The two senators intended to give visibility to their criticism not only of the U.S. delegation's abstention at Lake Success but of the Truman administration's general policy towards the Franco regime, which they portrayed in the session as a champion of anti-communism and a democracy (presumably simply because it was not communist). They also denounced that the United States had voted in line with its Western allies, particularly Great Britain and France. They pointed out that both countries had socialist governments but, even so, were trading with Franco's Spain, while the United States was being excluded from that market. For example, Spain was purchasing cotton from

---

they have many powerful friends in Washington and this matter will resolve itself very soon." File 23600, AFNFF.

[205] Lequerica to Martín Artajo, 29 June 1949, Ministry of Affairs Record Group, file number 82–05987, AGA.

[206] *New York Times*, 9 May 1949.

[207] *New York Times*, 9 May 1949.

[208] At the request of McCarran and Brewster, both articles were incorporated into the Senate's *Journal of Sessions*.

Egypt: that is to say, a sterling area, ultimately supported by the dollar. The debate was lengthy and the only dissenting voice was that of the Democratic senator from Virginia, A. Willis Robertson, who noted that perhaps the lack of religious freedom in Spain might be hindering relations between the two countries (which was, of course, true). However, after hearing McCarran and Brewster's blunt – and false – explanations on the matter, he believed them.

McCarran also raised the issue of official loans. He claimed that Acheson had assured the Appropriations Committee that "the granting of credit to Spain is an uncertain and risky business" and then argued against him, stating that "trade between Spain and Great Britain last year amounted to the respectable sum of $450 million." He felt that this showed that Spanish credit was sound. In his opinion:

> while pounds sterling were in widespread use in trade between these two nations, the United States [...] spent last year, and will spend this year also, the sum of $5,000 million to stabilise the exchange rate of the currency of Great Britain. Consequently, Spain's uncertain and dangerous credit is made good and wholly reliable by the guarantee of the American dollar through an intermediate party, in this case Great Britain.

He concluded his argument by returning to the issue of Spain purchasing cotton from Egypt, which prompted an intervention from Burnet R. Maybank, a Democrat from South Carolina, who introduced himself as "coming from the cotton-producing industry." He said that both he and Connally, the chairman of the Foreign Relations Committee and senator for Texas (another cotton state), had submitted a bill to the Banking and Currency Committee, authored by the latter, urging the Export-Import Bank to grant loans to Spain on similar terms to those granted to other countries, such as Italy and France. And he thanked McCarran for initiating the debate on Spain that day.

For his part, McCarran explained one of the reasons why he supported Spain:

> [I]n the last two years Nevada has become a major competitor in the production of cotton fiber and is surprisingly already rivalling the states of California and Arizona. So, all the representatives of both the West and the Great American South [...] today have the same interest in defending the countries that can buy our cotton and wish to know exactly where the final destination of our raw material is to be.

Maybank then explained that Spain had traditionally purchased the finest and best quality cotton, and Kenneth S. Wherry, a Republican from Nebraska, added that the United States had lost sales of 300,000 bales of cotton to Spain as a result of the UN resolution of December 1946. And that, when he had asked why Spain had not been admitted as a beneficiary of the Economic Cooperation Administration, Acheson had replied that:

> [S]ome countries in Europe [...] were opposed to Spain being included in the group of beneficiaries, and so he asked: why should we go to all the trouble of restricting the granting of loans to Spain if it pays its debts and, likewise, why should we put up with the ECA beneficiary nations preventing us from extending our aid to Spain by imposing conditions that are not imposed by the United States?

Immediately, McCarran intervened again, saying that he was also unable to explain

> why a democratic nation and a democratic and God-fearing people – and no one can deny that the Spanish people have had both these qualities for time immemorial – should be deprived of its right to receive the benefits of the ECA enjoyed by many other European nations, especially when the aim and purpose we are pursuing is that all nations should again be able to stand on their own two feet and be self-sufficient within a short period of time [...] If Spain is willing to join the Atlantic Treaty, if it wishes to be a member of the democratic nations of the world, as it has said that it does, why should we turn our backs on a great people, a great nation, and a great government precisely at a time when the United States is trying to bring together as many elements and resources as possible for our protection and to prevent a possible war?

And in reference to the Chase loan, which he did not mention by name, he added that in the last twenty-four hours a large private American bank with its headquarters in one of the large cities of the United States had just granted Spain a loan of considerable importance, which was in stark contrast with the administration's official position of not allowing public loans.

The debate then moved on to military and defense issues, with McCarran and other senators pointing out Spain's strategic importance. McCarran said that:

> I am neither a strategist nor a military expert [but] all strategists agree that there is nothing more essential to the military success of the North Atlantic Treaty – if indeed it aspires to military success – than the Iberian Peninsula. Nothing is more decisive and essential than the Iberian Peninsula – the main body of which is Spain – in the event, purely hypothetical for the moment, that we needed to cross it to get to North Africa.

He went on to say that he would "go even further [...] Not only would I give Spain diplomatic recognition, I would also try to flatter and please them as much as possible, so that they will feel like coming with us and marching by our side."

THE STRUGGLE TO CHANGE U.S. POLICY TOWARD FRANCO'S SPAIN   141

He also referred to Acheson's oft-repeated claim that Spain was a fascist state, stating that he did not care

> in the least if some fool, some stranger or some government official describes the present regime in Spain as Fascist. I sincerely doubt whether there is anyone with sufficient authority to make such a claim and whether it can be demonstrated with facts.

He also wondered, as Senator Kenneth McKellar, a Democrat from Tennessee, had asked Acheson earlier, whether Spain was not recognized because it was a Catholic country. Acheson had rejected the insinuation. And he explained, quite indignantly, that the previous week one of the delegates to the UN – John Foster Dulles – had appeared before the Foreign Relations Committee and claimed that the twelve signatory countries of the Atlantic Pact had pledged to vote together at the UN. At that point, the president of the Committee, Connally, joined the meeting and he confirmed what Dulles had said. He was extremely critical of what had happened at Lake Success, and in general of the Truman administration's treatment of the Franco regime. He said:

> I have never supported the withdrawal of our diplomatic representation in Spain. At the last UN meeting in New York – which I attended as a delegate – I was a member of the Committee which was charged with studying the resolution submitted by Poland – which recommended the total withdrawal of ambassadors and all kinds of diplomatic representatives, condemning Spain to total isolation. I strongly opposed the Polish proposal within the Committee, but, after several days of wrangling, the American Delegation and our Secretary of State forced me to back down and ordered me to abide by the Delegation's vote. Against my true feelings, I had no choice but to agree. They knew, however, what I thought, for I did not hesitate to proclaim it repeatedly in the Committee and before the Delegation. I think it is illogical to maintain diplomatic relations with Russia, for example, while refusing to establish diplomatic relations with Spain. If there is indeed any danger of a threat to peace in either of these two countries, it is clear that the more serious of the two is not Spain.

However, he also said that he did not approve of

> the present form of government in Spain, nor, of course, of the government in Russia. But [...] it has never occurred to us to demand the approval of foreign governments for our political theories as a basis for recognition or for the sending of diplomatic representations. We maintained normal diplomatic relations with Japan when it was a totalitarian state governed exclusively by the edicts of the Emperor. We also maintained diplomatic relations with Tsarist Russia. We continue to maintain diplomatic relations with the present government

142   JOAN MARIA THOMÀS

of the USSR [Soviet Union] despite its political and social theories and doctrines.

And, as an explanation of what was happening with Franco's Spain, he said that it could only be understood by bearing in mind that:

> in some foreign nations there is a deep aversion to the Franco regime, and it is quite possible that the pressure exerted by these nations has influenced the decision of our State Department and some other countries to deny Spain full official recognition and the right to an embassy. It is true that we have a *chargé d'affaires* in Madrid, but this can in no way be compared to an embassy.

He concluded by saying that "we know that Spain's form of government is different from ours, but this is Spain's business and nobody else's. The Spanish people have a perfect and undeniable right to adopt the form of government they want." Subsequently, Brewster pointed to Moscow as the inspiration behind the "opposition to the recognition of Spain", as well as its "close relationship with the Republican government of Spain [in exile]." He noted that if the Republicans had won the Civil War, "Moscow would have succeeded in establishing a bridgehead in the most important territorial area of the European continent." And he raised one of the issues that mattered most to him – and on which he clashed with the Truman administration: before the Senate approves NATO membership, should it not give

> serious consideration to the resumption of diplomatic relations with Spain, if it is our sincere desire to make the Atlantic Treaty a genuine concert of all those nations that are most likely to prevent World War III or to achieve victory in it if it cannot be avoided.

But even if Spain were not to be admitted to NATO, he was in favor of normalizing relations. Senator Dennis Chavez – Democrat from New Mexico and the first Hispanic senator in the history of Congress – immediately responded in the same vein by comparing the diplomatic relations with Hungary and Spain. He said:

> Despite our protests about what was done to Hungary and Cardinal Mindszenty, and although the present Spanish regime has never done anything like that to anyone, the fact is that we have an ambassador and maintain relations with the nation where the Cardinal was so cruelly tortured. Yet we have not yet sent an American ambassador to Spain because of the influence of the USSR [Soviet Union] in France, England, Italy, and other places. I see no logic at all in such a policy, which seems to me to be totally lacking in sincerity.

And he added that if there were one government in the world

THE STRUGGLE TO CHANGE U.S. POLICY TOWARD FRANCO'S SPAIN 143

that had truly fought Communism, then that is the government of Spain under its present regime. So I see no reason why we should be helping France while its soldiers are killing Chinese people in China, or why we should be helping the Netherlands to set up a dictatorship in Indonesia, while claiming that "we do not like Franco's government", which is why we withdrew our ambassador.

Brewster agreed with him by saying that "we have not withdrawn our ambassador from Hungary or even from countries where Protestant clergy are persecuted." And he raised a subject of great interest to him: airports. He said that during his visit to Madrid the previous September he had been aware of British and French pressures and that, "apart from the cotton problem" – about which he declared himself ill-informed "since it is not produced in my state, Maine" – he had learned in Madrid that the "government of Spain urgently wished to normalize our air relations [...] and acquire American material and equipment, both aircraft and ground services, which will be indispensable auxiliaries for the functioning of our air forces." However, England was also interfering in this matter,

> trying not only to sell, but almost to force the Spanish to purchase outdated British material, not only aircraft but also air installations and material for airfields, trying to get rid of material that they know will be of no use in the future.

He also pointed out, again in relation to what had happened at Lake Success a few days earlier, the contradiction that "all last autumn and winter we were told that the United States would not take any action [...] but would support whatever proposal was put forward" in favor of the partial withdrawal of the December 1946 resolution. But when a proposal was made, they had not complied. And, in contrast to the State Department's stance on the matter, he ended by raising the question of the importance of having an ambassador in Madrid:

> As I understand from the newspapers, our Secretary of State does not seem to attach any great importance or significance to whether or not we have an ambassador in Spain. Does he really think the American people are so stupid? Does he want us to believe that – despite his great diplomatic experience – he is ignorant of the enormous difference between an ambassador and a mere *chargé d'affaires*? And if there is no such difference, why do we not appoint an ambassador in Madrid? Moscow attaches great significance to the issue. Poland also thinks it is important in the UN. Why are they both so keen to torpedo the proposal if it is of no importance? Even those with little understanding of international law know that an ambassador is quite different from a *chargé d'affaires*. The former can go freely to the head of state and to the foreign minister, while the latter cannot visit the former and has

limited access to the latter, at least as long as we continue behaving as we are doing towards Spain. As the illustrious representative of Texas and the chairman of the Foreign Relations Committee said, the ambassadors we have abroad are not at the service of the countries they are sent to but of our own. Why do we have an embassy in Moscow? Certainly not to serve the Soviets, but in the hope that it can inform us and keep us abreast of what is going on there. Why, then, do we not have an ambassador in Madrid to inform and advise us – not for the benefit of Spain, but in the service of America and all the vital interests we have there? For all these reasons, I believe that the Senate would not be wasting its time if it were to take an hour to inform itself properly and from a direct source of the reasons why we think as we do. I hope that the frank statement by the Chairman of the Senate Foreign Relations Committee will be echoed and welcomed not only in the remotest parts of this country, but also overseas, in the chancelleries of Paris and London. London needs to know that the American people are no longer willing to subordinate our most vital interests to the machinations of those whose ideology or selfish commercial interests further prolong an attitude which the American people must now put a decisive end to.

The debate did not result in a resolution being passed because the issue was not on the agenda, but some senators (for example, Taft) made statements to the press. The blunt response to these statements came on 11 May from the secretary of state and highlighted the increasing distance between Congress and the administration on the question of Spain. During a press conference, he read a declaration that described the Franco regime as fascist and Spain as not being subject to the rule of law. In particular, he said that Franco's Spain had been "established with the active support, and only with the active support, of Hitler and Mussolini"[209] and added that it was "a Government [...] which was patterned on the regimes in Italy and in Germany, and was, and is, a Fascist government and a dictatorship." And, to make things quite clear, he pointed out that this was not a simple question of word play but a political reality of a tangible lack of freedom, of which he went on to give four specific examples:

> One of the things that all dictators do – from the time of the French Revolution and before the French Revolution down to the present time – is to take anyone that they do not like and throw him in the *oubliette* [dungeon] and there he stays until he dies, or until they shoot him, or until they take him out. The fundamental protection against that in free countries is the writ of *habeas corpus*. Now, what does

[209] *New York Times,* 12 May 1949. All the following quotes are from the same source.

THE STRUGGLE TO CHANGE U.S. POLICY TOWARD FRANCO'S SPAIN 145

that mean? That means that anybody who is detained against his will may at any time get an order from the court that shall be produced in person before the court and that those who hold him must justify the fact that they are holding him under the provisions of law. There is nothing more fundamental in the preservation of human liberty than that ancient British tradition which is now incorporated in most of the procedures in the free world. That right does not exist in Spain. I suppose a second fundamental right, which is useful only if you have the first, is that if you are tried – and, of course, it follows from the writ of *habeas corpus* that you cannot be sentenced to prison unless you are convicted of some crime. The second right is that in being convicted of a crime you are convicted not by employees of the State but by your fellow citizens. That is the right of trial by jury. It means that no judge, even though he is independent, certainly no administrative official, can order you put in jail. The only people who can do that are ten in some parts of the world, twelve in others – citizens just like yourself – and if they listened to the testimony and say Joe Doakes goes to jail, then he goes to jail. That is fundamental. That right does not exist in Spain. Then there is the question of religious liberty, which is fundamental to a free exercise of the human personality. That right does not exist in Spain. Then there is the right of association – association in political activities, association in trade-union activities, association in benevolent activities. That right does not exist in Spain. I could go on, but what I want to draw to your attention is that these certain fundamental basic rights of the individual which make the difference between what we call "Free Europe" and the "Iron Curtain" countries, these rights do not exist in Spain, and the Spanish people are prevented from enjoying them by action of the Spanish Government.

From all this he concluded that it would be impossible for "Western European countries" to engage in any "intimate working partnership with such a regime in the economic field and in the defense field." He also took advantage of the opportunity to explain the principles behind the policy that was being applied, saying that "there must be some move to liberalize, that [...] Spain, which has never been a full-flowered democracy, must become so." Because, if not,

> what is the use of having Ambassadors? We give someone with a different title. It may raise the prestige of the individual a little bit, but what is the use of it all? It is important only if it becomes a symbol, and if it becomes a symbol of the fact that after all we don't care much about these rights, then it is a bad symbol. If it ceases to be a symbol it wouldn't make any difference to anyone whether you had an Ambassador or whether you didn't.

146   JOAN MARIA THOMÀS

He concluded:

> The fundamental thing is that American policy is to try to bring Spain back into the family of Western Europe. That is a family matter. You have to convince the Spaniards that they must take some steps toward that end, and you have to convince the Europeans that they have to take some steps. So that it isn't fundamentally a matter which can be brought about by American action, and therefore the policy of the American Government is one which I am quite sure is calculated to please neither groups of extremists in the United States – either those who say that we must immediately embrace Franco or those who say that we must cast him into the outermost darkness. But it is a policy directed toward working with the Spaniards and with the Western Europeans bringing about a situation where these fundamental liberties do exist in Spain and where the Western Europeans can bring Spain into the community.

And he finished by, quite rightly, saying "I have spoken at some length on this subject because it is so easy to confuse form with substance."

The press immediately picked up on the secretary's blunt talk. In the *New York Herald Tribune*, Homer Bigart, a prestigious journalist who had been awarded the Pulitzer Prize in 1946[210] and who had been denouncing the predicament of Protestants in Spain, said that it had been "the boldest official statement yet made on the explosive issue of Spain."[211] He made particular reference to the secretary's words that the United States "would shun the initiative in restoring full diplomatic relations with Spain because the Franco regime remained a symbol of Fascism" and that "the chief bar to lifting the diplomatic blockade was an emotional one. Spain had been built up as a symbol – the last living symbol – of a system the U.S. had fought to destroy." He also pointed out that considerable pressure was being exerted on the administration by groups of militant Catholics but also by groups of militant Protestants. The abstention in the UN had been the response.[212]

Acheson's problem was that the policy on Spain, as he had explained it in his statement, was based on sophisticated political and ideological arguments while the increasingly tense debate was gradually bringing more and more representatives in the two houses of Congress round to the pro-Spanish stance and transmuting to a game of goodies and baddies, anti-communists and pro-communists, which did nothing to reinforce the position adopted by the

---

[210] He was awarded another in 1951, this time with other leading war correspondents in Korea.

[211] Homer Bigart, "Acheson Bars Initiative on Spain by U.S.," *New York Herald Tribune*, 12 May 1949.

[212] Ibid.

secretary and the president. This can be seen in Taft's declarations mentioned above, published alongside Acheson's communiqué in the same issue and on the same page of the *New York Times*. Taft criticized the decision to abstain from voting on the Spanish question in the UN and urged Acheson "to shake loose from its Communist-front philosophy"[213] and to establish full diplomatic relations with Spain. He insisted that, in accordance with U.S. diplomatic doctrine and for strategic-military reasons, "there is no reason in the world why we should not grant full diplomatic recognition to Spain and send an Ambassador to Madrid." He was also in favor of the Export-Import Bank awarding official loans so that Spain could purchase cotton and wheat.

In a press conference on 2 June, President Truman responded by categorically stating his opposition to all this.[214] The reasons for this opposition were given in a "very confidential" internal memo "for top level officials of the Department" by Acting Secretary of State James E. Webb after the two men had met in the White House: the president not only had doubts about Spain's ability to repay the loans but also disagreed "about some of the policy aspects of the Spanish situation and particularly the treatment of certain religious minorities."[215] This issue was fundamental to his deeply rooted rejection of the Franco regime and it dictated his attitude toward Spain. And, of course, it was one of the issues that was dealt with by the embassy, the Spanish Lobby, and the members of the Spanish Bloc.

The Francoist Reaction

In Madrid, on 21 May, Acheson's press release prompted Spain to submit a *note verbale* in protest to the U.S. embassy. The note attributed the secretary of state's pronouncements to "an evident lack of information about the real situation in Spain," which was also directly connected to "the biased campaign of lies and falsehoods that Soviet Communism and European Marxist Socialism have been undertaking on Spanish affairs."[216] The note refuted the (alleged) distortions contained in Acheson's pronouncement about the organization of Spain and its ideological positioning. It questioned the allegations that the regime had been put in place with the assistance of Hitler and Mussolini, that Spain was a fascist and totalitarian state, and that civil rights were not respected. On the contrary, it claimed, Spain was a kingdom that had been endorsed in a free vote in 1947, with an elected parliament and elected town

[213] *New York Times,* 12 May 1949.

[214] Memorandum of the Acting Secretary of State, 7 June 1949, FRUS, vol. IV, 750.

[215] Ibid.

[216] Verbal note. 21 May 1949, Ministry of Foreign Affairs Record Group, file number 54–12434, AGA.

councils. It also denied that other Western European countries had refused to enter into trade and military agreements with Spain, and claimed that these agreements existed and/or were in the process of negotiation. It did not deny that some countries refused to allow Spain to take part in the Marshall Plan, but it did cite that Portugal was in favor. And as far as NATO was concerned, it simply stated that Spain had not applied to be a member.

Likewise, as far as bilateral relations were concerned, the note refuted that close collaboration was not possible on economic and military issues with the United States, pointing out that the embassy in Madrid, military authorities, and congressmen in the United States had been saying quite the opposite for some time. On the question of the lack of *habeas corpus* in Spanish legislation, it stated that a detainee had to appear before a judge at most seventy-two hours after arrest. Neither did Spain have any concentration camps, although other countries with which the United States had full diplomatic relations did. It also replied to Acheson's comment that juries did not exist in Spain, pointing out that they did not exist in many fully democratic countries, and mentioned that Spanish courts were equivalent to others, including military ones. And, on the issue of the rights of association mentioned in the secretary of state's communiqué, it merely stated that they were included in the Fuero de los Españoles (the Charter of the Spaniards) (a false argument since the charter was simply a declaration that required legal development). What the note had to say about religious freedom is particularly interesting because of the importance it had for President Truman and the deliberate mention of Senator Brewster's declarations in the session of 11 May:

> Article 6 of the *Fuero de los Españoles* clearly states: "Everyone shall have the right to their religious beliefs and the private exercise of worship." In Spain, although almost all Spaniards are practicing Catholics, there are 168 Protestant chapels, where barely 25,000 people (most of whom are foreigners) worship under the protection of the authorities. There are also several synagogues; there is an authorized orthodox chapel and even a mosque on Spanish territory. It is worth mentioning on this occasion the statement made on the 11th of this month in the US Senate by Mr. Brewster, who, after visiting and touring Spain freely, declared that "Franco's Government allows freedom of worship and belief and the practice of their liturgical ceremonies, without bothering them at all."[217]

The note recalled that during the Republic in Spain, liberty had turned into licentiousness and international communism had tried to exploit the situation and set up a regime. And it finished by referring to the unpleasant effect that Acheson's speech had had on Spanish public opinion and asking him, as soon

---

[217] Ibid.

THE STRUGGLE TO CHANGE U.S. POLICY TOWARD FRANCO'S SPAIN 149

as was convenient, to explain "the true state of the Spanish legal system, thus doing justice to the fact that he was well known for pursuing the truth."

The note did not go down well in Washington. If we are to believe what Director General of America Prat y Soutzo told Minister Martín Artajo about a discussion he had had on 24 May with Earle O. Titus, acting public affairs officer of the U.S. embassy in Madrid,[218] it had made a painful impression, more for its harsh form than for its substance. Apparently, Culbertson had gathered all the staff together to read and discuss it, and he felt that it should have taken the form of a memorandum of protest and demand for rectification, not a *note verbale*, and have been delivered by the *chargé d'affaires* to the State Department in Washington. However, what most concerned Prat was that Titus regretted that the *note* "compromised all the efforts that had been made to improve relations [...] and they were now forced back to the beginning of their task of rapprochement and appeasement." And he brought up a recurring theme in the relations between the embassy and the ministry: Lequerica's atypical visit to Washington was at the heart of all the problems. In fact, it was "the main obstacle to the improvement of Spanish-American relations." Prat reiterated that Culbertson had already told him exactly the same on other occasions: that "Lequerica had got into our embassy through the back door when the Spanish government must have been aware that the American government would not give him the *agrément* as Ambassador."[219]

After the events of Lake Success and Acheson's press release, in Madrid Culbertson wrote to the secretary requesting that the policy prior to the abstention in May be resumed. He said:

> It is my hope that the position adopted prior to the abstention decision, based as it was on sound and not emotional reason, will be readopted and that when the Spanish question comes before the UNGA [UN General Assembly] it can be finally done away with as a question before that body.

He also expressed his opposition to

> the idea that we should base policy on the concept of molding the rest of the world in our own democratic image. It would be fine if the nations of the world could thus be molded, but peoples the world over are not the same and won't mold the same. Certainly not the Spanish.[220]

[218] Ferrary, "Los Estados Unidos...", 281–334.

[219] Note for His Excellency the Minister of Foreign Affairs, 25 May 1949, Ministry of Foreign Affairs Record Group, file number 82–05987, AGA.

[220] The *Chargé* in Spain (Culbertson) to the Secretary of State, Confidential, Madrid, 22 June 1949, FRUS, vol. IV, 752–754. The paragraphs below come from this same source.

He went on:

> Internal Spanish objections to the Franco régime are, however, quite different in most respects than our objections. For instance, our objection to the Régime because it was helped to power by our recent enemies – Germany and Italy – plays no part in Spanish objection. On the other hand, Soviet assistance to the Republic is an element supporting Franco. We do not like Franco himself but here in Spain Franco as an individual has less opposition than the regime. As an example: Spain's economic difficulties are laid at the doorstep of the Minister of Industry and Commerce and not on Franco's. Monarchists object to Franco not so much because he is a dictator but because they feel Franco did not keep faith with them, they having fought with and supported Franco during the Civil War because they thought they were fighting for the restoration of the Monarchy. Another factor, and an important one, with regard to Franco is that while there is opposition and objection to him, there is no majority desire to see him thrown out on his neck because there is no visible alternative that could assure internal security.

On religious freedom, he wrote:

> We find religious intolerance in Spain repugnant to our democratic concepts. It is repugnant but when attacks are directed against that intolerance, they should be directed against the Spanish people and not against the Franco regime. The Homer Bigarts and others who keep this question stirred up at home do not draw that distinction. Franco is not to blame for all the things that are wrong here in Spain and, while he himself is a devout Catholic, there is no indication that he or his regime members support that old Inquisition spirit found in the Spanish Catholic Church and among the people. From the standpoint of religion, the Spanish church and people are bigoted and backward. Franco may be a dictator, but he would never get by with any crusade on behalf of Protestants. So, on religion I think we should give the devil his due.

And he finished by saying:

> Political repression and persecution in any form or degree go against the grain of American ideas and we therefore object to that side of the Spanish regime. We are more conscious of and impressed by this repression and persecution because of the Fascist origins and trappings of the Regime. Spain is a police state and, as one prominent Spaniard remarked the other day, it "is a country occupied by its own Army". However, the vast majority of the Spanish people are little, if at all,

THE STRUGGLE TO CHANGE U.S. POLICY TOWARD FRANCO'S SPAIN   151

affected by repression and persecution as practiced today. The peasant, the laborer, the clerk and on up the line are more concerned today with the actual problem of living than they are with the establishment of political liberties such as we know them. It is the economic situation in Spain and its economic inequalities that are of greatest importance today to the individual Spaniard and, I suppose, our basic interest lies more in the welfare and wellbeing of the people of Spain than in the individual who happens to be at the head of the State at any given time. The refusal of material aid to Spain punishes the Spanish people, not Franco and his cohorts or the rich. There are lots of very hungry folk in Spain today, and there are going to be more before the end of the year

I assume that our broad policy toward Spain continues to rest on our desire to see Spain integrated economically, politically, and militarily into the Western community of nations. To that end we expect Spain to take steps, more or less undefined, which would make her eligible for membership. In this connection we should frankly recognize that liberalizing measures adopted by Franco which might satisfy the United States would not, because of that fact, of necessity satisfy France and Great Britain. Probably would not, in fact, but even so are we in a position to indicate what conditions must be met by Spain? *Habeas corpus* and trial by jury were indicated by the Secretary in his statement to the press on May 11. Neither of these conditions takes into consideration Spanish legal history or practice. Conditions not equally applicable to all nations are not easily defended. And I do not mean by that that just because Franco may be a bit less of a sinner than someone else, he gains entrance into the Kingdom. As the Department knows, I have talked liberalization to these people but without success. The tragedy of Spain is that Franco takes no measures of an evolutionary character, and without evolution revolution is possible, and, in the event of Franco's death, I think probable. One would think that Franco, if he is honest and I think he is, would see that. However, he is stubborn and provincial, and so long as the nations of the world continue openly to condemn him, he may do a Samson and pull the temple down on himself. There is probably no problem any more difficult than one involving a desire to help a people who won't help themselves.

This was the state of things and they were not about to change. What would change, however, was the attitude of the Truman administration, beginning with Acheson and followed, reluctantly, by the president. But not immediately.

To finish, as well as the note we have just analyzed, the national delegate for syndicates Fermín Sanz Orrio gave another official response to the "injustice" suffered by the regime at the hands of Acheson. He wrote and published

152 JOAN MARIA THOMÀS

a pamphlet "refuting" the secretary's arguments, which was translated into English and distributed by the embassy in the United States.[221]

New Initiatives by the Lobbyists in the Pay of Spain in the House of Representatives, and by McCarran and Brewster in the Senate: McCarran and the Second Failure of Official Economic Aid to Spain

The embassy, its contractees, and the congressmen sympathetic to the Spanish cause returned to the fray in Congress less than a month later, at the beginning of June, this time not in the Senate but in the House of Representatives. The leading player now was one of the contractees, Father Thorning, who managed to get a good number of representatives to come out and make declarations in favor of Spain. The session was analyzed by the journalist Edward A. Harris in the *St. Louis Post Dispatch*, who also reported on the public appearance, "all of a sudden," of the "new lobby [...] until then unknown to the general public."[222] He pointed out the lobby's "intensity, ingenuity and resources" and compared it with "the perpetual lobby of real-estate developers" and the "enthusiasm of those in favor of intervening in China."[223] In particular, he described how he had seen Thorning "standing at the door to the cloakroom" of the House acting "like a sort of prompter [and] addressing the representatives as they came in trying to convince them to give [short and fervent] speeches" in favor of a change in policy on Franco's Spain.

The first of the speeches was given by the Democratic representative for Texas Omar T. Burleson, "one of the guests at Lequerica's dinners." Harris pointed out that "most of those who spoke in favor of Franco that day were southern Democrats" and made particular mention of John W. McCormack, Democrat representative for Massachusetts, who had said that "national interest makes it imperative to recognize Spain. From the military point of view, Spain is the key to the Iberian Peninsula." Likewise, Gosset, Democrat representative for Texas, said that "Franco was at the head of the most stable government in Europe"; John E. Rankin, Democrat for Mississippi, contended that "Franco went ahead and took on Communism," and L. Mendel Rivers, Democrat for South Carolina, argued that "our interests demand recognition." Harris said that they had all spoken of "anti-Communism and America's national interests" but only after they had been convinced that "Spain is prepared to import at least 250,000 bales of surplus cotton in the South," so it seemed that "King Cotton held greater sway over their economic calculations than

---

[221] Fermín Sanz Orrio, National Syndical Delegate, "An Open Letter to Dean Acheson," 2 June 1949, Presidency of the Government Record Group, file number 54–08916, AGA.

[222] E. A. Harris, "We have no need for Franco any more but they are still lobbying for him in Washington," *Saint Louis Post Dispatch*, 4 June 1949.

[223] Ibid. All the citations below come from this same source.

THE STRUGGLE TO CHANGE U.S. POLICY TOWARD FRANCO'S SPAIN   153

Dictator Franco." He was also convinced that "Franco [...] was anxious to import large amounts of wheat from this country, paid for by an American loan, of course."[224] This, too, was inspiring more than one congressman to convert to the pro-Franco cause. The overall context, it was claimed, was one in which "the Cold War with Russia makes Spain essential in terms of military strategy," an argument that Harris questioned even though he understood Spain's vital importance at a time that the North Atlantic Treaty had just been signed. He also challenged the argument that the Pyrenees were the "abrupt protective defense" of the West. In this case he quoted the journalist Walter Lippman, who had written that

> the only way of ensuring that nobody in Europe would fight if the Russians were to march in is to tell the Europeans that the United States expects to withdraw quickly from the Elba to the Rhine, from the Rhine to the Seine and from there to the Pyrenees. It would be like preparing to defend the United States against a Japanese invasion by fortifying Long Island.[225]

He also presented arguments against the change in policy on Spain: for example, that it was Franco not the United States who urgently needed the change to save the regime. In support of this argument, he quoted the Democrat representative for California and anti-Francoist, Helen Gahagan Douglas, who had said: "We shall never defeat Communism, here or in Spain, if we trust in the happy deceit that it is enough to be anti-Communist."

Harris correctly identified the forces that were pressing to "normalize" relations with Franco's Spain:

> Franco's envoys who are working for him in this country [that's to say, the embassy]. Economic pressure groups, particularly attractive to the southern representatives. Sincere religious groups that believe that Franco's anti-Communism compensates for other less attractive aspects. Paid, professional lobbyists.

He also mentioned characters such as James Farley, the high-ranking Coca-Cola executive.[226] And he portrayed Lequerica as the mastermind behind the whole set-up:

---

[224] Ibid.

[225] Lippmann concluded that "our true objective is to prevent war by making the risks prohibitive and successful aggression impossible, and then by negotiation and compromise with the Soviet Union to end the military partition of Europe": W. Lippmann, "Common sense and the problem of Spain," *Daily Mail,* 18 May 1949.

[226] Ibid.: He made particular mention of his "passionate support [for Franco]" and pointed out that "he can still make himself heard in the legislative chambers. Farley was the architect of Franklin D. Roosevelt's two consecutive, winning election

> Ambassador of Spain at large [...] who came for a lunch in Washington and has been eking out his stay ever since. He has been in the capital for over a year now and he is still organizing impressive dinners for members of Congress and the Government, preaching in favor of recognition, loans, trade and inter-state comradeship [...] How long his visit to this country is going to last does not seem to be a concern for either Lequerica or the State Department.[227]

But he was very much concerned by this and other issues. The speeches in the House of Representatives were little more than high-flown but innocuous pro-Spanish declarations reported by Harris. But one month later, on 11 July, an increasingly enterprising McCarran, fully committed to the fight against Truman and assisted by Senator McKellar, managed to get the Senate Appropriations Committee to approve an aid package of $50 million for Spain and include it in the Marshall Plan budget. Before he did so, he had informed *Chargé d'Affaires* Baráibar of his intentions.[228] So he managed to sneak Spain into the aid package through the back door "provided, that nothing herein shall be construed to require Spain, as a condition to the furnishing of such assistance, to adhere to a joint program for European recovery."[229] It was his first attempt at such a thing and his initial success would be only temporary. But in 1950 and 1951, his success was definitive. And from this point on he was undoubtedly being "subsidized" by Lequerica.

The aid he had procured included the following:

> For expenses necessary to enable the President to extend assistance to Spain, including expenses of attendance at meetings concerned with the purposes of this appropriation; purchase and hire of passenger motor vehicles; purchase, maintenance and operation of aircraft; payment of damage claims pursuant to law [...]; health service program as authorized by law [...]; transportation of privately owned automobiles; exchange of funds without regard to section 3651 of the Revised Statutes; and loss by exchange; $50,000,000, of which not to exceed 350,000 shall be available for administrative expenses; such assistance to be provided in accordance with applicable provisions of the Economic Cooperation Act of 1948.[230]

---

campaigns, and he is spending a lot of time in the capital working for Franco from his base at the Mayflower Hotel. He recently visited Franco in Madrid."

[227] Ibid.

[228] Telegrams on 1 and 7 July 1949 from the Spanish Embassy in Washington in ANFF, file 177. Cited in Suárez Fernández, *Francisco Franco* ..., vol. IV, 363.

[229] United States Senate, Office of the Legislative Counsel, McCarran Papers, University of Nevada-Reno Archives and Nevada Historical Society Archive. I would like to thank the archivists Jacquelyn K. Sundstrand from the University of Nevada and Sheryln Hayes-Zorn, of the Nevada Historical Society, for their help.

[230] Ibid.

THE STRUGGLE TO CHANGE U.S. POLICY TOWARD FRANCO'S SPAIN   155

The fact that he had been coordinating with Lequerica became clear when, on the day after the vote, Lequerica turned up at the State Department and asked Assistant Secretary for Economic Affairs Willard L. Thorp, "Where do I go to get my fifty million dollars?" Thorp replied that the vote had been for aid in the form of programs and projects and not money, but the very next morning he received a call from McCarran reproaching him for his attitude. McCarran also phoned his immediate superior, Secretary Acheson himself, and rather threateningly asked him "Are you giving them [the Spaniards] what they want?"[231] All this was in response to Acheson's hurried public announcement that there were more deserving causes for the money than Franco, while the administrator of the Marshall Plan, Paul G. Hoffman, warned of how disappointed the Allies would be if Franco were eventually provided with the financial aid.[232]

Despite the huge stir caused by McCarran, the $50 million aid package that had just been passed soon disappeared into thin air: on 4 August, the plenary of the House rejected it by fifty-five votes against to thirty-six.[233] The pressure exerted by Acheson and the possible veto by the president had prevailed. During a press conference on 14 July, when a journalist had asked the president "Will you approve the $50 million out of the European Cooperation Administration (ECA) for aid to Franco?," he had responded simply "I would not. Period." And in response to further questioning on the issue ("Would you say why, Mr President?"), he had explained his administration's policy on Spain and the Western European bloc in the following words:

> Because we are not on friendly relations with Spain at the present time, and there is a certain way in which that situation can be developed. If the other European countries vote to take Spain in, and they can convince us that Spain is to come in, that's a different matter. The matter has been put up to that European organization by Portugal some time ago, and no action has ever been taken on it.[234]

The Spanish embassy protested the very next day. *Chargé d'Affaires* Baráibar went to the State Department where he was received by Deputy

---

[231] M. J. Ybarra, *Washington Gone Crazy. Senator Pat McCarran and the Great American Communist Hunt,* Hanover, Steerforth Press, 2004, 475.

[232] Telegram from *Chargé d'Affaires* Baráibar to the Ministry and note to the Office of Diplomatic Information, 12 and 13 July 1949, AFNFF, file 177 cited in Suárez Fernández, *Francisco Franco ...,* vol. IV, 364.

[233] Shannon, "The Franco Lobby...".

[234] July Press Conference, *Public Papers of the Presidents of the United States. Harry S. Truman,* 1949, Washington D.C., United States Government Printing Office, Washington, 1964, 375.

156   JOAN MARIA THOMÀS

Assistant Secretary Thomson and by William Dunham, of the Spanish desk. He said:

> The Spanish Government has of course the greatest respect and consideration for the President and the Government and people of the United States. His Government was therefore disappointed and regretted the President's statement that relations between Spain and the United States were unfriendly. On the contrary, he said, Spain has the greatest desire to cooperate with the United States and maintain friendly relations.[235]

And he asked for his message to be passed on to Secretary Acheson. In the meantime, on 8 June, Clark and McCarran had organized a meeting between Lequerica, Baráibar, and Merry del Val on the one hand and the Republican senator Vandenburg on the other. Vandenberg had been chairman of the Committee on Foreign Relations until the previous 3 January, and told them that the withdrawal of ambassadors caused by the 1946 resolution had been utterly ridiculous.[236]

Things were not going well for the Francoists with the Truman administration and this was made evident once again when McCarran told Lequerica in confidence (a confidence that, of course, he did not keep) that the president would not be sending an ambassador to Madrid until Spain allowed Protestants full freedom of worship.[237] Still smarting from his recent failure, McCarran – who some sectors of the press were now calling the ambassador from Nevada[238] – continued to fight his private crusade. He announced that in the course of a forthcoming trip to Europe he would meet with Franco to discuss Spain being given diplomatic recognition by the United States and the possibility of a loan. This prompted the president to respond in the press, saying that McCarran "in his trip represented nobody in the United States Government" and that he could speak with Franco and with anyone else but he could not reach any agreements on behalf of the government.[239]

Neither McCarran, Brewster, nor the lobbyists in the pay of Lequerica had managed to make any significant changes in Washington by this point. The Truman administration had made no effective or tangible change in terms of improving relations with Spain either, despite the intentions of the U.S. delegation in the UN and the award of loans to Spanish companies by the

---

[235] July 1949, FRUS 1949, vol. IV, 754.

[236] Telegram from Lequerica to Minister Martín Artajo, 9 June 1949, AFNFF, file 179, cited in Suárez Fernández, *Francisco Franco ...*, vol. IV, 361.

[237] A. Marquina Barrio, *España en la política de seguridad occidental 1939–1986*, Madrid, Ediciones Ejército, 1986, 270.

[238] *The Reporter*, 13 September 1949.

[239] *New York Times*, 16 September 1949.

official Export-Import Bank. The private loan from the Chase was certainly a success. But there was considerable tension between the pro-Franco sectors in Congress and the State Department and the president because of Spain's scheming, the congressmen in Spain's pay, the "subsidies," and Spain's friends. In April, this tense situation prompted the State Department to initiate an operation to have Lequerica removed from Washington, played out largely during the second half of 1949 and the beginning of 1950 by the most militantly anti-Franco sector of the State Department but also by Culbertson in Madrid and, much more unexpectedly, sectors of the Spanish Ministry of Foreign Affairs who were not on good terms with the "inspector."

The First Attempt to Remove Lequerica from Washington:
Baráibar's Dismissal as Chargé d'Affaires and His Replacement
by Propper de Callejón

Lequerica's activity since the beginning of 1949, in conjunction with the lobbyists in the pay of Spain, and the effect it was having on Congress, had raised the alarm in the State Department, particularly that part of it dealing with relations with Spain. This activity came on top of the fact that Lequerica had supported Dewey in the electoral race of the previous year, and that ever since he had arrived in the country he had been engaged in intense social activity in U.S. political circles. In reaction to all this, the State Department questioned his diplomatic status as a tactic to prevent him from residing in the United States apparently as an "inspector" but in reality as the Spanish ambassador in the shade. This may not have been on the instructions of Acheson or one of his assistants,[240] because on more than one occasion he showed that he was rather unaware of the issue, but an initiative of the Iberian desk and the sections on which it depended. The main players were Hickerson, Achilles, and Durham in Washington[241] and Culbertson in Madrid with, if we are to believe Lequerica, unexpected support from within the Palacio de Santa Cruz.[242]

Let us not forget that his visa had been granted on the understanding that his inspection would be temporary and only last one or two months. Subsequently, in 1949, he had made an application for an extension of two and four months more. And in the meantime the embassy had tried to get him included on the list of the members of the Spanish diplomatic staff when Baráibar asked the

---

[240] Or, at least, we have found no documentary evidence that it was.

[241] In this respect, see Dunham's reference to John Wesley Jones, who became *chargé d'affaires* in December 1950 after Culbertson left on 15 December 1950: "Our past efforts to needle the Spanish Government into recalling Lequerica," U.S. Embassy Madrid, Classified General Records 1940–1963, RG 84, NARA-2.

[242] Letter from Lequerica to Martín Artajo, 25 October 1950, file 9532, AFNFF.

158 JOAN MARIA THOMÀS

State Department in what position he should be.[243] Nevertheless, the debates in Congress and the tension with McCarran had put a new complexion on the situation, and it was decided that a discreet attempt would be made to force him to leave the United States. To this end, Culbertson submitted a whole series of requests from Washington to the Spanish Ministry of Foreign Affairs.

The first movements in this particular battle – which the United States would not stop fighting until February 1950 – had been made shortly before the UN meeting in Lake Success in April 1949, when Culbertson had asked the ministry what the department wanted him to find out: How much longer was Mr Lequerica going to be staying in Washington?[244] The department had persistently phoned Culbertson (on 21, 28, and 30 April) in an attempt to get this information. Subsequently, after he had received the *note verbale* in response to Acheson's declarations, he asked again when the "inspector" applied for a visa for his private secretary.[245] Also in this month he had told the ministry that Lequerica "would never be given the *agrément* [as the real ambassador]."[246] Likewise, another official from the embassy, Titus, told Director General of América Prat y Soutzo that

> the biggest obstacle to the task of rapprochement and appeasement [between the United States and Spain] was the presence of Mr Lequerica in Washington, who had got in through the back door and who the Spanish government must have known would never be given the agreement as ambassador by their North-American counterparts.[247]

The campaign against Lequerica intensified on 6–7 June when Culbertson informed the Palacio de Santa Cruz that he had just been sent a letter from the State Department in the diplomatic bag ordering him to respond to the questions he had persistently been asked about Lequerica's stay in Washington. And on 23 June, when he coincided with Prat at a dinner with friends, he inquired yet again and was simply told that his question had been sent to the minister. To this Culbertson replied that the State Department was making no attempt

> to hide from me that if Mr Lequerica – whom neither I nor the Department have anything against; on the contrary, I am on warm,

[243] State Department to German Baráibar, Minister Plenipotentiary – *Chargé d'Affaires* a.i. of Spain, 3 November 1948, Presidency of the Government Record Group, file number 82–05987, AGA.

[244] Letter from Culbertson to Martín Artajo, 6 July 1949, Ministry of Foreign Affairs Record Group, file number 82–05987, AGA.

[245] Ibid.

[246] Ibid.

[247] Note for the Minister of Foreign Affairs, 25 May 1949, Presidency of the Government Record Group, file number 82–05987, AGA.

THE STRUGGLE TO CHANGE U.S. POLICY TOWARD FRANCO'S SPAIN 159

friendly terms with him – should stay any longer in Washington, things will get very ugly and measures will be taken to remove him from North-American territory. I am sure you realize that this would create a difficult situation and put Spain's prestige on the line. I repeat: We have nothing personal against Mr Lequerica but we do have something against the way in which he gained entry to the embassy by using a subterfuge that my government cannot tolerate.[248]

He added that the U.S. government expected a solution to be found within "a reasonable period of time" given that

Mr. Lequerica's presence in Washington has created uncase within the Diplomatic Corps, especially among the representatives of the European powers, and he pointed out something that I had already heard through other channels: that the staff of the French Embassy has refused to come to our Embassy since the day Mr. Lequerica moved in.[249]

Culbertson had read the three official telegrams about Lequerica to Prat, and the first of them also to Under Secretary Carlos de Miranda and Director General of Foreign Policy José Sebastián de Erice. He also mentioned several letters sent by the department, one of them in the diplomatic bag. Of these three letters, one referred to Lequerica as "an ambassador in waiting."[250]

The remarkable thing about this case is that the requests made by Washington and Culbertson in Madrid may have been instigated by sectors opposed to Lequerica within the ministry itself – in particular by Prat, the former ambassador in Washington, Francisco de Cárdenas, and even, if we are to believe Lequerica's version, *Chargé d'Affaires* Baráibar in the embassy in Washington. Even the minister of foreign affairs could hardly be said to be a fan either because Lequerica had a direct relation with Franco and aspired to take over his post.

As soon as he became aware of the department's needs, Culbertson acted speedily. After discussing the situation with Franco, they both agreed that Lequerica needed to be relieved of his position in the United States and decided that he should be sent as ambassador to Buenos Aires.[251] And this is what Lequerica was told by the minister on 27 June 1949. That is to say, he

---

[248] Confidential note for His Excellency, 24 June 1949, Ministry of Foreign Affairs Record Group, file number 82–05987, AGA.

[249] Ibid.

[250] Highly confidential and reserved note for His Excellency, Minister de Prat, 7 July 1949, Ministry of Foreign Affairs Record Group, file number 82–05987, AGA.

[251] To substitute José María de Areilza who was tired of the post. On why he was fed up and his desire to further his political career in Spain after the signature of the 1946 agreements and the 1948 Protocol, see Rein, *La salvación de una dictadura* ....

160 JOAN MARIA THOMÀS

was being given an honorable discharge after the Spanish government had succumbed to pressure from Culbertson and the State Department, perhaps with some surreptitious assistance from Lequerica's enemies within the ministry. This decision was taken with the aim of normalizing diplomatic relations with the United States.

At first Lequerica accepted the proposal, but then initiated a counterattack by denouncing his enemies within the ministry and, of course, Culbertson, Durham, and other members of the State Department. From a letter he wrote to his brother Enrique, and which the police made sure was also delivered to Franco, we know that he had been initially attracted to the idea of the new position, that he had even agreed that his situation in the United States was an "anomalous" one, and that the success of his mission, although assured, would take time:

> The *Generalísimo* has offered me the embassy in Buenos Aires. [José María de] Areilza [ambassador in the Argentine Republic] is about to leave and it's available. I was quick to say yes, as I always am in these cases, but what do you think? In favor: in regimes with authority there's no room for valiant, parliament-type attitudes. I certainly think of Jordana y Varela's wise move. I would be thrilled to get to know Buenos Aires as more than just a tourist. And it would also give me the chance to see Chile, Peru and Brazil. How can I miss this opportunity? It would do me good to get involved in political madness with important colonies and in the main country that speaks our language. What is more, I adore everything Hispano-American so Argentina is very inviting. The political and economic issues of the mission do not worry me in the slightest. I should add that I believe in the success of the mission here, but in the long term. My situation is anomalous.[252]

But the letter of acceptance of the new position – "with the greatest pleasure and honor"[253] – which he sent to Martín Artajo was the beginning of a full-blown attack on his adversaries in an attempt to prevent his transfer and remain in Washington. And it turned out well for him. In the letter he twisted what Norman Armour had said about his going to the United States a year and a half before, and suggested that he had had his support. But, above all, he tore into the members of the ministry who were on the United States's side in so far as his case was concerned:

[252] Report, 4 August 1949, file 2093, AFNFF.

[253] Personal and reserved letter from Lequerica to the Minister, 29 June 1949, Presidency of the Government Record Group, file number 82–05987, AGA. The paragraphs below come from the same source.

THE STRUGGLE TO CHANGE U.S. POLICY TOWARD FRANCO'S SPAIN 161

I find it extremely harmful to the national interest that I am being withdrawn in this way […]. Extremely harmful and quite undignified. I find it outrageous that some conversations with Mr Prat and a few largely indirect instructions from Culbertson, all stage-managed by Cárdenas, who I am sure would not dare to say that he is in agreement with the [State] Department, can lead to a former minister of Franco's being removed from the office to which he was sent after arduous negotiations, and <u>fully aware</u> [underlining in the original] of what he was going for, with <u>no time limit</u> [underlining in the original], as Armour has told me a thousand times. There has been a complete lack of consideration for my person and no strength of mind at a key moment for our policies. I have constantly been on the receiving end, and I have made my thoughts on this issue clear to him, of Cárdenas, with the support of Undersecretary Miranda and others. Truly a sad state of affairs.

He then described all the work he had been doing with sympathetic congressmen and others:

The injustice of the whole thing is made worse by the fact that, after all the effort, when we now have a parliamentary movement on our side which is proving to be decisive and I have even made direct contact with the [State] Department, I am told today that you are going to reinforce diplomatic relations in the next UN Assembly by proposing freedom of diplomatic relations with pretexts and bad language.

He also mentioned that "my relation with influential and secret military bodies has never been better" and that "Our friends will be extremely upset." He then went on to accuse Baráibar of disloyalty and of taking active part in the plan:

In my opinion, leaving Baráibar in charge is outrageous. He was – I could feel it – a part of this Culbertson–Cárdenas plot to get rid of me, of which you clearly approve. It surprised me that when we were speaking of salaries the Undersecretary paid close attention to a paragraph in your letter about what the minister-counselor would be paid when there were absences and substitutions. You need a steady nerve to leave the whole shebang in his hands at this critical time. Never again will we see such a case of inaction. What Prat from the French embassy says about whether they are coming or not could only have occurred to him. Nobody is coming here from France or from anywhere else. Economy, indescribable salaries agreed on between colleagues and total passivity. If getting rid of me makes up for all this, my sense of justice makes me feel very sorry. Even if we assume that I were to leave, someone more capable and solid should remain. It's a disgrace, that's what it is.

162 JOAN MARIA THOMÀS

And he finished by asking the head of state and the minister to reconsider:

> To sum up, in my opinion, the proposal you are making is appalling, deplorable and damaging to Spain. I can't imagine how much plotting and scheming has been involved. But please bear in mind what I have to say, Your Excellency, and consider your options. The [State] Department should speak out, but not in casual conversation with insignificant people. Culbertson is Cárdenas. I am not scared of facing up to the problem right here. But even if we assume that there have been indirect instructions, are we really still in the time of the deceased García Prieto, for example, when we have to accept foreign impositions on matters of our dignity and sovereignty? Conclusion: Do not worry about all of this. Allow me to finish things off. We are almost there. When I have done so, I shall leave so that the Under Secretary, Cárdenas and all the others can breathe a sigh of relief. But now we should not take this regrettable step back, sacrificing a tremendous amount of work just to satisfy a desire for revenge and petty jealousies only on the strength of a conversation with Prat! Dear Artajo, advise José María [de Areilza] to be patient for a little while longer.[254] This is up to you but I advise you as a friend.

In response to this letter, Martín Artajo ordered Prat to call Culbertson to clarify the position of the United States. This he did on 5 July. He insisted that Lequerica should leave and added that

> to calm all the excitement produced in the [State] Department and the diplomatic corps, it would be preferable for Mr Baráibar, who gets on well with the Department and enjoys their trust, to remain in charge of the embassy until October or November, when he believes that diplomatic relations between Spain and the United States will have returned to normal after the exchange of ambassadors.

And he offered to write a letter to the minister, the draft of which he would send to Prat.[255]

While all this was going on in Madrid, Lequerica had set to work in Washington to find out who was plotting against him in the State Department and the reasons behind Culbertson's repeated requests for him to leave the country. On 5 July, he phoned the minister to inform him that, according to his contacts in the State Department, "the alleged intensification of the animosity [...] against my person is false." He described all that had happened as a

[254] On his desire to be relieved, see note 233.

[255] Highly personal and reserved note for His Excellency the Minister, de Prat, 7 July 1949, Ministry of Foreign Affairs Record Group, file number 82–05987, AGA.

THE STRUGGLE TO CHANGE U.S. POLICY TOWARD FRANCO'S SPAIN 163

strategy of his U.S. and Spanish enemies,[256] as a conspiracy between sectors of the State Department, Culbertson, and Spanish diplomats.

Martín Artajo gave him "a summary of Franco's point of view" and said that he would be sent a letter. But on that same day he received another communication from Lequerica telling him of a meeting with Undersecretary of State James E. Webb, who had pointed out that

> despite what has been said, nothing was sent in the diplomatic bag and our wishes are quite the opposite of what was apparently expressed in conversation [...] There is no reason at all to change the current situation. In fact next week I will be informed of the position of France and the Benelux countries at the next UN Assembly.

He concluded his message by asking the minister to "pass the information on to whoever needs it [that is to say, Franco] and I advise that all plans be halted until the underlying reasons can be fully clarified, which I hope will be soon."[257]

Whether this was true or not, he was playing his cards in Washington. He was aiming higher than Hickerson, Achilles, Durham, and Culbertson, so he felt he could talk his way out of the plot against him. Also on 5 July, the minister had received Culbertson's letter in which he reiterated the request for Lequerica to be withdrawn and once again mentioned the telegrams sent by the State Department in April, the conversations he had had with the high-ranking officials in the Spanish ministry, and his fear that "the State Department will begin to get impatient about my long delay in answering the messages received."[258] However, this time, before sending the letter to Franco, he put a question mark next to this last statement and added a note that would turn out to be fundamental: "It is not clear that there has been any further pressure from Washington."

Weighing up all the arguments, Franco and Martín Artajo decided to listen to Lequerica and not to withdraw him from the U.S. capital. What is more, the minister managed to get the "inspector's" visa renewed in July, although the ministry instructed him to consider the possibility of going on visits to Caracas, Havana, Bogota, and Montreal, to justify the title that appeared in his passport. He followed these orders immediately by going to Ottawa and Montreal in Canada and making the most of the opportunity to take a break from the intense pressure he had been under.[259]

---

[256] Handwritten note from Martín Artajo to Franco, 6 July 1949, file 23598, AFNFF.
[257] Telegram from Lequerica to Martín Artajo, 5 July 1949, file 23598, AFNFF.
[258] Letter from Culbertson to Lequerica. 6 July 1949, file 23598 AFNFF.
[259] Cava Mesa, *Los diplomáticos de Franco* ..., 308.

164 JOAN MARIA THOMÀS

The fact that he was not withdrawn from Washington was a triumph. He immediately began to take reprisals, and managed to have Germán de Baráibar[260] replaced as *chargé d'affaires* with another of his former subordinates in Vichy, Eduardo Propper de Callejón, who arrived in Washington on 19 September. From his time in Vichy, he knew the newly appointed head of the State Department's Division of Western European Affairs, Douglas McArthur II, nephew of the general of the same name who was married to Laura Louise, one of the daughters of Vice-President Barkley. Therefore, he was the brother-in-law to one of the embassy lawyers, Truitt,[261] married to Marian Frances, the vice-president's other daughter. McArthur was subordinate to Hickerson but he became a mainstay for the Francoists in the department and tipped the balance that had existed between the two factions up to that point.

While all this was going on, in Spain Culbertson's direct contact, Prat y Soutzo, had acted on his behalf and proposed to Martín Artajo a wide range of political and economic reforms along the lines of what the State Department had been demanding from Madrid. On 1 August, he wrote to his immediate superior with the following proposals for both the forthcoming meeting of the UN assembly in September and the meetings in Madrid in the same month between representatives of the U.S. syndicate AFL and the financier Bernard Baruch:[262]

> Abolition of the Special Tribunal against (sic) the Masons and Communism. The Masons hold a lot of power in the UN and one of their leaders is Baruch. Communism can be abolished in the ordinary courts but Freemasonry can only be fought with the weapons at their disposal and not by a court.
>
> The announcement that a decrease of 50% in the number of attorneys appointed by the Head of State in the Spanish parliament will be proposed to the Spanish parliament and subject to referendum. The decision on what the percentage will be should be taken by universal suffrage, with no restrictions on the people who could be candidates or on political opinion.
>
> The announcement of a bill on the freedom of press and association that would reinstate, with only the essential modifications, the Law of Associations that has not been repealed. There should be some sort of

---

[260] He was appointed *chargé d'affaires* in Cuba in the same month of September 1949: Letter from Lequerica to Martín-Artajo on 17 September 1949, Ministry of Foreign Affairs Record Group, file number 82–05987, AGA.

[261] Ibid.

[262] Cited in A. Marquina Barrio, *España en la política de seguridad occidental 1939–1986,* Madrid, Ediciones Ejército, 1986, 275–276. The excuse for the letter was to tell him about Prince Max de Hohenloe's impressions of the Spanish question.

THE STRUGGLE TO CHANGE U.S. POLICY TOWARD FRANCO'S SPAIN   165

clause that limits the freedom of those texts that may be detrimental to the security of the state, public order and the respect due to religion, morality and good habits.

The announcement, in somewhat vague terms, of new legislation on free trade and of changes to adjust and adapt the Spanish economy to the economies of Western Europe, suggesting that Spain prefers multi-lateral agreements to bilateral agreements.

The use of non-state channels to insist on religious tolerance, extending or apparently extending religious freedom not only to Protestants and Jews but also to the Orthodox Church, and authorizing the celebration of sacraments such as marriage in their churches to have civil effects.[263]

None of this was actually acted upon. Quite apart from the non-viability of the proposals, which questioned some of the political foundations of the Franco regime (such as its radically anti-democratic nature), the minister had confidence that Lequerica, the embassy, the paid lobbyists, and the sympathetic congressmen would gain greater support in the legislature and bring about a change in the policy on Spain. He was also confident because the armed forces were interested in setting up bases in Spain. And he was not mistaken. The change would come, but not in 1949, as we shall see.

Complaints about the Activities of the Pro-Francoists in the United States by U.S. Anti-Francoists

As well as the failed attempt by the State Department to have him removed from the country, another effect of the increasing activity of Lequerica, the embassy, the professional lobbyists, and the pro-Franco congressmen was that the U.S. anti-Francoist press started to publish articles against them. A good example of this was a new article published by former Secretary of the Interior Harold Ickes in *The New Republic* in which he attributed the policy of the State Department on Spain to the presence within it of pro-Francoists. Only this, he believed, could explain what for him was Secretary Acheson's incomprehensible attitude and why nothing was being done about Lequerica's scheming and continued presence in the country. He said the following:

When Secretary Acheson took over, there were high hopes that he would put the career boys in their place and that he would really take control of the department in which they had been running hog-wild. The easy infiltration of these Spanish Nazis who as implicitly take orders from Franco as does any Communist from the Cominform,

[263] Ibid. See also Viñas, *En las garras del águila...*, pp. 65–67.

justifies the suspicion that Secretary Acheson either does not know what is going on in his own department or is no more able to cope with it than were some of his predecessors. Time is running out on him.

For Ickes, "we are living in diplomatic concubinage with Franco," proof of which was the fact that they tolerated Lequerica who "came here more than a year ago to 'inspect' the embassy" and who recently "dispossessed a member of the Spanish Embassy of his home. Apparently, his intention is to favor us for an indefinite period." And he wondered:

> Should he not register as a lobbyist? By what specious reasoning can the State Department justify the presence here of a non-accredited representative of Franco who, as Spanish Ambassador to Vichy at the time of our defeat at Corregidor, exultantly gave a state dinner to celebrate, with enemies of the United States, the crippling blow struck by Japan?

He was to repeat this accusation in the future. And the accused took great pains to deny it.

However, he also mentioned the activities of Senator McCarran and the paid lobbyist Clark. He pointed out McCarran's "murderous attempt to cut the appropriation for ECA" while he attempted "to carve as much as $50 million out of the vitals of that bill in order to hand it over to the dictator of Spain who is desperately in need of money to maintain his trigger-happy soldiers in luxury." He said that he was "usually so crude in his operations that it is easy to fathom his tricks."[264] And he contrasted Clark's previous membership of the Truman Committee with the $50,000 per year that he was being paid by the Spanish embassy for acting as "Spanish Legal Counsel to the Division of Cultural (cultivating?) Affairs." He explained that "the 'cultivating' in which he and De Lequerica are particularly interested relates to such men on the Hill." He had McCarran and others he did not name in mind, one of whom was undoubtedly Brewster, all doing "a good job for Franco in 'cultivating' the belief that it would be a Christian act on our part to irrigate Spanish culture to the extent of $50 million as a beginning." He also mentioned Merry del Val, pointing out:

> [W]hile De Lequerica makes himself cozily at home on the Hill, Pablo Merry del Val, who at least is listed as a counselor of the Spanish Embassy, slips from cocktail party to cocktail party, ingratiating himself not only with thirst-quenching Senators and Representatives but with the self-anointed social elite of Washington.

---

[264] Harold Ickes, "A State Department...." 8 August 1949. All the citations below are from the same source. Ickes continued accusing Lequerica, Propper and others in his other article published in *The New Republic*, 12 December 1949, file 12506, AFNFF, as we have mentioned above.

THE STRUGGLE TO CHANGE U.S. POLICY TOWARD FRANCO'S SPAIN   167

He may not have been aware of the pro-Franco maneuverings undertaken by Farley or his friendship with McCarran,[265] or he may have decided not to mention them, but he could have done. Jim A. Farley was on the board of Coca-Cola, former chairman of the Democratic National Committee until 1940 (until he fell out with Roosevelt because he would not accept him as a candidate for a third term of office), a Catholic, and a great Franco supporter, with whom Ickes himself was at loggerheads.[266]

Lequerica spoke to Minister Martín Artajo about Ickes, describing him as "a good friend of the Spanish Reds, particularly [Álvarez del] Vayo, and saying that Truman had had to get rid of him from the Ministry because of his Soviet sympathies. He's an old (75) lunatic, fanatically anti-Spanish and anti-Catholic." He also looked into the origins of some of the information contained in this and other articles and how Ickes was connected to Culbertson and the men responsible for European and Spanish affairs in the department. It was while he was doing this that he found out that Dunham, chief of the Spanish desk, had not only spent some time in Madrid with Culbertson but that he had once been Icke's personal secretary. And he announced that once he had finished his investigations he would take his finding to "our friends here [...] who are so insistent on discovering the philo-Communist influences in the public administration,"[267] surely a (sinister) reference to the Republican senator, Styles Bridges, John Parnell Thomas (chairman of the House Un-American Activities Committee), and the Republican senator for Wisconsin, Joe McCarthy,[268] soon to become a friend of Lequerica's.

The relationship between Dunham and Culbertson, and between Culbertson and his friend in the Spanish ministry, revealed to Lequerica how Ickes was getting some of the internal Spanish information he was using in his articles. One such piece of information had been the appointment of Propper de Callejón in France[269] frustrated "by the Communist opposition" and which had been

> no more than an attempt because Propper lacks any real political weight. Here we could not understand how the former Red minister [a reference to Ickes] had got hold of this information because such

---

[265] Letters from McCarran to Farley, 12 September 1950 and 13 August 1951, Farley Papers Boxes 20–21, Manuscript Division, Library of Congress.

[266] Letter from Ickes to Farley, 27 February 1948, Farley Papers, Manuscript Division, Library of Congress.

[267] Letter from Lequerica to Martín Artajo, 8 August 1949, Ministry of Foreign Affairs Record Group, file number 82–05987, AGA.

[268] On McCarthy, see. J. C. Giblin, *The Rise and Fall of Senator Joe McCarthy,* Boston, Clarion Books, 2009; D. M. Oshinsky, *A Conspiracy so Immense. The World of Joe McCarthy,* Oxford, Oxford University Press, 2005; T. C. Reeves, *The Life and Times of Joe McCarthy. A Biography*, New York, Stein and Day, 1982.

[269] Ickes, "The State Department's Siesta."

168   JOAN MARIA THOMÀS

news, not entirely accurate but with a basis in fact, would never have
transcended the inner echelons of the Santa Cruz Department. I see
that perfectly now. Just as I see that as soon as the campaign against
Propper failed in the Red-Department weekly papers, he moved on
to other things.[270]

Another U.S. Attempt to Have Lequerica Withdrawn from Washington

In December 1949, there was another attempt to have Lequerica withdrawn
from the United States. Culbertson sent a letter to Prat, director general of
América, reminding him that he had not responded to his requests for clari-
fication of the inspector's situation in Washington.[271] Prat sent it on to Under
Secretary Miranda, who refused to send it on to Martín Artajo. So Prat did,
which prompted Culbertson to think that "the question seems to be such a hot
potato that no one in the Spanish Foreign Office wants to touch it."[272] As a
result, an initial response was drafted, which Prat changed before sending it to
the minister, who also made some changes. But whatever the case may be, the
final text, delivered to Culbertson in February 1950, brooked no debate. The
strategy this time was quite different from the previous occasion, when Franco
and Martín Artajo had initially opted to give way. Now they denied ever having
said that Lequerica was initially going to stay only for two months and then
for four months more, and they gave him the title of "ambassador-inspector
(or ambassador-at-large as he is called in North America)," which would
allow him to live wherever his home country wanted and for an unlimited
time. They also resorted to barefaced lying and stated that Lequerica had
never "communicated directly with the State Department" or with "the other
embassies, because that is the function of the *chargé d'affaires*." And they
even went so far as to say that "he has been careful to abstain from all personal
and private contact with the authorities of the United States on all political
and economic matters entrusted to the embassy." At the same time, the text
attributed all the criticism of Lequerica "to the malicious interpretations of
newspapers in the hands of emigrants [exiles] and the far left-wing." And
then they moved onto the attack by saying:

> It is curious to say the least that the North-American *chargé d'affaires*
> is surprised by the interest and time taken by a foreign government
> to publicly and loyally find out about the activities of a nation such

[270] Letter from Lequerica to Martín-Artajo, 8 August 1949.

[271] Culbertson to the Secretary of State, 7 February 1950, U.S. Embassy Madrid,
Classified General Records 1940–1963, RG 84, NARA-2.

[272] Culbertson to the Secretary of State, 16 February 1950, U.S. Embassy Madrid,
Classified General Records 1940–1963, RG 84, NARA-2.

THE STRUGGLE TO CHANGE U.S. POLICY TOWARD FRANCO'S SPAIN 169

as the United States, which plays a leading role in world affairs, and the activity in the country of the Spanish diplomatic and consular representatives.

After all, they argued, Washington was home to the headquarters of the Organization of American States (OAS) and New York was home to the headquarters of the UN. And they insisted in their criticism by pointing out that

> in a country in which so many strangers and often undesirables have permanent residence, it is least fitting to attempt to limit the stay of an ambassador from a friendly country, a person who acts in an impeccable and highly proper fashion, even though he may not have been given any particular accreditation by the government in Washington.[273]

Culbertson was deeply unhappy about the response, and he asked the department to throw in the towel on this question, at least in Madrid, "unless instructed otherwise."[274] Washington, however, was another thing. If Lequerica were to present an application to renew his visa there, he hoped that the department "can and will bring this question to a showdown." When the time came, the department did not act as he had hoped because, throughout 1950, as we shall see, things began to change with respect to Spain. But before we see exactly how they changed, let us take a look at the other initiatives of the embassy and the paid congressmen during the rest of 1949.

The 1949 Francoist Offensive in the United States

After the failed attempts to have him withdrawn, Lequerica was in a stronger position than ever before in Washington, so the embassy (now reinforced with Propper), the paid lobbyists, and Lequerica himself decided to launch a full-scale offensive to bring about a change in U.S. policy on the Franco regime. They did so by exploring the possibility of a rapprochement between Patrick F. Clark and President Truman, and trying to reach as many members of the two houses as possible. The main idea was known as the "Plan Otoño", which consisted of organizing and paying for a group of senators and representatives to visit Spain.

Likewise, other trips to Spain were independently organized for congressmen, the executives of companies interested in improving relations and even the military (the first ever official visit). All of this was simply the manifestation of the importance the "Spanish question" was acquiring in the United States

---

[273] February 1950, file 13776, AFNFF.

[274] Culbertson to Secretary of State, 16 February 1950, U.S. Embassy Madrid, Classified General Records 1940–1963, RG 84, NARA-2.

now that it was affecting the armed forces and the Secretary of Defense Louis Johnson,[275] and numerous congressmen and businessmen. With the exception of the aforementioned "Plan Otoño," these trips were paid for by Congress or the travelers themselves. In fact, in the second half of 1949 it was all the rage to visit Spain as a part of more extensive tours around Western Europe. We could say that it was a real case of "Spanish fever."

Senator McCarran's visit to Spain was a mixture of the "Plan Otoño" and the initiatives of the congressmen. It was an added extra to a trip he made to several European countries to investigate the situation of the displaced persons and to find arguments to oppose the proposed extension of the 1948 law. Likewise, in his capacity as chairman of the Joint Committee on Foreign Economic Cooperation – known as the Watch-dog Committee – he called meetings to discuss U.S. aid.[276] His visit included an audience with Franco, which proved to be the beginning of a personal relationship between the two men, particularly prized by Franco, that was to last until McCarran's death.

All the visits to Spain mentioned above and the pressure from the military were a considerable thorn in both the Department's and President Truman's side. The same could be said of the embassy in Madrid where Culbertson was overwhelmed by the number of visits from leading U.S. citizens and rightly felt that they were interfering in the official policy that he was taking great pains to apply. For his part, Captain Mercer, whose goals were quite different from those of the *chargé d'affaires*, regarded the arrival of a squadron of the U.S. Navy in Ferrol with Admiral Connolly in command as a military success. The embassy had split down the middle between the "civil" section and the "military," a direct reflection of the discrepancies between the State Department and the armed forces on all issues referring to Spain.

Meanwhile, Lequerica was still striving to get loans for Spanish businesses from the Export-Import Bank, with encouragement from the lobbyist Max Truitt, although up to that point he had had no success, sometimes being turned down point blank by Truman. And both Truitt and Clark went on trips to Madrid to make contacts.[277]

[275] On Johnson, see K. D. McFarland-D. L. Roll, *Louis Johnson and the Arming of America. The Roosevelt and Truman Years*, Bloomington, Indiana University Press, 2005, in which there is not a single mention of Spain, Franco, or Lequerica.

[276] Box 54, folder 1, McCarran Papers, Nevada Historical Society.

[277] Letter from Lequerica to Martín Artajo, n.d., but probably in September 1949. The letter announces Max O. Truitt's trip to Madrid, Ministry of Foreign Affairs Record Group, file number 82–05987, AGA.

THE STRUGGLE TO CHANGE U.S. POLICY TOWARD FRANCO'S SPAIN 171

Rapprochement with President Truman and the Protestant Question

One of the main obstacles to the more cordial relations Spain was pursuing with the United States was the Franco regime's refusal to allow freedom of worship, an issue of great personal interest to President Truman himself. The embassy, the paid lobbyists, and the sympathetic congressmen made various attempts to convince the president that there was no truth in the accusations being leveled at Spain in this respect. They never achieved their aim and the debate remained alive until the end of Truman's term in office, although it would not prevent U.S. policy from changing direction because of more pressing strategic factors. But to Truman's irritation it was to be an unresolved point of conflict with Franco's government which, in turn, was under pressure from the Spanish Catholic Church, one of the mainstays of the regime.

Unfortunately for the Francoists, however, the president's fundamental anti-Francoism had another *raison d'être*: the relentless persecution of Freemasonry by the regime. For as well as being a devout Baptist who was often sent information and complaints about what was happening in Spain to his church, Truman was also a leading Freemason who had been bestowed the thirty-third degree when he was elected president and appointed the grand master of the Grand Lodge of Missouri.[278]

The president's status as a Freemason was also fundamental to Franco, whose anti-Freemasonry convictions were central to his political thought.[279] In 1940 he had enacted specific legislation to repress the organization (Law on the Repression of Freemasonry and Communism) which, despite its name, had focused almost exclusively on Freemasonry. In fact, Truman's membership of the Masonic brotherhood was the reason for many of Franco's personal and rather peculiar interpretations of U.S. policy, which he even published in the national press under the pseudonym Jakim Boor. On 9 August, in *Arriba*, the main newspaper of the single-party FET y de las JONS (the Falange), he wrote the following:

> When he occupied the Presidency on the death of the previous president [Roosevelt], Mr. Truman, who comes from a long line of masons, drew closer to his desired goal when he was bestowed the highest degree of American Freemasonry. Then the Brotherhood took advantage of the elevation of the United States to the leading position

---

[278] Edwards, *Anglo-American Relations* ..., 42–44. Within Freemasonry, the thirty-third degree is an honorary degree, conferred by invitation only, for members who have demonstrated extraordinary service to Freemasonry or society.

[279] J. Domínguez Arribas, *El enemigo judeo-masónico en la propaganda franquista (1936–1945)*, Madrid, Marcial Pons Historia, 2009.

in Western government, as a result of the victory [in 1945] and as a direct consequence of the offensive against Spain.[280]

Truman's concern for the predicament of Protestants in Spain and, generally speaking, for the lack of any real religious freedom was increased by the hard-hitting articles published in the *New York Herald Tribune* and *Time*. The journalist, Homer Bigart,[281] wrote that, ever since the pastoral letter by the archbishop of Seville Cardinal Segura in 1947 comparing Protestantism with atheist communism, Protestant churches had been subject to attacks of vandalism while Franco's government toughened its policy on Protestants as a whole.

We know Truman's opinion on all this because of the letters he wrote to his friend James A. Farley, a Democrat, a Catholic, and a leading pro-Francoist, in response to the U.S. abstention in the UN vote on Spain in May. Just a few months before, Farley had had an audience with Franco in Madrid[282] (not for the first time and also not for the last) and since then he had quite openly done everything in his power to change U.S. policy on Spain, including complaining to Truman about the vote cast in the UN. Truman had explained why he did not like either Franco or his regime, one of the main reasons being the religious question as part of the more general lack of freedom in the country. He took pains to point out that, as far as he was concerned, the essential liberties were those described in

> George Mason's Bill of Rights and embodied in our organic law, the Constitution of the U.S. [...] throughout [the] entire history of our nation, the least minority among us has been guaranteed full religious freedom, which embrace complete liberty of conscience and education, freedom of speech and of press, and right of assembly [...] Anything less than that, whether in Spain or Hungary or Bulgaria, whether behind the Iron Curtain or outside of it, is an unwarranted and indefensible abridgment of civil and religious freedom.[283]

[280] J. Boor [Francisco Franco], "Alta masonería," *Arriba*, 9 August 1949, cited in J. Ruiz, "Menos Camboyas, Caperucita. Reflexión sobre la represión franquista, 1939–1953," *Dictatorships & Democracies*, vol. 8 (2020), 93.

[281] In one of the articles published in *Time* – on 7 March 1949, entitled "Religion: Protestants in Spain" – he had stated that "a Protestant in Spain today is a second-class citizen [...] He is not allowed to practice his faith in public. The chapel he attends must not display any exterior evidence that it is a place of worship. It cannot advertise its existence, not even with a bulletin board. It cannot be listed in the public directories." According to him, a Protestant clergyman "suffers much the same type of persecution as the Roman Catholic clergy endure in Communist Hungary" even though in Spain they were not thrown into prison: *Time*, 7 March 1949.

[282] Letter from Farley to Franco, 3 December 1948, Farley Papers, box 20, Manuscript Division, Library of Congress.

[283] Letter from Truman to Farley, 16 May 1949, OF 422 Miscellaneous, HSTPL.

Religious freedom, then, was central to his way of thinking.

It was certainly true that in Spain between fall 1947 and summer 1948 the Catholic hierarchy, with the support of the press and high-ranking government officials, had launched an anti-Protestant campaign in response to their concern about the growing numbers of non-Catholic faithful. Their aim was to effectively comply with article 6 of the Charter of the Spaniards, which proclaimed that

> the profession and practice of the Catholic religion, which is the religion of the Spanish State, shall enjoy official protection. Nobody shall be prevented from having their religious beliefs nor from worshiping in private. Ceremonies and external religious manifestations other than those of the Catholic faith shall not be permitted.

That is to say, the anti-Protestant campaign was in compliance with an article that did not permit non-Catholic rites of worship outside the strictly private sphere, which even called into question the existence of churches of other confessions.

Aware of the president's opinion and after finding out about a conversation he had had in June with Under Secretary of State Webb, Acheson had sent him a memorandum[284] in support of his own stance on the policy on Franco's Spain. The memorandum pointed out the delicate situation in which the Spanish government found itself, caught between the Catholic hierarchy who insisted on the aforementioned article 6 being respected to the letter, and the awareness that the lack of effective freedom of worship was an obstacle to the normalization of diplomatic relations that Spain was so anxious for in the international sphere, in democratic Europe and the United States. For the Secretary of State, the question was "inherently delicate and highly charged" as was the case with other issues involving the Franco regime, which always tended to generate "more heat than light."

His memorandum was based on an analysis by the embassy in Madrid a year before, after Culbertson and other officials had had conversations with a spokesman of the Protestant groups in Madrid. One of his conclusions was that

> if the Spanish government were pressed into declaring itself openly on the question of the interpretation of Article 6, which the Catholic bishops have unsuccessfully been urging it to do, the result would probably be a strictly literal interpretation of the Article.

This result, he said, would be given "the publicity accorded to this problem in the foreign press, and particularly in the United States." And, in fact, there had been an increase in

---

[284] D. Acheson, "Statement on The Catholic Church and Religious Minorities in Spain," 7 July 1949, PSF, HSTPL.

174 JOAN MARIA THOMÀS

the vigilance of the Church and the sensitivity of the Spanish Government to such an extent that any effort to raise the issue of religious freedom greater than that permitted by Article 6 would undoubtedly result in forcing the Spanish Government into a strict interpretation.

For all these reasons, the embassy was skeptical about getting results in the short term and stated:

> The dilemma in which the Spanish Government finds itself over these problems is admittedly difficult if not impossible to resolve under present conditions. In view of the background of Spanish tradition and culture in the Catholic religion, it is perhaps too much to expect the early realization of complete religious freedom, as we know it, in that country. Certainly, Spanish pride and resistance to outside interference in their affairs militate against the establishment of greater religious freedom in Spain through foreign pressure. This is essentially a problem for solutions by the Spaniards themselves for if religious and other freedoms are to be successfully developed in Spain, they must emerge from within the country. The greatest hope of a movement in that direction lies in the gradual and progressive development of more democratic principles and institutions, both in belief and in practise. A broadly free and democratic government is, of course, almost unknown in Spanish history, and unlikely of attainment in the near future. But, although its development in Spain must necessarily be estimated in terms of generations, evolution toward democratic government appears to offer the only ultimate solution to the many difficulties, such as the restriction of religious and other freedoms from which Spain is suffering today.[285]

The embassy also admitted that, despite the privileges and protection that the Catholic Church enjoyed and that were described in the basic laws of the regime, "non-Catholic religious minorities do exist in Spain and are, in practice, sometimes granted greater than a literal interpretation of the laws would allow." This did not mean that there was no *de facto* discrimination of Protestants and non-Catholics in general, which affected other civil rights. So the 25,000–30,000 Spanish Anglicans, Baptists, and Seventh-Day Adventists, with their 161 churches and their ceremonies in ffity private homes, who received subsidies from the United States (the Baptists in particular), Norway, Switzerland, and Sweden could not have their marriages or family salary supplements recognized by Francoist legislation, nor could they become civil servants. Likewise, the 1,000–1,500 Jews only had two authorized synagogues with an extremely limited capacity, where they were not allowed

[285] Ibid.

THE STRUGGLE TO CHANGE U.S. POLICY TOWARD FRANCO'S SPAIN 175

to hold ceremonies or marriages, which were not legally recognized. But the government did tolerate the distribution of religious texts, the clandestine sale of bibles, and the restricted circulation of non-Catholic religious newspapers. Nothing else. The British government, for example, had been unable to get permission from the Spanish authorities to reopen their ten Anglican chapels.[286]

However, this cold, realistic account of the religious question in Spain, with its correlate of the continuing U.S. official policy that exerted moderate pressure on the Franco regime for political and economic changes, did not have the slightest effect on the president's hostility. But it surely awoke his interest because he now had more details about what was happening. This newfound interest first became evident in the course of the interview that the president granted to the lobbyist Clark, the first attempt by the Francoists to explain their viewpoint to Truman. And it was confirmed in a subsequent interview requested by the president himself.

Thanks to the mediation of Vaughan, Clark was received at the White House on 13 September 1949. At the time, Vaughan was being accused of accepting gifts for favors, which did not have any consequences then but that would reappear in the final stage of Truman's presidency.[287] Apparently, before the meeting Clark was a little wary because he thought he would be coming up against a hostile president, but this turned out not to be so. During the interview, Clark explained that he was planning to go to Europe and stop off in Spain during his travels, which was not entirely true because Spain was his one and only destination. When the president mentioned that he had heard

[286] Ibid.

[287] Letter from Lequerica to Martín Artajo, 16 September 1949, Ministry of Foreign Affairs Record Group, file number 82–05987, AGA. In it he says that Vaughan was "particularly grateful [to Clark and the Spanish embassy] [...] for the discrete approach of the Spanish press to his affair." This must have been a reference to fact that he had had to appear before a Congress committee to explain why he had done favors and cut deals by exploiting his close connection with the president. Other members of the president's staff had also had to appear before the committee made up of the Republicans Joe McCarthy, Karl Mundt, and Margaret Chase Smith, and with Senator Hoey as chairman. If we believe Vaughan himself when he was asked about the affair years after the event "there were three other Democratic members of the committee, but they never attended hearings – they were too interested in other things. I was getting a lot of abuse in the press about numerous matters and I went in one day to the President and said, 'It's more important that your administration have a bit of tranquility than it is that I stay around here, so if I should ask to go on inactive duty, it might relieve the situation.' 'Harry,' he said, 'you and I came in here together and we're going to leave together and I don't want to hear any more of this damned foolishness about you wanting to resign.' So, I never brought the matter up again": Oral History Interviews, General Henry H. Vaughan, HSTPL. Vaughan was investigated once again at the end of Truman's presidential term for having accepted gifts to get into the White House.

news of "great persecutions of Protestants" in the country, Clark denied there were any and said that this news had been greatly exaggerated by self-interest and anti-Francoist propaganda. Truman showed that he trusted him by saying, "Charlie, you and I have worked and investigated together on the Truman Committee. This time investigate for me and report back when you return."[288] Clark was delighted with "the friendship and trust"[289] the president had shown him and with the opportunity to explain Franco's side of the argument to the president, appropriately disguised as his own work.

However, two days later, the president called the journalist Constantine Brown,[290] an expert in diplomatic relations, to the White House because he knew that he was also going to be traveling to Madrid and he wanted to ask him for another report. What he did not know was that Brown was a friend of Lequerica's and, more than likely, a recipient of his "subsidies." So, after the meeting, Brown went straight to tell Lequerica all about it. Brown had also been asked by Defense Secretary Johnson to prepare a trip to investigate the possibility of a visit between 28 October and 1 November as part of a tour of European capitals that would also take him to Japan.[291] This was one more sign that the armed forces had become one of the spearheads pressuring for a change in policy on Spain and that the secretary was prepared to play a major role in this endeavor. This contravened the policy of the State Department and led to a disagreement between the two departments and their corresponding secretaries. The president, however, supported Acheson and, when he found out about the planned trip, he confronted him by saying, "I've been told you are going to Spain." Johnson responded, "Yes, I am, because when I accepted the Defense Department, you gave me the freedom to carry out my policy and that includes this visit to Spain."[292] Finally, on 7 September, Truman, with Acheson in support, forbade him from going.[293]

When he saw Brown, the president put his contempt for the Francoists into words. "How stupid these Spaniards are. Only from me can they expect anything at all and all they do is antagonize me. They are harshly persecuting Protestant Baptists of whom I am one." And, just as Clark had done before, Brown tried to downplay the accusations by suggesting that "there has been

---

[288] Telegram from Lequerica to Martín Artajo, 16 September 1949, Ministry of Foreign Affairs Record Group, file number 82–05987, AGA.

[289] Ibid.

[290] Lequerica to Martín Artajo, 16 September 1949, Ministry of Foreign Affairs Record Group, file number 82–05987, AGA. In 1935, with Drew Pearson, Brown had written a popular book, which was critical of U.S. foreign policy since the 1920s, *American Diplomatic Game* (D. Pearson and C. Brown, *American Diplomatic Game*, Garden City, Doubleday, Doran & Company, Inc., 1935).

[291] Marquina, *España en la política de seguridad...*, 279.

[292] Ibid., 278.

[293] Hualde, *El "cerco" ...*, 283.

THE STRUGGLE TO CHANGE U.S. POLICY TOWARD FRANCO'S SPAIN 177

considerable exaggeration and tendentious propaganda." At this point Truman asked him to prepare a report for him: "When you go to Spain, get direct information about the situation and report back to me. And do not allow yourself to be influenced by anyone." To this Brown laughed and responded, "Of course not, Mr President. I'll not be influenced by the Spaniards or by the embassy [of the United States in Madrid]. You are very aware of which Department interests it serves." Truman had also laughed in response to this and the journalist continued, "Let's rely on our experienced FBI agents. They are safe [...] but I do not believe that there is any basis in what you have been told." The president insisted and said that "also in South America the Spaniards are spreading anti-North American propaganda" which Brown tried to deny by saying "I'm sure they are doing nothing of the sort; don't believe all the reports issued by the State Department on this." And he went on:

> The Spaniards would be crazy to try to fall out with you and the United States. On the contrary, [Spain] is a country that is only trying to be pleasant to us and we really need their friendship. I speak to you as a North American and you know as well as I do that all branches of the military consider Spanish collaboration to be a real strategic necessity. Even on questions of lesser importance [the Spaniards] have been more respectful to you than to the other European nations.

He mentioned an incident concerning refrigerators – about which we know nothing – and finished by saying that the State Department's attitude to Spain had been heavily influenced by the "March–Heyneman [sic] lawsuit which has been used to attack the Spanish government. Heyneman [sic], currently hostile to the Spanish administration, has in his employ men such as Messersmith and Hooker and, to some extent, Foster Dulles."[294]

He was referring to a lawsuit that had been submitted to the Spanish judicial system in February 1948 and which ten years later would pit Spain against Belgium in the International Court of Justice in The Hague.[295] The lawsuit had come about as a result of the company Barcelona Traction Light & Power (known as La Canadiense) being declared bankrupt. It involved the Spanish financier Juan March,[296] who had filed for the company's bankruptcy at a court

[294] Lequerica to Martín Artajo, 16 September 1949, Ministry of Foreign Affairs Record Group, file number 82–05987, AGA.

[295] In 1958, which resulted in a favorable verdict for Spain.

[296] On March and the Barcelona Traction affair, see M. Cabrera, *Joan March (1880–1962)*, Madrid, Marcial Pons, 2011, 362 ff. On the Barcelona traction affair, see J. Ll. Sureda Carrión, *Fantasía y realidad en el expolio de Barcelona Traction. Apunte para una biografía de Juan March Ordinas*, Barcelona, Civitas-Thompson Reuters, 2014. On the bankruptcy judge, see A. M. Jordà, "El juez de Reus o el amargo sabor de la calumnia," *Diari de Tarragona*, 25 November 2016.

in Reus, and Dannie Heineman,[297] from the majority shareholder, SOFINA. Heineman was connected to various former and current members of the U.S. diplomatic service: George Strausser Messersmith – former ambassador in Mexico and Argentina and at that time an executive in Mexico DF for the Mexican Light & Power Company,[298] which also belonged to SOFINA; Robert G. Hooker Jr., associate chief of the Division of Eastern European Affairs; and John Foster Dulles, member of the U.S. delegation at the UN and Republican senator for New York in 1949 who, as we know, Lequerica had been accusing of following Heineman's orders after the delegation's abstention in the previous month of May. Truman said that he knew absolutely nothing about all of this, and asked to be sent an informative note.

These events revealed the quality of the contacts (or the tentacles well-greased with "subsidies") working for Lequerica, the embassy, and the paid lobbyists, which had now surfaced in the vicinity of the centers of power (in this case the most powerful of them all, the presidency itself). After the interview, Brown went to get the note from Lequerica, who dictated it to him as quickly and as briefly as he could "despite the considerable complexity" of the matter and the fact that it was to be given to the president of the United States.[299]

The "inspector" had been worried about the Barcelona Traction problem ever since the beginning of the dispute. After speaking with Heineman the year before, he had attempted to persuade the Spanish government to be considerate and reach an agreement on this and other issues involving SOFINA and Spain (such as the Compañía Hispanoamericana de Electricidad-CHADE). But to no avail. In fact, Heineman had threatened to do "a lot of damage to Spain if the Spanish government does not ensure that justice is done."[300] What is more, after a recent interview between the press attaché, Cacho Zabalza, and the member of the U.S. UN delegation Corrigan, Lequerica had been sent a message telling him that Spain should clear the way "of powerful enemies who are cautious but tenacious" if they were to make any progress in the United States. More specifically, Spain "needed to put aside the problem of Barcelona Traction and suspend, at least during the UN sessions, all judicial action or intervention in the affair." For Corrigan, "Spain has already paid over the odds for any services provided by Mr March and is now the victim of his unbridled ambition."[301]

---

[297] On Heineman, a U.S. citizen of German origin, see L. Rannieri, *Dannie Heineman. Un destin singulier 1872–1962*, Brussels, Racine, 2005.

[298] Letter, 16 December 1949, George G. Messersmith Papers, University of Delaware Archives.

[299] Lequerica to Martín Artajo, 16 September 1949.

[300] Letters from Lequerica to the Minister of Foreign Affairs, 28 July 1948 and 10 January 1949, Archivo Suanzes, cited in Cabrera, *Joan March ...*, 379–380.

[301] Visits from Cacho Zabalza to New York on 6 September 1949. Telegram from Lequerica to Martín Artajo Washington, 7 September 1949, Presidency of the Government Record Group, file number 82–05987, AGA.

THE STRUGGLE TO CHANGE U.S. POLICY TOWARD FRANCO'S SPAIN 179

Returning to the question of the Protestants, Lequerica and his sympathetic congressmen continued preparing reports and making political use of testimony from U.S. citizens living in Spain to question that there was any discrimination against them. In this regard, after twice visiting Spain, once as a guest of the "Plan Otoño" and once with his wife in the previous month of August,[302] Brewster asked Max H. Klein, president of the American Chamber of Commerce in Spain, who lived in Barcelona, to send him a letter-cum-report giving his version of what was really happening with the Protestants in the country. As Brewster had suspected, when he eventually received the report,[303] it was highly biased because Klein was a Catholic not a Protestant.[304] At no point was this mentioned – in fact, Klein seemed to suggest quite the opposite – which gave the text greater credibility. Brewster passed it on to Clark, who sent it to President Truman together with a personal letter[305] and two other reports that had been sent to the group of traveling congressmen and to Clark himself, one of which was highly critical and the other more moderate. The first was by John David Hughley Jr., representative in Spain for the Foreign Mission Board of the Southern Baptist Convention. And the second was by E. K. Haselden, leading elder of Milan del Bosch 97 Assembly in Barcelona.

Having visited Spain with the congressmen as part of the "Plan Otoño" and being received personally by Franco, Clark decided not to send the president the report he had asked for but the three texts just discussed and a personal letter in which he asked for a new interview so he could explain in person what, so he claimed, he had been told by the Generalísimo himself ("to take back an expression of General Franco's feeling regarding the religious situation, as well as other matters. The writer would prefer to discuss the Chief of State's [Franco] message orally. The writer arrived at a certain conclusion which he would also prefer to give orally").[306] But Truman refused to meet with him. By that time he must have been aware of his proximity to Lequerica, and the report by Hughley confirmed his point of view, even though Clark's

---

[302] Document sent by Spain's *Chargé d'Affaires* Germán Baráibar to the Spanish frontier authorities requesting that they assist Senator Brewster and his wife Mrs Dorothy Brewster, who were traveling to Spain: Washington, 25 August 1949, Ralph Owen Brewster Papers, Bowdoin College Library.

[303] Letter from Max H. Klein to Honorable Owen Brewster, 5 October 1949, Ralph Owen Brewster Papers, Bowdoin College Library.

[304] Lowi, "US Bases in Spain"…, 679.

[305] Letter from Charles Patrick Clark to the president enclosing his findings of a recent survey on freedom re "Worship in Spain" as applied to Protestants, 11 November 1949, Miscellaneous 422 cross-reference sheet, HSTPL. I am grateful to the HSTPL archivist and social media coordinator Tammy K. Williams for being so kind as to send me a copy of this file during the period of restricted access to the archive because of the COVID-19 pandemic.

[306] Letter from Charles Patrick Clark to the president enclosing….

180 JOAN MARIA THOMÀS

accompanying letter had tried to discredit him, because it coincided with his own Baptist sources of information.

Clark said that Hughley had admitted that

> in preparing this report, he had consulted no other clergymen of the Baptist or any other denomination, nor did he seek their views in the matter. This was confirmed by every minister interviewed, all stating that they were not consulted, nor had they seen the report until shown [by Clark himself]. [They believed that] the language was too strong and went too far. [...] His business and religious movements had never been interfered with by Spanish governmental authorities [...], he could cite no example of governmental interference with freedom of Protestant worship [although] he could cite incidents of civilian interference (by youths). [...] His visitor's visa has never been picked up by the government and he had never been asked by responsible government officials to leave Spain despite the general feeling that his actions and writings had been inflammatory, incitational, provocative, duplicitous, misleading and lacking in truth.

It is hard to believe that Hughley could have said these words, and it raises doubts about Clark's intentions. On the other hand, Clark sang the praises of the reports by Haselden and Klein and told the president that his interview with Franco had lasted an hour and that they had discussed "Freedom of Worship, particularly as applied to Protestants; So-called Jewish problems; and The Labor Situation."[307] And he requested the new interview mentioned above that was never to take place.

This put an end to the possibility of influencing the president and the decisions he would take to solve the Spanish question. The only channel left open was the legislative one, supported by pressure from the armed forces. So Lequerica, the lobbyists in the pay of the embassy and, of course, the sympathetic congressmen set to work in both the houses of Congress.

Loans for Spanish Companies and the Controversy with the Ministry of Trade and Industry

The strategy employed by Lequerica and the embassy to deal with all the applications for loans being made by Spain and Spanish public and private companies was to channel them all through the law firm Cummings, Stanley, Truitt & Cross. As Lequerica wrote to Minister Martín Artajo, "like all countries in the world, we are surrendering ourselves to the interest and care of specialized attorneys from here, who are ready to profit from the situation."[308]

---

[307] Ibid.

[308] Lequerica to Martín Artajo, 17 September 1949, MAE R-20210–10, cited in Cava Mesa, *Los diplomáticos de Franco ...*, 313.

THE STRUGGLE TO CHANGE U.S. POLICY TOWARD FRANCO'S SPAIN 181

For this reason, Lequerica attempted to give a high profile in Spain to Max O. Truitt, the partner in the law firm who spent most time on Spanish matters. We do not know for sure whether he actually traveled at this time to Spain, but we do know that Lequerica asked Martín Artajo to receive him, have an in-depth conversation and introduce him to all the right people. He argued:

> [I]f we are to get ourselves out of this economic dead end, put him in touch with the people who have the most influence because the economic situation, about which I am quite optimistic, is being delayed somewhat because of influential managers, or so it seems to me.

It was Truitt who had suggested that Spain approach the Export-Import Bank. Lequerica was critical of some of the bankers he knew such as "Barth of the Chase National, Oswald and other Spanish friends" of whom he said "that they were slightly inclined to the monopoly and tried to scare everyone else off."[309]

However, the Ministry of Foreign Affairs did not agree that everything should be channeled through the Cummings law firm,[310] and the other ministers involved in economic matters continued to send applications through the Ministry of Trade and Industry, the Ministry of Agriculture, or the National Institute of Industry directly to governmental and private organizations in the United States. For his part, Minister of Trade and Industry Juan Antonio Suanzes had been working on *Chargé d'Affaires* Culbertson for several months. He had sent him a "Note on Orientations for Economic Policy"[311] in which he not only calmed his possible "nationalizing" fears with respect to the increasing importance of the INI – which he was in favor of – but also suggested the possibility of a loan of $1,300 million over five years from the United States, starting with a first instalment of $200 million, of which $110 million would be used to import industrial equipment, $30 million to create transport infrastructure, and $60 million to purchase nitrogenous fertilizers. He also proclaimed the end of autarky and argued that U.S. capital should have a place in Spanish companies. Culbertson had proved to be receptive, so Suanzes sent Andrés Moreno – the chief executive of the Banco Hispano Americano – to negotiate the possibility of a loan. But to no avail.

In fact, Suanzes and Lequerica ended up clashing some months later when Tomás Boada, count of Marsal and president of the Empresa Nacional Torres Quevedo, visited Washington. Lequerica took him to visit Achilles in the State

---

[309] Letter from Lequerica to Martín Artajo, n.d.

[310] In the margin he wrote "This is not the case" with reference to the need for intermediate lawyers who would be paid for their time: Lequerica to Martín Artajo, 17 September 1949, MAE R-20210–10, cited in Cava Mesa, *Los diplomáticos de Franco ...*, 313.

[311] March 1949: A. Ballestero, *Juan Antonio Suanzes 1891–1977*, León, LID, 1993, 218 ff.

182 JOAN MARIA THOMÀS

Department and Emery, the vice-president of the Export-Import Bank. During the first visit, the department's director for Western Europe listed the regime's structural economic issues that he believed should be changed, and he pointed out once again that the official policy for awarding loans was based on their economic viability and the perspectives of repayment. During the second visit, they discussed the possible conditions of a loan of $50–70 million over ten years but did not agree on anything in particular because Boada had no specific instructions. However, the discussion was leaked to the U.S. press, which damaged the image of Spain and put paid to the discreet nature Boada's trip. Upset by Lequerica's interference, on 11 November Suanzes got the Council of Ministers to disapprove of the inspector's actions.

The Congressmen's Trip to Spain Organized by the Embassy and the Paid Lobbyists: The "Spanish Fever" of Trips by Congressmen, Businessmen, and the Military

During the summer of 1949, Lequerica, the embassy, and Clark designed the Plan Otoño", a trip to Spain paid for by the Madrid government for a group of selected sympathetic businessmen – "the champions of our cause," according to Lequerica – who were invited to "find out for themselves how to defend it."[312] The trip was clearly a bribe and a reward: on arriving in Spain, every traveler was given a cash bonus to the tune of $5,000 – $4,000 in U.S. currency and $1,000 in pesetas – and the congressmen's wives were included in both the trip and the cash bonuses. And McCarran, who eventually had to pull out, even planned to take two personal secretaries with him. All of this put considerable strain on the funds of a regime that was running chronically short of foreign currency. When Martín Artajo agreed to the plan,[313] he made it clear to Lequerica that in the short term they would be unable to incur any more expenses.[314] What is more, the program of activities was of the highest level

---

[312] Lequerica to Martín Artajo n.d., Ministry of Foreign Affairs Record Group, file number 82–05987, AGA.

[313] Authors such as Marquina or Hualde include visits by the military and others in the Plan Otoño.

[314] Martín Artajo's telegram to Lequerica, 1 September 1949, Presidency of the Government Record Group, file number 82–05987, AGA, says: "In principle I approve of the general lines of the Plan Otoño although the quantities seem excessive since the cost of the ticket will never be more than $1,000 plus companion, which is dead weight, very costly and makes the trip more expensive. Merry must come as soon as possible with three embassy secretaries to prepare Plan details with the Ministry under direct orders from me. I now urgently require the ministries of the Treasury and Commerce to send money order to the General Consulate New York for $140,000 by virtue of Council of Ministers agreement. Of this amount, $65,000 must remain in the Consulate account as repayment for monies already advanced to Your Excellency so that New York Consulate can cover outstanding debts with Ministry of the Treasury.

THE STRUGGLE TO CHANGE U.S. POLICY TOWARD FRANCO'S SPAIN 183

imaginable and included an audience with the head of state, meetings with ministers and other official visits in Madrid, Barcelona, and Bilbao, as well as numerous opportunities for leisure, recreation, and sightseeing.

The first official list of guests was, of course, headed by those who were the leading pro-Francoists in the Senate (that is to say, McCarran and Brewster). McCarran was planning to travel with his wife, his relative and political secretary Verner Adams, and his personal secretary Eva Adams,[315] who was to go on to have a successful career in the civil service. Finally, however, he could not travel as a member of the group. He did, however, share the voyage from New York with them, in his capacity as chairman of the Joint Committee on Foreign Economic Cooperation because he had he had been tasked with going on a fact-finding mission for the reform of the 1948 Displaced Persons Act (which he opposed). He had proposed his three-week trip to the Senate, but it was only agreed to and paid on 12 September, very close to the departure date of the "Plan Otoño" group. Once in Europe, he visited Spain and Franco after the group had already been, as we shall see below. Brewster did travel and was at the head of the group. He was introduced by Lequerica as "a wholehearted friend of ours since the beginning of our recent campaign" and someone who "the embassy largely owed the support not only of the other Republican senators but even of some leading Democrats."[316]

The group of travelers was made up of the following members: James T. Richards, Democrat representative for South Carolina, Protestant, and the acting president of the Foreign Affairs Committee who, according to Lequerica, had made "a long and entirely apt intervention in the House to cut the loans for the rearmament of Europe in half in favor of Spain"; Eugene Keogh, Democrat representative for New York, a Catholic, "a wholehearted friend of Spain's and a skillful strategist" in Congress, "of great prestige" and a member of the Interstate Commerce Commission and the Foreign

---

The remaining $75,000 will be paid to you to cover the $72,000 mentioned in your letter and Merry's trip and extras. I also require money order for 450,000 pesetas from the Ministry so that the amounts indicated by Your Excellency can be given to the travelers at the frontier. I must point out to Your Excellency that as we are making an extraordinary effort to collect $140,000 in foreign currency, any further money orders will be practically impossible so I earnestly request that until new notice you abstain from incurring any more expense in foreign currency. Also, the expedition to Spain, and above all, your zeal and diligence, allows us to hope for a positive outcome, even though we may have to wait for the rest of the project. Artajo" Apparently, in a previous communication Lequerica had asked the minister to be extremely discreet about the cost of the trip: "But for God's sake, do your usual tactful best to avoid anything that might suggest disinterest in the trip. It would not be practical – my God, what a scandal – and it would not be fair." Cited in Cava Mesa, *Los diplomáticos de Franco ...*, 311.

[315] Ibid.

[316] Ibid. All the citations below are from the same source.

Affairs Committee; Harold D. Cooley, Democrat representative for North Carolina, a Protestant and the chairman of the Committee on Agriculture, whom Lequerica described as "a leading member of Congress whose understanding of agriculture may be of great use to us"; and William R. Poage, Democrat representative for Texas, a Protestant and also a member of the Committee on Agriculture. The representative Arthur J. Klein, a Democrat for New York, a Jew – Israelite in Lequerica's terminology – and member of the Interstate Commerce Commission and the Foreign Affairs Committee, who was expected "to show great interest in the Jewish problem in Spain," was unable to travel, and was replaced by Abraham J. Multer, also a Democrat for New York and a Jew. Another member of the group was the Democrat representative for Pennsylvania, the Catholic William J. Green Jr., from the Armed Forces Committee, who was traveling on the understanding that he would deliver a report to the committee on his return to the United States. And, finally, there was another Catholic Democrat, the representative for Kentucky, Noel J. Gregory, who was a member "of the most important house committee, Ways and Means, which, as well as its most important task, was responsible for selecting committee members from among the representatives in the house." He was also a specialist on issues of irrigation and reservoirs "because he had an in-depth knowledge of the Tennessee Valley project."

As a whole, the group should have been made up of two senators and seven representatives, eleven men and seven women, the most notable of whom were "the unconditional friends of ours [...] the senators McCarran and Brewster, Congressman Keogh and the chairman of the Foreign Affairs Committee, Congressman Richards." They were to be accompanied by the organizer, Clark, who was the "leader of the expedition," and by Pablo Merry del Val, the embassy's advisor for cultural affairs. Lequerica had tried to get authorization from the ministry – apparently without success – to include the embassy's secretary, Jaime de Piniés, in the group because he worked closely with both himself and Merry in their dealings with the congressmen, and he was well known and appreciated.[317]

---

[317] The letter from Lequerica to Martín Artajo, 5 September 1949, Presidency of the Government Record Group, file number 82–05987, AGA, says: "Piniés knows most or all of the travelers personally. Because of his special political preparation and active enthusiasm, he has constantly attended lunches and meetings with senators and congressmen, and has even worked personally with the Capitol. Senator McCarran is an enthusiast of his, and never misses an opportunity to ask me about this intelligent young secretary, who has also provided him with information for his work. With Richards, the second ranking member of the House Foreign Affairs Committee, he also had numerous conversations. He has personal dealings with Brewster, Keogh and, I believe, practically all the others. So they would be delighted to meet Piniés. And in my opinion, it would be extremely useful to have him with them at this juncture. Baráibar, Propper and Merry are also of the same opinion."

The group stayed in Spain for thirteen days. They arrived by train in Port Bou on 27 September 1949 after leaving New York by ocean liner on 14 September and then traveling by train through France. They returned home via Irún on 10 October and then went back through France before boarding for the United States. The travelers were provided with a total of $72,000 and, when they reached the border at Port Bou, 450,000 pesetas. With this money, distributed as we have mentioned above, each member of the group had to pay for their accommodation and other expenses. Everything else (excursions, transfers, trips, and meals) was paid for by the Spanish government.[318] That is to say, although the congressmen seemingly paid for their own lodging, they were the recipients of yet another official Spanish subsidy.

The group spent the first stage of their journey (27 September–1 October) in Catalonia. They stayed at the Hotel Ritz in Barcelona and visited the city, local industry (where they met leading industrialists and businessmen), cotton plants, factories making agricultural machinery and fertilizers, waterfalls and electrical grids, the potassium mines in Suria and Cardona, and farms. They were taken sightseeing and introduced to local culture on trips to the Costa Brava (Girona) and the Benedictine monastery of Montserrat.[319] And, of course, there was also time to meet "leading Catholics, Protestants and Jews." After Barcelona, on 2 October, some of the group traveled to Bilbao by night train and others by plane. It was during the train journey that one of the anecdotes of the trip took place: two of the members of the group had their money and some of their clothes stolen. In the Basque capital, they stayed for two days in the Hotel Carlton, and their program of visits included mining and industrial centers, blast furnaces, electricity companies, and meetings with industrialists and bankers. From Bilbao, the group went on to Madrid, with a stopover in Burgos to visit the cathedral. Once in the capital, where they stayed in the Ritz, they met with Franco and his ministers and visited the National Social Security Institute and the Ministry of Employment. Several receptions were held in their honor: a lunch at the American Chamber of Commerce, with 400 guests, during which the minister of trade and industry, Suanzes, and the director general of the Banco Exterior de España, Arburúa, made a toast for improved trade relations between the two countries; a cocktail party hosted by the Banco Hispano Americano at the city hall; and a lunch organized by the Bank of Spain. They were also invited to attend a bull fight and a festival of dance and song by the Women's Section of the Falange, and they were taken sightseeing to El Escorial and Toledo.[320]

[318] Lequerica to Martín Artajo, n.d., Ministry of Foreign Affairs Record Group, file number 82–05987, AGA.

[319] "Visita de congresistas americanos," *La Vanguardia Española*, 1 October 1949: Brewster Papers, Bowdoin College Library.

[320] Marquina, *España en la política de seguridad...*, 282–283.

186   JOAN MARIA THOMÀS

The robbery on the train on 5 October involved the representatives Keogh and Richards,[321] and occurred when the train had stopped at the station in Casetas (Zaragoza). They were asleep and had hung their trousers next to the window, through which the thieves extracted them with a fishing rod. In total, they lost $5000 and Richards's trousers (Richards had to borrow some new ones to leave the train when they arrived at their destination).[322] However, the Spanish police acted promptly and managed to retrieve the trousers and $3800 after a shootout in Zaragoza in which the ringleader was seriously injured. But the most important aspect of the incident was that it revealed that politicians in the United States had been paid by the Franco regime. Richards and Keogh declared that "the money was intended to pay the fares of a group of Congressmen now touring Spain,"[323] which was used against the regime by the anti-Franco sectors of the country.

During the trip, Brewster and Clark were informed about the situation of the Protestants in the country and picked up the reports mentioned in the section above. Mulder was informed about the Jews. Green and Keogh were in contact with the military authorities. And all members of the group collected numerous documents about the country's economic predicament and its financial needs.

As well as the "Plan Otoño," the strategy of the embassy and the paid lobbyists benefitted from other trips made by U.S. citizens also seeking to improve relations between the two countries. The activity was such that it could be described as a real "Spanish fever" of official, semi-official, and private trips by congressmen, the military (a squadron of the U.S. navy), and businessmen interested in doing business with Spain.

There was one trip, however, that was raising some concern, even though Lequerica had pulled all the strings he could (through Clark and Truitt) to have Spain included on the list of countries to be visited. It was a trip made by a group of senators, also in September, after they had attended the thirty-eighth conference of the Inter-parliamentary Union in Stockholm and visited other European capitals. Apparently, Lequerica himself had managed to add Spain to their itinerary after London, Brussels, Amsterdam, Copenhagen, Stockholm, Oslo, Berlin, Geneva, Vienna, Trieste, Athens, Rome, Madrid, Paris, Le Havre, Bremerhaven, and Cherbourg, and he insisted that they be given an official

---

[321] According to Marquina, the travelers involved were Brewster and Keogh. Marquina also states that only senators had gone on the trip: namely, Brewster, Cooley, Multder (sic), Green, Poagh (sic), Richards, Clarck (sic) and Keogh, which again seems to be mistaken. He makes no mention of the organization of the trip by Lequerica and the Spanish embassy in Washington: Marquina, *España en la política de seguridad...*, 282–283.

[322] "2 Congressmen Robbed $5000 on Spanish Train," *The Washington Post*, 6 October 1949, Brewster Papers, Bowdoin College Library.

[323] "Congressmen Regain $3800; Stolen Pants," *The New York Times*, 8 October 1949, Brewster Papers, Bowdoin College Library.

THE STRUGGLE TO CHANGE U.S. POLICY TOWARD FRANCO'S SPAIN 187

welcome by the authorities.[324] The aim of the trip was to monitor how the money from the ECA was being spent.[325]

According to Lequerica, it was "a group of senators who were mostly members of Senate committees, particularly the armed forces, and included some of great prestige and far-reaching influence."[326] The problem now was that, unlike the trip organized by the embassy, the group of travelers consisted of friends ("half of them have tried to help us economically without knowing Spain") but also "systematic enemies." In general, Lequerica explained to Minister Martín Artajo, they were people who

> are taking advantage of their vacations [...] to find out in person and in the field what economic needs Europe has. Their study of conditions, their observations and the opinions they form will directly be turned into the activities of the parliamentary commission and the award of loans for Europe. And not only for the immediate future. The criteria they put forward about any country or any problem will last for many years.

For all these reasons, he asked the minister to treat them with "the utmost care and the greatest effort" and give them "every opportunity on all things but, insofar as it is possible, prevent them from coming into contact with people who may have an unduly negative influence on them." He warned him that "Above and beyond their financial interests, on this occasion the Protestant issue will be a major concern." So he specifically asked "that all means possible be used to take care of Spanish Protestants." He also warned the minister that the "real friends" in the group needed to be told about the "dreadful state of the civil side of the US embassy [in Madrid], who would not leave them alone for a minute." Once again, in the opinion of Lequerica and the ministry, there was a clear difference between the civil and the military sections of the U.S. embassy in Madrid, the latter of which was headed by the navy captain Mercer.

The group was made up of various senators, one of whom was McKellar, a Democrat from Tennessee and president of the Finance Committee who, according to Lequerica,

> was fully and at all times on the side of Senator McCarran during the Committee's discussions on the loan for Spain. On several occasions he spoke to the press in favor of granting the loan [...] saying that,

---

[324] Cava Mesa, *Los diplomáticos de Franco* ..., 310.

[325] Ibid. Cava Mesa cites the article by M. Childs, "Washington Calling," *The Washington Post*, 9 September 1949.

[326] Telegram from Lequerica to Martín Artajo, 26 August 1949, Ministry of Foreign Affairs Record Group, file number 82–05987, AGA.

188   JOAN MARIA THOMÀS

despite being an old Protestant, Spain should be heeded. He is an
elderly man of 80, admirably young.[327]

Another senator in the group was John L. McClellan, a Democrat for
Arkansas, chairman of the Committee on Expenditures in Executive
Departments and member of the Financial Committee, "a close personal
friend," who had voted for the initiative in favor of Spain in the previous
July. A third, Millard E. Tydings, was a Democrat for Maryland who was also
on the Finance Committee. Of him, Lequerica said that although "at first his
opinions on Spain had been very favorable [...] and he is always most polite in
all personal dealings" and that they were on friendly terms, he had eventually
become less publicly committed and even voted against the proposal. Lequerica
interpreted this change to be the result of the "influence his father-in-law,
the left-wing Ambassador [Nathaniel Penistone] Davies, has on him." Other
travelers in the group were Homer Ferguson, a Republican for Michigan and
member of the Finance Committee and the Judiciary Committee, who had
voted in favor of the proposal to help Spain; Willis Robertson, Democrat for
Virginia, member of the Finance Committee and the Committee on Banking
and Currency, who had voted against and was, according to Lequerica, "under
Protestant influence"; Richard B. Russell, Democrat for Georgia, member of
the Finance Committee and the Armed Services Committee, who had voted
in favor of the Spanish proposal despite being the representative of a highly
Protestant state; and Leverett Saltonstall, Republican for Massachusetts, also
a member of the Finance Committee and the Armed Services Committee. Of
him, Lequerica said that he belonged

> to one of the three best families in Boston whose importance has not
> diminished. The Saltonstalls have been involved in North American
> politics for many years. The role they have played can be compared to
> that of the Cecil family in England. Deeply Protestant and a puritan,
> he voted against the Spanish proposal probably because of his deep-
> seated Protestantism.

Also traveling with the group were Edward V. Nye, a Republican for
Minnesota and member of the Agriculture and Forestry Committee, who voted
against the Spanish proposal; Harley M. Kilgore, a Democrat for West Virginia,
a member of the Finance Committee and the Judiciary Committee who also
voted against (Lequerica believed "because he was a close friend of President
Truman" and he had always proved "to be hostile to our interests"); Guy Gordon,
a Republican for Oregon and a member of the Finance Committee and the

---

[327] Annex to the telegram from Lequerica to Martín Artajo, 26 August 1949,
Ministry of Foreign Affairs Record Group, file number 82–05987, AGA. The citations
below are from the same source.

THE STRUGGLE TO CHANGE U.S. POLICY TOWARD FRANCO'S SPAIN 189

Foreign and Insular Affairs Committee, who had voted in favor; Theodore F. Green, a Democrat for Rhode Island and a member of the Finance Committee and the Foreign Affairs Committee, of whom Lequerica said the following:

> Although he is over 80 years old, he is in good health, and he often shows off about his choreographic skills. He is susceptible to praise, refined and profoundly left wing. He acts against Spain's interests. He voted against the proposal for economic aid, probably for religious reasons. Very wordly, may God spare us from his falling into the hands of armchair opponents to the regime.

And the group was completed with Elmer Thomas, a Democrat for Oklahoma and a member of the Finance Committee and the Agriculture and Forestry Committee, who had voted in favor of the proposal of aid for Spain and whose "agricultural knowledge could be very useful to us"; and, finally, Milton R. Young, a Republican for North Dakota, also a member of the Finance Committee and the Agriculture and Forestry Committee, and who had also voted in favor of the Spanish proposal.

More explicit in his analysis of the dangers of this group's visit to Spain was the press attaché, Cacho Zabalza, who was concerned because he regarded them all as "loose cannons [*versos sueltos*] who get involved with unscrupulous elements and get up to no good."[328] He described the group in the following terms:

> Senator McKellar, an old friend of ours and old in age because he's over 80. McClellan voted with him. Tydings, our enemy, voted against although after what he said in the Finance Committee it seemed that he was in favor. Ferguson is a friend. He voted in favor. Robertson, a great Protestant, voted against. Russell ran the risk of losing everything for us because he represents such a Protestant state as Georgia and he voted in our favor. Saltonstall, a Republican Protestant, voted against. Nye did likewise, against. Kilgore is very hostile because of his friendship with the president. Guy Gordon, a friend, voted in favor. Green, 80 years old, voted against and responds well to praise. Thomas, a good friend, is interested in agriculture and his knowledge in this area is very important. And it may work in our favor. He voted for us. As did Young.[329]

---

[328] Quite unlike the "Plan Otoño" group, about whom he said "I hardly worry about because they are accompanied by our adviser Mr. Clark and Merry has been asked to be with them throughout their visit, just to be on the safe side": Letter from Mr. Cacho Zabalza, Washington, to Mr. Lojendio, 30 August 1949, San Sebastián, 7 September 1949, Diplomatic Information Office, Ministry of Foreign Affairs Record Group, file number 82–05987. The citations below all come from the same source.

[329] Ibid.

190   JOAN MARIA THOMÀS

He concluded:

> Most of these loose cannons cannot do us too much harm, but you
> know how things are; if someone out there moves in on them, after
> the pressure by our "Reds" who have managed to find representation
> in the Scandinavian congress […], they might have the truth of what
> they see and observe twisted for them. I should stress that we have
> open doors not iron curtains like [Marshal] Tito and all the others.[330]

Whatever the case may have been, the importance of the thirteen senators
was made clear, since four of them were the chairmen of Senate committees.
Lequerica was quick to point out that seven of them had voted in favor of
the Spanish proposal the previous month of July, and that some of these
were Democrats and had had to accept the consequences of "disobedience
and going against the guidelines laid down by the party in power." And on
other issues, only one of the travelers was a Catholic while all the others were
Protestants,[331] which could hardly be said to be an advantage.

Apart from the "Plan Otoño," this was the most important group that traveled
to Spain, although, as we have mentioned above, there were many others. This
"Spanish fever" was caused by the incipient but progressive change in feeling
toward relations with Franco and his regime among congressmen, sectors of
the U.S. administration, and businessmen, who were gradually beginning to
come round to the armed forces' way of thinking. One example of this change
was the first official visit by U.S. navy vessels to a Spanish port (Ferrol) on
3 September.

The visit was a significant sign of the pressure the military was bringing to
bear on the president and the secretary of state and, since Secretary Johnson
had not been allowed to visit Madrid, it was a real declaration of intent.
The naval squadron consisted of the cruisers *Columbus* and *Juneau* and the
destroyers *Stribling* and *Bordelon*, the first of which had Admiral Richard
Connolly, commander of the North Atlantic and Mediterranean fleet, on board
as well as three other admirals – Henderson, chief of staff of the fleet; Foskett,
commander of the cruiser division; and Walter Moore – as well as Harper, the
general of an army division, and Richie, the general of an air force brigade. Of
course, the Franco regime took great pains to give them a tremendous welcome
and, although Connolly did not have an official meeting with Franco, he did
coincide with him in the city bull ring, after he had sailed to La Coruña on
his yacht *Azor*.[332] Subsequently, Admiral Moore and the colonel of the marine
infantry Crawford Murray flew to Madrid from Lugo where they were joined

---

[330] Ibid.

[331] Analysis of the group. Annex to the telegram from Lequerica to Martín Artajo,
26 August 1949, Ministry of Foreign Affairs Record Group, Signature 82–05987, AGA.

[332] *El Faro* (Ceuta), 4 September 1949; *Los Sitios* (Gerona), 4 September 1949.

THE STRUGGLE TO CHANGE U.S. POLICY TOWARD FRANCO'S SPAIN 191

by Rear Admiral Manning and an officer from the marine infantry. Everything seems to suggest that in the capital they had meetings with high-ranking members of the military, probably set up by Mercer, who must have been elated by his success. On Admiral Connolly's return to the United States, he had interviews with several congressmen and President Truman himself.[333]

Other travelers in the month of September were the chief executive of Coca-Cola James Farley[334] and James J. Murphy, Democrat for New York and an active pro-Franco Catholic.[335] And in October Lequerica announced the visit of several senators from the Appropriations Committee who wanted to interview Franco and take part in a hunt. The ministry replied that their first wish could not be granted but that their second could.[336] They had been traveling around Europe for five weeks and were all of the Democrat party: Chavez (New Mexico), Stennis, Thye (Mississippi), McClellan (Arkansas), Robertson (Virginia), and Thomas (Oklahoma). And on their return to the United States they all declared that Spain should be given diplomatic recognition and economic aid.[337] For its part, the U.S. embassy announced the arrival of another group of twelve members of the House of Representatives, who were welcomed at Barajas airport by Director General of American Policy Prat y Soutzo and other high-ranking officials from the Ministry of Foreign Affairs. Among other things, they visited the president of the Regency Council, Minister of Trade and Industry Juan Antonio Suanzes, and Minister of National Education José Ibáñez Martín. And, since hunting had also apparently become part of the "Spanish fever," they also participated in two shoots. However, they did not manage to see Franco or the minister of foreign affairs as they had planned, because they were both on an official visit in Portugal.[338]

Particular mention should be made of McCarran's visit to Madrid on a private trip with Charles S. Dewey and their respective wives. After traveling from Paris, they were in the city from 29 October to 8 November. They had come to Europe on the same ocean liner as the congressmen of the "Plan Otoño" on a fact-finding mission for the reform of the 1948 Displaced Persons Act (which they opposed). McCarran had traveled in his capacity as chairman of the Joint Committee on Foreign Economic Cooperation and Dewey as agent general.[339] Before arriving in Madrid, they had taken in West Germany,

[333] Ibid.

[334] Marquina, *España en la política de seguridad...*, 282.

[335] Ibid., 280.

[336] Ibid., 286.

[337] *New York Times,* 2 November 1949.

[338] Marquina, *España en la política de seguridad...*, 288.

[339] The other members of the Joint Committee were Tom Connally (Texas), Walter F. George (Georgia), Styles Bridges (New Hampshire), and N. Alexander Smith (New Jersey). Tour of Spain and Europe 1949, 82–11/IV/1, box 28, Eva B. Adams Papers, University of Nevada, Reno.

Austria, and Italy, where McCarran had an audience with Pope Pius XII in the Vatican and requested that his two daughters, both nuns, be transferred from California to Washington (apparently their mother superior had refused to give permission despite the intervention of Cardinal Spellman).[340] And, after leaving Spain, they went on to Great Britain and Ireland to continue with their task of classifying refugees and determining economic aid, which involved interviewing the members of various governments. McCarran made the most of the opportunity to try to further Franco's cause. During his interview with the president of the Council of Ministers, the radical socialist Henri Queuille, he argued that France should work on improving its relations with Spain. He made little progress, however, because the president explained that

> it would be a bit shocking to the French to immediately accept a closer relationship with the Spanish government which was in opposition to all French thinking. [Although he] appreciated [...] the necessity of coming to some understanding at as early a date as was politically possible and stated that already commercial relationships existed between Spain and France.[341]

The visit to Spain was not on his agenda as a member of the Joint Committee; as we have seen, it was more a personal question. So both he and Dewey paid their own travel expenses to the border[342] where they were picked up by a reception committee of official cars sent by the Ministry of Foreign Affairs with Pablo Merry del Val, his introducer from this point on, at the

---

[340] Ybarra, *Washington Gone Crazy* ..., 472.

[341] Queuille did not agree: "His answer to the present policy or France in regard to Spain was that it would be a bit shocking to the French to immediately accept a closer relationship with the Spanish government which was in opposition to all French thinking. He appreciated however the necessity of coming to some understanding at as early a date as was politically possible and stated that already commercial relationships existed between Spain and France." Notes by Senator McCarran, 26 September 1949, 82–11/IV/1, box 28, Eva B. Adams Papers, University of Nevada, Reno. He also saw Jean Monnet, author of the plan of the same name and then head of the Planning Division of Modernization and Equipment of French Industry. Notes by Senator McCarran, 23 September 1949, 82–11/IV/1, box 28, Eva B. Adams Papers, University of Nevada, Reno.

[342] "I'm going into Spain with Mrs McCarran and Mr and Mrs Dewey. They will have to bear their own expenses while in Spain because there are no counterpart funds, and I will have to bear mine, which is alright. I understand that the Spanish government will extend certain courtesies but that we will have to take care of our own gasoline expenses and hotel and living accommodations. That too is alright." Letter from McCarran to Eva Adams, 26 October 1949.

head. Beforehand, McCarran had met with Ambassador Aguirre de Cárcer[343] in the Hotel Crillon in Paris, who had given him his formal invitation. Also present were the duke of Alba and the manager of the Morgan Bank, Nelson Dean Jay.[344] When the small group of travelers reached Madrid, where they stayed for three days, McCarran had audiences with Franco, Primate Pla y Deniel, and most government ministers. He was shown what the regime was doing to improve social conditions and which public infrastructures they were putting in place, and McCarran was so impressed that he became even more convinced of his pro-Franco sympathies. A good example of this was that he did not hesitate to claim that, if Spain had received aid for these purposes from the United States or any other country, in terms of reconstruction it would be ahead of all the countries he had inspected. His exact words were the following:

> From my study of France, Western Germany and Italy I would say that Spain has kept abreast of all of these countries in her advancement and improvement. Hundreds of miles of bridges have been put in, hundreds of miles of roads improved, reconstruction of buildings and construction of new buildings –all stand as a monument to Spanish determination. All of this without a dollar of aid from any country. However, it must be said in all seriousness that unless some economic assistance is rendered to Spain within a very short time, many of the strides of advancement made during the years since the Civil War in Spain will have been lost. The Spanish authorities and the Spanish people cannot understand the attitude of America. They seem depressed with the fact that we would recognize and aid Tito, and not recognize and aid Spain. They seem depressed that we

[343] Notes by Senator McCarran, 23 September 1949, 82–11/IV/1, box 28, Eva B. Adams Papers, University of Nevada, Reno.

[344] At a reception, he had met the duke of Alba, who had been very critical of Franco for not having kept his promise to make way for Don Juan de Borbón once the Civil War was over, as he had promised him and other royalists. Notes by Senator McCarran, 23 September 1949, 82–11/IV/1, box 28, Eva B. Adams Papers, Adams Papers, University of Nevada, Reno. In Fontainebleau, he had dined at the home of Nelson Dean Jay, manager of the Morgan Bank in Paris, who had had experience of negotiating loans with Spain during the Primo de Rivera dictatorship. McCarran said that "Jay was quite outspoken in his belief that the decision of the United Nations to withdraw diplomatic representation from Spain only strengthened Franco's hand and the Spanish people took it as a personal offence." Likewise, "he believed that Franco looking to the return of King Juan might have made some arrangements for some sort of parliamentary form of government. This is probably to be hoped for now but has been delayed by the action of the United Nations." Notes by Senator McCarran, 25 September 1949, 82–11/IV/1, box 28, Eva B. Adams Papers, University of Nevada, Reno.

194 JOAN MARIA THOMÀS

would aid Germany and have Germany put into the United Nations, and not extend a friendly hand toward Spain. With one voice they claim that they do not want gifts, they want nothing given to them, what they want is an opportunity to have credit and credit in such amounts that they can pay back when they promise to pay, that is all that Spain is asking. They look upon gifts with disdain, they pray for credit. England has but recently extended credit in the amount of 1,300,000,000 pesetas and probably more. This of course is backed up by American dollars given to Great Britain. France has entered into a trade agreement with Spain, and this again is supported by American dollars given to France. In other words, England and France are building up trade with Spain to the detriment of the United States. Spain wants millions of tons of cotton; she needs heavy machinery in great quantity, roadbuilding machinery, cement machinery, textile machinery, all of which could come from the United States; and in every instance they want to purchase from the United States rather than from any other country. Other countries are taking advantage of this. If Spain had dollars, she would be far ahead of any country in Europe that I have visited.[345]

But he had been even more impressed by his conversation with Franco:

My visit with Franco was exceedingly interesting and I was most agreeably surprised to learn the nature and kind of man that he is. He has been frightfully slandered and maligned by some agencies evidently with design. I had contact with nearly all the members of his cabinet and went into their plans of operation and their method of government in detail. Their social security laws are in advance of those in America today. The housing that is being constructed by the government for the workers in the various plants is superior to the housing that is being built in America any place that I have seen. As regards social security again, in most industries the entire social security is paid by the employer and in some instances it is as high as 112 percent of the earnings of the employee. There is, of course, poverty in Spain as there is in all countries. We don't have to go out of New York to see that, but in proportion to the population there is, I would say, a minimum of poverty – not to say that the people live on a very high caloric intake, but nevertheless they seem to be happy and intent on going forward.[346]

[345] McCarran to Adams, 9 November 1949, Tour of Spain and Europe 1949, 82–11/ IV/1, box 28, Eva B. Adams Papers, University of Nevada, Reno.
[346] Ibid.

THE STRUGGLE TO CHANGE U.S. POLICY TOWARD FRANCO'S SPAIN 195

And, of course, the contacts that Merry had set up for him with members of the general public had the desired effect on McCarran, who came away with the impression that the regime and its leader had massive popular support:

> I found the sentiment of the people of Spain from the lowest in stature to the highest, outspoken in praise of Franco's regime and of Franco himself. The only opposition that appears to Franco is the Communist regime that maintain a school at Toulouse in France and educate young misguided Spaniards to carry forward sabotage and destruction across the line near the French–Spanish border, and of course the Communist regime from Russia. What is more, there is a very decided opposition to aiding Spain coming from Mr. Attlee's government. Attlee took a heavy part in the Civil War in Spain and was one of the outspoken, encouraging agencies of the Communist regime in Spain.[347]

During the voyage in the company of the "Plan Otoño" group, however, McCarran realized that Clark was concerned about his plan to go to Madrid during his Joint Committee fact-finding mission and he began to distrust him. He explained his impressions to his administrative secretary, Eva Adams, in the following terms:

> I am a little afraid, although I have nothing to support this statement, that the group that went in under Clark, that is the group that was guided by Mr Charles Patrick Clark, for some reason or other made it difficult for some of us who are following up to go to Spain. This of course is strictly confidential because I haven't anything to support it, but certain straws in the wind make me think that there is a wind. I am glad that you are writing to Mrs McCarran and myself here, that's just the right thing to do. I hope you will tell us all the news about home and sister Margaret and Patricia and sister Mary Mercy. Charles Patrick Clark telephoned me in Rome saying that he was leaving for America. He was then in Paris. He said that he had left certain documents with "Mary del Valle" – this is his brother, a fellow who used to be secretary to the former Pope – in Spain, but where "Mary del Valle" is is more than I know. I think maybe it is some more double talk on the part of Mr. Clark. I got a lot of that coming over on the boat, and a lot of other things that I will tell you when I see you. Suffice it to say, treat the gentleman civil but cool. Give him no information. Deal in his own methods: double talk.[348]

---

[347] Ibid.

[348] Letter from McCarran to Eva Adams, 26 October 1949, 82–11/IV/1, box 28, Eva B. Adams Papers, University of Nevada, Reno.

As expected, when he returned from his trip to Europe he spoke out loudly in favor of Franco and of granting Spain loans. His arguments for normalizing the diplomatic relations between the United States and Spain were the following:

> Moral. To correct the injustice to Spain resulting from the cessation of full diplomatic relations.

> Military. To assure the United States of Spanish friendship in the Cold War with Russia, with resulting improvement of our military, naval, and air strength vis-a-vis Russia.

> Economic. To promote the exchange of goods and services between the United States and Spain and thus strengthen the economies of both countries.

> Diplomatic. To promote further our relations with Latin America whose culture derives from Spain.[349]

McCarran's trip to Spain was not the last made by congressmen, who nearly always took advantage of the final days of other visits to Europe to stop off in the country. The number of visits even prompted Martín Artajo to complain to Lequerica about the lack of warning about some of the new arrivals.[350] And *Chargé d'Affaires* Culbertson complained again to the State Department about the situation being created and the catastrophic consequences for the policy they wanted to implement.[351] He also complained about the U.S. navy's visit because of the political importance given to it by the Spaniards and the fact that it, and other similar visits, was delaying any change in the Franco regime.[352] In response to his complaints, Acheson felt obliged to telegraph him to confirm that they were still implementing the same policy. In fact, it is quite feasible that Mercer's dismissal as naval attaché was the direct consequence of Culbertson's complaints. Indeed, on 10 November, a new military attaché arrived in Madrid.[353]

However, the divide separating the pro-Franco congressmen and the Pentagon from the secretary of state and President Truman was increasingly evident, and, what was much worse for the last two, Franco was very aware of this situation because the congressmen had made sure that he was kept

---

[349] Resumption of Full Diplomatic Relations with Spain, 82–11/IV/1, box 28, Eva B. Adams Papers, University of Nevada, Reno.

[350] Marquina, *España en la política de seguridad...*, 293.

[351] Ibid., 283.

[352] Ibid., 284–285.

[353] Ibid., 293. Marquina claims that Mercer was the head of the CIA in Spain, which we do not believe to be true, as we have mentioned above when citing Alfred Conrad Ulmer.

up to date. In December, Averell Harriman, the coordinator of the Marshall Plan – European Recovery Plan (ERP) – and former ambassador in Great Britain and the Soviet Union was given the following information by one of his collaborators in Europe:[354]

> Franco seems to have come to the conclusion that, regardless of the hostile attitude of the United States and the Department of State, he will be able to obtain American credits for Spain, either through the Export-Import Bank or (which seems to him more likely) through the ECA. This belief stems from the following: Last summer, during the visit of the United States Fleet, several high-ranking naval officers spoke quite openly – not only to him but to other Spaniards as well – of the necessity for the United States to control naval bases in Spain and islands owned by Spain. Some months ago, two unidentified American generals visited Franco and also spoke quite openly of the necessity of Army and Air Force bases in Spain to defend the Continent against Russian attack. During the recent visits of Senators and members of Congress to Spain, several of them stated at parties that despite the attitude of the Department of State and the United Nations, they (the Senators and Representatives) really represent the government and they will see to it that Spain receives adequate financial support from the United States.[355]

All of this left Undersecretary Miranda and Prat feeling quite "overwhelmed" and reinforced Franco's belief that Lequerica was working too closely with the State Department and not enough with Congress, despite paying Clark an annual salary of $50,000.[356]

At the end of 1949, the anti-Francoists in the United States were still denouncing the shortcomings and ambiguities of the State Department's policy on Spain and how Franco was taking advantage of this situation. On

---

[354] Jan F. Libich, former OSS agent decorated for his action in Hungary in 1944 and who at that time was working as assistant at the Office of Special Representation in Europe of the Mutual Security Agency, in Paris. He had obtained the information from conversations held in Madrid between 5 and 15 December 1949, the most important of which was with a contact who was a "close friend of Generalissimo Franco, with whom I spent several days on a hunting trip in the mountains near Madrid." Memorandum from Jan F. Libich to Mr. Harriman, Eyes Only, 17 December 1949, Harriman Papers, Library of Congress.

[355] Memorandum Jan F. Libich.

[356] Ibid., "Franco is not satisfied with the services of his representative in Washington Marchese Lequeitio (sic), who pays $50,000 a year for the services of a contact man and lobbyist, a Washington lawyer by the name of Clark (initials unknown). He is of the opinion that Lequeitio (sic) works too much with the Department of State, which is hostile to Spain, instead of working on public opinion and Congress."

12 December, in *The New Republic*, Harold Ickes once again pointed out the contrast between some clearly anti-regime declarations made by the secretary (for example, on 30 May he had said "the United States must withdraw from the initiative of reestablishing full diplomatic relations with Spain") and the reality of putting up with the presence of Lequerica, Propper, Mendoza, and others from the Vichy period. He also harked back to the meal organized by Lequerica to celebrate the Japanese victory at Corregidor[357] and he denounced the activity of "Senator McCarran of Nevada, the Machiavelli of Coca-Cola James A. Farley, and other more or less distinguished or distinguishable politicians with their own private interests."[358] And he now included in his criticism both the Chase National Bank of New York for having loaned Spain $25 million and Admiral Connolly for having visited Ferrol, all to the benefit of "shameless Franco."[359]

1950

Action Taken by José Félix de Lequerica, the Embassy and the Paid Lobbyists in 1950

Lequerica and the embassy very soon got a return on their activity of the previous year. As soon as they were back in the United States many of the congressmen who had traveled to Spain, whether as members of the "Plan Otoño" or not, made statements to the press and/or radios, or intervened in their respective houses or in joint debates in favor of changing U.S. policy on Spain. Economic stakeholders, particularly from the cotton sector, also applied greater pressure in Congress, with new interventions by President Truman and the Texan senator Tom Connally, who was working closely with the Export-Import Bank, the Chase National, and the National Bank.[360] Likewise, some sectors of the Spanish Bloc gave fresh impetus to pro-regime propaganda: Carlton Hayes published a new book, *The United States and Spain. An Interpretation*,[361] which, unlike *Misión de guerra en España*, was brazenly pro-Franco. For him, the Spanish question had become one of his favorite topics.[362] The importance Lequerica gave to Hayes's support was made clear by the fact that he asked Martín Artajo for Minister of National

---

[357] Harold Ickes, *The New Republic* 12 December 1949.

[358] Ibid.

[359] Ibid.

[360] Hualde, *El "cerco"* ..., 275.

[361] New York, Sheed & Ward, 1951.

[362] And it continued to be until his death in 1964. See the letter from Hayes to Clark on 3 May 1961: "Your subject is a favorite one with me, namely, Spain and the need of promoting close friendly relations between the US and the Spanish People. We owe Spain a great deal for the historic role it has played in the American Continent and

Education José Ibáñez to award him an honorary degree from the University of Salamanca.[363] At the same time, the embassy encouraged U.S. citizens to send pro-Franco letters to the press,[364] and Franco expected that other letters he had received should also be published in the United States. José María Doussinague, former director of foreign policy of the Ministry of Foreign Affairs and author of *España tenía razón (1939–1945)*, went on a book tour of the United States and Canada to promote the English translation. Both the tour and the translation were funded by the ministry.[365] And General Willoughby, a leading member of the bloc, spent his time writing letters from Japan, where he was stationed, to the government in Madrid explaining his pro-Franco activity in Washington and to senators Vandenberg, McCarran and Cain insisting that justice be done with Spain.[366] The Spanish Bloc was increasingly attracting some businessmen who aspired to be intermediaries and others who hoped to take advantage of the change in policy on Spain.[367]

Less visible, but equally determined, was the pressure exerted by the military, who executed a *de facto* pincer movement with senators McCarran, Brewster, and other pro-Franco congressmen in the period immediately preceding the outbreak of the Korean War on 25 June. In April, high-ranking officers of the armed forces attempted to influence the Allied Conference of Ministers of Foreign Affairs that was going to be held in London, crucial for the integration

---

latterly as a bulwark against atheistic communism." John D. Lodge Papers. Hoover Institution Archives. Stanford University (California).

[363] He was never actually awarded the degree, but in 1952 he received the Grand Cross of Alfonso X the Wise: "I presented Ambassador Hayes with the Cross of Alfonso X. I found him quite well, and as passionate and animated about Spain as ever. We spent three extraordinarily pleasant days with them. The people from these small villages are really quite curious; they are highly cultured and in general very sympathetic to our country and its Regime. During mass, the Catholic priest of Afton called me the Ambassador of His Excellency's and repeated the name 'Franco' a number of times in the midst of thoughtful and fair praise. I was impressed with the tone of American life even in a town of fewer than 1,000 inhabitants. The cocktail party given by Carlton Hayes for fifty or sixty guests seemed just like a Washington party. According to the ambassador, this town was repeated many thousands of times all over North America, and was the true basis of life in this country." Lequerica to Martín Artajo, 6 November 1952, Presidency of the Government Record Group, Head of State, file number 72–07660, AGA.

[364] Lequerica to Erice, director general of Foreign Policy, 7 January 1950, Presidency of the Government Record Group, file number 82–07487, AGA.

[365] Lequerica to Erice, director general of Foreign Policy, 25 May 1950, Ministry of Foreign Affairs Record Group, file number 82–07487, AGA.

[366] Lequerica to Erice, director general of Foreign Policy, 4 January 1950, Ministry of Foreign Affairs Record Group, file number 82–07487, AGA.

[367] Lequerica to Erice, director general of Foreign Policy, 14 August 1950, Ministry of Foreign Affairs Record Group, file number 82–07487, AGA.

200 JOAN MARIA THOMÀS

of Spain into the Western defense system either bilaterally or as part of NATO. Secretary Johnson, the chairman of the Joint Chiefs of Staff, General Bradley, and Admiral Connolly all made it clear to Secretary Acheson that Spain was the last European bastion in the event of a communist offensive in the West, an argument that the State Department and the president[368] considered to be counterproductive to relations with their European allies, particularly France. Likewise, Bradley, General Hoyt S. Vandenberg (chief of staff of the air force) and a representative of Admiral Forrest P. Sherman (the U.S. navy chief of naval operations and also a member of the Joint Chiefs of Staff) approached the Senate Appropriations Committee to explain the ineffectiveness of the North Atlantic Treaty and argue for Spain to join the efforts to defend Europe.[369] This full-scale military offensive was brought to a sudden halt on 15 June when the president announced that the sections on Germany and Spain in the document Johnson had submitted to the National Security Council (NSC 72) were of an excessively "military nature."[370] He went on to approve Acheson's proposal of drafting two new memoranda on Spain, one for himself and the other for NSC. However, this was only ten days before the outbreak of the Korean War, the first armed conflict of the Cold War, which was to have an indirect influence on relations with the Franco regime and lay the foundations for the Truman administration's definitive change in policy toward Spain.

Meanwhile, in response to the increase in public interest in the "Spanish question," the Secretary of State sent a letter to the chairman of the Senate's Foreign Relations Committee, Connally, on 18 January 1950.[371] In it, and for the first time, he stated what the United States planned to do about the ambassadors and the admission of Spain to the UN specialized agencies. He denounced that

> the Spanish question has been so exaggerated by controversy that it now has a place among the current problems of our foreign policy that is out of all proportion to its intrinsic importance. The propaganda and the pressure both here and abroad have kept the controversy alive, and have served to stimulate the emotions rather than rational thought.[372]

[368] Hualde, El "cerco" ..., 289–291.

[369] During one of these meetings, Secretary Johnson also mentioned that "politically this was really quite complex because of the persecution of Protestants in Spain": Lequerica to Martín Artajo, 19 April 1950, AFNFF.

[370] Cited in Hualde, El "cerco" ..., 291.

[371] This was the (correct) interpretation that Lequerica transmitted to Madrid: it was the result of the flood of statements on the issue in the recent months.

[372] Washington, 19 January 1950, "Letter from the US Secretary of State, Mr. Acheson, on the Spanish question," Ministry of Foreign Affairs Record Group, file number 82–07487, AGA.

THE STRUGGLE TO CHANGE U.S. POLICY TOWARD FRANCO'S SPAIN 201

He also revealed in public that he was in favor of repealing the 1946 UN resolution, which would pave the way for the exchange of ambassadors between Washington and Madrid, and that "there is no sign of an alternative to the present [Spanish] government," which enjoyed "a strong internal position" and "the support of many who, although they would prefer another form of government or head of state, fear the chaos and the civil war that would inevitably be the result of any movement" to overthrow it. He accompanied all these arguments with a demand for internal changes, although he made no mention of the regime's fascist nature.

In the secretary of state's opinion:

> Spain is a part of Western Europe that should not be permanently isolated from the normal relations in the zone. There are, however, some obstacles to this. For reasons of the nature, origin and history of the present Spanish government, Spain is still unacceptable to many of the nations in Western Europe as an associate in cooperative projects such as the European Recovery Program and the Council of Europe. We believe that on this issue the nations of Western Europe should have the final say. If they are to be successful, these programs require the closest possible collaboration among the participants and are designed to strengthen and develop the democratic way of life, in opposition to the threats posed by Communist expansion. This is a policy on which we and the nations of Western Europe have all agreed. It is not merely a negative reaction to Communism. Rather, it is a positive program to sustain and strengthen democratic freedoms – politically, economically and militarily. In this framework, the involvement of the present Spanish government, unless and until there has been some indication of evolution toward a more democratic regime, would weaken rather than strengthen the collective effort to safeguard and reinforce democracy.

He deduced that there was a need for the United States to continue striving

> to persuade the Spanish government that its own interests as a member of the international community, and particularly as a member of the community of Western Europe, require steps to be taken toward democratic government with the highest hopes for the enjoyment of basic human rights and fundamental freedoms in Spain [...] The decision on which measures can and should be adopted must, of course, be taken only by the Spanish.

He pointed out the difficulty "of regarding Spain as a member of the free Western community if there is no substantial progress toward any increase in civil freedom, religious freedom and the freedom to enjoy the basic rights of organized work." He reinforced this argument by saying that one of the first acts of the new International Confederation of Free Trade Unions [had been] to issue a resolution condemning the present government of Spain and opposing any aid to Spain until the moment at which democratic rights and full trade-union rights have been restored and workers find themselves once more in a position to contribute to the recovery of the country.

Indeed, the previous December, shortly after had come into being, the International Confederation of Free Trade Unions passed a motion to oppose any sort of aid to the Franco regime and Spain's inclusion in the Marshall Plan and NATO. This opposition was given further support in February at the congresses of the two leading U.S. trade unions, the American Federation of Labor (AFL) and the Congress of Industrial Organization (CIO), which had also sent their agreements to Acheson and Truman.[373]

With respect to the U.S. decision to support the repeal of the 1946 resolution, Acheson said:

[I]n the General Assembly last spring, the majority of members voting on the Latin-American resolution concerning Spain expressed the desire to revise the 1946 resolution in the sense of allowing members freedom to decide whether they should return their ambassadors or ministers to Madrid. It is the opinion of this Government that the anomalous situation with respect to Spain should be resolved. The United States is therefore prepared to vote in the General Assembly in favor of a resolution which would leave members free to send an ambassador or minister to Spain if they so desire. We would do this for the reasons I have already indicated and in the hope that this aspect of the Spanish question can no longer be used by hostile propaganda to create unnecessary divisions within the United Nations and among our own people [...] but our vote would not in any sense signify approval of the Spanish regime. It would simply indicate our desire, in the interests of orderly international relations, to return to normal practice in the exchange of diplomatic representations.

In other words, he was in favor of exchanging ambassadors. He also stated that he was in favor of allowing Spain to take part in UN specialized agencies

if they felt that Spain's membership would contribute to their efficiency. We believe that membership in these bodies should be determined, as far as practicable, on a technical rather than political basis. It has already been found on a number of occasions that the work of these organizations has been undermined by Spain's inability to accept the obligations and restrictions, as well as the privileges, of the activities.

[373] Cited in Hualde, *El "cerco"* ..., 287–288.

THE STRUGGLE TO CHANGE U.S. POLICY TOWARD FRANCO'S SPAIN 203

Finally, he stated that public and private subsidies to companies were quite acceptable but refused to entertain the idea of official aid of a general nature. And he once again argued that Spain needed to make important changes to its economic policy:

> The success of mutually beneficial economic relations between the United States and Spain depends entirely on the equal collaboration of both sides. Unfortunately, however, little progress has been made. The United States sincerely wishes to facilitate normal business and trade with Spain, but ultimate success depends on the cooperation of the Spanish Government in taking constructive steps to promote its trade and attract foreign investment. In order to assist these activities, the United States offered to negotiate a new treaty of friendship, trade and navigation. So far the Spanish Government has shown no interest in such agreements. Efforts have also been made to induce the Spanish Government to simplify its import and export controls and its foreign exchange system, which is based on a multiplicity of exchange rates, with a view to establishing an exchange rate which would enable Spanish goods to compete, particularly in the dollar market. Efforts have also been made to induce the Spanish Government to lift the 25% restriction on the participation of foreign investors in Spanish companies and to give existing foreign investments better treatment, all of which are now obvious obstacles to the inflow of investments into Spain. As far as these problems are concerned, we have pointed out to interested Spaniards and to the Spanish Government that the current critical situation in the Spanish balance of payments in dollars appears to stem from difficulties that could be substantially rectified by action of the Spanish Government. To date, however, this Government has done little in this regard. In the Department's view, the steps to be taken to foster mutually beneficial economic relations between Spain and the United States are a matter for the Spanish Government.[374]

At the time, he was unaware that in the following April and July McCarran would manage to force the award of an official loan to Spain, first by the direct approach and then by senatorial strategy.

The letter was well received by Lequerica, who immediately understood the progress it meant, and he explained it to Minister Martín Artajo in this positive light just when he was having to cope with the State Department questioning the legality of his stay in Washington. This attempt was clearly a sign that he, the paid lobbyists, and the sympathetic congressmen were a thorn in the side of the anti-Franco sector of the department. However, ever since his time as minister of foreign affairs, and thanks to people such as Hayes and

---

[374] Washington, 19 January 1950, "Letter from the US Secretary of State, Mr. Acheson, on the Spanish question."

his old and new contacts with diplomats and officials, Lequerica knew that the department was a complex organization and that, within it, he had enemies but also friends and supporters. And just as he always had done, he continued to cultivate these friends and supporters. Foremost among them was Douglas McArthur II, head of the Division of Western European Affairs; but among the others who showed no hostility to him there was also Under Secretary for Administration John E. Peurifoy – the department's number three – for whom Lequerica held a banquet when he stepped down to go to the embassy in Athens.[375] It was during this banquet that Peurifoy himself announced that in October or November Lequerica would cease to be "ambassador in waiting" – as he was referred to jokingly but without malice by some of the press – and finally occupy the position he aspired to (or rather yearned for).[376] He was now in the position that he was not sure that he would ever be appointed, not because of the *agrément* but because of the enemies he had made in the Palacio de Santa Cruz. Meanwhile, in Washington, the name on everyone's lips as favorite to be ambassador in Madrid was Admiral Leahy, his old friend from Vichy, who was recovering at the time from a serious illness. Even so, he was prepared to accept the appointment, and was expecting it, because of his close relationship with President Truman.[377]

In parallel to his letter and in preparation for the recovery of full diplomatic relations, Acheson began to develop a program within the State Department to improve how the general public in Spain perceived the United States. To do so, he commissioned the design of the first "country paper" from the U.S. Information and Educational Exchange Program (USIE), which would be the first step in a whole package of measures for Spain.[378]

The Debate on the Protestant Question in Spain on 10 March

As part of his exploitation of the results of the "Plan Otoño" and aware of President Truman's inflexibility on the Protestant question, on 10 March Brewster raised the Protestant question in Congress and denied that there was no freedom of worship in Spain. He read some sections of Max Klein's report, and referred to contacts of his own and of others in Spain. However, the Protestant question and the general situation in Spain was discussed most

---

[375] Attended by five senators and representatives, as well as the ambassador of Brazil. Lequerica to Martín Artajo, 20 April 1950, file 21314, AFNFF.

[376] Handwritten letter from Lequerica to the Head of State, 25 October 1950, file 9532, AFNFF.

[377] Lequerica to Martín Artajo, 20 April 1950, file 21314, AFNFF.

[378] L. Delgado Gómez-Escalonilla, "La maquinaria de la persuasión. Política informativa y cultural de Estados Unidos hacia España," *Ayer,* vol. 75 (2009), 113–114; see also P. León Aguinaga, "Los canales de la propaganda norteamericana en España 1945–1960," *Ayer*, vol. 75 (2009), 133–158.

THE STRUGGLE TO CHANGE U.S. POLICY TOWARD FRANCO'S SPAIN 205

extensively by the chairman of the House of Representatives' Committee of Foreign Relations, Richards, who contested the Truman administration's policy of scrutinizing the Franco regime's politics and economy, pointing out that it did not do the same for any other country. He supported the points of view proffered by Brewster and Mulder, who had looked into the situation of the Jews, by quoting from the report written by Clark.

The New Senate Initiatives in Favor of Loans for Spain in April and June: Finally, Results of $62.5 million

As well as the debate on Spain just mentioned, there were two other initiatives in connection with the granting of loans to Spain, instigated by Lequerica and involving Brewster and McCarran. One of them was successful, largely thanks to McCarran. But, before looking at them in detail, we should say that at this time Lequerica and the embassy were also taking representatives of Spanish companies to visit public and private U.S. banks,[379] or sending letters of introduction and/or recommendation to Minister Martín Artajo from U.S. businessmen and journalists who were traveling to Spain either to negotiate possible deals with the Ministry of Trade and Industry or to report favorably on the country.[380] However, Suanzes and Martín Artajo were making new plans. After the trip to Spain organized by the embassy in the United States for congressmen, and in agreement with Culbertson, they decided to make the most of the situation and send Mariano Yturralde, the director of economic policy of the Ministry of Trade and Industry, on an economic mission to Washington. They had hoped that the mission would be a secret one but it did not turn out like that. The aim was for him to negotiate a loan from the Export-Import Bank for industrial projects and the purchase of wheat, bearing in mind that in April 1950 this bank had granted a loan of $125 million to Argentina.

Lequerica, probably upset by the idea, was categorically against the director's trip because he felt that it was not the moment, that the amount of the loan and the purpose to which it would be put had not been well thought through, and that it was not in line with his attempts with the congressmen to obtain future industrial aid for Spain. After Yturralde had reported back to his superiors about Lequerica's attitude, he was ordered to carry on with his preparations so he had to communicate with the two ministers without the embassy knowing about it.[381] More importantly, on 18 January 1950 the Export-Import Bank announced that it would be willing to discuss the possibility of a $25 million loan for purchasing fertilizers, mining products, and electric

---

[379] Lequerica to Martín Artajo, 15 April 1950, file 21287, AGA.
[380] Lequerica to Martín Artajo, 22 April 1950, file 21345, AGA.
[381] Ballestero, *Juan Antonio Suanzes ...*, 223–225.

generators. In the area of private finance, Suanzes and Barth directly negotiated a loan from the Chase for the purchase of 55,000 tonnes of wheat between March and June 1950.[382] All of this opened up a divide between Lequerica and the minister, and increased the existing tensions with the economic ministries, evidence of which came when Lequerica wrote to Suanzes in an attempt to take the credit for the goodwill shown by the Export-Import Bank. In the margin Suanzes wrote "Impertinent buffoon."[383]

This was the state of affairs until Lequerica's work with the sympathetic congressmen began to bear fruit in the form of loans for Spain that were for greater amounts than the ones just mentioned. It was a two-stage process. The first stage in April ended in failure; the second, in July, in success. In the first, McCarran and Brewster took advantage of the debate on the Foreign Economic Assistance Act – which proposed that the Export-Import Bank should be assigned $3,366,450,000 to use as loans to foreign countries – to submit an amendment that included the award of $100 million to Spain. Immediately, the president of the Foreign Relations Committee, Connally – who had close ties to the cotton industry – expressed his approval. This set the alarm bells ringing for Secretary Acheson and President Truman, who were quick to inform him that they were categorically opposed to it. Acheson even gave him his arguments in writing, in another letter that was also made public. In response, Connally went back on what he had said, although he sympathized with the spirit of the amendment and suggested, as Acheson himself had done in his letter, that Spain could apply for a loan directly to the Export-Import Bank. Of course, as we know, this was something Spain had already done. McCarran and Brewster's proposal was finally rejected by forty-two votes to thirty-five.

Lequerica tried to sell Martín Artajo the idea that the proposal and the tightness of the vote had been a success. However, the minister was as dissatisfied with the whole affair as Franco was, and he made no bones about telling Lequerica that instead of feeling happy he should be upset about the amendment ending in failure.[384] Madrid was getting increasingly agitated about the lack of results after such an investment in the Spanish embassy in Washington, and on the following 20 May there was an incident between Culbertson and Suanzes when they were both attending a formal dinner at the residence of the minister of the Swiss embassy in the presence of other foreign representatives. Irritated by what had happened in the Senate, the U.S. *chargé d'affaires* referred to Lequerica's political activity in Washington in the most derogatory terms and he also railed against some of the projects of the Spanish

[382] Ibid., 226.

[383] Ibid., 225.

[384] Handwritten note from Martín Artajo to Franco, 27 April 1950, file 21318, AFNFF.

Ministry of Trade and Industry – such as the refinery in Cartagena or the project to manufacture cars with FIAT – because of their nationalizing intent. And he even compared the Spanish and Yugoslavian dictatorships.[385] Suanzes responded so violently and was so critical of U.S. interference in Spanish politics that Culbertson got up and left the room. He had to be convinced by the ambassador from Brazil to return.[386] That is to say, Suanzes had had to defend Lequerica, who he did not get on with, against Culbertson, who was worried about the changes in U.S. policy that were calling into question everything he had been doing up to that point.

Meanwhile, in the United States, the most pro-Franco senators who were working with Lequerica and the paid lobbyists[387] had not ceased in their endeavors, and, at the end of July, in his capacity as chairman of the Appropriations Committee, McCarran submitted another amendment in favor of Spain, this time to the bill for supplementary funds of $4 billion that had been urgently requested by Truman for foreign aid. The amendment was for the amount of $100 million and this time, after being reduced to $62.5 million, it was passed by a clear majority of sixty-five votes to fifteen. Immediately afterwards, it was passed by the House of Representatives by a narrower margin: 164 votes to eighty.[388] And on 6 September 1950 the General Appropriations Act for 1951, of which the amendment was a part, was signed by the president. The Spanish amendment pained him and he had received many requests from trade unions, anti-Franco citizens, and the Republican Spanish government in exile not to sign.[389] In fact, on the very day of the

[385] According to the embassy in Madrid, "many of Spain's present difficulties are due to the Government's growing participation in industry, its excessive tempering with [...] The correction of practically all of this lies within the power of the Government. Most of them are not, strictly speaking, our business, and corrective measures could not successfully be made pre-requisites of economic assistance by the United States": Madrid Embassy, Department of State, "Spanish Government. Policies and Practices Contributing to Economic Difficulties of Spain, and Possibility of Making their Correction Prerequisite to the Extension of Financial Assistance by the US," 2 August 1950, RG 59, 852.10/8–250. I am grateful to Pablo León Aguinaga for this document.

[386] Ballestero, *Juan Antonio Suanzes ...*, 227–228.

[387] According to the columnist Drew Pearson, Defense Secretary Johnson had also been working behind the scenes. Among the plotters he pointed to Truitt and Clark working with Brewster, McCarran and Keogh: D. Pearson, "Behind the scenes," *The Washington Post*, 7 August 1950 in Stephen J. Spingarn (Administrative Assistant to the President) Papers Box 20, HSTPL.

[388] Hualde, *El "cerco" ...*, 306.

[389] See letters and telegrams from Jacob S. Potofski, General President Amalgamated Clothing Workers of America, Walter Kazmiesowski, University of Syracuse, Álvaro de Albornoz and Pascual Morán, Official File OF 410–0, box 1419, HSTPL.

signature, he expressed his discontent in public and said that Spain would only be granted loans if it was in the U.S. interests.[390]

What had happened? It should not be forgotten that the aid to Spain was part of the general budgetary regulation, so not passing it would have been a considerable problem for the president, and this is what McCarran[391] had been astute enough to see. At Lequerica's request, he was immediately congratulated by the Spanish government and by Brewster.[392]

The bill was passed for many reasons, not for a sudden change in the opinion of the houses in favor of Spain. Without a doubt, one of these reasons was the new anti-communist climate generated by the outbreak of the Korean War the previous month. Another was that McCarran had secretly met with representatives of the Pentagon in the Senate.[393] That is to say, the armed forces and the pro-Francoists in Congress were not converging only in theory; they were reaching agreements in practice. And yet another was the opposition of the Republican party and some sectors of the Democratic party to the president's decision to mobilize the armed forces for this new war without convening Congress, so there was a general desire to punish him where it would hurt most.[394]

The award of public loans to the Franco regime was a key moment because it was the first victory of the pro-Francoists in Congress over the State Department and the president. The victory was crushing; McCarran gloated in the press and criticized Truman for his public statements on the

[390] He said: "I also feel obliged to comment upon the provision of the bill which authorizes loans for the purpose of assistance to Spain. I do not regard this provision as a directive, which would be unconstitutional, but instead as an authorization, in addition to the authority already in existence under which loans to Spain may be made. Spain is not, and has not been, foreclosed from borrowing money from this Government. Money will be loaned to Spain whenever mutually advantageous arrangements can be made with respect to security, terms of repayment, purposes for which the money is to be spent, and other appropriate factors, and whenever such loans will serve the interests of the United States in the conduct of foreign relations": Statement by the President Upon Signing the General Appropriation Act, 6 September 1950, *Public Papers of the Presidents of the United States. Harry S. Truman*, Washington D.C., U.S. Government Printing Office, 1965, 616.

[391] Memorandum, The McCarran Amendment, 2 August 1950, Ministry of Foreign Affairs Record Group, file number 82–07487, AGA.

[392] Eduardo Propper de Callejón to Owen Brewster, 11 August 1950, Ministry of Foreign Affairs Record Group, file number 54–12668, AGA.

[393] Pat McCarran, "Why Shouldn't the Spanish Fight for Us?," *Saturday Evening Post*, 28 April 1951. McCarran spoke about the meeting one year after the event, as we can see. He did not give the names of the officers who attended: Lowi, "US Bases in Spain,"..., 681.

[394] Hualde, *El "cerco"* ..., 298 and 306.

day of the signature,[395] while Acheson had to put up with criticism from the British and the French.

Meanwhile, a euphoric Lequerica made constant mention of the success in his letters to Martín Artajo and pointed out that the loan could be used to purchase both industrial materials and basic foodstuffs such as wheat.[396] He also noted that there had been a considerable increase in the number of intermediaries and companies approaching the embassy to do business (but also an increase in the number of undesirables and opportunists).[397]

However, what was really decisive for Spain was not the loan but that the United States had become embroiled in a new war, alongside its two main military allies and many other countries after the UN resolution and mandate, with the frontal opposition of the Soviet Union. In this new situation, the armed forces exerted greater influence over the president, who became much more involved in the field of foreign policy by attending National Security Council meetings and being in closer contact with the Joint Chiefs of Staff. All this was to the detriment of the State Department. And while the focus on Korea was paramount, the president, the senior military leaders,[398] and Paul Nitze, head of the Policy Planning Staff since Kennan's departure in 1949, were convinced that the Soviet Union was preparing for a conflict in a new theater, but not for a Third World War. This meant that they needed to improve their defensive strategies, especially in Europe, which involved reinforcing and rearming not only the German Federal Republic but also Spain, which, in the event of a Soviet invasion, could have been the West's last defensive redoubt, together with French North Africa. So Spain now became a priority. This state of affairs benefitted the U.S. pro-Francoists inside and outside the State Department to the detriment of the policy of Acheson, the Iberian desk, and Culbertson in Madrid, all of whom saw that they were gradually losing their grip. And it also led Truman to greater realism.

---

[395] Cutting from *Diario Nueva York*, n.d., "McCarran dice el Presidente no puede eliminar ayuda a España", Ministry of Foreign Affairs Record Group, file number 82–07487, AGA.

[396] Note for His Excellency: phone call from Mr Lequerica, 16 November 1950, file 11987, AFNFF.

[397] "Calderón has spoken to a lawyer and former US civil servant. One of the numerous individuals willing to save us with their good connections, eye for a business opportunity, etc. Who we are finding every step of the way…it is madness now to start new explorations": Lequerica to Erice, 9 August 1950, Presidency of the Government Record Group, file number 82–07487, AGA. Ibid., 14 August 1950: "that's quite enough of illustrious and spontaneous individuals who, with their good connections and influence, or business nous, want to save us because, as you rightly point out, it would be madness to begin these explorations." Presidency of the Government Record Group, file number 82–07487, AGA.

[398] Hualde, *El "cerco"* …, 297–306.

210 JOAN MARIA THOMÀS

At the same time, throughout the summer of 1950, leading congressmen such as Senator Harry Cain, of the Armed Forces Committee, made new trips to Madrid, where he met with Franco and Martín Artajo. The embassy's military attaché, Colonel Miller, gave assurances that there would soon be a change in relations with Spain.[399] And, at the beginning of fall, leading organizations such as the American Legion, with three million members and now associated with the rapidly growing Spanish Bloc, made declarations in favor of fully establishing relations of all kinds with Spain.[400]

More Results: The Partial Lifting of the 1946 Resolution in the UN

This was the situation when, on 4 November, the 1946 UN resolution on Spain was partially lifted. Shortly before the vote, Lequerica had said that he was quietly confident that the vote would go in Spain's favor. In a letter to Franco at the end of October, in the midst of the fifth General Assembly that had started on 19 September, he had said, "I am assuming that the UN vote will very probably be a happy one, but I cannot be absolutely sure."[401] At this time, there were reasons for optimism because the United States was prepared for change despite the opinions of its two main allies, Great Britain and France. Throughout the summer of 1950 the three countries had been working to reach an agreement on repealing the sections of the resolution on the withdrawal of ambassadors and Spain's admission to the UN's specialized agencies, although with no success. Washington's strategy was not actually to make a proposal but to give its vote to any other delegation or delegations that recommended partial repeal. However, the Labour government in Great Britain and the French government were more inclined not to support the normalization of relations with Spain until democratic elections had been held and a constitutional regime had been established.[402]

Lequerica and the embassy, in particular the press attaché, Antonio Cacho Zabalza, worked tirelessly to have the resolution lifted. At first, they concentrated on the Latin American delegations that were preparing proposals (Bolivia, El Salvador, and the Dominican Republic) and, in the words of Lequerica, tried to unify them. This had pleasantly surprised the U.S. delegation, with whose chairman, Warren Austin, the Francoists in Lake Success had a smooth relationship, now led by the State Department[403] despite the opposition of the Spanish desk. Several different Latin American proposals would have spelled

[399] Ibid., 302.

[400] José Pérez del Arco, the consul in Los Angeles, 14 October 1950, Ministry of Foreign Affairs Record Group, file number 54–08871, AGA.

[401] Handwritten letter from Lequerica to Franco, 25 October 1950, file 9532, AFNFF.

[402] Hualde, El "cerco" ..., 311–313.

[403] Letter from Lequerica to Martín Artajo, also sent to the Head of State, 25 October 1950, file 9532, AFNFF.

disaster for Spanish interests so the press attaché, Cacho Zabalza, had set about bringing them all together. Lequerica gave the following explanation to the Spanish minister of foreign affairs:

> On this memorable occasion, Cacho Zabalza decided that the *ad hoc* committee should include the Hispano-American proposal about Spain on the agenda. As you will recall, after Belaunde had promised to put it on the agenda himself, he then refused because he was frightened that if he did he would be accused of bias in favor of Spain. This led to a very tricky vote on procedure, not content, which you had wisely advised us to avoid and which I was also very much against. But without it, Belaunde's lack of conviction would have abandoned the whole thing to its fate, to be decided by the whims of the great international debating chamber. Minister Propper was cowering in the corridors, too afraid to consult me – and, even if he had, I too would probably have been too afraid to permit taking such a risk – and at this point good old Cacho took it upon himself to get the Dominicans and Ambassador Castro to take the delicate decision to propose the debate. Thank God, it was approved by 25 votes against 15. This was the starting point of our success. Despite being only procedural, if the vote had gone against us, it would have looked like a defeat for Spain but the result was just what we needed for the resolution that we have been striving for. The Muslim world voted against, for the reasons I stated at the time in my telegram. However, Cacho had calculated our support very well, and his stroke of audacity was decisive in our winning the battle.[404]

Now that there was a proposal that needed to be voted on, the U.S. delegation took decisive action. They moved quickly, ignoring French requests to postpone the debate until 1951, with Republican senator Henry Cabot Lodge as their spearhead, backed up by two other members of the delegation, John Foster Dulles and the Democratic representative John Sparkman, described by Lequerica as "a great friend of ours and very close to Keogh and the parliamentary group that supports Spain."[405]

Even so, this time Spain had been unable to say which members of the delegation planned to vote as they had done in 1949. According to Lequerica, "maybe [Ernest A.] Gross and [Benjamin V.] Cohen, and the widow herself [in reference to Eleanor Roosevelt], although I doubt she will."[406] The general attitude of the U.S. delegation was to "give support and keep their word that they would vote, but not to take the initiative in public or, apparently at least, not put any pressure on voters." The presence of pro-Franco friends in the

---

[404] Letter from Lequerica to Martín Artajo, 7 November 1950, file 9533, AFNFF.
[405] Ibid.
[406] Ibid.

212 JOAN MARIA THOMÀS

delegation and some like-minded officials from the State Department[407] – who had also kept Lequerica informed – had contributed to the general progress being made, although adversaries such as Dunham did everything they could to delay any change. But the fundamental difference was that Acheson had changed his mind.[408] About all this, Lequerica said the following:

> Decisive in this good result has been the presence in the North-American delegation not only of these political friends but of officials from the State Department who are kindly disposed toward Spain […] Having served for some considerable time on the boards of directors of factories, I am very aware of how useless it is for suppliers to make fair claims if they do not have the support of the group of officials and employees who are responsible for the daily decisions on administrative issues. The greatest of pressure is ignored and the request is buried with a smile. So on this occasion it has been a great help to have always been kept abreast of the intentions of delegation number one, to have had some say in action to be taken and to have had constant access to information without which we would still be wondering whether the Spanish question was going to be raised in December or not or whether it would be put off until the extra Assembly in spring. At the risk of being tedious, I insist on all this so that the North-American position is clear. Approval and support but no visible effort.[409]

What is more, according to Lequerica, if it had not been for the United States, they would not have won the vote. In reply to the question "If the United States had cooled off again and announced that it was going to abstain even with no hostile intent, would it have been possible to win the vote?" he

---

[407] "Strong pressure from Dunham in the Spanish Office [Iberian desk], who told Secretary Piniés he tends to delay agreements on Spain until the very end of the Assembly and thus delay sending an ambassador for as long as possible and making the present interim position last as long as possible." Lequerica to Martín Artajo, 9 April 1950, Ministry of Foreign Affairs Record Group, file number 54–08871, AGA.

[408] "Senator Brewster, with whom I conferred at length yesterday, deems it necessary to maintain pressure […] Now, in view of serious Senate discussions on State Department conduct, Secretary Acheson is endeavouring to maintain good relations with influential parliamentarians, inform them and listen to their advice, an opportunity we must seize. More effective than the appointment of Foster Dulles, who Your Excellency will not have forgotten because of his [previous] dealings at the UN." Military advisors of the President also took some trouble with the Embassy. Admiral Souers, for example, "special advisor to President Truman, who would be in and out of his office several times a day," who attended a reception organized by Lequerica: Lequerica to Erice, Director General of Foreign Policy. 16 October 1950, Ministry of Foreign Affairs Record Group, file number 82–07487, AGA.

[409] Ibid.

THE STRUGGLE TO CHANGE U.S. POLICY TOWARD FRANCO'S SPAIN 213

said "after seeing such malice and spite, categorically no."[410] But Spain won, to the annoyance of the opposing sector of the Iberian desk and Culbertson,[411] who must have felt that he had been backing a winner because on 7 October the State Department had published a new volume of Nazi documents just as it had done on the day of the resolution against Spain in 1946. On that occasion, the documents had been about the relations between Franco and the Axis powers; now they were about the years of the Civil War and investments in Franco's Spain by Germany to the tune of $200 million. The intention was clear.[412]

The proposal presented jointly by Bolivia, El Salvador, the Dominican Republic, Honduras, Nicaragua, Peru, and the Philippines had been passed by thirty-eight votes in favor, including the United States, to ten against and twelve abstentions. Among these abstentions were France and Great Britain,[413] two countries which, again according to Lequerica, were influenced by the Spanish opposition, particularly "the strong Prieto group of pseudo-monarchists and pseudo-Catholics, with the support of the left-wing trade unions."

The Spanish embassy spared no expense to thank the Latin American ambassadors who had helped bring about the success,[414] and they were all given gifts of about $1000 apiece.[415] Neither had it spared any expense at

---

[410] Ibid.

[411] "Culbertson probably hadn't expected such a quick result from the Madrid group [...] This group and its spokesman in Washington had made people here believe in some mixed government or some other Greek-style solution to destroy Spain. With this in mind they tried to stop the UN solution. The vote has been a game changer and they are making no attempt to conceal their fury." Lequerica to Martín Artajo, Top Secret, n.d., Ministry of Foreign Affairs Record Group, file number 82–07487, AGA.

[412] Lowi, "US Bases in Spain,"…, 688.

[413] Hualde, El "cerco" …, 313.

[414] At the moment of victory, he singled out three Latin American protagonists. On the one hand, the [Brazilian] ambassadors Muñiz and Castro. "For what they did after the proposals had been cleared and standardized. They watched over our affair in permanent contact with us, with very happy results. On the other hand, General Romulus, very agile and skillful, stopped Indonesia voting against and probably also changed Burma's attitude thanks to his personal prestige. The great speech in Rio (prepared on his behalf by the excellent 'ABC' correspondent Massip) made a deep impression on the voters in the Assembly and helped matters along. In short, everything was going very well, but could also be derailed at any moment and when they would be straightened out again only God knows. The world situation and its dangers would have been skillfully exploited by the Franco-English coalition against us to put off for another year our rehabilitation in the face of the iniquity of the 46th." Lequerica to Martín Artajo, Top Secret, n.d., Ministry of Foreign Affairs Record Group, file number 82–07487, AGA.

[415] As can be understood from the following fragment of the letter from Lequerica to Minister Martín Artajo. And which also shows the extent of the expenditure, which

214 JOAN MARIA THOMÀS

any stage of the process and the cost of the partial suppression of the 1946 resolution was estimated to be $20,000.

The paragraphs on the origins of the Franco regime and the condemnation by the UN remained in place, so the 1950 resolution had not been fully revoked by the 1946 resolution. But Lequerica saw that the vote raised the possibility of Spain becoming a member of the Organization. He proposed this possibility to Martin Artajo and Franco, albeit cautiously because he was well aware of their reluctance in this respect. In a letter he said:

> [D]espite the caution and healthy indifference that have been standard features of the policy you have followed in recent years, it seems to me that we can also set about preparing our entry into the organization. Whatever we may think of it, we should not forget that it is the favorite instrument of U.S. policy and even Cardinal Spellman says special prayers in the hope that it will be successful.[416]

The End of the Beginning: The Appointment of Ambassadors to Madrid and Washington and Admiral Sherman's Visit to Franco

After the partial lifting of the UN's 1946 resolution, work began on exchanging ambassadors, a question that the U.S. administration responded to promptly despite the relative reluctance of President Truman. On the same day that the resolution had been partially lifted (4 November) he had jokingly answered a

---

can hardly have been reassuring for him: "Calculation of expenses: In my haste to catch the courier tomorrow, Wednesday, and since I have to leave for New York today, I am not yet able to give you a calculation of our expenses at the UN. I can, however, repeat what I wrote to you last month about our abandonment at a critical moment. As at critical moments, there has been no lack of trustworthy people in Spain prepared to advance the small sums needed, some of whose names I sent you in letter No. 228. The Ritz-Carlton has still not charged us, and I dare not, even for curiosity's sake, ask how much their accounts will amount to. The anticipated sum for everything so far, all included, is no more than eleven. Secretarial expenses essential for the rapid notification of the affairs will be around a thousand. We still need to make some well-deserved gifts to the three or four most important friends, which should amount to no more than three or four. I dare not think how much the Ritz bill will be, but all in all I think everything will be under twenty. I think we shall be able to let you know in a private letter in the near future. And with my warmest congratulations on the great effort made by our diplomacy in the world, the fruits of which we are now reaping, and for the determination to support our policy, I remain your friend and subordinate, and send you my affectionate greetings: Ibid. One of the 'trustworthy people' who loaned money may have been a Sephardic Jew, Olivar (to be exact, $25,000)": Lequerica to Martín Artajo, file 6941, AFNFF.

[416] Ibid.

THE STRUGGLE TO CHANGE U.S. POLICY TOWARD FRANCO'S SPAIN 215

question about the possibility of appointing an ambassador to Madrid in the following way: "I have no thought on that idea at all. It is going to be a long, long time before there is an ambassador to Spain, and you will have plenty of time to think it over."[417] Nevertheless, on 22 November the State Department officially notified the Spanish Ministry of Foreign Affairs that they wanted to apply for the *agrément* for a new ambassador.[418] And on 8 December the director of the Office of Western European Affairs, Homer M. Byington Jr. – in the absence of *Chargé d'Affaires* Propper[419] – notified the embassy official Espinosa that the State Department had sent a telegram to Madrid ordering Culbertson to apply for the *agrément* in the name of Stanton G. Griffis, until then ambassador in Argentina.

This meant that Admiral Leahy had been discounted, probably because of his health problems, and a Spanish-speaking ambassador had been chosen. He was one of Truman's personal friends, a member of the board of directors of the Paramount film company, with experience of doing business with Spain, and he had been behind the campaign to seek support for Truman's 1948 election campaign in Hollywood. He was a major donor himself and, since 1947, the president had been rewarding him with embassies.[420] He was a former employee of the Office of Strategic Strategies, had spent a few weeks in Spain in 1943, was an ardent anti-communist, and proved to be an outstanding pro-Francoist. In compliance with the president's instructions, he tried to obtain concessions on religious freedom from the Spanish government, the major obstacle to the relations between the two countries, while sponsoring agreements between the Motion Picture Export Association of America, of which he was a member, and Spain, as he had already done in other countries where he had been ambassador.

On 16 December he was formally appointed, and on 20 December he was given the *agrément*, although the appointment was not made effective until 1 February 1951 and his credentials were not presented to Franco until 1 March.[421]

---

[417] *Public Papers of the Presidents of the United States. Harry S. Truman,* 1950, 697.

[418] Hualde, *El "cerco"* ..., 318.

[419] *Chargé d'Affaires* Propper was in Scranton on this day at a concert of the Coros de Mallorca. Telegram from Lequerica to Martín Artajo, 8 December 1950, file 7266, AFNFF.

[420] In Poland, Egypt, Argentina, and now Madrid: León Aguinaga, *Sospechosos habituales...*, 298.

[421] Stanton G. Griffis, *Lying...*, 283; Griffis arrived in Spain on 15 February via Cadiz, and managed to get his friend Clarence Dillon to ask Luis Bolin, director general of tourism, for permission to dredge a channel to the quay so that his cars could be disembarked: Griffis to Dunham, 27 February 1951, U.S. Embassy Madrid, Classified General Records 1940–1963, RG 84. On Bolín, see Carlos Larrinaga (ed.), *Luis Bolín y el turismo en España entre 1928 y 1952*, Madrid, Marcial Pons, 2021.

This delay delighted the president and was partly caused by him because, after accepting the post, Griffis had requested a two-month vacation starting from the moment he finished in Buenos Aires. Upset by the swiftness with which the department had worked, Truman granted the request. In the interview between the two men, he had said "that's exactly what I want. I do not want you to go for the present, so soon after what I said a few weeks ago. I have been overruled and worn down by the Department."[422] He immediately went on to express his concern about the situation of the Protestant churches in Spain, an issue that remained – and would continue to remain – unresolved, and which had delayed, not prevented, the change in U.S. policy toward Francoist Spain. In fact, in the interview in which he granted him the two-month leave, the president had told him:

> I don't know if you have any [religious convictions], but I am a Baptist and I believe that in any country man should be permitted to worship his God in his own way. The situation in Spain is intolerable. Do you know that a Baptist who dies in Spain must even be buried in the middle of the night.[423]

Indeed, this was his major concern: the lack of freedom in Spain and, particularly, the lack of religious freedom. Aware of the president's concern, Griffis took this issue very seriously.

But the policy had finally changed, and in this change the president had played a role, albeit a reluctant one. Lequerica explained it to Martín Artajo in the following words:

> The "Washington Post" itself, in response to Truman's comment [about the "long, long time"], clearly says in its editorial of 5 November "that the sending of ambassadors cannot be delayed much longer. Now that the Assembly has taken action, the gap must be filled." Because of the consideration he has for masonry, international socialism and even Indalecio Prieto and Trifón Gómez imposed by the workers' societies here, it is up to the President to cast doubt on the resolutions favorable to Spain that have now become legal and to which he himself contributed with his signature.[424]

---

[422] Stanton G. Griffis, *Lying in State*, New York, Doubleday, 1952, 269.

[423] Ibid., 269.

[424] And he added: "It is not worth dwelling too long on these affectionate sweet nothings directed to agonizing Spanish socialist legitimism, comparable to those of former sovereigns speaking about their dethroned colleagues with no chance of return": Letter from Lequerica to Martín Artajo, 7 November 1950, file 9533, AFNFF.

THE STRUGGLE TO CHANGE U.S. POLICY TOWARD FRANCO'S SPAIN 217

Although he must have felt that he was in a stronger position after the success at the UN, Lequerica was still concerned about his appointment as ambassador in Washington. Just two weeks before the vote in the Assembly, he had been assailed by doubts and was afraid that Cárdenas and other enemies of his in the ministry would once again join forces with Culbertson and begin their scheming against him. In an attempt to stop this, on 25 October he had written a personal letter to Franco explaining his fear and mentioning the "only danger" that he believed could prevent him from "finishing off" the task entrusted to him in the United States: "a new plot along the lines of the passport incident" (although he did add "I do not believe it to be probable"). He was very wary and did what he could to stop himself being alienated by providing Franco with arguments in his defense. For example:

> Deciding not to submit credentials – the only task I came here with – would invalidate 70% of everything we have achieved and suggest that here people are worn down by serving Your Excellency and the regime. It would seem to say that Francoists respond to the bad, complicated times; but as soon as the situation improves, they pack up and go home because they are Francoists and leave it up to others who are cold, neutral and hostile to abandon or betray the regime in the face of the United States.

He also pointed out that he would regard not being appointed as a personal affront:

> Neither will I pretend, Your Excellency, that expelling me just when we are about to reap the rewards of two and a half years of hard work would not be a terrible personal humiliation and affront, an unprecedented snub no matter how much it is sugarcoated. Now that the formalities of the credentials have been completed, I will hasten to explain to Your Excellency and the Minister how I see the present and future situation although, as always, I submit willingly to your superior resolutions.[425]

In another letter to Minister Martín Artajo – but fully aware that the head of state would also read it – he used a more professional tone and made an effort to provide evidence that the State Department looked favorably on him and his appointment as ambassador. He claimed to have gone to Washington on Franco's orders "for as little or as much time as I saw fit and to present

---

[425] Handwritten letter from Lequerica to the Head of State, 25 October 1950, file 9532, AFNFF.

my credentials at the first opportunity."[426] As "evidence" of the U.S. readiness to appoint him, he cited what Peurifoy had said at the February lunch he had organized in his honor, and the fact that Hickerson, who at one time had been so hostile and so in tune with Culbertson, had told Constantine Brown just a few days previously that he regarded him as the future ambassador. This view, so he claimed, was shared by other members of the department such as O'Shaughnessy and Dunham.[427] He also boasted that Hickerson, also in conversation with Brown, had summed up Lequerica's two and a half years in Washington by saying:

> [A]t the end of the day, he said that I was Spanish and my attitude had to be judged with this in mind [...] In other countries – though not, I feel, in Spain – they are used to seeing certain people forget what nationality they are when they deal with the United States.[428]

All this led him to embark on a self-complacent story about the attempts by the department and the Spanish Ministry to have him dismissed:

> Many of the attempts at interrupting our mission to fully champion the policy of the Spanish regime originated from Spain. I still remember that in July 1949, they tried to make Your Excellency believe that the State Department refused to accept my being here any longer and even submitted a report from some Spanish official describing details of a conversation with the US *Chargé d'Affaires* to oppose the renewal of my passport. The facts were soon provided, however, and I do not forget that Your Excellency was quick to accept them. Today a similar approach would be even less well founded. In my opinion the Department's struggle for the Spanish representation to be understanding and neutral, somewhere between the political position of the Spanish Government and the intrusive reforming political pretensions of the United States, is over for the time being and only a change in the Spanish attitude could revive it. As in almost all work, my mission in Washington has produced some results, but perhaps this is the principal one. I have limited myself to following Your Excellency's instructions from the first day and even before that, and what I know that Your Excellency, the Head of State, believes. There is no other way. Understanding and innocuous people do not yield. Ultimately the directors of American policy find it useful to deal with those who represent the thought of a Government and serve it thoroughly and actively.

---

[426] Letter from Lequerica to Martín Artajo, also sent to the Head of State, 25 October 1950.

[427] Ibid.

[428] Ibid.

THE STRUGGLE TO CHANGE U.S. POLICY TOWARD FRANCO'S SPAIN 219

He also took advantage of the opportunity to once again trumpet the success of not backing down in the face of democratizing pressures:

> It seems to me that there are two dangers threatening the world today: the first, obvious and monstrous, is Communism. The second, purely objective, but with serious consequences is the attempt by officially influential North-American schools of thought to impose political norms to the liking of this powerful country on friendly countries, defenders of civilization. In a pragmatic order, an imposition such as this nullifies the efforts of nations by delivering them into the hands of perfectly ineffective, false government directives; but it also takes away their dignity because they accept the spiritual interference of one nation in the private affairs of another. These recommendations of liberalization and democratization, and the threats of economic punishment if they are not heeded – as in the case of Greece – are, after Communism, the most serious danger to international life at the present time. I believe that the fortitude shown by the Government of His Excellency the Head of State during five years of continuous assaults is an immense service to all countries and to the United States itself. In the latest conversations with Mr Byington and Hickerson himself, Minister Propper de Callejon frankly told them to refrain from trying to advise Spain on domestic policy and making these matters the subject of debate. Of course we have the advantage of already having refused to do so; but I cannot but compare this attitude, at once of great dignity and good political sense, with some conversations I heard on my arrival here, in which a former ambassador in Madrid and a good personal friend [Norman Armour] no less said that His Excellency the head of State should form a Government with Madariaga and Prieto!! This is the same advice given to Chiang Kai-shek, with highly regrettable results. For this outcome alone it was well worth the trouble of having to put up with many personal hostilities and difficulties, nearly all of which have been overcome. And I am fully aware that "personal" issues, whether they concern Your Excellency, your ministers or other more subordinate agents, are purely political but in a less important guise, because "personal issues" always bring into play passions that can be exploited by the adversary. Even our own friends have attempted to use this ploy. Constantine Brown always reminds me that Hickerson asked him time and time again to remind his influential friends in Madrid of the need to change the representative in Washington for someone more acceptable to the taste of the Department. Even the excellent Farley (and in this case I would not be surprised if the suggestions came from the Spanish Coca Cola) was made to say on occasion that it would be better to have some aristocrat as the Spanish representative [surely a reference to Cárdenas] who was more accommodating and more to

> the American taste. Our own concerns aside and in the context of the general political situation, I believe we can congratulate ourselves on the change in this aspect of our relations with the United States.[429]

And he was quite right, although he ignored such fundamental international aspects as the deterioration of the Cold War and the outbreak of the Korean War, which had prompted Truman and Acheson to change their policy toward the Franco regime. Even so, after Byington's call to Espinosa, Lequerica ordered him to go at once to the State Department and say that "the Spanish government wished to simultaneously request the *agrément* as Spanish ambassador in the United States for myself." And he did not waste a second in telegraphing Martín Artajo to recommend that "the approval of the two names, if it is to come about, should be simultaneous." At the same time he gave his opinion on Griffis – "he is an important businessman of no particular political significance, except for his great friendship with the President" – and recommended that the *agrément* be granted to him ("there is not the slightest reason in his past or present in relation to Spain to oppose his appointment").[430]

All this activity did him some good, but he was still, rightly, very wary. Martín Artajo had discussed his doubts about Lequerica with Culbertson in the middle of December, shortly before Culbertson went back to the United States on leave[431] (never to return to Madrid because he was posted as head of mission in Mexico City), and this discussion had created some expectations in the Iberian desk that Lequerica would not finally be appointed by Madrid as the ambassador. Martín Artajo's doubts had been aroused by the fact that Suanzes's undersecretary, Suñer, had criticized Lequerica to Dunham[432] and others because of his handling of Spain's interests in the United States and that at times the relationship between the "inspector" and Minister Martín Artajo was somewhat tense because it was rumored that Lequerica wanted to take over from him.[433] Whatever the case may have been, Lequerica's appointment as ambassador in Washington was now a question that had to be answered only by Madrid. In line with the change in policy, Washington was no longer making any objections and, in the Spanish capital, the criteria of the head of state prevailed over any doubts the minister of foreign affairs may have had.

---

[429] Ibid.

[430] Ibid.

[431] Dunham to John Wesley Jones, *Chargé d'Affaires*, 15 December 1950, U.S. Embassy Madrid, Classified General Records 1940–1963, RG 84, NARA-2.

[432] Ibid.

[433] Ibid. Rumors also reached the U.S. vice-consul in Seville that Martín Artajo himself could be the new ambassador in Washington: Wilson to Jones, 5 February 1952, U.S. Embassy Madrid, Classified General Records 1940–1963, RG 84, NARA-2.

THE STRUGGLE TO CHANGE U.S. POLICY TOWARD FRANCO'S SPAIN 221

Hence, Lequerica was soon confirmed as ambassador to Washington. But not before he had purged some of the members of staff in Washington who he did not believe to be of the same persuasion.[434]

The news that Lequerica had been granted the *agrément* was filtered to the press by the president's friend and military aide, General Vaughan[435] after Acheson had reminded Truman that Lequerica's activities, "and particularly the lobbying in which he has engaged, have on occasion created difficulties for the Administration."[436] On 14 January 1951 Lequerica was relieved of his functions as "inspector of embassies and legations" and appointed ambassador of Spain to Washington. He presented his credentials to President Truman on 17 January. And he immediately began to gloat about Culbertson's comeuppance. He pointed out that the press had made no mention of his activities in France during the war, and he boasted that Senator Dennis Chavez, the Democratic representative for New Mexico, had organized a lunch in his honor that had been attended by all the Latin American ambassadors, even the one from Mexico,[437] a country with no diplomatic relations with Spain.

However, Lequerca got a little carried away by the euphoria of the moment and, in his response to Truman's address during the presentation of credentials and afterwards in his declarations to the journalists awaiting him, he said such things as "Spain is willing to join all those countries that represent civilization and a love of peace," and that it had an army of 400,000 men that could become one million or more in the fight against communism. His words did not go down well with the government in Madrid, and he was called back to Spain at once to account for them, where he was very probably reproved by Martín Artajo. But the consequences did not go much further than this: he had the support of both Franco and – to a lesser extent – his minister and he had achieved a lot, particularly the financial package of $62.5 million awarded in September of the previous year. And Spain still needed him to achieve a lot more.

At the beginning of 1951, the Spanish government was clearly nervous, and the delay in the arrival of the new U.S. ambassador merely made the situation worse. So Martín Artajo ordered Lequerica to visit Griffis and tell him to bring

---

[434] Like the minister plenipotentiary and trade adviser Luis García Guijarro, who was sent to Madrid by Lequerica and who told John Y. Millar, of the Office of Western European Affairs of the State Department that Lequerica "wants to be the dominant personality in the Embassy and is eliminating the people who are not subservient to him." The Americans described García as "oriented to the CEDA-line." Millar to Culbertson, 4 August 1950, U.S. Embassy Madrid, Classified General Records 1940–1963, RG 84, NARA-2.

[435] Cava Mesa, *Los diplomáticos de Franco* ..., 319.

[436] Acheson to Truman, 22 December 1950, OF 1.417, HSTPL

[437] Ibid.

to Madrid all the signed documentation of the loan in the same conditions as all the other countries affected by the general law of the Economic Cooperation Administration, even though it was to be provided by the Export-Import Bank. Underlying this demand was the little faith Minister of Trade and Industry Suanzes and Undersecretary Tomás Suñer had in the deal, because they were well aware of the bad blood between Lequerica and the Iberian desk, the body they believed the Export-Import Bank would end up consulting.[438] However, their greatest concern was how they would be allowed to use the $62.5 million. They were afraid that they would not be able to spend it on consumer products such as cotton, fertilizers, fuel, and tractors but be forced by the conditions of the "pure" Export-Import Bank loans to invest in projects that could generate or save sufficient amounts to cover the repayments.[439]

Finally, McCarran managed to find a solution to these concerns. He organized a meeting with Deputy Secretary of State Carlisle Humelsine, Dunham from the Spanish desk, chairman of the board of the Export-Import Bank, Herbert E. Gaston, Paul B. Porter from the ECA, himself and ... Lequerica. In the meeting he gave them all a piece of his mind. The fact that the Spaniard had been allowed to attend was denounced as scandalous by the press and even McCarran agreed that it had been "a little out of line."[440] He may have wanted to show Lequerica, his "sponsor," how hard he was working.

But the meeting broke the deadlock and a bilateral agreement was signed that made it possible for Franco to pass two laws on 9 February and 16 March 1951. The agreement stipulated the interest rate, a twenty-five-year repayment period and, what was of most interest to the Spanish government, the possibility of using the loan to purchase consumer articles in both the public and the private sectors.[441] This was clearly a step in the right direction, albeit a limited one, because the amount of the loan by no means covered all the Franco regime's economic needs.

Another issue that was overcome in this initial stage of bilateral relations was the thorny problem created by the application of the new Internal Security Act – also known as the Subversive Activities Control Act – which classified Spain as a "totalitarian state" so the U.S. embassy and consulates in the country could not issue visas. It was agreed that from this point on they would be allowed to do so.[442]

---

[438] Ballestero, *Juan Antonio Suanzes* ...., 229. Which is exactly what happened: see Memorandum to the Secretary by Perkins (Europe), Assistant Secretary Thorp, Fisher, 11 September 1950, Harriman Papers, Library of Congress.

[439] Ibid., 228.

[440] *Washington Post*, 1 June 1951, 1.

[441] Ballestero, *Juan Antonio Suanzes* ..., 231.

[442] "Congratulations on being granted the agrément by the American government and thus officially consecrating the function that you have been carrying out so brilliantly as ambassador of our country there": Erice to Lequerica, 28 December 1950, Ministry of Foreign Affairs Record Group, file number 82–07487, AGA.

Progress was also made on the issue that most concerned President Truman. Nevertheless, there was no change in legislation, the only step that would really have satisfied him and the Protestant communities in Spain. In particular, in the course of a long interview, Franco promised the ambassador that

> he would tomorrow instruct Cabinet and through them all Civil Governors that interpretation of Spanish law on non-Catholic religious services must be greatly broadened including full right of non-Catholic services which did not disturb the peace, specifically permitting open funerals for non-Catholic dead.

Griffis interpreted these words as hope of "religious freedom in Spain."[443] He asked several civil servants to make a study of the situation of the pastors and churches of the Southern Baptist Convention (the object of the report by Hughley). He told the president that the problem was that the Protestant churches were working in a highly insecure environment because they were tolerated more in some provinces than in others and the level of tolerance depended on the influence the bishops had over the civil governors. He assured him that he would follow up on the instructions given by Franco. And well aware of Truman's hostility to Franco he also denied ever having said "I bring the hearty good wishes of President Truman and the American people to the people of Spain,"[444] a sentence that the U.S. press claimed he had uttered to Franco. As can be seen, he was prudent in the extreme when dealing with President Truman.

The State Department's Definitive Change in Attitude in 1951

As he had promised after Truman's criticism, on 15 January 1951 Acheson submitted a new version of the document NSC 72 with a proposal for a definitive change of strategy toward Spain. This new document was also a response to the Joint Chiefs of Staff asking new Secretary of Defense General Marshall to obtain updated information about Spain's military capacity from the embassy in Madrid so that they could evaluate the possibilities of Spain joining NATO or entering into a bilateral agreement.

The new document, NSC 72/2, entitled "Policy of the United States toward Spain," recognized the strategic importance of the Iberian Peninsula and argued that Spain should be part of the plans to defend Western Europe, although it also recognized that this would present political complications because the European Allies were against it. The United States should make Spain ready to play its role by increasing the potential of the Spanish armed forces with

---

[443] Letter from Griffis to Truman, 5 April 1951, OF 419–0, box 1418, HSTPL. The letter includes the "Memorandum Situation Baptists in Spain."

[444] Ibid.

necessary supplies and, above all else, ensuring that the United States had their own air and naval bases in the country. Once the Joint Chiefs of Staff had modified the document with their proposal that Spain should join NATO and that U.S. strategists should be allowed to contact the Spanish armed forces, it was sent on as NSC/3 to the State Department where it underwent further modification to become NSC/4. At this point it was approved by Truman. Griffis was immediately informed of its content and told by Acheson that his mission in Spain should focus on getting Spain to join the Western European community. For this to happen, he had to do various things: (1) convince Franco to stop creating tension between the United States on the one hand and Great Britain and France on the other; (2) follow the United States Information and Educational Exchange Agency program[445] to disseminate pro-U.S. propaganda in Spain; (3) attempt to get the prevailing economic controls relaxed and do away with the 25 percent limit on foreign capital in Spanish businesses; and, finally, (4) if Franco agreed to a NATO-focused Western defense, notify him that the United States was prepared to provide military support.[446]

This was the state of affairs when, in May, the consensus on the Spanish question that the State Department had been striving for was suddenly shattered. Acheson wanted to save face with Great Britain and France, while Marshall and the Joint Chiefs of Staff wanted to speed up contacts with Spain so that they would be rewarded with their air and naval bases as soon as possible.[447] A joint meeting was held on 6 June attended by Admiral Forrest P. Sherman – chief of naval operations and member of the Joint Chiefs of Staff – who was one of the staunchest supporters of change with respect to Spain and who Griffis had invited to visit the country.[448] Out of this meeting came NSC/5 and the decision not only to notify London and Paris but also to enter into bilateral talks with Spain even if France and Great Britain were against the idea.[449]

On 16 June, and once again at the suggestion of Griffis, William D. Pawley, assistant to the secretary of state and political advisor to General Bradley, traveled to Europe to visit Minister Martín Artajo in Madrid with

---

[445] See Memorandum by Dorsey Fisher, 26 October 1951, Dorsey Fisher Public Affairs Officer USIE, U.S. Embassy Madrid, Classified General Records 1940–1963, RG 84, NARA-2.

[446] Hualde, El "cerco" ..., 322 ff.

[447] Acheson to Culbertson, 27 June 1950, U.S. Embassy Madrid, Classified General Records 1940–1963, RG 84, box 2, NARA-2.

[448] Letter from Griffis to Sherman, 26 April 1951, U.S. Embassy Madrid, Classified General Records 1940–1963, RG 84, NARA-2. Griffis had also dined with Secretary Marshall and the leaders of the Joint Chiefs of Staff (Sherman included) in Washington in the previous month of February: Ibid.

[449] Hualde, El "cerco" ..., 330–331.

THE STRUGGLE TO CHANGE U.S. POLICY TOWARD FRANCO'S SPAIN 225

the ambassador himself and Director General of Foreign Affairs Erice. During the meeting, Pawley, who had just been to Paris to see General Dwight D. Eisenhower, the supreme allied commander in Europe, explained that the Joint Chiefs of Staff were willing to help rearm the Spanish armed forces and asked the minister about Spain's attitude to taking part in the defense of Europe beyond its frontiers, a bilateral agreement with the United States, and joining NATO in the future if the British and the French could be convinced. Speaking on behalf of Eisenhower, he regretted that

> the current political circumstances do not allow him [Eisenhower] to come to Madrid and speak directly to His Excellency the Generalissimo and his general staff, or to go to Greece or Turkey since none of the three countries were members of the North Atlantic Treaty.[450]

Pawley, a personal friend of Truman's, also brought up the Protestant question. Martín Artajo was quite prepared to discuss military issues but he gave absolutely nothing away about religion and simply refused to accept that there was no freedom of worship in Spain. He repeated the government's usual arguments and referred to the Charter of the Spaniards. Ten days later Franco agreed to start bilateral military talks with the United States.

Meanwhile, on 10 July France and Great Britain submitted an aide-mémoire to President Truman in which they objected to the United States negotiating with Franco on political and moral grounds even though they recognized the strategic importance of Spain. Truman was "greatly impressed" by the arguments, most of which he agreed with, and almost gave them his support because he was still no further forward on the question of religious freedom in Spain. Neither had he made any progress on the issue of Freemasonry and he had already started to receive letters from leading Freemasons concerned about the change in policy toward Spain.[451] However, he was outnumbered by Marshall and Acheson, Admiral Sherman and General Bradley, and Congress, which was sending members of the Senate Foreign Affairs and Armed Forces Committees to Europe to work on issues of economic and military aid. They even had an appointment with Franco arranged for 13 July. Finally, on 11 July, the president approved the new policy.[452] A few days later, when he was questioned by the press, he recognized that he had indeed changed the

---

[450] Note from a conversation between Martín Artajo and Ambassador William D. Pawley, adjunct to the Secretary of State and Political Advisor of Lieutenant General Bradley on his mission to Europe, 16 June 1951, Ministry of Foreign Affairs Record Group, file number 82–07496, AGA.

[451] Letter from Brother Thomas J. Harkin, Past Grand Master of North Carolina to the president, 30 July 1951, OF 410–0, box 1418, HSTPL.

[452] Hualde, El "cerco" ..., 338.

policy toward Spain as a "result of advice by the Department of Defense."[453] And beforehand Acheson had done the same, saying that "military authorities are in general agreement that Spain is of strategic importance to the general defense of Western Europe. As a natural corollary to this generally accepted conclusion."[454]

Nevertheless, the president was still reluctant and, after receiving letters from Freemason friends denouncing the lack of religious freedom in Spain, he wrote the following:

> I've never been happy about sending an Ambassador to Spain, and I am not happy about it now, and unless Franco changes his treatment of citizens who do not agree with him religiously, I'll be sorely tempted to break off all communication with him in spite of the defense of Europe.

Although by this time Griffis had been in Madrid for several months, there had been no progress on the religious question. Truman recalled that before Griffis had set off for Spain, he had told him:

> Franco's attitude in these matters is exceedingly obnoxious to me. [...] there was a time, and I think it still exists, when Protestants couldn't have public funerals. They are forced to be buried at night and are allowed no markers for their graves. They are buried in plowed fields like potters' fields. I think in these modern times when we are doing everything we possibly can for religious freedom that it is a very bad example to be set before the world.[455]

As can be seen, the religious question in Franco's Spain and relations with the country in general were still the source of considerable controversy.[456]

Truman's approval completed the three-year shift from the "kick-Franco-out-now policy" initiated at the beginning of 1948. It had been a long and tortuous process involving the press, the Catholic Church and, above all, senators and representatives who defended their own personal interests, the economic interests of their states, and their ideology. And in some cases they

---

[453] *New York Times*, 20 July 1951, 4.

[454] Department of State Press Release 639, 18 July 1951,

[455] President to Secretary of State, 2 August 1951, OF 419–0, box 1418, HSTPL.

[456] See, for example, the letters received for and against the policy by Republican Senator Robert A. Taft, Taft Papers, Library of Congress. The historian Richard Herr, of the University of Chicago, wrote letters of complaint from Paris on 31 August 1951 to Senators Taft, Connally, Brewster, Douglas and others, using the living conditions in Spain as his main argument and the fact that if during the previous world war there had been no need for an alliance with Franco, there was no need for one now, either. Richard Herr to Senator Robert A. Taft, 31 August 1951, Taft Papers, Library of Congress.

had been spurred on by Lequerica, the embassy, and the paid lobbyists, and their policy of greasing congressmen's palms with "subsidies". However, although their aim had been achieved, it was not thanks to them; the decision to change had been taken by the president and his administration on the basis of strategic factors in which the Francoists had played no role at all.

What is more, there was still a lot of work to do. The loan of $62.5 million had still not been issued, and Lequerica complained that Spain and the sympathetic congressmen could not enjoy the benefits of what they had fought long and hard for. The new loan for $100 million granted in October 1951 was to take even longer to issue and had been granted thanks to McCarran including it in the Mutual Security Act, a maneuver that had again outraged Acheson and the president, but that eventually came into effect. This financial package had been arranged by McCarran and maybe some other members of Congress who Lequerica had mobilized with "subsidies" and other perks after several months during which the ministry had provided no funds for these needs. Lequerica had also been working unofficially on some sectors of the administration and the State Department although we do not have any details.[457]

It seemed at first that the military talks would make quick progress but they soon slowed down and did not conclude until the agreement was signed on 26 September 1953. They had started when, as part of a longer trip to southern Europe in representation of the Joint Chiefs of Staff, Admiral Sherman had traveled secretly to Madrid where he met Franco on 16 and 18 July 1950. As we have seen, Sherman, together with Marshall, had played a decisive role in convincing President Truman to change his mind.[458]

In this interview with the Generalissimo they agreed to initiate contacts on bilateral cooperation on issues of defense. In response to Franco's insistent demands for economic aid, Sherman promised that the Department of Defense and the Joint Chiefs of Staff would submit to Congress the necessary requests for a joint economic and military aid package for Spain.[459]

---

[457] This is clear from the following paragraphs of the telegram sent by Lequerica to Martín Artajo, 7 September 1951: "We still have the Appropriations Committee, which will take specific decisions favorable to Spain, but we must immediately resume our activities which, as Your Excellency knows, are at a total halt today. [...] Your Excellency knows that, in addition to the parliamentary solution, I can suggest other effective and, I believe, decisive actions we can take in the upper echelons of the Administration and the State Department. [...] . They have been used with great success in the past and I trust that we will be able to use them again." Cited in Viñas, *En las garras...*, 130.

[458] T. Draper "Los castillos de España del Pentágono," *The Reporter,* 30 October 1952, Presidency of the Government Record Group, Head of State, file number 72–07660, AGA.; Lowi, "US Bases in Spain,"..., 692.

[459] Memorandum of conversation. General Franco, Marqués de Prat, Ambassador Griffis, Admiral Sherman, 16 July 1951, Records of the Office of Western European

228   JOAN MARIA THOMÀS

The admiral's sudden death on 22 July in Naples did nothing to stop the agreement from being put into practice, and the Joint Chiefs of Staff appointed a team of six high-ranking officers to initiate the negotiations. Significantly they were headed by a general of the U.S. air force, James W. Spry.[460] In parallel, another commission was set up for the economic issues, headed by Sidney C. Sufrin, of the Business and Economic Research Center of Syracuse University. It analyzed the investments made with the loan of $62.5 million in 1950, and studied the economic conditions of the country and its capacity to repay other credits and receive future investments.[461] However, "in order to assure successful negotiations for military facilities" the U.S. government decided to minimize "the question of economic assistance in order to safeguard our best bargaining weapon until such time as negotiations were begun."[462] In fact, the negotiations for what would finally be the Pact of Madrid did not begin until April 1952 with the new ambassador, Lincoln McVeagh, only appointed in March, assisted by a new group of military experts and the Mutual Security Agency, again led by a U.S. air force general, August W. Kissner. Beforehand, Griffis had asked to be dismissed[463] so that he could return to his private life. His time in office had created various problems for the State Department, some of which were quite disagreeable.[464]

The talks did not finish until the very day of the signature (26 September 1953), by which time there was a different ambassador, James C. Dunn, who had taken up the post on 9 April of the same year. The agreement required the United States to provide Spain with economic aid and, in return, they would be allowed to set up their own military bases on Spanish territory, although formally under Spanish sovereignty. It also contained secret clauses

---

Affairs. Records of the Spanish and Portuguese Desk Offices, Subject Files Relating to Spain and Portugal 1942–1953, box 6, RG 59, General Records of the Department of State, NARA-2.

[460] Hualde, El "cerco" ..., 344. On the disappointment of the U.S. military when they saw the lack of effectiveness of the Spanish army, and the Spanish demands, see Draper, "Los castillos de España del Pentágono".

[461] Hualde, El "cerco" ..., 347.

[462] "Unfavorable remarks about Western European countries," n.d., U.S. Embassy Madrid, Classified General Records 1940–1963, RG 84, NARA-2.

[463] Griffis to Truman, 3 January 1952, U.S. Embassy Madrid, Classified General Records 1940–1963, RG 84, NARA-2.

[464] He had brazenly announced his pro-Franco leanings, which went against the guidelines that had been laid down, and he was the cause of many embarrassing situations with the wives of diplomats and high-ranking Spanish and foreign officials in Madrid, as the embassy itself reported to Washington: "Unfavorable remarks about Western European countries," n.d., U.S. Embassy Madrid, Classified General Records 1940–1963, RG 84, NARA-2.

that seriously compromised Spanish sovereignty, which was somewhat contradictory considering the Francoists' proud ultranationalism.[465]

Despite the best efforts of the pro-Franco ambassador to make progress on the Protestant question, satisfy the president, and bring the negotiations to a speedy conclusion, the Franco regime made no concessions in this respect or any other concerning domestic policy. In fact, by October 1951 Griffis had already thrown in the towel as far as achieving change was concerned. He gave the following explanation to the secretary of state:

> The Spaniards are a very proud people. They will resent more quickly than almost any other country any attacks on or efforts to change their way of life and their way of government [...] there is a little to do but keep a strictly hands-off policy on Spanish internal affairs, except when, as and if in private and unofficial conversations I can call the attention of Spanish officials to the great impetus they could give to American public opinion by even slight relaxations on policies which are considered fascistic in our country.[466]

The regime's resistance to change gave rise to new tensions between Truman and the pro-Francoist congressmen. It also generated new controversies in the U.S. press and media between those in favor of the new policy toward Spain and those against, particularly because Franco refused to back

---

[465] Viñas, *En las garras....*

[466] Griffis to Secstate, 18 October 1951, U.S. Embassy Madrid, Classified General Records 1940–1963, RG 84, NARA-2. Years later, on 4 April 1961, he complained to Clark of how the United States had wasted the chance of being on good terms with Spain. He wrote: "It is my feeling and my strong feeling that, next to England, Spain is our staunchest, safest, most loyal, and potentially useful ally in the fight against Communism. The years since the beginning of my tenancy of the Ambassadorship in Madrid have been years of almost futile struggle to persuade the American people to abandon their old prejudices against Franco and his regime and to convince them of the importance of aiding and cultivating the Spanish people and its government for our own safety in the future. Philosophically, we have probably made some advances in this battle, but financially we have been stupid and niggardly. [...] Fortunately, my great desire to see Military and Air Bases in Spain and to convince the Spanish government that if they abandon their requirements the tourists would become one of their great industries have come true, but it is a bitter pill to me to see almost Communistic nations receive large assistance from our government and Spain held down too little or nothing. This is a real, a very great problem for the American people to create an understanding in their minds of how important Spain and its government is to us. There should be a new appraisal of the situation and that appraisal, if honest, would develop the theory that Spain is our second-best friend, our most hopeful investment and our safer protection against dangers with overwhelm us on every side": John D. Lodge Papers, Hoover Institution Archives, Stanford University.

down on any domestic issues or the (non-existent) political freedoms of the Spaniards, including religion. General Vaughan suggested to Lequerica that an exchange of letters between the president and Franco might help the situation. It did not. In fact, at the beginning of 1952 Truman once again spoke out harshly against Franco.[467] And meanwhile, the talks carried on. The agreement was finally signed by the Republican General Dwight D. Eisenhower because Truman was no longer the president of the United States, which must have been a relief to him. But that is another story.

Conclusions

In its first fifteen years of life, the Franco regime benefitted from two "non-interventions"[468] by the European powers and the United States. The first was in 1936; the second in 1945. The first contributed to Franco's victory in the Civil War; but the second isolated Spain internationally and turned the country into a semi-pariah for five years (from 1945 to 1950). From the perspective of U.S. policy, this five-year period can be divided into two different stages, the second of which began at the end of 1947 and finished at the end of 1950, when the UN repealed much of its 1946 resolution (which had recommended withdrawing ambassadors from Madrid, thus initiating the diplomatic isolation of Franco's Spain) and the United States decided to enter into bilateral talks. However, Spain never had access to the North Atlantic Treaty or the Marshall Plan despite the fact that the latter was one of its initial aspirations. This meant that it was not involved in either of the two great strategic projects backed by the United States in Europe, which meant that Spain was out on a limb. This is the period dealt with in this chapter.

At this time, the United States insisted that Truman's reluctant change in policy in January 1948 was dependent on Franco making liberalizing reforms. This Franco never did, which meant that the change took three years before it came into effect and, when it finally did, it was the result not of the work put in by the Francoists in Washington, the sympathetic congressmen, the paid lobbyists, or the so-called Spanish Bloc, as Lequerica said it was, but of a U.S.

---

[467] See President Truman's press conference, 7 February 1952, "Attack on President Truman Continued by Falange Papers," 12 February 1952; Memorandum of Conversation Robert E. Wilson Sevilla Viceconsul-Santos M. Molins Zurita, pastor of the Reformed Spanish Church, Seville; "Reaction to ex-Ambassador Griffis's Recent Statements on Religious Intolerance in Spain and other matters," 28 February 1952, and other documents in U.S. Embassy Madrid, Classified General Records 1940–1963, RG 84, NARA-2.

[468] Joan Maria Thomàs, "La larga sombra de la Guerra Civil: España y las grandes potencias (1939–1953)," *Dictatorships & Democracies. Journal of History and Culture*, vol. 8 (2020), 11–26.

decision largely based on the outbreak of the Korean War and the escalation of the Cold War. The decision to change was also taken because the United States was very aware that the conflict in Korea was not going to be the major one in the short and the medium term; there would be others in Europe prompted by the Soviet Union's now established role as a nuclear power. This state of affairs made it necessary for the United States to have air and naval bases on Spanish soil. Increasingly involved in strategic military issues, President Truman decided to authorize bilateral talks with the Franco regime, subordinating the personal revulsion he felt for Franco's anti-communist but fascist, or semi-fascist, Spain to his general political strategy of anti-communism.

This does not mean that the Francoists did not have some success with their U.S. policy. The most significant was the result of the sympathetic congressmen working with Lequerica and the embassy to obtain the first official U.S. aid package for the Franco regime since 1939. It consisted of $62.5 million as part of the General Appropriations Act for 1951, passed on 6 September 1950. The package had been opposed by Acheson and Truman but it was pushed through even so. Lequerica's "subsidies" to members of the press and his frenetic activity did much to improve public opinion on Spain, although this change came about in a general atmosphere of increasing anti-communism, facilitated by simplification and polarization.[469] The second great success was not down to the Francoists but to the Truman administration. On 4 November 1950 the UN resolution of 12 December 1946 was lifted, a decision that was followed by Lequerica being appointed ambassador in Washington and Stanton G. Griffis ambassador in Madrid, and, in August 1951, by the beginning of talks in Madrid after Sherman had met with Franco the month before. These talks were not completed until the very day of the signature of the Pact of Madrid on 26 September 1953.

Franco had started maneuvering to ingratiate himself with the Allies in the last stages of the Second World War, at the end of 1943 and the beginning of 1944, in an attempt to avoid any sort of punishment for his support of the Axis powers. Since August 1944, in his capacity as minister of foreign affairs, Lequerica had played an important role in this policy. However, after the end of the conflict, he was dismissed because he had been an ambassador in Nazi-occupied France and Franco needed to present a new image before the victorious Allies, which he decided to do by promoting the president of Acción Católica Martín Artajo and giving greater importance to the national Catholic sector. At the same time, he made an effort to cover up the most obvious fascist features of his new state. Nevertheless, none of this had been of any use to Franco or had pulled the wool over the Allies' eyes even for a moment: in 1945 Spain had been stopped from joining the UN and the following year had been put into diplomatic isolation. It

---

[469] Montero-León, *Los Estados Unidos y el...*, 324 ff.

had also been excluded from the North Atlantic Treaty and the Marshall Plan, despite Portugal's attempts on Spain's behalf.

Franco was convinced of the inevitability of a future confrontation between the Western Allies and the Soviet Union, and of the military importance – which he tended to exaggerate – of Spanish territory in the defense of the "free world." At the national level, he exploited the (alleged) injustice of the way in which Spain was being treated to bring the country together, and he organized press campaigns and mass demonstrations focusing on himself as a leader and his policies. But even as he portrayed his regime as the victim of a lack of understanding, and constantly trumpeted in the national and international press that "the truth" would finally prevail and Spain's (anti-communist) merits would be recognized, he, his government, and particularly the minister of foreign affairs strived to piece together an international policy that would bring the country out of diplomatic isolation. Spain was suffocated by economic problems and desperately needed the 1946 UN resolution to be lifted. To this end, Franco sought to increase the very little international support he had by means of a specific policy targeting the Latin American and Arabian countries. He saw the United States as a chance of obtaining the aid he needed to ease the problems of supply and modernizing the economy. For these reasons, Franco and Martín Artajo, who were well aware of the support they had in some sectors in the United States and of the interest of the U.S. armed forces to have bases on Spanish soil, decided that Lequerica should travel to Washington to work on changing U.S. policy toward Spain and obtaining the much-needed aid. Any change of this sort inevitably required the 1946 sanctions to be lifted because it was unthinkable that the United States would enter into any agreements with the Franco regime without first re-establishing diplomatic relations. As soon as he got to Washington, Lequerica used the diplomatic contacts he already had and the ones he soon made in combination with the funds at his disposal to employ professional lobbyists (two individuals and a prestigious law firm) to "subsidize" (that is to say, pay) journalism companies, make donations to the Catholic church and pay people, some of whom were probably congressmen.

Working alongside them was what we have referred to as the Spanish Bloc, the group who ever since the Civil War had been expressing their support of Franco and the regime for political-patriotic, ideological, religious, or cultural reasons, or because they represented companies, consortia, or banks interested in re-establishing, increasing, or improving their economic relations with Spain. They had continued to give their support after the end of the Second World War because they believed that Spain had been treated unfairly by the UN in 1945. Also on their side was what was known as the Spanish Lobby, those sectors that were working from within Congress for a change in U.S. policy toward Spain. Above, we have criticized the fact that, from the very moment this concept was formulated by political scientists, historiographers, and journalists, there has been a tendency to assume not only that there was some form of stable coordination but also that it was led by the lobbyists in the pay of the embassy. Although the work put in by these lobbyists both inside and outside Congress cannot be denied, this coordination and leadership never existed. We have also discussed the fundamental role played by senators Brewster and McCarran, who worked hand in hand with Lequerica to present debates, make proposals, and apply for aid for Spain, and we have pointed out the possibility that McCarran may even have been paid by Lequerica to do so.

The "inspector" worked intensely in Washington, using a variety of strategies to increase congressional and non-congressional support for the change in U.S. policy toward Spain. Throughout his time in the capital, he fostered relations with the State Department and other sectors he knew to be sympathetic, or at least not hostile. He also engaged in the important task of attracting members of Congress by means of projects such as the "Plan Otoño" and extending support for Spain. He made approaches to the armed forces, the Republican party, the Catholic Church, and some sectors of the press. And in an attempt to lift the 1946 resolution, which had been passed largely due to the United States, he was in contact with the U.S. delegation and several Latin American delegations at the UN. His scheming in Congress or with members of the armed forces or the State Department created some difficult moments for the State Department and the president. Lequerica's interlocutors at the Iberian desk did not find it easy to defend the official policy of requiring internal reforms in Spain because they were trapped between the schemes of the pro-Francoists and the militant anti-Francoists. Several years later, the head of the desk, William Dunham, explained the situation in the following terms:

> Participating in negotiations as politically controversial as the ones with Spain were in those days was not without its own hazards. There were those in Congress, in organizations like the Lincoln Brigade, and other groups adamantly opposed to any dealings with Spain who mounted continuing campaigns against any agreements with "Franco Spain." Anyone so engaged was regarded as a Fascist. On the other hand, there were those in the Congress and other groups outside government who saw business benefits they could reap once these agreements were completed and they regarded as a Communist or a Communist "sympathizer" anyone they thought was driving too hard a bargain. I remember Senator McCarran hailing several of us up to a committee he was on to explain a cable he had got somehow. I had drafted it, Livie Merchant had signed it, and the Senator was suspicious that we were up to something that would be harmful to one of his constituents, the Wells Fargo Co. It was some very incidental matter that had nothing to do with that company, but the senator's

immediate conclusion that we were "up to something" was symptomatic of the suspicions many business people had that their interests in future business in Spain were being overlooked.[470]

Dunham also gave the following accurate description of Lequerica:

> The Spaniards had their own "lobby" set up. They had sent a high ranking official to their Embassy in Washington to encourage such suspicions about anything and anyone they thought was trying to drive too hard a bargain. Jose Felix de Lequerica, whom we all regarded as Ambassador-in-waiting, was a typical wardheeler politico, ebullient, tricky, overtly friendly but untrustworthy, and capable of any underhanded maneuvers that would advance his cause. In short, a man well-suited to his task.[471]

Lequerica's way of working, his personality, and his character were behind the tensions with Minister of Trade and Industry Suanzes and, to a lesser extent, with Martín Artajo, although he could always rely on the latter, and of course Franco, for support. The anti-Francoist sectors of the State Department, in agreement with the *chargé d'affaires* in Madrid Culbertson and apparently with the support of Lequerica's enemies at the Ministry of Foreign Affairs (e.g. the former ambassador Cárdenas) or at the embassy itself in Washington (e.g. *Chargé d'Affaires* Baráibar) attempted to have him withdrawn from Washington. But they did not manage it, and Lequerica came out stronger from the confrontation.

The change in U.S. policy gave rise to a long negotiation for a bilateral agreement – something that Spain had always aspired to[472] – in the course of which Spain was granted military support and loans that were for much smaller amounts than they had hoped for in exchange for intolerable (if they had been public knowledge) and secret transfers of sovereignty, quite unexpected considering the ultra-nationalism that was such a feature of the Franco regime.

The Francoists did not win the day in the United States. The policy toward Spain changed because the president and his government decided to change it for the reasons we have discussed. Lequerica, the embassy, the lobbyists, the sympathetic congressmen, the Spanish Lobby, and the Spanish Bloc were

---

[470] Association for Diplomatic Studies and Training Foreign Affairs Oral History Project, Foreign Affairs Series, WILLIAM B. DUNHAM, 1996, Copyright 1999, ADST.

[471] Ibid.

[472] On the reluctance to bilaterality, see Dunham to Culbertson, 29 April 1949, Records of the Office of Western European Affairs, Records of the Spanish and Portuguese Desk Offices, Subject Files Relating to Spain and Portugal 1942–1953, box 6, RG 59, General Records of the Department of State, NARA-2.

at times a considerable nuisance for Truman and Acheson. But the president and the secretary did not change their policy in response to action taken by Congress and the Francoists; they changed it for other reasons, which took precedence over their policy to force Franco to carry out liberalizing reforms in his regime. The fact that these reforms were never made meant that they too failed.

Sources

Archives

Archivo de la Fundación Nacional Francisco Franco (ANFF)
Archivo General de la Administración (AGA)
Archivo General de la Universidad de Navarra
Bowdoin College Library. Brunswick (Maine)
Georgetown University Archives
Library of Congress
Mudd Manuscript Library. Princeton University
National Archives and Records Administration (NARA-2)
Nevada Historical Society. Reno
Rare Books and Manuscripts Library. Columbia University. Carlton J. H. Hayes
    Papers
Harry S. Truman Presidential Library (Independence, Missouri)
Hoover Institution Archives. Stanford University (California)
University of Delaware Archives
University of Nevada Reno

Bibliography

Aline, condesa de Romanones, *El fin de una era*, Barcelona, Ediciones B, 2010.
Baldwin, H. W., "US 'Frontier' is Issue," *New York Times*, 10 October 1948.
Ballestero, A., *Juan Antonio Suanzes 1891–1977,* León, LID, 1993.
Benet, J., *Lluís Companys, afusellat,* Barcelona, Edicions 62, 2005.
Bernardo, I. y Goiogana, I., *Galíndez: la tumba abierta. Guerra, exilio y frustración,* Bilbao, Sabino Arana Fundazioa, 2006.
Bigart, H., "Acheson Bars Initiative on Spain by U.S.," *New York Herald Tribune*, 12 May 1949.
Boor, J. [Francisco Franco], "Alta masonería," *Arriba*, 9 de agosto de 1949.
Bowen, W. H., *Truman, Franco's Spain, and the Cold War,* Columbia, University of Missouri Press, 2017.
Briggs, P. J., *Making American Foreign Policy: President–Congress Relations from the Second World War to the Post-Cold War Era*, Lanham, Rowman & Littlefield, 1994.
Buruma, I., *Año Cero. Historia de 1945,* Barcelona, Pasado y Presente, 2014.
Cabrera, M., *Joan March (1880–1962)*, Madrid, Marcial Pons, 2011.
Cava Mesa, M. J., *Los diplomáticos de Franco. J. F. de Lequerica. Temple y tenacidad (1890–1963)*, Bilbao, Universidad de Deusto, 1989.

Chapman, M. E., *Arguing Americanism: Franco Lobbyists, Roosevelt's Foreign Policy and the Spanish Civil War*, Kent, The Kent State University Press, 2011.

Childs, M., "Washington Calling," *The Washington Post*, 9 September 1949.

Collado Seidel, C., *España, refugio nazi*, Madrid, Temas de hoy, 2005.

Collado Seidel, C., *El telegrama que salvó a Franco. Londres, Washington y la cuestión del Régimen (1942–1945)*, Barcelona, Crítica, 2016.

Costigliola, F., "After Roosevelt's Death: Dangerous Emotions, Divisive Discourses, and the Abandoned Alliance," *Diplomatic History*, vol. 31, n. 1 (January 2010), 1–23.

Costigliola, F., *Roosevelt's Lost Alliances: How Personal Politics Helped Start the Cold War*, Princeton, Princeton University Press, 2012.

Crassweller, R. D., *Trujillo. La trágica aventura del poder personal*, Barcelona, Bruguera, 1966.

Delgado Gómez-Escalonilla, L., "La maquinaria de la persuasión. Política informativa y cultural de Estados Unidos hacia España," *Ayer*, vol. 75 (2009), 97–132.

Diccionario de la Real Academia de la Historia, "Jose Felix de Lequerica and Erquicia," http://dbe.rah.es/biografias/12004/jose-felix-de-lequerica-y-erquicia.

Domínguez Arribas, J., *El enemigo judeo-masónico en la propaganda franquista (1936–1945)*, Madrid, Marcial Pons Historia, 2009.

Dorley Jr., A. J., *The Role of Congress in the Establishment of Bases in Spain*, Ph.D. dissertation, St. John's University, 1969.

Douglas, M., "Remembering Julian Pitt-Rivers. A personal note," en Honorio M. Velasco (coord.), *La Antropología como pasión y como práctica. Ensayos in honorem Julian Pitt-Rivers*, Madrid, CSIC, 2004.

Draper, Th., "Los castillos de España del Pentágono," *The Reporter,* 30 de octubre de 1952.

Edwards, J., *Anglo-American Relations and the Franco Question 1945–1955*, New York, Oxford University Press, 1999.

Ferrary, Á., "Los Estados Unidos y el régimen de Franco, 1945–1973. De la 'kick-Franco-out-now-policy' al 'solving the 'Spanish Problem': modernización y apertura exterior," *Memoria y civilización. Anuario de Historia*, vol. 21 (2018).

Ferrell, R. H. (ed.), *Truman in the White House. The Diary of Eben A. Ayers*, Columbia, University of Missouri Press, 1991.

Ferrell, R. H., *Harry S. Truman and the Cold War Revisionists*, Columbia, University of Missouri Press, 2006.

Foreign Relations of The United States, 1948, Western Europe.

Foreign Relations of The United States, 1949, Western Europe.

Foreign Relations of The United States, 1950, Western Europe.

Franco Salgado-Araujo, Teniente general Francisco, *Mis conversaciones privadas con Franco,* Madrid, Planeta, 2005.

Gaddis, J. L., *Estados Unidos y los orígenes de la Guerra Fría 1941–1947*, Buenos Aires, Latinoamericano, 1989.

Gaddis, J. L., *The Cold War. A New History*, London, New York, Penguin, 2005.

Giblin, J. C., *The Rise and Fall of Senator Joe McCarthy*, Boston, Clarion Books, 2009.

Gilmore, R. W., *The American Foreign Policy-Making Process and the Development of a Post-World War II in Spanish Policy, 1945–1953: A Case Study*, Ph.D. dissertation, University of Pittsburgh, 1967.

Griffis, S. G., *Lying in State*, New York, Doubleday, 1952.

Guixé Corominas, J., *La República perseguida. Exilio y represión en la Francia de Franco (1937–1951)*, València, PUV, 2012.

Harris, E. A., "Ya no nos hace falta Franco, pero continúa el pasilleo en Washington a favor del dirigente español," *Sant Louis Post Dispatch*, 4 de junio de 1949.

Hayes, C. J. H., *Wartime Mission in Spain, 1942–1945*, New York, The Macmillan Company,1945.

Hayes, C. J. H., *The United States and Spain. An Interpretation*, New York, Sheed & Ward, 1951.

Hayes, C. J. H., *Misión de guerra en España*, Zaragoza, Prensas de la Universidad de Zaragoza, 2018 (presentación de Joan Maria Thomàs).

Herrero García, P., *La labor como embajador de José María de Areilza en Argentina, los Estados Unidos y Francia*, Tesis doctoral, Universidad San Pablo-CEU, 2018.

Hualde Amunarriz, X., *El "Cerco" aliado. Estados Unidos, Gran Bretaña y Francia frente a la dictadura franquista (1945–1953)*, Bilbao, Universidad del País Vasco, 2016.

Ickes, H., "The State Department's Siesta," *The New Republic*, 23 May 1949.

Ickes, H., "A State Department Shell Game," *The New Republic*, 8 August 1949.

Jarque Iñíguez, A., *"Queremos esas bases" El acercamiento de Estados Unidos a la España de Franco*, Alcalá de Henares, Universidad de Alcalá, 1998.

Jordà, A. M., "El juez de Reus o el amargo sabor de la calumnia," *Diari de Tarragona*, 25 de noviembre de 2016.

Kennan, G. F., *Memoirs 1925–1950*, New York, Pantheon Books, 1983.

Larrinaga, C. (ed.), *Luis Bolín y el turismo en España entre 1928 y 1952*, Madrid, Marcial Pons, 2021.

León Aguinaga, P., *Sospechosos habituales. El cine norteamericano, Estados Unidos y la España franquista, 1939–1960*, Madrid, CSIC, 2010.

León Aguinaga, P., "Los canales de la propaganda norteamericana en España 1945–1960," *Ayer*, vol. 75 (2009), 133–158.

León Aguinaga, P., "The Chase Bank, the WCC and the (Financial) Rehabilitation of Spain in the Early Cold War," *SAHFR – Themed session on CAPITALISM. Panel: "International Bankers, Offshore Merchants, and Foreign Diplomats: Change and Continuity in U.S. Foreign (Spanish–American) Relations from the Great Depression to the Bretton Woods Age,"* 2021.

León Aguinaga, P. (ed.), *Philip W. Bonsal. Diario de un diplomático americano en España, 1944–1947. Estados Unidos ante la dictadura franquista*, Zaragoza, Prensas de la Universidad de Zaragoza, en forthcoming.

Liedke, B. N., *Embracing a Dictatorship. US Relations with Spain, 1945–1953*, London, Macmillan Press, 1998.

Lippmann, W., "Common Sense and the Problem of Spain," *Daily Mail*, 18 May 1949.

López Zapico, M. A., "Against All Odds. El diplomático Juan Francisco de Cárdenas durante la Guerra Civil española y el primer franquismo," en Antonio César Moreno Cantano (coord.), *Propagandistas y diplomáticos al servicio de Franco (1936–1945)*, Gijón, Trea, 2012.

Lowi, Th. J., "U. S. Bases in Spain," in Harold Stein (ed.), *American Civil-military Decisions. A Book of Case Studies*, Tuscaloosa, University of Alabama Press, 1963.

McCarran, P., "Why Shouldn't the Spanish Fight for Us?," *Saturday Evening Post*, 28 April 1951.

McFarland, K. D. and Roll, David L., *Louis Johnson and the Arming of America. The Roosevelt and Truman Years*, Bloomington, Indiana University Press, 2005.

Marquina Barrio, A., *España en la política de seguridad occidental 1939–1986*, Madrid, Ediciones Ejército, 1986.

Martín Aceña, P., *El oro de Moscú y el oro de Berlín*, Madrid, Taurus, 2001.

Messenger, D. A., *Hunting Nazis in Franco's Spain*, Baton Rouge, Louisiana State University Press, 2014.

Messer, R. L., *The End of an Alliance: James F. Byrnes, Roosevelt, Truman, and the Origins of the Cold War*, Chappel Hill, University of North Carolina Press, 1982.

Montero Jiménez, J. A. y León Aguinaga, P., *Los Estados Unidos y el Mundo: la metamorfosis del poder americano (1890–1952)*, Madrid, Síntesis, 2019.

Mota Zurdo, D., *Un sueño americano: el gobierno vasco en el exilio y Estados Unidos (1937–1979)*, Tesis doctoral, Departamento de Historia Contemporánea, Universidad del País Vasco, 2015.

Offner, A. A., *Another Such Victory: President Truman and the Cold War 1945–1953*, Stanford, Stanford University Press, 2002.

Oshinsky, D. M., *A Conspiracy so Immense. The World of Joe McCarthy*, Oxford, Oxford University Press, 2005.

Pearson, D., "Behind the Scenes," *The Washington Post*, 7 August 1950.

Pearson, D. and Constantine, B., *American Diplomatic Game*, Garden City, Doubleday, Doran & Company, Inc., 1935.

Pérez-Part Durbán, L. y Fernández Arribas, G. (eds.), *Holocausto y bienes culturales*, Huelva, Universidad de Huelva, 2019.

Portero, F., *Franco aislado. La cuestión española (1945–1950)*, Madrid, Aguilar, 1989.

Public Papers of the Presidents of the United States. Harry S. Truman, 1948, Washington D.C., US Government Printing Office, 1965.

Public Papers of the Presidents of the United States. Harry S. Truman, 1949, Washington D.C., US Government Printing Office, 1965.

Public Papers of the Presidents of the United States. Harry S. Truman, 1950, Washington D.C., US Government Printing Office, 1965.

Rannieri, L., *Dannie Heineman. Un destin singulier 1872–1962*, Bruxelles, Racine, 2005.

Reeves, Th. C., *The Life and Times of Joe McCarthy. A Biography*, New York, Stein and Day, 1982.

Rein, R., *La salvación de una dictadura. Alianza Franco-Perón 1946–1955*, Madrid, CSIC, 1995.

Rodríguez Lago, J. R., "'Aliados pola forza. Redes para unha victoria'. Os Aliados e os Estados Unidos na Galicia da II Guerra Mundial," *Xornadas Galicia e a II Guerra mundial*, Consello da Cultura Galega, 13–14 de abril de 2021.

Rubottom, R. R. and Murphy, J. C., *Spain and the United States Since World War II*, New York, Praeger, 1984.

Ruiz, J., "Menos Camboyas, Caperucita. Reflexión sobre la represión franquista, 1939–1953," *Dictatorships & Democracies*, vol. 8 (2020), 77–94.

Sánchez González, I., *Diez años de soledad. España, la ONU y la dictadura franquista 1945–1955*, Sevilla, Universidad de Sevilla, 2015.

Scowcroft, B., *Congress and Foreign Policy: An Examination of Congressional Attitudes Toward the Foreign Aid Programs to Spain and Yugoslavia*, Ph.D. dissertation, Columbia University, 1967.

Serrano Suñer, R., *Entre el silencio y la propaganda. La Historia como fue*, Barcelona, Planeta, 1977.

Sesma Landrín, N., *Un yanqui en la corte del general Franco. Charles A. Willoughby y la larga marcha hacia los Pactos de Madrid (1947–1953)*, documento de trabajo 2013/5, Seminario de Historia Departamento de Historia Social y del Pensamiento Político UNED/Departamento de Historia del Pensamiento y de los Movimientos Sociales y Políticos UCM/Instituto Universitario de Investigación Ortega y Gasset, 2013.

Shannon, W. V., "The Franco Lobby. A Jumble of Cotton, Silver, Cork, Generals, Society Pages, and Cocktails," *The Reporter*, 20 June 1950.

Smith, W. Th. Jr., *Enciclopaedia of the Central Intelligence Agency*, New York, Facts and File, 2003.

Suárez Fernández, L., *Francisco Franco y su tiempo*, vol. IV, Madrid, Azor, 1984,

Sureda Carrión, J. L., *Fantasía y realidad en el expolio de Barcelona Traction. Apunte para una biografía de Juan March Ordinas*, Barcelona, Civitas-Thompson Reuters, 2014.

Termis Soto, F., *Renunciando a todo: el régimen franquista y Estados Unidos desde 1945 hasta 1963*, Madrid, Biblioteca Nueva, 2005.

Thomàs, J. M., *La batalla del wolframio. Estados Unidos y España de Pearl Harbor a la Guerra Fría (1941–1947)*, Madrid, Cátedra, 2010 (English version: *Roosevelt, Franco and the End of the Second World War*, New York, Palgrave-Macmillan, 2011).

Thomàs, J. M., "Ramón Serrano Suñer. El personaje real y el personaje inventado," en Adrián Gómez Molina y Joan Maria Thomàs (coords.), *Ramón Serrano Suñer*, Barcelona, Ediciones B, 2003.

Thomàs, J. M., "La larga sombra de la Guerra Civil: España y las grandes potencias (1939–1953)," *Dictatorships & Democracies. Journal of History and Culture*, vol. 8 (2020), 11–26.

US Congressional Record, vols 1948–1950, US Congress.

Viñas, Á., *Los pactos secretos de Franco con Estados Unidos. Bases, ayuda económica, recortes de soberanía*, Barcelona, Grijalbo, 1981.

Viñas, Á., *En las garras del águila. Los pactos con Estados Unidos, de Francisco Franco a Felipe González (1945–1995)*, Barcelona, Crítica, 2003.

Weil, M., *A Pretty Good Club. The Founding Fathers of the US Foreign Service*, New York, Norton, 1978.

Whitaker, A. P., *Spain and Defense of the West: Ally and Liability*, New York, Council of Foreign Relations/Harper&Brothers, 1961.

Ybarra, M. J., *Washington Gone Crazy. Senator Pat McCarran and the Great American Communist Hunt*, Hanover, Steerforth Press, 2004.

4

"In Support of Our Prestige and Our Values": The Spanish Lobby and Local Politics in the United States, 1945–1955

WAYNE H. BOWEN

Introduction: The City of Angels

Los Angeles was in many ways an unexpected place for the government of Francisco Franco to achieve a foreign policy success. Far from Washington, D.C., outside the traditional Northeast U.S. corridor of political influence, and on the wrong side of North America for close ties of trade and travel with Europe, Los Angeles was at most an afterthought in U.S. and Spanish diplomatic circles prior to the Cold War. Although Los Angeles had been founded during the time of Spanish rule in the late eighteenth century, it had not been under the authority of the Spanish empire since 1821, when Mexico gained its independence from Madrid through successful rebellion. Los Angeles's initial Spanish and Catholic heritage had over time been subsumed by internal migration of Protestants from within the United States, although there remained a significant Spanish-speaking minority of Mexican Americans and Mexicans with some connection to the prior experience as well as contemporary Mexico through local churches, historical and cultural events, and cross-border travel.[1]

San Francisco had long been the city considered the international center for California and where Spain had traditionally operated a consulate. Indeed, it was in San Francisco that the organizing sessions of the UN were held in spring and summer 1945. Spain was a particular object of attention, excluded from membership based on the Franco regime's origin through support from Nazi Germany and Fascist Italy. Spain's consul in the city at the time of the UN meeting, Francisco de Amat, sent back reports to Spain lamenting at the unfair treatment, comparing it to other countries over whom there were

---

[1] C. Sterling, *Olvera Street: Its History and Restoration*, Los Angeles, Mario Valadez, 1947, 7–9.

also membership eligibility questions, including Poland and Argentina, and some neutral states such as Sweden and Portugal. Spain's diplomat noted the effective work by Spanish Republican exiles to influence delegations from Europe and Latin America, collaborating closely with both the Mexican and Soviet delegations, as well as organized progressive, socialist, and communist groups in San Francisco throughout this effort.[2]

While Spain did attempt cultural outreach in the Bay Area, there was little success outside of Catholic institutions, given San Francisco's long-term reputation as "a center for radical activity" and as a West Coast hub of support for Spanish Republican exiles after 1939.[3] Some groups even protested when the Spanish consulate tried to work with the San Francisco public library system to put on an "Exposition of the Contemporary Spanish Book," with anti-Franco editorials and complaints that reduced attendance and discouraged potential event sponsors. In the city, complained Amat, "the enemies of Spain work with free hands." Short of resources and faced with a hostile local environment, there were clear limits on possibilities for public events, even ones focused exclusively on religious and cultural themes.[4] Over the next decade, the Spanish consulate (later consulate-general) in San Francisco did put on other events, but primarily on a small scale, within the confines of Catholic churches, taking advantage of ecclesiastical protection, or within the confines of higher education at friendly private institutions such as Stanford University and Catholic Church-affiliated Santa Clara University.[5]

Unlike San Francisco, Los Angeles at this time was relatively isolated from global affairs and did not have the same base of activists engaged on the issue of Spanish foreign policy. Politics in Los Angeles in the late 1940s and early 1950s focused on issues such as crime, economic development, industries such as Hollywood, aerospace, and agriculture, and the status of labor under the *bracero* program for temporary workers from Mexico.[6] Even so, with its Hispanic heritage, conservative politics, vibrant economy, and dynamic Roman Catholic Church, Southern California proved the most successful region for

---

[2] *Archivo General de la Administración (AGA)* (10)025 Estados Unidos. Consulado de España en San Francisco, 54/12.122. Report, Francisco de Amat, Consul, San Francisco to Ministerio de Asuntos Exteriores. "Informe sobre la conferencia de San Francisco," 28 June 1945. J. M. Thomàs, *Roosevelt, Franco, and the End of World War II*, New York, Palgrave Macmillan, 191–193.

[3] E. Smith, *American Relief Aid and the Spanish Civil War*, Columbia, University of Missouri Press, 2013,72.

[4] *AGA* 54/12.122. Letter, 4 June 1947, Amat to Ministerio de Asuntos Exteriores. Letter, 15 July 1947, Amat to Ministerio de Asuntos Exteriores. Report on the "Exposición del Libro Español Contemporáneo" in San Francisco.

[5] *AGA* 54/12.122. Various letters and reports, Spanish Consulate, San Francisco, to Ministry of Foreign Relations, Madrid, 1945–1953.

[6] M. Prouty, *César Chávez, the Catholic Bishops, and the Farmworkers' Struggle for Social Justice*, Tucson, University of Arizona Press, 2006, 11.

Spanish diplomatic efforts in the United States in the early moments of the Cold War. Indeed, the example of the Spanish consulate in Los Angeles, led by an ambitious young Spanish diplomat, would serve as a case study for other efforts by Spain to develop closer ties with the United States through dedicated outreach, collaboration with supportive local groups, and a focus on cultural ties, rather than political questions.

Most of the research on the Spanish Lobby, the efforts by the Franco regime and its allies in the United States to restore friendly relations between the two states, has appropriately focused on high-level foreign relations. Spanish diplomats applied significant resources to lobby administration officials and members of Congress, coordinating with conservative and Catholic senators and congressmen, military and business leaders, favorable media, and high ecclesiastical figures, groups categorized by historian Joan Maria Thomàs as the Spanish Bloc, to influence public opinion and government policies. Opposed by the Truman administration, major factions within the Democratic party, and pressure groups such as trade unions, the Spanish Lobby and its allies in the Spanish Bloc nonetheless made steady progress during the emerging Cold War. This was especially true at the local level where, in cities such as Los Angeles, Spanish diplomats enjoyed earlier and more pervasive acceptance by cultural, political, economic, and religious elites.

Local Diplomacy, Local Conflicts

Consular efforts on the West Coast also focused on restoring Spain's legitimacy as the traditional leader of Hispanic culture in the Americas. One conflict emerged over the legacy of Christopher Columbus, with a bitter fight between Spanish and Italian diplomats over rival claims over this historic figure. Although born in the republic of Genoa in the Italian peninsula, Columbus sailed under the banners of the Spanish monarchs King Ferdinand and Queen Isabella. This dual legacy made little difference in the fifteen and sixteenth centuries, when loyalty was to dynasties and religions, rather than to ethnicities and nations. However, to Italian Americans, Columbus had come to represent their arrival as full-fledged American citizens, with the elevation of Columbus Day as a federal holiday in 1937 the result of years of lobbying by Catholic groups, most especially the Knights of Columbus.[7]

Despite the identification of Columbus Day with Italy in the United States, Spain hoped to associate this day more closely with Spain, connecting it to the Día de la Hispanidad, or Día de la Raza, celebrated in Spain and in much of Latin America. For 1949, the consulate staged a series of events, beginning

---

[7] E. Bartosik-Vélez, *The Legacy of Christopher Columbus in the America: New Nations and a Transatlantic Discourse of Empire*, Nashville, Vanderbilt University Press, 2014, 147.

THE SPANISH LOBBY AND LOCAL POLITICS IN THE UNITED STATES 243

with religious processional at "La Placita," a historic Spanish church in the heart of Olvera Street, an original Spanish district. The day continued with a reception at city hall and a small banquet at the Beverly Hills Hotel, although without much press coverage in local media.[8] The Italian consulate even invited Del Arco to their own event, to which he responded that he would be leading his own. Given the formal tone of the letter and the reply, it is not clear whether relations were civil at that moment between the two consulates, but no doubt the Italians understood Spain was advocating the restoration of a Spanish role in the commemoration of the day.[9]

In 1950, the event was much larger, and received coverage not only in California, but in Madrid, in the monarchist daily *ABC*. The Spanish banquet was large, with over 250 guests, including all accredited Latin American consuls in Los Angeles, Archbishop Francis McIntyre, Los Angeles Mayor Fletcher Bowron, and Los Angeles County Sheriff Eugene Biscailuz. The program for the event was titled "Día de la Raza: Conmemoración Hispánica del Descubrimiento de América" (Day of the Race: Hispanic Commemoration of the Discovery of America). Jaime Del Amo, honorary Spanish vice consul, spoke of the "historic injustice" that the day was associated more with Italy than with Spain.[10] Del Arco declared the event thereafter a "great success," but complained about the lack of coverage by major media in the region. Only *La Opinión*, a Spanish-language newspaper, and the *LA Evening Herald Express* featured stories about the Spanish event, compared to widespread newspaper and radio coverage of Columbus Day activities in the Italian American community.[11]

Indeed, the Italian version of the day was much larger, with "Columbus Day Civic Ceremony" taking place on the steps of the Los Angeles City Hall. With remarks from the mayor, county sheriff, the lieutenant governor of California, chairman of the Los Angeles County Board of Supervisors, Italian consul, other diplomats (but not from Spain), the band of the Los Angeles Police Department, and a leading role by the Knights of Columbus and Federated Italo Americans of Southern California, it was a rival event that drew more prestige, elected officials, and attention.[12] Del Arco expressed his

---

[8] *AGA*, 54/11.753. Letter, 13 September 49, Del Arco to Jaime Del Amo, President of Del Amo Foundation, and Honorary Vice Consul of Spain in Los Angeles. *Los Angeles Times*, 13 October 1949.

[9] *AGA* 54/11.753. Letter, 11 October 1949, Del Arco to Mario Pettaros, Vice Consul of Italy, Los Angeles.

[10] *AGA*, 54/11.753. *ABC*, Madrid, 23 October 1950. Program, "Dia de la Raza: Conmemoracion Hispanica del Descubrimiento de America," 12 October 1950.

[11] *AGA*, 54/11.753. Letter, 13 October 1950, Del Arco to Ministerio de Asuntos Exteriores.

[12] *AGA*, 54/11.753. Program, "Columbus Day Civic Ceremony," Los Angeles City Hall, 12 October 1950.

244 WAYNE H. BOWEN

ongoing frustration at Italian grandstanding about Columbus Day, indicating to the Spanish Foreign Ministry that he had "a couple of clashes with the Italians, dedicated as they are to frustrating, in whatever way they can, our commemoration."[13]

Spain in U.S. Foreign Policy and Domestic Politics

At the national level, the Franco regime had long enjoyed the support of the hierarchy of the Catholic Church in the United States. Even some religious orders normally considered progressive, such as the Jesuits, advocated on behalf of the regime, noting the anti-clerical positions of the Spanish Republic, as well as the destruction of religious institutions and the executions of clergy in Republican-held territories. The leading Jesuit publication, the magazine *America*, from early in the Spanish Civil War, denounced "the blood-drenched agents of Moscow," and their campaign of "liquidation of priests and nuns."[14] As early as summer 1939, *America* was calling for a normalization of relations with Spain, minimizing the potential for a Spanish alliance with Nazi Germany, and describing Franco as the nation's "guiding genius."[15] Later issues during the later stages of the Second World War and during the early Cold War called for Spain's entry into the UN, membership in the NATO access to U.S. markets and credit, and more generally allowing "Spain back in the family of nations."[16]

Historians such as Boris Leidtke, Stephen Byrnes, Jill Edwards, María Jesús Cava Mesa, Joan Maria Thomàs and others have presented an effective analysis of the slow integration of Spain into the U.S.-led Cold War defensive and political system, a development initially opposed by President Harry Truman. These volumes and others chronicle the domestic political struggles within the United States during the early years of the Cold War, as American and allied leaders argued over the appropriate place for Spain in the world, with debates in the UN, NATO, in relation to the Marshall Plan (European Recovery Program) for aid to Europe and within the political systems of each nation. While some nations, such as the Soviet Union and Mexico, called for more active intervention to overturn the regime, in the West there was much

---

13 712*AGA*, 54/11.753. Letter, 18 September 1950, Del Arco to Alfredo Sánchez Bella, Director, Instituto de Cultura Hispánica, Madrid.

14 G. McGowan, "Farewell Fifth Column! Long Live the Sixth Column," *America*, 12 February 1938, https://www.americamagazine.org/content/history-america-0, accessed 15 September 2021.

15 Unsigned editorial, "A Trustworthy Nation," *America*, 17 June 1939.

16 J. LaFarge, "The Future of Spain," *America*, 30 December 1944; unsigned editorial, "The UN and Spain," *America*, 27 April 1946; unsigned editorial, "Are Catholics Consistent?," *America*, 12 March 1949; unsigned editorial, "Cooperation with Spain," *America*, 24 February 1950; unsigned editorial, "Church-State in Spain," *America*, 22 March 1952.

THE SPANISH LOBBY AND LOCAL POLITICS IN THE UNITED STATES 245

less enthusiasm for this option, outside of a French coalition government that initially included communists. The French were a notable exception, however, as even adamant anti-Francoists such as Harry Truman and Clement Attlee did not advocate direct military intervention or even recognition of a government-in-exile based on Spanish Republicans.[17]

Despite efforts by their supporters in the United States to urge recognition of former elements of the Spanish Republic as a government-in-exile, analogous to the approach the Allies took with Poles, the Free French, and other during the Second World War, this strategy came to naught. The ongoing incapacity of Spanish Republican exile groups to form a broad coalition of all parties, minus the communists, that could form "a serious and credible alternative for the replacement of the Franco Regime" was one key element that over time undermined the original intent of the global pressure campaign against Spain. Absent a viable replacement for the Francoist system, the West feared either a reemergence of a new Spanish Civil War or, especially given the strength of pro-Soviet parties in France and Italy in the late 1940s, a communist victory in Spain.[18] This was also reflected in campaigns within Congress and in the broader political context of the United States to denounce Spanish Republican groups and their allies, especially those that had worked in coalition with the U.S. and Spanish communist parties, as threats to national security in the late 1940s and early 1950s. These pressures weakened support for Spanish exiles among former supporters, including U.S. labor unions, progressives within the Democratic party, and civil rights groups, all of which feared being identified as pro-Soviet amid the Cold War and legitimate concerns about U.S. national security in the face of this global struggle. What seemed acceptable in the mid-1930s, aligning with other liberal and leftist movements to support the Popular Front government in Spain, and the Republican coalition during the Spanish Civil War, was no longer acceptable, given that both had included the Spanish Communist party, and accepted aid from Stalin's Soviet Union.[19] Other supporters, such

---

[17] B. Leidtke, *Embracing a Dictatorship: US Relations with Spain, 1945–1953*, London, Macmillan Press, 1998; S. Byrnes, *Shedding the "Garb of Idealism": Truman Administration Policy Toward Spain and Yugoslavia*. Ph.D. dissertation, University of Texas at Austin, 1993; J. Edwards, *Anglo-American Relations and the Franco Question*, Oxford, Oxford University Press, 1999. M. Cava Mesa, *Los diplomáticos de Franco: J.F. de Lequerica, temple y tenacidad (1890–1963)*, Bilbao, Universidad de Deusto, 1989; J. M. Thomàs, *Roosevelt, Franco, and the End of World War II*, New York, Palgrave Macmillan, 2011.

[18] J. Barras, *Políticas de las exilados españoles, 1944–1950*, Paris, Ruedo Ibérico, 1976, 289–290.

[19] E. R. Smith, *American Relief Aid and the Spanish Civil War*, Columbia, University of Missouri Press, 2013, 118–121, 123–127.

as Claude Bowers, former ambassador to the Spanish Republic, had retired from active politics and no longer campaigned against Franco.[20]

New York was the center of support within the United States for the Spanish Republic and the cause of resistance to the Franco regime after the end of the Spanish Civil War. The city provided approximately 20 percent of the 2800 Americans who served in the pro-Republic International Brigades during the conflict, and after the Spanish Civil War was the home for organizations such as the Veterans of the Abraham Lincoln Brigade, which continued to oppose the Franco Regime.[21] With institutions such as NYU and Columbia University hosting refugee Spanish Republican scholars, "New York City was clearly the central American local of Spanish culture in exile."[22] New York was also a frequent meeting place during the Second World War for exile groups, such as the Basque government in exile, where it could count on local supporters for logistics, fundraising, and publicity.[23] New York had a club for Basque men, the Central Vasco-Americano, and an active community, including José Antonio de Aguirre, former leader of the Basque separatist government, who arrived in New York in December 1941 with his family, another exile from Franco's Spain. Granted an academic posting at Columbia University, Aguirre spent the war years in New York and traveling internationally supporting the Allied cause, encouraging enlistment by exiled Basques, and fundraising for the war effort, with the expectation that this support would contribute to the anti-Franco cause after the defeat of the Axis.[24]

This enthusiasm in New York began to wane after the end of the Second World War, especially given the decreasing interest among the Allies for intervention against the Spanish government. Indeed, while a January 1945 rally at New York City's Madison Square Garden drew 16,000, and featured national union leaders, members of Congress, media leaders, and celebrities by 1950 a similar event could only attract 1000 attendees.[25] An editorial from early

[20] P. Sehlinger and H. Hamilton, *Spokesman for Democracy: Claude G. Bowers, 1878–1958*, Indianapolis, Indiana Historical Society, 2000, 253.

[21] Smith, *American Relief ...*, 18, 35, 39, 106. *FAQ*, Veterans of the Abraham Lincoln Brigade, https://alba-valb.org/who-we-are/faqs/, accessed 22 September 2021.

[22] R. Gray, "Spanish Diaspora: A Culture in Exile,"," in "Remembering the Spanish Civil War," special issue, *Salmagundi: Quarterly of the Humanities and Social Sciences*, n. 76–77 (Fall 1987–Winter 1988), 77.

[23] M. Kurlansky, *The Basque History of the World*, New York, Penguin, 2001, 228, 229–230.

[24] J. A. de Aguirre, *Escape Via Berlin: Eluding Franco in Hitler's Europe*, Reno and Las Vegas, University of Nevada Press, 1991, 5. "History of Euzko-Etxea of New York," https://newyorkbasqueclub.com/our-history, accessed 23 September 2021.

[25] S. Payne, *The Franco Regime, 1936–1975*, Madison, University of Wisconsin Press, 1987, 383. *Volunteer for Liberty*, January 1945, Supplement 4, New York: Veterans of the Abraham Lincoln Brigade, 3–4, https://alba-valb.org/wp-content/uploads/2020/04/Volunteer_Supplement4_Jan_1945.pdf, accessed 22 September 2021.

1946, published in *Volunteer for Liberty*, the newsletter for the New York-based Veterans of the Abraham Lincoln Brigade, could proclaim at the fifteenth anniversary of the declaration of the Spanish Republic (April 1931) that the movement was "confident that the 16th anniversary would be celebrated in Madrid."[26] Others made more concrete plans, with the Basque government in exile holding a meeting in New York City of their full government February 1945, preparing for what they expected would be an Allied-backed return to Spain; Aguirre himself returned to Europe the following month, courtesy of a U.S. army air forces bomber.[27] Similarly, in 1947, one exile leader noted hopefully his assessment that "the Franco Regime is not going to last much longer."[28] Even though the immediate post-war years from 1945 to 1947 saw many exiles confident "that the Caudillo's days were numbered," few would make such an observation after 1950.[29] The heady wartime days, when advisors to President Franklin spoke openly about an invasion of Spain either prior to or as part of the 1942 landings in North Africa, were by the early 1950s a distant memory as the "fragile" coalition against Franco began to fade with the early Cold War.[30]

New York was not the only city where supporters of the former Spanish Republic had been active. In cities such as Chicago, Detroit, and San Francisco, they had been quite successful at raising financial support, volunteers, and awareness during the Spanish Civil War. In Southern California fundraising efforts in Los Angeles and Hollywood also supported making pro-Republican films such as the 1937 documentary *The Spanish Earth*, which involved celebrities such as Orson Welles, Lillian Hellman, John Dos Passos, and Ernest Hemingway. While during the Spanish Civil War this was a cause popular in Hollywood, the anti-Franco cause did not have the same capacity to rally enthusiasm or resources within the United States after the Second World War, especially in the anti-communist environment of the Cold War. Indeed, the film industry went through a quite thorough purge of communists and their sympathizers in the late 1940s and especially early 1950s, with major studios

---

[26] Harold Smith, "The Fifteenth Anniversary of the Spanish Republic," *Volunteer for Liberty* (April 1946), New York, Veterans of the Abraham Lincoln Brigade, https://alba-valb.org/wp-content/uploads/2020/04/Volunteer_For_Liberty_V6_No12_April_1946.pdf Accessed 22 September 2021.

[27] Aguirre, *Escape Via Berlin*, 6, 9.

[28] "Speech of Antonio Mije Made To A Special Meeting of International Brigaders, 25-2-47," *Volunteer for Liberty* (April 1947), New York, Veterans of the Abraham Lincoln Brigade, https://alba-valb.org/wp-content/uploads/2020/04/Volunteer_Vol9_No4_April_1947.pdf, accessed 22 September 2021.

[29] P. Preston, *Franco: A Biography*, New York, Harper Collins, 1993, 536, 541.

[30] D. Tierney, *FDR and the Spanish Civil War: Neutrality and Commitment in the Struggle that Divided America*, Durham, North Carolina, Duke University Press, 2007, 141, 146.

reluctant to retain anyone tainted with ardent leftist credentials.[31] Indeed, the shift in movies was often quite stark; from *The Spanish Earth*, California filmmakers moved to movies such as *I Was A Communist For the FBI*, an Oscar-nominated documentary from 1951.[32]

The most emblematic connection between newly anti-communist Hollywood and the Franco regime was the naming of former Paramount Studies executive Stanton Griffis in 1951 as the first ambassador to Spain since the UN-sponsored international diplomatic boycott of 1946. Griffis retained strong ties to California's film industry through membership in the Motion Picture Association of America and the Motion Picture Export Association of America, promoting U.S. films in Spain, convincing the Spanish government to increase by almost 60 percent the number of Hollywood movies licensed annually in Spain (from 78 to 135), and encouraging American filmmakers to consider Spain actively as a site for low-cost cinematic productions and as a distribution hub for Europe and Latin America.[33]

While Hollywood quickly muted its advocacy during the Cold War, theirs were not the only voices raised in concern about the Franco regime during this period. Other historians have also catalogued the efforts by groups within the United States, such as mainstream Protestants, to oppose the integration of Spain into the Western security structure and the United States, in large part because of the regime's documented persecution of Protestants, a concern also embraced by the Baptist Harry Truman.[34] Other tensions between the United States and Spain, including the slow-walking by the Franco regime of the repatriation into Allied hands of German citizens, including Nazi officials, diplomats, and long-term residents of Spain, diminished U.S. enthusiasm for warmer ties. Indeed, at various times U.S. diplomats referred to the Franco regime's lack of compliance with these repatriations as a stumbling block to better relations, with the hiding of potential German war criminals a point of ongoing contention. While this issue became less important as the Cold

---

[31] R. Rhodes, *Hell and Good Company: The Spanish Civil War and the World It Made*, New York, Simon and Schuster, 2015, 177–178, 237–238; *The Spanish Earth*, Internet Movie Database, https://www.imdb.com/title/tt0029594/, accessed 19 September 2021.

[32] M. Walker, *The Cold War: A History*, New York, Henry Holt, 1994, 69; "I Was A Communist for the F.B.I.," Internet Movie Database, https://www.imdb.com/title/tt0043665/, accessed 19 September 2021.

[33] W. Bowen, *Truman, Franco's Spain, and the Cold War*, Columbia, University of Missouri Press, 2017,123. D. Norton, "Hispanidad and the Hollywood ambassador: friendship, kinship and the rearticulation of Spanish national identity before the pact of Madrid," *Journal of Spanish Cultural Studies*, vol. 19, n. 1 (2018), 46–47, 55.

[34] R. Shaffer, "Religion and International Relations: The *Christian Century's* Protestant Critique of the U.S. Embrace of Fascist Spain," *Journal of Church and State*, vol. 59, n. 4 (Autumn 2017), 588–607.

War escalated, and after most Nazis and their assets were finally handed over through a process known as Operation Safe Haven, it remained a sore point between the two nations until the early 1950s. Indeed, some U.S. diplomats expressed open frustration at the United States opening to Franco, given the many unresolved cases of Germans in Spain. Many of these holdouts, including non-Germans such as the former Nazi collaborator and Belgian Rexist leader Léon Degrelle, remained permanently in Spain, protected by friends in the government and Falange.[35]

In the context of the early Cold War, while the United States rushed to accommodate pro-Western dictatorships and absolute monarchies elsewhere to form a broad global coalition against the Soviet Union, Harry Truman attempted to hold a firm line against Francisco Franco. Against the advice of his own military and diplomatic team that a partnership with Spain was essential to U.S. security, Truman refused to bend. Recoiling from Franco, who he saw as "as bad a dictator" as Hitler, Mussolini, or Stalin, Truman also resisted what he saw as unethical pressure from U.S. corporations eager to trade with Spain, American Catholics focused the official religion of the state, and conservative politicians who cared more about the Cold War than freedom for the Spanish people.[36] For the first few post-war years, Truman's "visceral reaction to Franco" meant that even close aides were reluctant to raise the issue of Spain, fearful of the president's response.[37] To the end of his presidency, Truman remained "the leading exponent of anti-Franco feeling in the government."[38]

Over time, however, the president yielded to internal pressure from his national security officials, as well as the successful efforts by the Spanish Lobby. By 1949, despite Truman's reluctance, there began to be open discussions about integrating Spain into the Cold War security architecture. By 1951, these multi-agency and department reconsiderations, promoted especially by the newly-formed U.S. Department of Defense, accelerated past the point of potential reversal.[39] Global events, including the beginning of the Korean War in 1950, and invasion of the pro-U.S. South by the Soviet-backed North, crystalized for many Americans, including Truman, that the Cold War was a struggle requiring all available allies, no matter how distasteful. Indeed, these sentiments were reflected in Spain, where Spanish veterans of the Blue Division, a volunteer unit

---

[35] D. Messenger, *Hunting Nazis in Franco's Spain*, Baton Rouge, Louisiana State University Press, 2014, 35–36, 67, 160–161, 162–164, 168–170.

[36] R. Ferrell, *Truman in the White House: The Diary of Eben A. Ayers*, Columbia and London, University of Missouri Press, 1991, 6 May 1949, 309–310.

[37] Byrnes, *Truman Administration Policy Toward Spain and Yugoslavia*, 164.

[38] A. Whitaker, *Spain, and the Defense of the West: Ally and Liability*, New York, Praeger, 1961, 23.

[39] Bowen, *Truman, Franco's Spain, and the Cold War*, 96, 124.

250 WAYNE H. BOWEN

of soldiers within the German army that had fought against the Soviet Union during the Second World War, presented themselves at the U.S. embassy to volunteer to fight communism again, this time in East Asia.[40]

From the Spanish Civil War to the end of the Second World War, the primary cities in the United States that focused on Spain were, not surprisingly, Washington, D.C., and New York City. While high politics and international diplomacy were the main activity in the capital, New York City played a dominant role as a center for Spanish exiles, as well as the main nexus for communications and the press, as well as the primary hub for culture, non-profit organizations, and higher education throughout the United States. The well-organized opposition to the Franco regime among the U.S. media, universities, labor unions, and grassroots of the Democratic party, championed most vocally by former first lady and U.S. diplomat Eleanor Roosevelt, were a concern for the Spanish government and even for Franco personally.[41]

The Los Angeles Exception: Consul Pérez del Arco

At the local level, however, Spain's efforts were arguably successful much more quickly than at the national level. This was consistent with overall efforts by the Spanish government to employ a "direct appeal," bypassing high-level official U.S. government channels, especially in the State Department, in favor of contacting more favorable audiences, including at the local level.[42] Effective leadership at the level of Spain's consulates, especially on the West Coast, showed positive results as early as 1947, when Spain was still considered a pariah by the Truman administration in Washington, D.C., with ongoing meetings between the U.S. State Department and Spanish exiles.[43] In Los Angeles, by contrast, Spain's diplomats were welcomed at public events, Catholic commemorations, Chamber of Commerce galas, and civic activities organized by the city of Los Angeles, among other groups.

In late 1947, José Pérez del Arco, a Spanish diplomat working in New York, who would later become consul in Los Angeles, provided a memo to the Spanish government, describing the political climate for Spain and outlining potential areas for attention. Given the "calumnious anti-Spanish campaign" by exiled Spaniards and their supporters dating back to the Spanish Civil War, the situation toward the Franco regime was basically hostile. However, in the United States, Pérez del Arco saw a "favorable conjuncture" to change this

[40] L. Suárez Fernández, *Francisco Franco y su tiempo*, vol.4, Madrid, Azor, 1984, 413–414.

[41] Ibid., 25.

[42] R. Hadian, *United States Foreign Policy Towards Spain, 1953–1970*, Ph.D. dissertation, Santa Barbara, University of California at Santa Barbara, 1976, 4.

[43] Thomàs, *Roosevelt, Franco, and the End of World War II*, 194.

attitude. There was rising interest in the United States in Spain and its history, the new Fulbright program that could sponsor educational exchanges, and there were numerous educational institutions, universities, and publications with centers focused on Spanish language and civilization. While he understood the focus on New York, with its 400,000 Spanish speakers and concentration of cultural organizations, most Hispanic associations and cultural institutions in New York were "under the absolute control of the exiled Red groups," thus encouraging a focus on more favorable areas. Additionally, he advocated closer collaboration with potentially friendly conservative and anti-communist organizations, such as the Knights of Columbus, Catholic war veterans, Chambers of Commerce, and the American Legion. These ideological allies just needed encouragement, guidance, support, materials, and current information about conditions in Spain to counteract the influence of Spanish communists.[44]

Indeed, it was the presence of communists among the Spanish Republicans that provided a successful way to split the exile community, already divided by geography, with substantial communities in Mexico, France, the United States, and the Soviet Union. While some former Republican Popular Front leaders, such as Juan Negrín, were willing to forge a broad front that included the Spanish Communist party, other exiled politicians, such as the socialist Indalecio Prieto, were virulently opposed, arguing that Spanish communists had betrayed the Republic to the Soviet Union and would cripple any effort to gain international support for anti-Franco forces in the post-war era. Prieto spoke adamantly against endorsing either one of the remaining dictatorships, "the Falangist totalitarianism or the Communist totalitarianism" by the exile movement.[45]

Spain's diplomats outside Washington, D.C., operated with highly restricted staff numbers and resources. Their primary tasks were to provide services to Spanish citizens in the United States, as well as facilitate the initially limited numbers of U.S. travels to Spain. Much of their efforts, especially in the New York consulate, always the largest, were focused on approving or denying visas, providing addresses for next of kin for deceased Spaniards in Spain and the United States, facilitating the shipments of commercial materials to and from Spain, acting as a clipping service for articles that mentioned Spain, which would then be sent to the Spanish embassy in Washington, and forwarding information or materials requested by the consulate for U.S. citizens or organizations.[46]

---

[44] *AGA*, 54/11.752, Memo, October 1947, José Pérez del Arco, "Notas sobre posible acción del Instituto de Cultura Hispánica en los Estados Unidos."

[45] O. Glondys, *La guerra fría cultural y el exilio republicano español*, Madrid, CSIC, 2012, 48–50.

[46] *AGA*, (10)024,002 Estados Unidos. Consulado de España en Nueva York. Caja 54.4315, Órdenes Recibidas del Ministerio, 1944–1946.

Another key role played by the consulates in New York, Chicago, San Francisco, and Los Angeles, was the provision of information requested by the Spanish government. For example, in early 1947, the Franco regime purchased 300 copies of *Wartime Mission in Spain*, by Carlton Hayes, former ambassador to Spain. This book, supportive of closer ties with Spain, was a powerful counterpoint to the attitude of the Truman administration. Seeing its values in the public debate, the Spanish government ordered its consulate in New York to buy these copies and ship them to Spain, for further distribution to key communicators, educational institutions, and others involved in influencing of public opinion and political actions in the United States.[47]

In mid-1948, the Spanish Foreign Ministry acted on some of the recommendations of Pérez del Arco, requesting and receiving permission from the U.S. State Department to open a new consulate in Los Angeles. His argument, that Los Angeles could not be adequately served by distant and much smaller San Francisco, was effective, even during the penury of the Spanish Foreign Ministry. The more liberal and globalist politics of San Francisco, as exemplified by the convening of the founding conference of the UN in that city, including its accompanying exclusion of Spain, were also contributing factors in this argument. Los Angeles, which had boomed during the Second World War, had become the fourth largest city in the United States, with almost two million residents, with its higher wages, reputation as a land of opportunity, and sunny climate attracting a wave of migration during and after the Second World War.[48] After a scramble to find office space on a limited budget, with a maximum of $159 per month authorized, the new consulate officially opened on 1 December 1948, at 606 South Hill Street, in the financial district, under the leadership of the new consul, José Pérez del Arco, a diplomat transferred from the New York consulate.[49] The new consulate has responsibility not just for the city and county of Los Angeles, but all of Southern California from the Mexican border north to Santa Barbara, San Luis Obispo, and Kern counties. The consulate in San Francisco, which in 1949 would be upgraded to a consulate-general with direct oversight for the Western United States, oversaw the northern and the remainder of central California.[50]

---

[47] *AGA*, (10)024,002 Estados Unidos. Consulado de España en Nueva York. 54.4316. Ordenes Recibidas del Ministerio, 1947–1948. Letter, 18 March 1947, Director General de Relaciones Culturales to Consul of Spain, New York City.

[48] A. Rolle, *California: A History, Second Edition,* New York, Thomas Y. Crowell Company, 1969, 593, 596–597.

[49] *AGA*, (10)022 Estados Unidos. Consulado de España en Los Angeles. Caja 54/11.751. Letters and telegrams, August–December 1948, between Spain Ministry of Foreign Affairs and Consulate of Spain, Los Angeles.

[50] *AGA* 54/11.752. Letter, 12 August 1949, Del Arco to Germán Baraibar, Chargé d'affaires, Spanish Embassy, Washington, D.C.

THE SPANISH LOBBY AND LOCAL POLITICS IN THE UNITED STATES 253

Pérez del Arco began his tenure with great anticipation, writing to a friend back in Madrid, the director of the Instituto de Cultura Hispánica, about his plans and initial perspective on Los Angeles:

> My first impression is magnificent. This city, with such a rich Spanish atmosphere, has a tremendously surprising vitality, especially when coming from New York City, and offers, to my way of seeing, abundant possibilities to develop an intense cultural labor. There are here such a diversity of elements sufficient to coordinate an effective work in support of our prestige and our values, historical and current; I think that if I am not able to achieve this, it will be more due to my failure than because of a lack of a receptive atmosphere.[51]

Indeed, Pérez del Arco did find a receptive atmosphere. He seemed ideally prepared to work in Los Angeles, a city rising in confidence and profile, fueled by burgeoning aerospace, defense, agricultural industries, as well as the glamour of Hollywood. A profile of Pérez del Arco by the Associated Press described him as "small, dapper and fast-talking," a veteran of the defeated army of the Spanish Republic who had become converted to the righteousness of the Franco regime, "because only through him was Spain saved as a nation". Indeed, Del Arco was one of more than twenty former diplomats of the Spanish Republic recruited to serve in Franco's foreign service, bringing as they did the enthusiasm of converts to the cause.[52] At the young age of thirty-three, Pérez del Arco had been entrusted with this significant diplomatic role, in which he saw his task as "lecturing himself hoarse trying to convert Americans to friendship with Spain."[53]

Pérez del Arco quickly cultivated an extensive network of collaborators, including groups willing to share their membership lists with the consulate. Among these were the Historical Society of Southern California, Del Amo Foundation, Pan American Friendship Club (Hollywood Chapter), Club de Damas Pan-Americanas, American Association of Teachers of Spanish (Los Angeles chapter), San Diego Historical Society, Ateneo Hispánico de California, Plaza de Los Angeles (Olvera Street), and the University of Southern California chapter of Sigma Delta Pi, the National Collegiate Hispanic Honor Society.[54] His efforts also benefited from the conservative inclinations of the local media, not just pro-Republican Hearst papers such as the *Los Angeles*

---

[51] *AGA*, 54/11.752. Letter, 27 December 1948, Del Arco to Alfredo Sánchez Bella, Director, Instituto de Cultura Hispánica, Madrid.

[52] "Consul Suggests Linking of Santa Barbara's Fiesta and That of Seville, in Old Spain," *Santa Barbara News-Press*, 5 January 1950.

[53] *AGA*, 54/11.754. Ralph Dighton "Consul in Los Angeles Talks Frankly of Franco," *Pasadena Star News*, 29 May 1949.

[54] *AGA*, 54/11.754. Membership lists, 1949–1950.

Herald-Express, but even the much larger *Los Angeles Times*, were more right-wing in their editorial positions than many East Coast publications.[55]

One immediate partner for the new consulate was the local Catholic archdiocese of Los Angeles. While the opinions of U.S. Catholics had long been divided over the Franco regime, the Church hierarchy was much more supportive. Indeed, one of the early public events sponsored by the consulate was a celebration banquet for the Reverend Joseph McGucken, auxiliary bishop and vicar general of the archdiocese of Los Angeles, awarded the "Encomienda de Numero de la Orden de Isabel la Católica," Spain's highest civilian honor. General Francisco Franco granted this award for the bishop's services "on behalf of Los Angeles residents of Spanish descent."[56] Bishop McGucken, who had supported the Nationalist side in the Spanish Civil War, accepted the award with "deep gratitude" to "His Excellency, the Chief of the Spanish State, along with the expression of my intention to do everything in my power for the Spanish speaking people in this territory, and for the preservation of their ancient and honored Catholic culture." This strong endorsement for Franco was an early sign of the continued alliance with the Catholic Church in the United States, even when the U.S. government continued to express open hostility.[57] McGucken, while being pro-Franco, was also well-known in Southern California for his ties with Mexican and Mexican-American parishioners, advocating for more Spanish-speaking priests, charitable outreach, and civil rights.[58] Given his prestige, popularity and importance within the Catholic Church, the bishop served as an effective "defense attorney," rallying public support at the local level in support of a Franco regime under attack by the U.S. government and anti-Franco forces, especially among the national media, progressives within the Democratic party, unions, and allies of the exiled Spanish Republicans.[59]

Indeed, the archdiocese of Los Angeles was of rising importance within the U.S. Catholic Church. While relatively poor in resources compared to more established Catholic regions in the Northeast, the Church in the late 1940s and early 1950s was in the midst of a building boom of both parish churches and parochial schools not only to accommodate the existing population, but a Los

[55] Rolle, *California: A History*, 611.

[56] *Los Angeles Evening Herald and Express*, 22 March 1949.

[57] *AGA*, 54/11.752. Letter, Bishop Joseph McGucken to Spanish Consul, 12 September 1948; Memo, 9 September 1948, Carlos Manzanares, acting consul of Spain to Rev. Joseph McGucken.

[58] J. Burns, "The Mexican Catholic Community in California," in Jay Dolan and Gilberto Hinojosa (eds.), *Mexican Americans and the Catholic Church, 1900–1965*, Notre Dame, Indiana, University of Notre Dame Press, 1994, 130, 198, 207.

[59] Á. Ferrary, *El franquismo: minorías políticas y conflictos ideológicos, (1936–1956)*, Pamplona, EUNSA, 1993, 230–231.

THE SPANISH LOBBY AND LOCAL POLITICS IN THE UNITED STATES 255

Angeles that was growing three times as fast as the overall U.S. population, with Los Angeles County becoming the largest in the nation by population.[60] An indication of the significance of the Los Angeles Church came in 1952, when Archbishop James McIntyre was named a cardinal: the first U.S. member of the College of Cardinals not just from California, but from the entire Western United States. An ardent conservative, throughout his long career as archbishop of the Los Angeles archdiocese (1948–1970) he was known for his anti-communism, advocacy for traditionalist theology, and opposition to radical politics.[61]

In May 1949, Los Angeles hosted the annual conference of the International Federation of Women Lawyers (Federacion Internacional de Abogadas (FIDA)), an organization of female attorneys and judges. Representatives of twenty-five nations gathered to discuss law, the profession, and international developments to promote legal education, court access, and other issues relating to women and the law. Founded in Mexico in 1944, it had members from Latin America, the United States, Africa, Europe, and Asia, sending more than 150 delegates to the Los Angeles conference. Among the local dignitaries attending was Los Angeles Mayor Fletcher Bowron, who hosted a reception for the attorneys at Los Angeles City Hall. One of the key organizers and presenters was María Teresa Segura Pérez del Arco, attorney, and wife of Spain's consul in Los Angeles. Her talk on "Social Protection for Families in Current Spanish Legislation," in which she highlighted the influence of "Christian morality" within Spain's legal system was well received, and she was elected incoming vice-president for the international organization. For a Spanish citizen to become a leader in FIDA was perhaps a surprise, within the context of the international diplomatic boycott of Spain and its exclusion from UN membership. The election of Segura, however, was an early signal of the success of Spanish efforts to emphasize cultural and religious ties, rather than contentious political and diplomatic questions in public engagements at the local level in Los Angeles.[62]

Unlike in New York City, where anti-Franco academics dominated institutions such as Columbia University and NYU, in Los Angeles there was more openness for Spain's diplomats. Pérez del Arco was an invited guest

[60] The population of Los Angeles grew 49.8 percent during the decade between 1940 and 1950. Overall U.S. population growth was 14.5 percent during this same period. Rolle, *California: A History*, 602.

[61] K. Starr, *Golden Dreams: California in an Age of Abundance, 1950–1963*, Oxford. Oxford University Press, 2009, 135–136, 182–185.

[62] *AGA*, 54/11.752. Nota, "Sobre la V Conferencia de la Federación Internacional de Abogadas celebrada en Los Ángeles de 14 a 19 de mayo de 1949"; "Lady Lawyers of 24 Nations Gather Here," *Los Angeles Evening Herald Express*, 16 May 1949; *La Opinión*, 19 May 1949.

at the celebration of the twenty-fifth anniversary for USC's Eta chapter of Sigma Delta Pi, the national Spanish-language honor society. This banquet, on 19 November 1949, at the famous West Hollywood nightclub and restaurant "Ciro's," featured Father Pedro Peñamil, a native of Spain and professor of Spanish language at Loyola University. The honor society, which shared its membership lists and organizational events with the Spanish consulate, offered opportunities to win support among future teachers of Spanish.[63]

The close relations with these societies were an indication of how Spain was beginning to overcome the legacy of the Spanish Civil War in the United States, which had caused partisans of the Spanish Republic and of Nationalist Spain to divide over relations with the victorious Franco regime. By 1950, other associations in Los Angeles began to accept Spain as legitimate as well. Benevolent organizations such as the Sociedad Española de Beneficia Mutua and the Casa de España began to include the Spanish consulate in their events, despite opposition from some members who opposed the Franco regime. As one Hispanic civic leader noted, commenting on the time passed since the Spanish Civil War: "Now we are in 1950, very far from that terrible crisis for our fatherland; anyone that wants to preserve the intransigence from that time […] is out of touch with reality."[64]

Spain also played a significant and public role in the annual festival in honor of the Virgin of Guadalupe, held on 12 December 1949, at the historic Church of Our Lady Queen of the Angels (Iglesia de Nuestra Señora la Reina de los Ángeles), the first Catholic church in the city. The presence of Spanish officials at this ceremony was especially meaningful given the Virgin's role as patron of Mexico, a state hostile to Franco. Even so, both Pérez del Arco and his wife were allotted seats at the head table, and the consul delivered comments, the only diplomat invited to do so. The consul no doubt took pleasure in the remarks of prominent local Catholic lay leader Joseph Scott, who in his remarks denounced the "the international anomaly of the exclusion of Spain, bulwark of world anticommunism, from the United Nations." No doubt, the consul of Mexico and others from the Mexican and Mexican American community were less enthusiastic. The prominence of Spain at the event was a victory for the consul, who provided full details on the commemoration to the Spanish embassy in Washington, D.C.[65] While at the international level relations between Mexico and Spain remained tense, with Mexico an ardent opponent of normalization with Spain, in Southern California the Mexican

---

[63] *AGA*, 54/11.752. Memo, 23 November 1949, from Perez del Arco to Spanish Foreign Ministry.

[64] *AGA*, 54/11.751. Letter, 10 February 1950, Sabina Zubuieta, Sociedad Española de Beneficia Mutua, to Gabino González.

[65] *AGA*, 54/11.752. Letter 14 December 1949, from Perez del Arco to Spanish Embassy, D.C.

THE SPANISH LOBBY AND LOCAL POLITICS IN THE UNITED STATES 257

and Mexican American population "reflected an intense anticommunism that pervaded Catholicism in Los Angeles."[66]

Conservatism and Collaboration in Southern California

Indeed, politics in Southern California during the late 1940s and early 1950s were pervaded by anti-communism. While much has been made about the outspoken efforts by U.S. Senator Joe McCarthy, a Republican from Wisconsin, to elevate investigations of alleged communists in Washington, D.C. during this period, the same sentiments made their way West. Both the city and county of Los Angeles required loyalty oaths, requiring employees to attest that they were not communists. The California State Legislature launched its own hearings to uncover communists and their sympathizers, and Hollywood was the center of much concern in both D.C. and Sacramento. Communist books were removed from local libraries, and even faculty at the University of California were asked to sign a loyalty oath to the constitutions of the United States and the state of California.[67]

There was even some engagement on global issues in Southern California; protests in the early 1950s organized by the Catholic archdiocese, the American Legion, and Republican women's clubs against the alleged globalism and socialism of UNESCO (United Nations Educational, Scientific, and Cultural Organization) led the Los Angeles Unified School District to ban pro-UNESCO curriculum. This issue and others related to fears of globalism and UN-led socialism had broader implications, with the 1952 and 1954 election seeing successful school board campaigns by candidates that had made their opposition to UNESCO a key platform in their runs for office. Even long-term Los Angeles Mayor Fletcher Bowron, the Republican chief executive of Los Angeles, was not safe from accusations of excessively progressive politics: he lost his party primary to Norris Paulson, a fellow GOP candidate in 1952. Paulson, who went on to serve as mayor until 1961, had accused Bowron of liberalism, a lack of anti-communist zeal, and excessive collaboration with Democrats.[68]

In spring 1950, Pérez del Arco began what would be his greatest propaganda success: a public lecture series about Spain. This series, sponsored by the General Petroleum Corporation, whose auditorium was the venue, featured speakers on Spanish history, culture, religion, and politics. Although free to attend, guests had to request tickets from the consulate in advance, an approach that enhanced the aura of exclusivity, while at the same time enabling the consulate to screen out known or potential opponents of the Franco regime.

---

[66] Burns, "The Mexican Catholic Community in California," p. 186.

[67] J. Caughey and N. Hundley, Jr., *California: History of a Remarkable State*, 4th edition, Englewood Cliffs, Prentice-Hall, 1982, 389–390.

[68] Starr, *Golden Dreams*, 200.

Using the membership lists and personal contracts he had accumulated in his first year, Pérez del Arco invited thousands of potential attendees, for a location with a capacity of only 250. For the next two years, every lecture was filled with a capacity audience, with requests for tickets arriving at the consulate in numbers that the staff was unable to accommodate. Prominent members of historical societies, chapters of the Knights of Columbus, lay Catholic societies, professors and teachers of Spanish, consular officials from Latin American nations working in Los Angeles, and local elected officials all sent requests for tickets. These aficionados of Spain hoped for a rare opportunity to hear prominent scholars, visiting Spanish dignitaries, or even Pérez del Arco, a dynamic and charismatic speaker in his own right. For a city increasingly focused on celebrities, the consul's invitation to an exclusive evening lecture by a world-famous academic was a clever public relations move, which made Spain not a pariah, as it was in Washington, D.C. and at the UN, but a preference. The lectures, such as the consul's, spread the message that Spain mattered, that the Franco regime was legitimate, and that its history and culture were in demand: Franco himself could not have hoped for a better outcome, and the congratulations from the Spanish embassy made clear the support for these events.[69]

By 1950, the inclusion of Spain in major public events no longer drew notice as anything unusual; indeed, organizations, local governments, and corporations, from the Los Angeles Chamber of Commerce to the city of Los Angeles, to American Airlines, regularly invited Spain's consulate to participate. As Americans began to travel internationally for tourism and business in the post-war era, the consulate began to receive request for letters of introduction and visas to Spain. Prominent U.S. citizens, such as the banker Edward A. Dickson, president of the Western Federal Savings and Loan Association, the Historical Society of Southern California, and chairman of the board of regents for the University of California, even asked Pérez del Arco to arrange personal audiences with General Franco during a visit to Spain. Dickson had been a frequent attendee of Spain's lectures and, as a devout Catholic, had attended Church events with consular officials. While requests such as this one was unlikely to be accommodated, as a low-level Spanish diplomat was not able to set the Caudillo's calendar, they were an indication of the high esteem in which Angelinos held the consul as tourism from LA to Spain began to accelerate.[70]

The consulate also facilitated group tourism and pilgrimages to Spain, assisting with visas, travel arrangements, and events, in collaboration with the Catholic Church in the United States and Spain, religious orders such as

[69] *AGA*, 54/11.752. Multiple letters, memos, schedules, and requests for tickets, 1950–1951.

[70] *AGA* 54/11.752. Letter, 19 April 1950, Edward A. Dickson, to Pérez Del Arco.

THE SPANISH LOBBY AND LOCAL POLITICS IN THE UNITED STATES 259

the Claretians, and the Instituto de Cultura Hispánica in Madrid. Although much has been made of political trips by congressional delegations during this period, the visits by ordinary (albeit wealthy Catholic) Americans to Spain had at least as significant an impact, as returning visitors came back with stories of Spanish hospitality, transformative spiritual experiences, their safety within Spain, and the low costs for food, lodging, and travel, especially compared with other Western European destinations.[71] Airlines such as Trans World Airlines, hoping to take advantage of growing interest in Spain, purchased program ads in events sponsored by the consulate, reminding Angelinos that "it would be marvelous if you could visit Spain."[72]

The consulate's efforts in Los Angeles were so successful, that other cities in central and Southern California began to reach out to Pérez del Arco, asking for contacts in Spain, suggestions for speakers, and invitations to public events. The most significant of these potential linkages was with the city of Santa Barbara, a wealthy coastal town that since 1924 had hosted an annual celebration, "Old Spanish Days," commemorating the Hispanic tradition with a parade, a rodeo, Spanish food, and music. City leaders, including Mayor Morris Montgomery, suggested a partnership with the Spanish city of Seville, host to an even more famous "Feria de Sevilla."[73] Luis Bolín, Spain's director of tourism, invited Montgomery and other city leaders to visit Spain to develop this idea intending by the "invitation an expression of friendship and good-will, a bond which we trust will be strengthened in years to come." The Spanish government did not offer to pay for travel, but instead to welcome the delegation upon their arrival and take care of everything, including lodging, meals, and transportation, from that point onward. While the mayor was not able to make the planned trip to Spain, Francis Price, president of "Old Spanish Days," did make the tourism pilgrimage, visiting Seville and other cities in April 1950. Returning to Santa Barbara, Price and his wife became strong advocates for the Franco regime and for closer ties, noting to the consul, "We have been singing the praises of Spain since our return."[74]

As a follow up, "Old Spanish Days" committed to financially sponsoring a visit by "Coros y Danzas," a Spanish troupe of folkloric dancers visiting the United States, and continued to promote a positive image for Spain as a benevolent nation, which in the past had contributed so much in a positive way

---

[71] *AGA* 54/11.752. Letter, 29 March 1950, Pérez Del Arco to Alfredo Sánchez Bella, Director, Instituto de Cultura Hispánica, Madrid. Bowen, *Truman, Franco's Spain, and the Cold War*, 86–87, 119–120.

[72] *AGA* 54/11.751. TWA advertisement in *Invitation to "Gran Baile de Gala,"* sponsored by the Sociedad Española de Beneficia Mutua, 30 September 1950, Sons of Herman Hall, 120 East 25th St, Los Angeles.

[73] https://www.sbfiesta.org/history-santa-barbara-fiesta.

[74] *Santa Barbara News-Press*, 23 March and 12 April 1950.

260 WAYNE H. BOWEN

to the history of California, and which continued as a friend of the community of Santa Barbara. "Coros y Danzas," affiliated with the Sección Femenina of the Falange, by now known officially by the more innocuous name of "The Movement" (El Movimiento) in Spain, was already a key part of Spain's international cultural diplomacy.[75] Indeed, Coros y Danzas performed throughout Southern California during a visit August and September 1950, including at the storied Hollywood Bowl, accompanied by the official Hollywood Bowl Orchestra, before an audience of 12,000, and at the Pasadena Civic Auditorium. Although efforts by Del Arco to extend the tour to other sites in the United States was vetoed by Spain, the visit was a real success for Spain's image and efforts at cultural diplomacy.[76]

Attempts by consular officials to duplicate the efforts of Los Angeles in San Francisco, Chicago, New York, and other cities were less successful. Longstanding organized opposition to the Franco regime by local officials, a stronger presence by Republican exiles, and influential radical groups, an alliance dating to the Spanish Civil War, mitigated against these efforts by Spanish diplomats to engage constructively in a way that supported the legitimacy of the Spanish government.[77] Whatever successes achieved or defeats faced by elements of the Spanish Lobby, the fundamental challenge was that Spain was a weak actor in the U.S.-dominated post-war international system. While there were limits to U.S. hegemony – Truman was, for example, unable to force Franco to reintroduce the monarchy or democratize, without being willing to employ military means to do so – the U.S. government was still the disproportionate global power during immediate post-war era.

It was not until late 1951 that the San Francisco consulate could speak of the "favorable evolution of political relations" and the decrease in agitation by anti-Franco forces. Arguing that San Francisco was still the cultural center of the West, even if Los Angeles had a larger population, consular officials asked for more funding and attention to their region, a request that came after the key achievements of the Spanish Lobby were well underway, with a U.S. ambassador again in Madrid, credits awarded to support trade with the United States, and even Truman promoting the integration of Spain into the U.S.-led system of military alliances.[78] Pleas for additional staff, raises

[75] *AGA*, 54/11.752. Letters, memos, and itineraries, 1949–1951, between Old Spanish Days, Pérez del Arco, and Luis Bolín.

[76] *AGA*, 54/11.753. *Santa Barbara News-Press*, 26 August 1950, 1. Program, "Coros y Danzas," 13 September 1950, Pasadena Civic Auditorium. Letter, 26 August 1950, Del Arco to Ministerio de Asuntos Exteriores. ABC (Madrid), 7 September 1950, 2. Telegram, 24 August 1950, Del Arco to Ministerio de Asuntos Exteriores.

[77] Smith, *American Relief Aid and the Spanish Civil War*, 39, 60–61, 72–77.

[78] *AGA* 54/12.122. Letter, 23 October 1951, from Jaime Jorro, Consul General, San Francisco to Ministerio de Asuntos Exteriores.

to accommodate the high cost of living in San Francisco, and proposals to fund large-scale outreach in northern California came too late, to a Spanish Foreign Ministry already celebrating its victories in Los Angeles and D.C.[79] Indeed, despite assurances from Spain's diplomats in San Francisco that the environment was becoming more favorable, even in mid-1951 the consulate faced a loud protest outside its front door, with several dozen young demonstrators denouncing Franco, calling for the release of political prisoners in Spain, and supporting recent labor actions in Barcelona and elsewhere. Indeed, even though the political situation did improve in San Francisco by the early 1950s, the Spanish consulate had to be prepared at every event for potential demonstrations, poor coverage in the local press, and editorials once again denouncing Franco and U.S. collaboration with his government. The stark differences between Los Angeles and San Francisco were clear.[80]

Local chambers of commerce played a key role in connecting local business and entrepreneurs with global capitalism. At luncheons, trade shows, receptions, and other events, small businesses interacted with large ones, and U.S. companies met with multinationals to discuss possible partnerships, export markets, trade policies, and politics at every level. In Los Angeles, under the Los Angeles Chamber of Commerce, "Global Trade Week" had become an annual event in 1927, "to increase community knowledge about the value of foreign trade" and connecting foreign markets to Southern California's agricultural and industrial products. Rather than an exhibition at a single site, the week most often included special exhibits throughout the city, focused on goods of international interest for export and import.[81] Spain's participation in 1950, for example, included a display of Spanish food at the main city branch of Farmers and Merchants Bank and an exhibit at Los Angeles Airport promoting tourism with the theme: "So you're going to Spain...!"[82] Although initially tourism by Americans to Spain was limited by strict rules on currency exchanges, liberalization of these policies in 1948 enabled a greater number of visitors to come to Spain. U.S. tourists were especially welcome, given their tendency to stay longer, spend more money, and return to encourage their friends to repeat the same travels.[83]

---

[79] *AGA* 54/12.122. Letter, 26 July 1951, from Jaime Jorro, Consul General, San Francisco to Ministerio de Asuntos Exteriores.

[80] *AGA* 54/12.122. Letter, 11 May 1951, Jaime Jorro, Consul General to Ministerio de Asuntos Exteriores.

[81] https://lachamber.com/pages/our-history/, accessed 27 August 2021.

[82] *AGA* 54/11.751. Materials related to Spain's participation in "World Trade Week," 21–28 May 1950.

[83] S. Pack, *Tourism and Dictatorship: Europe's Peaceful Invasion of Franco's Spain*, New York, Palgrave Macmillan, 2006, 48–51, 58.

262   WAYNE H. BOWEN

Los Angeles, however, did not have the established web of anti-Franco forces. With Fletcher Bowron as its long-serving Republican mayor (1938–1953), a powerful Catholic Church, Republican dominance in state politics, heritage as a former Spanish colony, and a relatively small community interested in international affairs, Los Angeles was fertile ground for a small and active Spanish Lobby. Indeed, in the absence of the cultural and intellectual prestige of established universities, East Coast cultural elites, mobilized anti-Franco forces, and proximity to New York and Washington, D.C., Franco's Spain found greater popularity there than anywhere else in the United States. At the same time, it is fair to say that what happened in California, other than what was captured in correspondence between Spanish diplomats, truly did stay in California.

The West, and especially the city and county of Los Angeles, may have been ahead of the East in fully readmitting Spain into the normal course of business, culture, and politics, but by no means was California yet in a position to set national trends. The future, which would see conservative Californians enter the White House, was yet to come. Even so, it was in the midst of the success of the Los Angeles Spanish Lobby that a young navy veteran, Richard Nixon, first entered Congress in 1947 to represent eastern Los Angeles County.[84] As a young congressman, Nixon would take on a prominent role investigating communists and alleged communists who had served in the U.S. government or in Hollywood.[85] Later, Nixon would serve as vice president under Dwight Eisenhower, during the administration that would finalize the 1953 agreements for U.S. bases in Spain. As president, Nixon would visit Spain in 1970 and embrace Franco, a gesture signaling in some ways the indirect final victory of the Los Angeles Spanish Lobby.[86]

Sources

Archives and newspapers

ABC (Madrid)
America (New York City)
Archivo General de la Administración (*AGA*), Alcalá de Henares, Spain
La Opinión (Los Angeles)
Los Angeles Evening Herald and Express
Los Angeles Times
Santa Barbara News-Press
Volunteer for Liberty (New York)

---

[84] P. Bullock, "'Rabbits and Radicals' Richard Nixon's 1946 Campaign Against Jerry Voorhis," *Southern California Quarterly*, vol. 55, n. 3 (Fall 1973). Starr, *Golden Dreams*, 203–204. Rolle, *California: A History*, 607–608. Walker, *The Cold War*, 2.
[85] Walker, *The Cold War*, 70–71.
[86] R. Eder, "Nixon, in Madrid, Stresses Its Role in Area Security," *New York Times*, 3 October 1970.

Bibliography

Aguirre, J. A. de, *Escape Via Berlin: Eluding Franco in Hitler's Europe*, Reno and Las Vegas, University of Nevada Press, 1991.

Barras, J., *Políticas de las exilados españoles, 1944–1950*, Paris, Ruedo Ibérico, 1976.

Bartosik-Vélez, E., *The Legacy of Christopher Columbus in the America: New Nations and a Transatlantic Discourse of Empire*, Nashville, Vanderbilt University Press, 2014.

Bowen, W. H., *Truman, Franco's Spain, and the Cold War*, Columbia, University of Missouri Press, 2017.

Bullock, P., "'Rabbits and Radicals' Richard Nixon's 1946 Campaign Against Jerry Voorhis," *Southern California Quarterly*, vol. 55, n. 3 (Fall 1973).

Burns, J., "The Mexican Catholic Community in California," in Jay Dolan and Gilberto Hinojosa (eds.), *Mexican Americans and the Catholic Church, 1900–1965*, Notre Dame, University of Notre Dame Press, 1994.

Byrnes, S. M., *Shedding the "Garb of Idealism": Truman Administration Policy Toward Spain and Yugoslavia*. Ph.D. dissertation, University of Texas at Austin, 1993.

Caughey, J. y Norris Hundley, Jr., *California: History of a Remarkable State*, 4th edition, Englewood Cliffs, Prentice-Hall, 1982.

Cava Mesa, M. J., *Los diplomáticos de Franco: J. F. de Lequerica, temple y tenacidad (1890–1963)*, Bilbao, Universidad de Deusto, 1989.

Edwards, J., *Anglo-American Relations and the Franco Question*, Oxford, Oxford University Press, 1999.

Ferrary, Á., *El franquismo: minorías políticas y conflictos ideológicos, (1936–1956)*, Pamplona, EUNSA, 1993.

Ferrell, R. H., *Truman in the White House: The Diary of Eben A. Ayers*, Columbia and London, University of Missouri Press, 1991.

Glondys, O., *La guerra fría cultural y el exilio republicano español*, Madrid, CSIC, 2012.

Gray, R., "Spanish Diaspora: A Culture in Exile," in "Remembering the Spanish Civil War," special issue, *Salmagundi: Quarterly of the Humanities and Social Sciences*, n. 76–77 (Fall 1987–Winter 1988).

Hadian, R. F., *United States Foreign Policy Towards Spain, 1953–1970*, Ph.D. dissertation, University of California at Santa Barbara, 1976.

Kurlansky, M., *The Basque History of the World*, New York, Penguin, 2001.

Leidtke, B., *Embracing a Dictatorship: US Relations with Spain, 1945–1953*, London, Macmillan Press, 1998.

Messenger, D., *Hunting Nazis in Franco's Spain*, Baton Rouge, Louisiana State University Press, 2014.

Norton, D., "Hispanidad and the Hollywood Ambassador: Friendship, Kinship and the Rearticulation of Spanish National Identity Before the Pact of Madrid," *Journal of Spanish Cultural Studies* vol. 19, n. 1 (2018), 71–92.

Pack, S., *Tourism and Dictatorship: Europe's Peaceful Invasion of Franco's Spain*, New York, Palgrave Macmillan, 2006.

Payne, S., *The Franco Regime, 1936–1975*, Madison, University of Wisconsin Press, 1987.

Preston, P., *Franco: A Biography*, New York, Harper Collins, 1993,

Prouty, M., *César Chávez, the Catholic Bishops, and the Farmworkers' Struggle for Social Justice*, Tuscon, University of Arizona Press, 2006.

Rhodes, R., *Hell and Good Company, The Spanish Civil War and the World It Made*, New York, Simon and Schuster, 2015.

Rolle, A. F., *California: A History, Second Edition*, New York, Thomas Y. Crowell Company, 1969.

Sehlinger, P., and Hamilton, H., *Spokesman for Democracy: Claude G. Bowers, 1878–1958*, Indianapolis, Indiana Historical Society, 2000.

Shaffer, R., "Religion and International Relations: The *Christian Century's* Protestant Critique of the U.S. Embrace of Fascist Spain," *Journal of Church and State*, vol. 59, n. 4 (Autumn 2017), 588–616.

Smith, E. R., *American Relief Aid and the Spanish Civil War*, Columbia, University of Missouri Press, 2013.

Starr, K., *Golden Dreams: California in an Age of Abundance, 1950–1963*, Oxford, Oxford University Press, 2009.

Sterling, C., *Olvera Street: Its History and Restoration*, Los Angeles, Mario Valadez, 1947.

Suárez Fernández, L., *Francisco Franco y su tiempo*, vol. 4, Madrid, Azor, 1984.

Thomàs, J. M., *Roosevelt, Franco, and the End of World War II*, New York, Palgrave Macmillan, 2011.

Tierney, D., *FDR and the Spanish Civil War: Neutrality and Commitment in the Struggle that Divided America*, Durham, Duke University Press, 2007.

Walker, M., *The Cold War: A History*, New York, Henry Holt, 1994.

Whitaker, A. P., *Spain and the Defense of the West: Ally and Liability*, New York, Praeger, 1961.

5

Toppling Franco? Great Britain, Spain, and the New World Order 1945–1951

EMILIO SÁENZ-FRANCÉS

> The ascent to greatness, however steep and dangerous, may entertain an active spirit with the consciousness and exercise of its own power: but the possession of a throne could never yet afford a lasting satisfaction to an ambitious mind.[1]

Introduction

On 24 October 2019, the remains of General Franco were exhumed from the Valley of the Fallen. This imposing mausoleum, built by the Franco regime and located to the north of Madrid, is perhaps the most important monument erected by the regime in all the years it held power in Spain. It is the "El Escorial" of the regime. Despite the government's decision to seek a new burial place for the Generalísimo, the valley still houses the remains of José Antonio Primo de Rivera, founder of the Falange movement, and those of no less than 30,000 Civil War combatants. Not for nothing did the Francoist propaganda of the time present the Valley of the Fallen as a monument to all the combatants who had lost their lives in the conflict.

The decision of the socialist government, which at the time had only been in power for a few months, led to a furious backlash and heated debate in Spain.[2] It attracted the attention of the international press and the live broadcast was followed with uncommon interest by over seven million people

---

[1] Edward Gibbon, *The History of the Decline and Fall of the Roman Empire*, ed. by David Womersley, 6 vols, London, Penguin Books, 1994.

[2] According to a survey by SIGMA DOS for El Mundo newspaper, 43.1 percent of those surveyed were in favour of the measure, with 32.5 percent against. Almost 20 percent were indifferent to the decision. A. Carvajal, "Encuesta El Mundo Sigma

in Spain.[3] The court battle that took place in order to impose the wishes of the government of Pedro Sánchez – in the face of resistance from the Franco family and the Benedictine community in the valley – had the predictable effect of generating renewed interest in the monument itself. In the months prior to the final removal of the remains of Franco, visits to the valley – which, like many other Spanish monuments, is overseen by the national heritage management agency, Patrimonio Nacional – multiplied exponentially. The Valley of the Fallen went from being an imposing but solitary example of "National Catholic" architecture in the bucolic heart of the Sierra de Madrid mountains to a meeting place for curious tourists or even a few nostalgic for Francoism, waving Franco regime flags. The turnstile personnel who controlled access to the monument were overwhelmed. Francoism and its controversies were back in fashion. Unleashed.

The arguments proffered in this debate were generally well known. And they became the center of Spanish social and political controversy with monotonous regularity. Apart from the last few hardliners still nostalgic for Francoism, no small part of Spanish society believes that the government decision was not only opportunistic, but also caused the collateral damage of reviving the ghost of the dictatorship and bringing it into the present when, after more than forty years of democracy, the period from 1939 to 1975 should be finally seen as Spain's history, not part of its present.[4] On the other hand, defenders of the government's decision offered the argument of the extreme exceptionality and abnormality of a cruel dictator, comparable to Hitler or Mussolini, honored in a fascist mausoleum, representing the last vestiges of his perverse legacy.[5]

Dos. Menos de la mitad de población aplaude la exhumación de Franco y un tercio se muestra en contra," *El Mundo*, 29 October 2019.

[3] The average television audience was over seven million viewers on the day of the exhumation of Franco, almost 5 percent more. "La audiencia media en TV superó los 7 millones de espectadores en la jornada de la exhumación de Franco, casi un 5% más," *Europa Press*, 25 October 2019.

[4] The Centro de Investigaciones Sociológicas (a Spanish public opinion research body) has not sought the opinion of the Spanish people about the dictatorship since 2008, shortly after the Zapatero government passed the Law on Historic Memory. At that time, almost 50 percent of those surveyed declared that the Civil War remained very vivid in the memory of the Spanish people. Almost 80 percent agreed that basic human rights were broken during Francoism, though almost 60 percent were of the opinion that "Francoism had good and bad aspects". Centro de Investigaciones Sociológicas, *Estudio 2760. Memorias de la guerra civil y del franquismo, CIS, 16–04–2008*, http://analisis.cis.es/cisdb.jsp?ESTUDIO=2760.

[5] From the perspective of the international press, see, for example, the *New York Times* article. R. Minder, "Plan to Exhume Franco Renews Spain's Wrestle With History," *New York Times*, 7 July 2018, https://www.nytimes.com/2018/07/07/world/europe/spain-franco.html?smid=tw-nytimesworld&smtyp=cur.

The appearance of the two sinister names, those of the two main leaders of the fascist aggression, was the argument that most excited the imagination and conjured up most passions in all of this complex dialectical tug-of-war that, furthermore, did not end with the removal of Franco from the Valley of the Fallen. A few months later, in September 2022, the government approved the Democratic Memory Law, which many found controversial, and that included heavy fines for those who promoted acts that glorified the dictatorship, as well as backing the closure of institutions such as the Francisco Franco Foundation, custodian of the personal archive of the general and, naturally, resolutely identified with his legacy.[6]

It is in this context of growing polarization that this chapter is written and, on writing it, we cannot avoid the fact that it is the moment to revisit reflections that are not new but, with the passing of time, can be contemplated more serenely and, we hope, more firmly, as they are supported by access to new documentary information and to the valuable work of many fellow historians. The volume to which this book belongs is sufficient proof. The debate continues and will continue in the future. Meanwhile, the level-headed work of historians is to continue throwing light and new interpretations on a convulsed period. It is on the foundations of knowledge gained through scientific effort that we can build a vantage point from which to contemplate the future with confidence.

The period from 1945 to 1951 was the only time in which the Franco regime felt that its existence and continuity were threatened. This continuity depended on the controversies and debates to which we have just referred. Things being so, the purpose of this chapter, which continues and develops the reflections contained in *De águilas y leones. Diplomacia británica en España 1939–1953. Tiempo de guerra y era de cambios*,[7] is to analyze the evolution over time of the relationships between the United Kingdom and Franco's Spain. We shall, at all events, focus mainly on the period 1945–1951 and, in doing so, we shall examine an aspect of the bilateral relationship which is collateral but of much greater importance. It is the process by which British diplomacy finally yielded the role of leadership in international politics to the United States, including policy towards Spain. It is a changing of the guard that, perhaps, had already been certified on a global scale in 1945, but which displays some particular characteristics. In addition to its close proximity, Spain remained an element of specific, enduring interest to British foreign policymakers. In 1945, Great Britain, under the Labour government of Clement Attlee and the foreign policy leadership of

---

6   The text of the draft law can be found at: https://www.mpr.gob.es/servicios/participacion/Documents/APL%20Memoria%20Democrática.pdf.

7   J. M. Thomàs, *Estados Unidos, Alemania, Gran Bretaña, Japón y sus relaciones con España entre la guerra y la postguerra (1939–1953)*, Madrid, Universidad Pontificia Comillas, 2016.

Ernest Bevin, may have thought that it still enjoyed strategic independence in the diplomatic terrain. Time would soon show that they were wrong.

***

In 1949, a British analysis of the scenario for a possible nuclear war fought by the United States and Great Britain against the Soviet Union established that a necessary condition for victory would be to count on Spain as a secure base of operations from which to launch a counter-attack against the communist forces, which would have been able to occupy a large part of continental Europe after the outbreak of the conflict. Two years later, in 1951, the British Chiefs of Staff were already openly considering Spain's entry into NATO. The diplomatic consequences were clear. Whether Francisco Franco's regime in Spain was palatable or not, strategic Cold War needs made it necessary to tolerate and compromise with the Caudillo. And so, in a way, a complex cycle of Hispano-British relations was closed – a cycle defined by the Second World War and the immediate post-war years. These were fourteen years in which the British empire was close to collapse but was saved, only to cede world supremacy to the United States and the Soviet Union. It was a period in which Spain was a significant, though fundamentally passive, piece on the world chessboard. A period in which Francoism could have remained a minor parenthesis in twentieth-century Spanish history. Great Britain was largely responsible for that not being so.

Spain and Great Britain 1939–1945. The Legacy of the War

The Second World War broke out as a result of German aggression against Poland's independence and ended with the principle of independence crushed by Soviet domination of East Europe.[8] For five years, what is without doubt the most ferocious war in the history of humanity was waged. It drove Nazi tyranny to the margins of history and gave birth to a new bipolar world in which the center of the great decisions was no longer located in Europe. It was a conflict undoubtedly defined to a large extent by the political leadership and inspiration of Winston Churchill, elevated once more to the waiting room of political power with the outbreak of the war and to the office of prime minister with the fiasco of the British intervention in Norway and the beginning of the irresistible German invasion of France in May 1940.[9] Churchill was also largely responsible for defining the basic lines of the crucial relationship between Britain and Spain in those years.

---

[8] See Basil Liddell Hart's initial reflections in his history of the Second World War: B. Liddell Hart, *The Second World War*, Barcelona, Qaralt, 2006.

[9] See J. Lukaks, *Cinco días en London, mayo de 1940: Churchill solo frente a Hitler*, Madrid, Turner, 2001.

GREAT BRITAIN, SPAIN, AND THE NEW WORLD ORDER

Before Churchill's arrival at 10 Downing Street, after the fall of France, ensuring Spain's neutrality in the conflict became much more urgently a key objective of Britain's international actions. This preoccupation was, apparently, more than justified. Spain, undoubtedly more fascinated by Italian fascism than German Nazism, mimicked every step taken by Mussolini, which led him to enter the war in June. On 12 June 1940, Spain modified its previous declaration of neutrality with a declaration of non-belligerence, interpreted at the time in all foreign ministries as a possible status of pre-belligerence.

The entry of Spain into the war would have been a devastating blow to Great Britain. If Franco had supported the Axis militarily in any naval action in the Mediterranean, the United Kingdom would have been seriously threatened and Gibraltar dramatically compromised. The war in Africa and Greece, the only theatres in which, until 1943, Great Britain was able to give battle (though often with little success), would not have taken place. In order to avoid that danger, the British government launched an ambitious diplomatic strategy based largely on an accurate perception of the deeper nature of the new political regime in Spain. Firstly, a heavyweight ambassador was sent to Madrid, one of the most prestigious politicians in the British political panorama at the time, who had stood out for his rivalry with Churchill himself. It was "Slippery Sam" Hoare, who had been one of the main appeasers during the 1930s and who, unable to occupy a relevant role in the domestic politics designed by Churchill, was able to undertake a clear, well-defined mission: to ensure that Spain did not enter the war. It was undoubtedly a top-level objective and also, undoubtedly, a maximum priority during those months in which Great Britain resisted alone the forces of the Axis.[10]

In Spain, Hoare applied the old policy of the carrot and the stick, with suggestive promises for the future regarding the enlargement of the Spanish protectorate in France after the war, and, above all, with leverage applied through supplies arriving by sea, on which Spain was totally dependent, and which were under the complete control of the powerful British navy. It should be highlighted that, at that time, Spain's relationship with the United States could at best be described as cold and distant. In the arduous process by which Churchill brought President Roosevelt into the terrain of the political needs that the war had created for his country, a not inconsiderable element was Britain's work in clearing the way for the signing of a trade agreement between Spain and the United States. Through this process, Spain's relations

---

[10] See S. Hoare, *Ambassador on Special Mission*, London, Collins, 1946. On the ambassador: M. Alpert "Las Relaciones Anglo-Hispanas en el Primer Semestre de la 'Guerra Caliente' La misión diplomática de sir Samuel Hoare," *Revista de Política Internacional*, vol. 160, 1978, 7–31 and J. A. Cross, *Sir Samuel Hoare. A Political Biography*, London, Jonathan Cape, 1977.

with the United States improved significantly, and the American embassy began to act in coordination with (and subordination to) the British, in a process by which, for political reasons, Franco's regime was able to obtain supplies of oil, of which there was a drastic shortage. Oil was essential in sustaining the Spanish economy. And not only that, Great Britain was aware that, should the case arise, the Chiefs of Staff in Madrid held the trump card, if all else failed, to prevent the entry of Spain into the war. So began a vast programme of bribes to the most important generals in order to incentivize their already generalized lack of enthusiasm for combat.[11]

At that time, Spain could in fact have significantly changed the balance of the war in favour of the Third Reich ... but finally did not do so. And it was not just through the skilful work of the crafty Hoare, or the Foreign Office's ability to understand the special rhythms that define Spanish politics and its needs. General Franco was not, in short, Benito Mussolini, whose fascination with Nazi Germany he never shared, except in purely military terms. His more generous disposition towards the Axis during the first part of the war was born more of the disdain and rancour felt by a large part of the Spanish right towards France and Great Britain, for having suffocated, they thought, any possibility of the renaissance of Spain as a great power in Europe. In the early phases of the war, Franco's aspiration was to make Spain the key to signing a quick peace deal. When it became clear that the Third Reich had become a military power capable of reducing what was supposedly the best army in Europe to impotence in just a few weeks, Madrid was perhaps more enthused by the thought of the defeat of the democracies than by the victory and domination of all Europe by Hitler. And we should not forget that the Führer had begun the war by means of a pact with the Soviet demon to destroy Catholic Poland. Franco was, ultimately, aware that war was a dark, dangerous business and that, leaving aside defiant speeches and bluster, his Spain was only imperial in an exercise of empty voluntarism, and that all he should preoccupy himself with was surviving. Just surviving.

Franco knew where the wheat that was feeding the Spanish people came from. The Third Reich might be impressive on land, but the seas still belonged to the British. Their famous navicerts, navigation certificates, were proof of that. The Caudillo was, in the end, a conscientious soldier who saw that the numbers did not add up.[12] The Spanish army was a force of perhaps a million men, but exhausted after a fratricidal war, poorly armed and worse fed, the

---

[11] See D. Smyth, "Les Chevallers de Saint-George; la Grande-Bretagne et la Corruption Des Généraux Espagnols (1940–1942)," *Guerres Mondiales et Conflits Contemporains*, n. 162 (April 1992), 29–54.

[12] See: R. W. Matson, "Neutrality and Navicerts: Britain, the United States, and Economic Warfare, 1939–1940," *The Journal of American History*, vol. 82, n. 2 (September 1995), 813–814.

perfect reflection of a people that neither wanted nor were able to suffer the impossible effort of joining the war. And Germany? Unlike the Italians, imperial in tone, Germany demanded rather than asked. There was no place for subtlety. That relationship was never a bed of roses.

Faced with this reality, Franco was ready to play his cards, and he was playing purely for survival – his own and that of his regime, that furious cauldron of arrogant generals, uncontrolled Falangists, and monarchist conspiracists. One flank, relations with the Allies, or at least with Great Britain, was never neglected, although the regime initially made the mistake of underestimating the potential role of the United States in the conflict and in future European history. It was not until 1943 that the error began to be remedied. Franco sent Juan Francisco de Cárdenas, a wily diplomat, to Washington, the details of whose work has still not been analyzed.[13] As regards Great Britain, since the Civil War, Franco's Spain had been represented by the duke of Alba. Without doubt, Alba was a very able diplomat who made very skilful use of his unrivalled personal connections to achieve the warmest possible diplomatic relations, bearing in mind Spain's obviously greater affinity with the Axis, and, from his privileged position, to seek a respectful British policy towards Spain that would encourage its neutrality. Though Alba had sent very unfavourable reports about Churchill in the months prior to his becoming prime minister, his attitude from then onwards evolved towards the greatest cordiality. Both, after all, shared the same interest in keeping Spain out of the war at all costs.[14]

For Franco, at that time, Germany clearly could not lose the war, but it was also evident that, the planned invasion of the British Isles having been cancelled, there was no clear way in which it could win. The Caudillo needed no more persuasion to remain on the sidelines, and his indecisiveness was bolstered by the melting pot of representatives of Nazi Germany in Spain, broken up into cliques and factions conspiring among themselves and, at times, against the regime itself. The more radical National Socialists among the German diplomatic presence in Madrid had, effectively, promised a change that gave power in Spain to the real Spain, the true Falangist Spain, that was willing and anxious to enter the war. Franco was aware of these movements, which threatened his position, and he moved decisively against them. Despite the understandable military fascination inspired by the Wehrmacht, he could expect little of Germany.[15]

---

[13] M. A. Lopez Zapico, "Against all odds. El diplomático Juan Francisco de Cárdenas durante la Guerra Civil Española y el primer franquismo," in *Propagandistas y diplomáticos al servicio de Franco (1936–1945)*, Gijón, Trea, 2012, 303–331.

[14] E. Sáenz-Francés, *Entre la Antorcha y la Esvástica. Franco en la Encrucijada de la Segunda Guerra Mundial*, Actas, Madrid, 2009.

[15] Ibid., 101–172.

The launch of Germany's invasion of Russia in June 1940 was to open a completely new chapter in the history of the Second World War. Spain would send its Blue Division, a division of the Spanish army that fought with Hitler against the Soviet Union, to Russia. Great Britain would be satisfied if Franco went no further. For now. The focus of the war effectively switched to the North, and Spain and the Mediterranean became backwaters, but that was just a momentary mirage. At the end of that year, after the Japanese attack on Pearl Harbor, the United States finally entered the war. Churchill succeeded, very skilfully and not without effort, in getting the Americans to accept an idea and a project drawn up by the British. It was the "Europe First" strategy: that it was necessary to first eliminate Nazism before focusing on Japan. The project: a vast military operation in North Africa which was initially given the name Operation Gymnast, but was soon renamed, much more appropriately, Operation Torch. Churchill basically persuaded the president that the Anglo-American forces were still not ready to give battle to Hitler in France. A longer path was needed, a path that would both expel from Africa and knock out the Führer's increasingly weak ally: Italy.

And, indeed, the Allied landings in North Africa in November 1942 represent one of the crucial moments in relations between the Allies and Spain during the Second World War. The operation, which was intended to bring the Americans into the European theatre, was a key development and nothing could be allowed to fail. Firstly, there was the objective of ensuring that the French forces in Morocco and Algeria did not react. That mission was entrusted to American diplomats. The more complex task was that taken on by Great Britain: to ensure the benevolent attitude of Spain. The landings included operations on the Atlantic seaboard of Morocco, but also others beyond the Strait of Gibraltar, in Oran and Algeria. As Sir Samuel Hoare said, that meant steering a course between two sharp Spanish knives, two particularly treacherous Spanish knives.[16]

That was perhaps Great Britain's finest hour during the war with respect to Spain, and it was, without doubt, a crucial time for General Franco. Spanish hostility to the landings would have made them unfeasible and would have brought the war to mainland Spain. Once the operation began, there was no lack of pressure on Franco from the Axis powers to allow them to use aerodromes in southern Spain, so that the Luftwaffe could operate in the area and, even worse, old maps from 1940 were dusted off in Berlin, against the possibility of undertaking a preventive operation on mainland Spain to shield the southern flank of Hitler's empire. Once more, Churchill's political calculations had been perfect. Skilful diplomatic strategy helped to ensure that his prediction came true: nothing moved in Spain in those days. Quite the contrary: the landings, thanks to the new Minister of Foreign Affairs – and

---

[16] Ibid., 336.

an old acquaintance of the Foreign Office – the count of Jordana, inaugurated a new era of cordiality between Great Britain and Spain while, during those months, the relationship with the Axis, split between a desperate Italy and a Germany that was heading irremediably towards the disaster of Stalingrad, experienced one of its tensest and most critical moments of the war.

And, in fact, 1943 was a turning point in the Second World War, both globally and as far as Spain was concerned. Until the summer, Franco and his regime were under the illusion that the gratitude of the Allies to Spain for its passivity during Operation Torch would protect the country from any complaint or recrimination. Churchill was happy to play that game, and he contained American dogmatism, which was already demanding a hard line with Spain, at least until operations in the North African theatre were over.[17] In July, Operation Husky, the invasion of Sicily, whose first consequence was the fall of Mussolini, was the dawn of a new relationship between the Allies and Spain. With Africa pacified and Italy heading straight for disaster, for many, not just in Washington but also in London, the time had come at last to deal with General Franco and his regime *as they deserved.*

From August 1943 on, the Allied attitude towards Spain hardened notably. Despite the improvement in the previous months, transcendental issues still arose between the two sides. Issues such as the Spanish occupation of Tangiers at the beginning of the war, which violated the international status of the city, and Spain's blind eye to the presence of a large network of German spies in the city and in all of Spain. Furthermore, thousands of Spanish soldiers continued to fight alongside German troops on the Russian front, an anomaly that, to the Allies, questioned Spain's declared wish to remain strictly neutral. And, even more importantly, Spain was one of the Reich's main suppliers of wolfram, a mineral essential for the production of armour plating for German vehicles.[18] Throughout the war, the legal and illegal trade in this mineral by Spain and Portugal, the largest producers in Europe, had grown spectacularly. The Allies tried to monopolize the market, which helped to accelerate price rises. It eventually became too costly for Britain and its allies to continue this system of preventive purchasing. The only option was to force Spain to stop the trade of this and other materials with Germany.[19]

While Churchill, Roosevelt, and the Canadian prime minister were holding a conference in Québec in August 1943, Sir Samuel Hoare, at his own initiative, laid out these questions in a meeting with Franco and rushed to leak to the press that the British ambassador had given nothing less than an ultimatum to Franco. Hoare had begun his private operation to rehabilitate himself as a public figure, as a prior step to his long-desired return to the frontline of British

[17] Ibid., 609–769.

[18] J. M. Thomàs, *La Batalla del Wolframio. Estados Unidos y España de Pearl Harbor a la Guerra Fría (1941–1977)*, Madrid, Cátedra, 2010.

[19] *Entre la Antorcha…*, 820 & ff.

politics, and he was willing to use Spain as a springboard. Hoare's initiative was not well received in the Foreign Office, but it was in tune with American sensitivities, firmly in favour of hardening Allied policy towards Franco.[20] Churchill had no love for Franco or his regime, but he was a realist, and he knew that there was no potential political benefit to be gained by destabilizing Spain. The fall of Franco could well push Spain back into chaos, complicating the wartime policy – and perhaps even post-war policy – in a scenario in which, as in 1936, the only priority for Great Britain was to maintain its strategic interests.

But the diplomatic hierarchy had changed. Until 1943, it was the British who called the tune in Spain. American ambassadors could only second the imperative provisions of Sir Samuel. By the end of 1943, the British eclipse was clearly visible. The United States was flexing its muscles as the power of the future, its economic and military capacity already marking it out as the undisputed leader of the Western Allies. And the United States was ready to impose its rules. Churchill, Hoare, and Anthony Eden, whose pasts had been informed by the idea of the greatness of the British empire, and who had made its defence the *raison d'être* of their political careers, had to drink from the bitter chalice and accept that, even though Britain won the war, its victory would bring with it the country's decline as the leading world power. The baton would be irreversibly handed over to the United States. And the future of Great Britain therefore depended on a solid, durable alliance with the American giant at all levels. The only country that could face up to the global threat that was already visible on the post-war horizon: Soviet Russia.

And so, it was the inexperienced Department of State, grudgingly followed by the U.S. ambassador in Madrid, Carlton Hayes, that started to lay down the lines of Spanish policy. With Franco, Hoare may have been a wolf, but he was wearing a skin that hid the old appeaser in him. When the Americans began to follow an extremely hard and demanding line with Spain, he was horrified. British policy at the time had to face up to the difficult role of tempering U.S. policy towards Spain. A political triangle that had previously borne fruit worked once again: Hoare, convinced that the end of his political career was in Spain, Viscount Halifax, another great appeaser, sent by Churchill to Washington shortly after Sir Samuel was sent to Spain (and for the same reasons), and the prime minister himself, thanks to his special, direct relationship with President Roosevelt.[21] The three had the same objective: to stymie the more radical U.S. policies with respect to Spain, and to work towards the achievement of the reasonable objectives that would finally relieve Franco of any debt with the Axis.

---

[20] Ibid, 863 & ff.

[21] On Viscount Halifax, see A. Roberts, *The Holy Fox. A Life of Lord Halifax*, London, Phoenix Press, 1999.

GREAT BRITAIN, SPAIN, AND THE NEW WORLD ORDER 275

At all events, late 1943 and early 1944 was a particularly difficult period for Spain. Franco refused to bow to Allied demands, because behind them he saw the ambition of the pro-monarchy generals who, buoyed by Allied successes, had begun to respectfully suggest to the Caudillo the need for a new design of the regime when the war was over that would favour the return of the king, and the formal establishment of a political system that was acceptable to the Allies. Franco thought that if he simply folded before the Allies, the result would only be to infuriate the conservative generals, whose position of absolute power within the regime would find itself under serious threat. The Caudillo knew that they had to resist, play for time and, meanwhile, use the support of the Falange, who were as needy as he was at that time of declining German fortunes. He did not hesitate to enter into his favourite game: confusion and deception. To the Allies, he even offered to replace the Blue Division with a flotilla of the Spanish navy that would join the war effort against Japan in the Pacific.[22]

And so, to the end, Spain resisted the withdrawal of the Blue Division, which would remain as the Legion until well into 1944. A drastic measure, in the shape of a total embargo of oil supplies to Spain during the early months of that year, was necessary to force Franco, reluctantly, to begin to give in to Allied demands. Only in April 1945 were Lufthansa flights between Germany and Spain finally suspended.[23] The embargo was considered to be an inadequate measure by many British politicians and, though many Labour members of the government coalition shared the fierce hostility of the Americans towards Spain, the majority response of the Conservatives was clear: despite all of its political deficiencies, the Spanish regime was more humane than the Russia of their ally, Stalin.[24] Churchill's vision prevailed, at least for a few months, in Great Britain. Parliamentary politics generally kept out of the matter rather than feed the fires of threats against Spain.

June 1944 saw the Normandy landings, which marked the beginning of the end of the world conflict. Just two months later, the count of Jordana, who had guided Spanish policy, with great success, since September,[25] died in San Sebastián. These two events, Operation Overlord and the death of the minister, marked the return of Spain to international insignificance. Land communication between Spain and the Reich was cut off shortly afterwards,

---

[22] F. Rodao, *Franco y el Imperio Japonés,* Barcelona, Plaza & Janes, 2002.

[23] Bowker to the Foreign Office, 17 May 1945, National Archives of the United Kingdom (NAUK) FO 371/39549.

[24] With respect to the diaries of Jock Colville, Churchill's secretary during the war, see J. Colville, *A La Sombra de Churchill, Diarios de Downing Street. 1939–1955,* Barcelona, Galaxia Gutenberg, 2007.

[25] F. Gómez de Jordana, *Milicia y diplomacia: Los diarios del Conde Jordana 1936–1944*, Burgos, Dossoles, 2002.

and there was no more reason to fear Spanish trade with Germany, or that the German spies in Spain could play any role in the progress of the war. Franco and his regime were relegated to a mere political quibble, a topic of conversation at the summits of the powerful. Stalin could speak of the peninsula and of the need, in due time, for the Caudillo to be called to account, and perhaps Portugal's leader Salazar too. But neither Roosevelt nor, especially, Churchill felt any enthusiasm for becoming bogged down trying to remedy the situation in the peninsula. Not yet. There were other priorities, and many of them concerned the voraciousness of the Soviet leader himself. Towards the end of the year, Samuel Hoare left Madrid, an unequivocal sign that Britain had no more interest in Spain.

When the war ended with the Allied victory and the birth of a new world, divided between Russians and Americans, Churchill chose Hendaye, on the border between France and Spain, for a few days' rest. The Spanish press speculated that the prime minister might visit San Sebastián. It was, above all, a desire for international blessing, and it gave way to enormous frustration.

Churchill sincerely appreciated Spain. His understanding, though without admiration or support, of Spain's policy during the Second World War was a faithful reflection of that reality. Over the years of conflict, despite all its faults, Spain did what Britain needed of it. Churchill was a realist and did not need any more than that. Despite his militant monarchism, he felt no need to settle private ideological scores when dealing with Franco and his regime. To have allowed any political engineering in the country would have gone against his deep-rooted sense of history. When he looked at Spain – whether during the suffering of the Civil War or in the years of the rise of Francoism –Churchill saw, above all, an unhappy people, the prisoners of the painful contradictions of their own history; a dilemma that, he was fully convinced, could only be resolved by the Spanish people themselves. In 1945, everything changed in London. The new Labour government elected in July was not without its brilliant politicians. As we shall see, the new prime minister himself, Atlee, and Ernest Bevin, the foreign secretary, are among the most illustrious of all British politicians of the twentieth century. But in these new times, the external pressures would be completely different, with a context that was unknown within the traditions of the Foreign Office and all British foreign policy in its recent history. Spain was to be one of the focal points where all of those changes, almost traumas, would become most visible. What Whitehall thought or planned would, day by day, become less important.

New Times at the Foreign Office?

With the departure, already mentioned, of Sir Samuel Hoare from the embassy in Madrid, and the arrival in the Spanish capital of his replacement, Sir Victor Mallet (the *chargé d'affaires* in the months until his appointment was Reginald

GREAT BRITAIN, SPAIN, AND THE NEW WORLD ORDER   277

James Bowker, an effective, level-headed career diplomat), a new chapter in
bilateral Hispano-British relations opened up, one that was defined by different
factors.[26] There was the approaching end of the war and the shift in the Allied
attitude to Spain after the war ended in Europe, above all with the Potsdam
conference and, related to that, the unexpected Labour victory that coincided
with the conference itself.

All of this would mean an intensification of international hostility towards
the regime and, with many ups and downs, of British hostility, too. A no less
transcendental change also took place in the U.S. embassy in Madrid, with the
departure of Carlton Hayes (lauded by the regime's authorities as a true friend
of Spain) and the arrival of his replacement, Norman Armour. Roosevelt, his life
rapidly draining away, gave instructions to the new ambassador in a document
that in later years was of special interest to those in charge at the Foreign Office:

March 10th, 1945.

My Dear Mr. Armour.

In connexion with your new assignment as Ambassador to Madrid I
want you to have a frank statement of my views with regards to our
relations with Spain. Having been helped to power by Fascist Italy and
Nazi Germany and having patterned itself along totalitarian lines the
present regime in Spain is naturally the subject of distrust by a great
many American citizens who find it difficult to see the justification
for this country to continue to maintain relations with such a regime.
Most certainly we do not forget Spain's official position with and
assistance to our Axis enemies at a time when the fortunes of war were
less favourable to us, nor can we disregard the activities, aims, organizations and public utterances of the Falange both past and present.
These memories cannot be wiped out by actions more favourable to
us now that we are about to achieve our goal of complete victory
over those enemies of ours with whom the present Spanish regime
identified itself in the past spiritually and by its public expressions
and acts. The fact that our government maintains formal diplomatic
relations with the present Spanish regime should not be interpreted
by anyone to imply approval of that regime and its sole party the
Falange which has been openly hostile to the United States and which

---

[26] The best study to date on the question is F. Portero, *Franco Aislado. La Cuestión
Española (1945–1950)*, Madrid, Aguilar, 1989. On the gradual transfer of protagonism
from the United Kingdom to the United States see C. Collado Seidel, *El Telegrama que
Salvó a Franco*, Barcelona, Crítica, 2016. Worthy of special mention is the magnificent
study of the question by Xavier Hualde: X. Hualde, *El Cerco Aliado. Estados Unidos,
Francia y Gran Bretaña ante la Cuestión Española*, Bilbao, Universidad del País
Vasco, 2016.

has tried to spread its Fascist party ideas in the Western hemisphere. Our victory over Germany will carry with it the extermination of Nazi and similar ideologies. As you know it is not our practice in normal circumstances to interfere on the internal affairs of other countries unless there exists a threat to international peace. The form of government in Spain and the policies pursued by that government are quite properly the concern of the Spanish people. I should be lacking in candour however if I did not tell you that I can see no place in the community of nations for governments founded on Fascist principles. We all have the most friendly feelings for the Spanish people and we are anxious to see a development of cordial relations with them. There are many things which we could and normally would be glad to do in economic and other fields to demonstrate the friendship. The initiation of such measures is out of the question at this time however when American sentiment is so profoundly opposed to the present regime in power in Spain. Therefore we earnestly hope that the time may soon come when Spain may assume the role and the responsibility which we feel it should assume in the field of international co-operation and understanding.

Very sincerely yours. Franklin D. Roosevelt.[27]

But let us return to the United Kingdom. British reports at the time about the Spanish attitude towards the Allied victory could not have given a more negative impression. On 29 May, Bowker informed London of the reaction in Zaragoza to the deaths of President Roosevelt and of Hitler. Apparently, private parties were held at which those present celebrated the death of the occupant of the White House while the German consulate in the city received repeated public condolences for the death of the Führer. This, according to the report, was partly due to the fact that the General Military Academy, whose instruction, the report noted, followed the German-Prussian model, was based in the city.[28] On 29 May, a *note verbale* of the U.S. embassy protested to the Ministry of Foreign Affairs regarding the aggressions and offences committed against the British and American flags flown in cities such as Lugo, Valladolid, and Santiago de Compostela, and at delegations of the Singer Sewing Machine Company, on the occasion of the victory in Europe.[29] On 20 June, the British also protested about a mass held in memory of Hitler in Santander.[30]

[27] Letter from Franklin D. Roosevelt to Norman Armour, 10 March 1945. Cited in a telegram from Viscount Halifax to the Foreign Office, 29 September 1945, NAUK, FO 371–49613.

[28] Translation of a report from Zaragoza (British Vice-Consul Zaragoza), 29 May 1945, NAUK, FO 371–49589.

[29] See Note Verbale of the U.S. Embassy to the Ministry of Foreign Affairs, 26 May 1945, NAUK, FO 371–49589.

[30] Aide Memoire of the British Embassy, 13 July 1945, NAUK, FO 371–49589.

GREAT BRITAIN, SPAIN, AND THE NEW WORLD ORDER 279

At that time, British and U.S. policy was to encourage profound, significant changes in the Francoist regime, though with no defined strategy as to how radical or deep that policy should be. On 19 June, a new report sent by Bowker to Anthony Eden speculated on the reasons why, even with the regimes of Hitler and Mussolini in ashes, Franco refused to initiate the reforms demanded by the British and Americans, which would require the dismantling of the fascist state apparatus. Among the reasons suggested by Bowker in his report was the Caudillo's resistance to change, since, in principle, all change, no matter how small, could weaken his pre-eminent position in Spain. Furthermore, the diplomat believed, Franco was genuinely convinced that he was called by providence to govern Spain and, from the perspective of that conviction, he felt safe, since the most probable future scenario was a war between the Western Allies and the Soviet Union.[31] In addition, and relevantly, Bowker noted that although the U.S. embassy followed the orders it received as closely as possible, it was no less true that the new ambassador, Norman Armour, was offering the regime a friendlier face than was desirable:

> It is no doubt, difficult to maintain cold reserve in the face of perpetual smiles and possibly Americans temperamentally are more susceptible to flattery than other [...] I am quite certain that the United States Ambassador has consistently spoken on the lines agreed in London and Washington in his conversations with General Franco's Minister, Señor Lequerica [...] But faced a week ago with an invitation to dine at the Pardo he did not feel able to send a refusal, despite the fact that such an invitation was quite unprecedented and the dinner would inevitably be given political significance. Mr and Mrs. Armour duly attended, to find the Minister of the Falange among the guests and, although Mr. Armour, at about 2.30 in the morning, after the guests have been treated to an exhibition of tapestries, had an opportunity of telling General Franco of his disappointment that no progress has been made with the modification of the regimen and the elimination of Falange in accordance with repeated representations, General Franco returned a soft if lengthy, answer to each point [...] the following day a notice duly appeared in the press to the effect that the Caudillo had entertained the United States Ambassador and his wife to an intimate and friendly dinner party. No doubt General Franco used the event to convince the generals once more that he could count on American support.[32]

The well-heralded inexperience of the American officials still constitutes the essential starting point in any analysis.

---

[31] See Bowker to Eden, 19 June 1945, NAUK, FO 371–49589.
[32] Bowker to Eden, 19 June 1945, NAUK, FO 371–49589.

280 EMILIO SÁENZ-FRANCÉS

There was no need to await the election of Clement Attlee to note the increased British interest in the possibilities of promoting political change in Spain, or at least to assess the capacity of the opposition to bring about that change itself. In April 1945, Harold Farquhar, the British consul in Barcelona, sent an extensive analysis of anti-Franco forces in Catalonia to the embassy in Madrid. The meticulous work of the consul revealed British diplomacy's renewed interest in movements that might bring down the Franco regime. The report gave a detailed analysis of opposition forces in Catalonia, listing communist movements (Unión Nacional Española, Alianza Catalana, Juventudes Combatientes); socialists and trade unionists (Alianza Nacional de Fuerzas Democráticas, Frente de la Libertad, PSOE, CNT, UGT, Movimiento Libertario, Confederación de Sindicatos Unidos, Partido Republicano Español, POUM, Frente de Libertad, Front Nacional de Catalunya/Bloque Catalán); and separatists (Bloque Catalán, Esquerra, Estat Catalá Proletari, Acció Catalana, Unió Democrática, Liberación Nacional Republicana, Frente Nacional). And all of this without entering into his reports on monarchists and Carlists, who enjoyed the most solid popular support, according to the consul.[33] At all events, as Farquhar well noted, the fragmentation of the opposition played into Franco's hands and none of those parties or unions, except the CNT, advocated the violent overthrow of Francoism.[34]

A few weeks later, at the beginning of July, James Bowker informed Churchill of an interview – widely covered by the media – granted by Franco to the director of foreign services of Associated Press. The Caudillo went so far as to declare his intention to hold municipal elections in Spain and to set up a council of the realm, as a prior step to the Restoration, "at the right time." These were surprising declarations, received with widespread skepticism, but which clearly laid out the unequivocal wish of the regime to urgently break all ties with the Axis and with Fascism.[35] Above all, he noted that Franco was angling to enter into one of the games at which he was a consummate expert, something we could call strategic procrastination.

Shortly after, following just that line and in a proactive defensive measure (similar to the promotion of the count of Jordana to the Ministry of Foreign Affairs in 1942), Franco was about to embark on a reshuffle, replacing José Félix de Lequerica with the more acceptable Alberto Martín Artajo,[36] at the same time abolishing the position of minister-secretary general of the Falangist movement. The number of Falangist ministers fell from seven to five.

---

33 See Farquhar to Bowker, 24 April 1945, NAUK, FO 371–49589.

34 See Bowker to Eden, 29 May 1945, NAUK, FO 371–49589.

35 Bowker to Churchill, 2 July 1945, NAUK, FO 371–49589.

36 On the political personality of Matín Artajo, see: F. Portero, "Artajo. Perfil de un Ministro en Tiempos de Aislamiento," *Historia Contemporánea* vol. 15 (1996), 201–224.

GREAT BRITAIN, SPAIN, AND THE NEW WORLD ORDER

According to the British *chargé d'affaires* in Madrid, this step was interpreted as a gesture to appease the monarchical sector of the regime.[37] A few days later, Bowker expanded his perspicacious analysis of the new government and the fundamental laws, the Fuero de los Españoles, which had been announced. He noted the fall of Lequerica as it was, among other reasons, a necessity in order to improve relations with France. The weight of Lequerica's track record as ambassador to the nefarious Vichy regime was too heavy, though the abilities of the slippery Basque politician were quite remarkable. His political activities, which are described in other chapters of this book, would still produce notable moments in the future as the person responsible for the creation of the Spanish Lobby in the United States. The replacement of the wily Lequerica, Alberto Martín Artajo, was very well received by the *chargé d'affaires* as a sensible Christian Democrat unencumbered by the filo-fascist flirting of the regime, as well as being sympathetic to Britain. Raimundo Fernández Cuesta (Justice) was portrayed as an unscrupulous opportunist, while Bowker linked the fall of Demetrio Carceller with the known cases of corruption associated with him.[38]

A few days later, with Sir Victor Mallet now installed as the new ambassador in Madrid (he had presented his credentials to Franco in San Sebastián at the end of July), an earthquake, to which we have already referred, shook British politics. In the general elections held for the first time since the outbreak of the war, the Labour party scored an historic victory, making Clement Attlee the new prime minister. Attlee would replace Churchill in the final sessions of the Potsdam conference. A much more wary attitude towards Spain and its regime was to be expected of the new government. The ideological viewpoint of Labour sympathies with respect to anti-Franco forces shifted from the monarchists to the much more fearsome republicans. The stable relationship, which was in any case anaemic, that existed during the Churchill era was coming to an end.

It is, therefore, necessary to focus on the figure of the new strongman in British politics – one who has been described as the best Labour prime minister of the United Kingdom in the twentieth century. Attlee was a calm individual whose political profile had been forged, among other elements, by the complex question of non-intervention in the Spanish Civil War.[39] The war had been the hinge on which his policy of opposition to rearmament swung towards positions, with respect to Spain, that were favorable to active support for the Republicans in the war. As Labour leader, he personally visited the International Brigades in Spanish territory. A battalion of the Brigades bore his

---

[37] Bowker to the Foreign Office, 22 July 1945, NAUK, FO 371–49589.
[38] See Bowker to Eden, 3 August 1945, NAUK, FO 371–49589.
[39] J. Bew, *Citizen Clem. A Biography of Atlee*, London, Riverrun, 2016, 201 & ff.

name.[40] In 1945, he became prime minister in a world very different to that of the 1930s. Great Britain was no longer an independent superpower, and the threat of the Soviet Union and post-war instability loomed over the country's future and that of all Europe. Its relationship with the United States would perhaps not be so poetic as that which had bound Churchill and Roosevelt. Attlee was a realist and, beyond the lack of enthusiasm he may have felt for some decisions coming from the White House or his apprehension with respect to the results of an aggressive policy of blocs, his main fear was that, eventually, the United States would revert to an isolationist foreign policy.[41] Great Britain was no longer in a position to fill that possible vacuum, and so, in the final analysis, leaving ideology aside, in foreign policy terms he had to cling desperately to the facts. It was no small matter, bearing in mind that his election had also raised doubts across the Atlantic, where this could be seen as the beginning of Great Britain's inexorable slide down the path of socialism.[42] Furthermore, apart from Spain, while the Atlee government was at the same time laying the basis of the modern British welfare state, combating post-war deprivation and moving forward in the reform of the Commonwealth, it also had to address the complex elements of the economic relationship with the United States such as the end of the Lend-Lease program.[43] There were too many fronts open and Spain, in a wider analysis, was just one more. It is true that, due to the historic significance of the Civil War in the recent history of the labor movement itself, Spain was one of the questions that most agitated the party's backbenchers and was most likely to be addressed from their ideological perspective.

Against this background, with the ascent of the Labour party to power, Francoism could only feel the greatest apprehension. This apprehension, naturally, was centered on the new foreign secretary, Ernest Bevin,[44] who would prove himself to be sensible, realistic, and efficient in the post. It is to another profile that we should be paying attention. In the often admirable world of British politics, Bevin was the candidate supported (apparently enthusiastically) for the post by no less than his predecessor, Anthony Eden. We have before us a man of contrasts, undoubtedly brilliant and with an atypical profile. Bevin was, to begin with, the closest friend and political ally of the new prime minister. Atlee himself, after his retirement, said quite clearly: "My relationship with Ernest Bevin was the deepest of my political life

---

[40] J. Bew, *Citizen Clem...*, 201 & ff.

[41] P. Weiler, *Ernest Bevin*, London, Routledge Revivals, 2016, 149.

[42] J. Bew, *Citizen Clem...*, 371.

[43] Ibid., 371 & ff.

[44] On the figure of Bevin, see A. Bullock, *Ernest Bevin. A Biography*, London, Oxford University Press , 2001; and also of interest: J. Saville, *The Politics of Continuity. British Foreign Policy and the Labour Government (1945–1946)*, London, Verso Books, 1993.

GREAT BRITAIN, SPAIN, AND THE NEW WORLD ORDER   283

[…] Ernest embodied, and indeed was the embodiment of common sense."[45] Though forged in the heat of the British trade union movement and of his ideological commitment, the strongman at the Foreign Office did not in many ways respond to the cliché of a typical Labour politician. On a worldly level, his style was far from that of a tough trade union leader:

> He was a committed democrat yet a tough authoritarian; a socialist yet an imperialist; a fervent patriot as well as an ardent internationalist; a trade union leader and working-class icon who became thoroughly middle class, even pan class. By the 1930s there was no cloth cap but instead a bowler hat, cigars, well-cut suits and an art deco apartment in Kensington. During the war, he even joined the Garrick Club. Yet, to the end, he was unseduced by money and status. The Garrick membership was mostly to hob-nob with actor managers from the world entertainment like J. Arthur Rank, Basil Dean and Seymour Hicks, pan-class impresarios like himself, who became his friends and even family connections.[46]

Even more surprising, if possible, was the imperialistic zeal shown by Bevin as foreign secretary, when he defended with unusual vigor the maintenance of British international power through the perpetuation of the greater part of the empire. There is consensus among historians on this point. Bevin believed that the only way in which Great Britain would not fall to the status of a second-rank power was to maintain the British imperial position in the Middle East and Asia, as the main benefactor power, and to support similar efforts by other European colonialist powers such as France and the Netherlands.[47] This surprising support for the continuance of empire was born, among other considerations, of a pessimistic view of the future of Europe with respect to the Soviet Union. Bevin, the Labour politician, knew that, to stop Moscow, the necessary, indispensable ally was the United States:

> Given this situation, the British had only one place to turn for help, the United States, which had emerged from the war as by far the strongest military alliance, however, relations between Britain and the United States were uneasy. American policy-makers had long disliked and resented British colonialism and regarded the sterling bloc, which tied present and former colonies to Britain economically, as a threat to the open world economy that they saw as the key to future American prosperity and world peace. Such attitudes complicated the Foreign Office's desire to "make use of American power for the purposes which we regard as good", as one official had put it toward the end of the war.[48]

[45] A. Adonis, *Ernest Bevin. The Labour Churchill*, London, Biteback, 2020, XIV.
[46] Ibid, XIII.
[47] P. Weiler, *Ernest Bevin*, 146 & ff.
[48] Ibid, 149.

Washington was also to the Labour party (as it largely was to the Conservatives) the capital of a young power that needed to be molded and guided. The analysis was not wrong. Until the arrival of George C. Marshall at the Department of State in January 1947, the structure and sophistication of the department could not be compared with the experience and pedigree of the Foreign Office. Truman's first secretary of state, Joseph F. Brynes, was a politically weak character, especially in comparison to his successors, Marshall, Acheson, and Stettinius. Brynes did not impose changes on the country's foreign policy to reflect its new global responsibilities. At the time, a senior U.S. diplomat described the Department of State as a marginalized, inefficient organization with excessively low morale.[49]

Soon, that young power would mature sufficiently to be able to dictate the policy of its allies ever more energetically. The case of Spain, in Bevin's international view, was not a keystone, but it was a faithful reflection of that reality. A useful microcosm to understand the vicissitudes of British foreign policy of the time.

Spain: Isolated… But With No Clear Strategy

But let us return to Spain. The final declaration of the Potsdam conference had explicitly excluded Spain from the "New World Order" that was beginning to emerge. The declaration by the U.S., U.K., and Soviet governments had advised against the entry of Spain into the newly created United Nations Organization, founded in April of that year in San Francisco:

> The three Governments feel bound however to make it clear that they for their part would not favour any application for membership put forward by the present Spanish Government, which, having been founded with the support of the Axis Powers, does not, in view of its origins, its nature, its record and its close association with the aggressor States, possess the qualifications necessary to justify such membership.[50]

As Victor Mallet would shortly inform London, the declaration, together with the Labour victory, had caused a real crisis within Spanish politics, as the British press attaché, Thomas Burns, confirmed in a private conversation with the new foreign minister, who was very concerned at the possibility that the Western powers might lend legitimacy to a provisional government

---

[49] See *El Cerco Aliado…*, 191.

[50] The Berlin (Potsdam) Conference, 17 July – 2 August 1945. (a) Protocol of the Proceedings, 1 August 1945, http://avalon.law.yale.edu/20th_century/decade17.asp, accessed 9 September 2021.

that was in favor of the restoration of the Republic. Mallet attached an incisive memorandum from Burns to his telegram, noting that the change of government in London had for the first time introduced the question of time, of urgency, into the complex equation of Spanish policy, during a period of internal movement that was at its most convulsive since the end of the Civil War. In his opinion, that sense of urgency for change should be left to do its work, without applying external pressure, and for the Spanish people to join together in support of the regime despite its disrepute, rather than a new Civil War. It should not be forgotten that, at almost the same time, in Mexico, the provisional republican government of José Giral was being established.[51]

On 8 August, Mallet sent a personal letter from San Sebastián, to where the government had moved for the traditional Ministerio de Jornada, the custom, continued by Franco, of government business being conducted in the Basque city by ministers accompanying the king, to Frederick Holler-Millar, a perspicacious diplomat who had recently arrived from Washington and was now installed as the head of the European desk at the Foreign Office. In the confidence of a personal letter, Mallet revealed his deepest perception of Spanish affairs as a recent arrival. In it, the ambassador reiterated the real fear of the regime of the possibility of British support for Juan Negrín or Indalecio Prieto, as traumatic replacements for Franco. Neither of them, in Mallet's view, enjoyed sufficient support in the country to constitute a serious option. Any false step in Spain, noted the ambassador, could trigger a new European conflict, and so it was in his opinion better to continue with the policy of containment of an abject, but ultimately inoffensive, regime, that was not even able to maintain a constant electricity supply in Madrid. After their first meeting, Mallet defined Franco as a "smiling villain – rather absurdly unlike the popular idea of a dictator with his Pekingese goggle eyes and fat tummy and short legs. Artajo is bulky and serious but probably a good chap, though a Jesuit."[52] In another personal letter, four days previously, to another illustrious official at the Foreign Office, Oliver Harvey, as well as highlighting the positive understanding he had with his U.S. counterpart (who traveled from Madrid to San Sebastián to receive him), Mallet noted that the Potsdam conference and the change of government in London had, without doubt, encouraged the generals to think in terms of a change of regime, should that become necessary.[53]

---

[51] Mallet to Bevin, 10 August 1945, NAUK, FO 371–49589. (Attachment to the memorandum of Tom Burns). Russia had shown special interest in including an explicit reference to Spain. See the note by D. Holler-Millar of 8 August, NAUK, FO 371–49613.

[52] Mallet to Holler-Millar, 8 August 1945, NAUK, FO 371–49613.

[53] Mallet to Oliver Harvey, 4 September 1945, NAUK, FO 371–49589.

286 EMILIO SÁENZ-FRANCÉS

On 7 August, a memorandum to the new foreign secretary, Ernest Bevin (regarding the resignation of the duke of Alba from his position as ambassador in London, following the petition made to that effect by Don Juan to the Spanish nobility), proposed that Bevin should inform Alba, as a fact, that it would be impossible to maintain a cordial relationship between the United Kingdom and Spain so long as Franco and the Falange remained in power.[54] An escalation that was perhaps symbolic, but coherent with the changes that the British had so far requested, which, as noted above, required a change in the nature of the regime, but not necessarily the removal of the Caudillo from power. One week later, on 15 August, Bevin informed the embassy in Washington of the willingness of different Latin American republics (Chile, Peru, Venezuela) to take some unspecified form of action with respect to Spain, but that possibly involved breaking off relations. Before taking any step, they wished to hear the opinion of the British government. The Foreign Office wanted to inform the Department of State of the (eloquent) response it was giving to these questions:[55]

> [T]he present British Government [...] would only be too glad to see the disappearance of the present regime from Spain. At the same time, they have no intention of intervening actively to bring about Franco's forcible removal or his replacement by any particular alternative government. They think the choice of any alternative form of government is a matter for the Spanish people themselves, and they think it is important to avoid any action which could be regarded as direct intervention in Spanish internal affairs. Any such intervention would, they think, only rally Spanish opinion behind Franco or, more likely, encourage the outbreak of civil war. The latter eventually must be avoided at all costs.[56]

On 20 August, Bevin spoke to Parliament for the first time about Spain, declaring the policy of the government. It was in the debate on the king's speech to both chambers, the first since Labour took power:

> May I now turn to a very popular subject -Spain- A good deal has been said in this Debate about General Franco and the Spanish question. I will briefly quote His Majesty's Government's view. It is that the question of the régime in Spain is one for the Spanish people to decide. I cannot go further than the declaration issued at the Berlin Conference, which makes it plain that while we have no

---

[54] Note for the Secretary of State on the Spanish Ambassador, 7 August 1945, NAUK, FO 371–49549.

[55] Foreign Office to Washington, 15 August 1945, NAUK, FO 371–49549.

[56] Foreign Office to Washington, 15 August 1945, NAUK, FO 371–49549.

GREAT BRITAIN, SPAIN, AND THE NEW WORLD ORDER 287

desire permanently to penalise the Spanish people, we cannot admit Spain into the club, unless she accepts the basic principles of the club. These are the rights of peoples freely to choose their own form of government. On the other hand, I am satisfied that intervention by foreign Powers in the internal affairs of Spain would have the opposite effect to that desired, and would probably strengthen General Franco's position. It is obvious from what I have said that we shall take a favourable view if steps are taken by the Spanish people to change their régime, but His Majesty's Government are not prepared to take any steps which would promote or encourage civil war in that country. In this, I know, I am voicing the views not only of myself but of many ardent Spanish Republicans.[57]

Nothing new, perhaps, or revolutionary under the pale London sun ... and perhaps, for that reason alone, Martín Artajo, who received the British ambassador shortly after hearing the speech on the BBC, could not hide his relief from Mallet. There was nothing in Bevin's words, despite the direct reference to Spanish Republicans, that supposed an imminent threat to the regime. Artajo, as well as being grateful for the reasonable tone used by Bevin, even hailed the speech as part of the long tradition of memorable addresses by British statesmen.[58] The minister, in effect, saw his government and his country as being on a knife's edge.

From September onwards, Mallet would speak with Martín Artajo on different occasions regarding the future of relations between the two countries.[59] In these talks, the direct intervention of the UN in Spain and support for revolutionary action to bring about political change in the country was ruled out, but all Spanish claims regarding the evolution of the regime, its peaceful nature, and the regime's legitimacy resulting from its domestic support or economic success were rejected.[60]

Meanwhile, the United States had opted for a much more aggressive policy, and Ambassador Armour had directly informed Martín Artajo that it was impossible to achieve positive relations between the two countries if Franco remained in power.[61] Harry S. Truman's hostility to the Franco regime, as was Roosevelt's previously, was radical.[62] The possibility of a change of regime

---

[57] The complete text of the speech can be found at: https://api.parliament.uk/historic-hansard/commons/1945/aug/20/debate-on-the-address#S5CV0413P0_19450820_HOC_31, accessed 15 September 2021.

[58] Mallet to the Foreign Office, 22 August 1945, NAUK, FO 371–49459.

[59] See Mallet to Bevin, 1 September 1945, NAUK, FO 371–49459.

[60] See Mallet to Bevin, 1 September 1945, NAUK, FO 371–49613.

[61] Mallet to the Foreign Office, 1 September 1945, NAUK, FO 371–49613.

[62] On this question, see the relevant contributions by Joan María Thomàs in this volume.

could be achieved, in British eyes, day by day, but to the Americans it was a more tangible (theoretical) possibility. The means, and their scope, were altogether different. The United States flirted with a frontal strategy; Britain favoured moderation and gradual change, despite the domestic pressures faced by the Labour government.

And so it was. Practically simultaneously with the opening of the political year in Madrid, the trade unions and other labor-leaning associations in Britain began to pressure the Foreign Office to cut all relations with Francoist Spain and not to enable the survival of fascism in Europe. To quote briefly just a few examples, the National Council for Civil Liberties wrote to Bevin on 4 September in this regard; on 24 September, representatives of the Transport & General Workers Union and the International League for the Rights of Man, on 19 October, both did the same.[63] The Foreign Office had to operate in a context in which its main ally, the United States, favored a more hardline policy, as did part of British public opinion, and the most belligerent of the Western Allies, France. Of all these, Great Britain was undoubtedly the most realistic but, even so, it was unable to do other than to join the policy then in vogue, to isolate Franco, or even to bring him down. The new world order did not appear willing to tolerate a stronghold of the past in Francoist Spain. The rapid escalation of tension between the blocs sparked by the Cold War helped to modify that panorama.

Against this background, Spain's period of international isolation began on 12 December 1946 with the decision of the main powers to recall their ambassadors from the country, the fruit of a resolution to that effect by the UN General Assembly. Before that, the siege surrounding Franco and his continuity in power saw significant events, mainly the condemnation of the regime on 4 March 1946 by the United Kingdom, the United States, and France, in the context of the escalation of tension between the regime and the French Republic, which led to the closure of the Pyrenean border in the autumn of 1945. Its text was fundamentally ambiguous, but did not lack extremely harsh words in some of its passages:

> The Governments of France, the United Kingdom and the United States of America have exchanged views with regard to the present Spanish Government and their relations with the regime. It is agreed that so long as General Franco continues in control of Spain, the Spanish people cannot anticipate full and cordial association with those nations of the world which have, by common effort, brought defeat to German Nazism and Italian Fascism, which aided the present Spanish regime in its rise to power and after which that regime was patterned.

[63] See NAUK, FO 371–49613.

GREAT BRITAIN, SPAIN, AND THE NEW WORLD ORDER

There is no intention of interfering in the internal affairs of Spain. The Spanish people themselves must in the long run work out their own identity. In spite of the present regime's repressive measures against the orderly efforts of the Spanish people to organize and give expression to their political aspirations, the three Governments are hopeful that the Spanish people will not again be subjected to the horrors and bitterness of civil strife.

On the contrary it is hoped that leading patriotic and liberal-minded Spaniards may soon find the means to bring about a peaceful withdrawal of Franco, the abolition of Falange, and the establishment of an interim or caretaker government under which the Spanish people may have an opportunity of freedom to determine the type of government they wish to have and to choose their leaders. Political amnesty, the return of exiled Spaniards, freedom of assembly and political association and provision for free public elections are essential. An interim government which would be and would remain dedicated to these ends should receive the recognition and support of all freedom-loving peoples.

Such recognition would include full diplomatic relations and the taking of such practical measures to assist in the solution of Spain's economic problems as may be practicable in the circumstances prevailing.

Such measures are not now possible. The question of the maintenance or termination by the Governments of France, the United Kingdom and the United States of diplomatic relations with the present Spanish regime is a matter to be decided in the light of the events and after taking into account the efforts of the Spanish people to achieve their own freedom.[64]

The antagonism of France towards Spain in the preceding months was, without doubt, a major headache for the Foreign Office, and undermined any willingness of the Western powers to coordinate their positions in the face of the radically hostile attitude of the Soviet Union and its satellites towards Spain. The declaration, it should be noted, stated that it was for the Spanish people to decide their own future and rejected any interference by the powers in that process, but also that, as soon as the country had a liberal democratic government, Spain would become fully integrated into the Western community of nations.

---

[64] U.S. Department of State, *The Spanish Government, and the Axis*, Department of State Publication 2483, European Series 8, Washington D.C., Government Printing Office, 1946, https://avalon.law.yale.edu/subject_menus/spmenu.asp.

Undoubtedly, the most significant development was that Moscow (with Poland as a proxy) took the Spanish question to the UN Security Council in April (as already mentioned). Thus began what we could call a magna-ceremony of international confusion that had, on the one hand, Spain at its center and, on the other, that brought to light how control of the threads of international diplomacy were slipping from the fingers of the Foreign Office. The story is well known. Though the question had germinated sometime previously (France had already shown enthusiasm for the possibility), it was in April 1946 that the Polish delegation, at the thirty-fourth session of the Security Council, asked for the "Spanish problem" to be included on the agenda, as a possible threat to peace or a potential source of aggression. In March, the British embassy in Washington had informed the Department of State of its government's opposition to taking the Spanish question to the Security Council, as suggested by the French government.[65] The American attitude was much less categorical in this regard.

After a tug-of-war in which the Security Council was split in two, it was agreed to create an investigative subcommittee to assess the threat that Spain might pose to world peace, of which Australia, Brazil, China, France, and Poland itself would be members.[66] One of the main fears of the Foreign Office was that the subcommittee could decide to turn its task into a public hearing on Spain and of its policy during the Second World War.[67] It appears that this option really was on the table, with names such as Samuel Hoare among the possible witnesses to be called. That would have converted its deliberations into a *de facto* courtroom.[68] It should not be forgotten that it was precisely at this moment when his famous memoirs *Ambassador on Special Mission* were first published.[69] The British government gathered information directly from the government in Madrid to submit to the subcommittee to demon-strate that any threat by Spain to world peace was very feeble. For example, it reported on the military capacity of the Spanish army in 1946. A telegram sent by Victor Mallet to the Foreign Office stated that it had, according to the Spanish authorities, 450,000 troops, of which 150,000 were concentrated on

---

[65] U.S. Department of State, Aide Memoire of the British Embassy in Washington, 18 March 1946, State Department 852.00/3–1846, https://history.state.gov/historical-documents/frus1946v05/d721, accessed 12 September 2021. On the U.S. attitude to the Spanish question, as addressed at the UN, see A. Jarque Iñiguez, "Estados Unidos ante el caso español en la ONU, 1945–1950," *REDEN: Revista Española de Estudios Norteamericanos*, n. 7 (1994), 157–174.

[66] See Cadogan to the Foreign Office, 25 April 1946, NAUK, CAB 121–541.

[67] On the Foreign Office and the work of the subcommittee, see NAUK, CAB 121–541.

[68] New York to the Foreign Office, 4 May 1946, NAUK, CAB 121–541.

[69] See Hoare, *Ambassador on Special Mission.*

GREAT BRITAIN, SPAIN, AND THE NEW WORLD ORDER

the border in the Pyrenees. According to the Polish authorities, the Spanish army apparently had over 200,000 troops just in Catalonia. Mallet's figures reduced this contingent to 60,000.[70]

Finally, though these and other dangers that might have destabilized the fragile Spanish position were averted, it is no less true that the resolution of the General Assembly of 12 December 1946 was a hard, almost unprecedented blow, exposing as perhaps never before the diplomatic underbelly of the Francoist regime. In effect, the resolution represented a net international condemnation of the regime, picturing it as a potential threat to peace, for which reason it should be excluded from any organization of the UN. At all events, what has certainly remained in the memory of those years was the departure from Spain of the greater part of the ambassadors accredited in Madrid.

It is no less true that what can be detected in a reading of Foreign Office documentation held in the U.K. National Archives is significant British frustration[71] with a process that they had not been able to control – a process in which the Soviet Union and its allies had played their cards much more skillfully and, above all, with nothing to lose. With respect to the United States, Xavier Hualde speaks of a calculated policy by which "Franco could be pressured, but only up to a point"[72], and never to the point of entering into the Soviet Union's game.[73] The British were, as we have seen, more fatalistic with respect to the results so far of addressing the Spanish case in the UN. A telegram to the Foreign Office from the ambassador in Moscow, Frank Roberts, who had been instrumental in Spanish affairs during the war, broached this reality more deeply, and at the same time addressed the ambivalent position of France with respect to the designs of the Soviet government.[74] In early April, Roberts wrote again, this time to Frederick Hoyer Millar, head of the European desk at the Foreign Office. The incisive Roberts noted that the Soviet strategy towards Spain was to create a climate in which the British and Americans designed their policy as a function not of their interests, but of their prior ideological position. They were achieving success in this task.[75] Roberts was a first-rate intellect, and his comment perhaps allows us to perceive a veiled criticism of his government and the interference in its actions that could be caused by pressure from the Labour bases to take a harder foreign policy line with Spain.

---

[70] See Mallet to the Foreign Office, 3 Mauy 1945, NAUK, CAB 121–541.
[71] See *El Cerco Aliado...*, 144 & ff.
[72] Ibid., 145.
[73] Ibid.
[74] Cfr. Roberts to the Foreign Office, 3 March 1946, NAUK, FO 371–60453.
[75] Cfr. Roberts to Hoyer Millar, 1 April 1946, NAUK, FO 371–60453.

During all of 1946, the British tried to extract some type of commitment from Martín Artajo with respect to possible regime change in Spain, which might relieve the tension at UN meetings. Franco, through his minister, went on procrastinating. The telegram from Victor Mallet to London, of 10 July, after a meeting between him and his U.S. counterpart with the head of Spanish foreign policy, is eloquent:

> In the course of my interview with Minister of Foreign Affairs yesterday my United States colleague and I asked if he could tell us anything more regarding the prospects of political evolution here. The minister who had just returned from a week-end in the country with Franco, said that closing of the French frontier and meetings of UNO had delayed political evolution by at least five months.[76]

Almost immediately, after the UN resolution, the United States decided not to replace its ambassador (until 1945, Norman Armour).[77] The embassy at the time was vacant. Normal relations between the parties would not be re-established until 1951. The British did the same, and Douglas F. Howard, a skillful diplomat, took control of the British mission in Madrid. In 1949, Robert Hankey would relieve him in the post. All of which are well-known events that it is not necessary to address here. Our objective, though, does include an analysis of how British policy was formulated in this situation, and how it was that from 1947 to 1949, the Foreign Office led a lukewarm, uncoordinated campaign to promote a peaceful change of regime in Spain in opposition to the short-term, as we shall see, but increasingly radical efforts of the Department of State.

1947. A Turning Point

The year 1947 was thus a turning point. And one that would show how far British foreign policy had become subsidiary, in both time and form, to U.S. policy. During that year, the United States would swing between considering relatively radical options to remove Franco, distilled in the meeting between Salvador de Madariaga and State Department officials on 10 March, to the emergence of a new realism coinciding with the appointment of George Marshall as secretary of state. The consequences of that change are known and were tectonic: the launch of the Truman Doctrine and the Marshall Plan, the passing of the new National Security Act and, with respect to Spain, the

---

[76] See Howard to the Foreign Office, 10 July 1946, NAUK, FO 371–60453.

[77] Armour would be appointed undersecretary of state by George C. Marshall, and it is evident that his first-hand knowledge of the Franco regime would help to mold the political change with respect to Spain that began a few months later.

start of a gradual redeployment from openly hostile positions towards the Franco regime. The consequences of that March meeting were, above all, a swansong. It was held with Marshall already in place at the Department of State and profound changes taking place in its organization and policies. But in the short term, the Americans appeared to be strongly backing regime change. That is how the situation was read in London. As Florentino Portero tells, on 7 April, the Department of State sent the Foreign Office a new proposal for action on Spain, which involved letting Franco know that both British and Americans considered it necessary for him to give up power rapidly (Winston Churchill was proposed for this important task). Contact would be established with the army and the opposition to facilitate the formation of an interim regime that would call elections and would receive the political and economic support of the British and American governments. Oil supplies to Spain would be embargoed as additional pressure.[78] In the following weeks, the Department of State constantly and intensively pressed Britain to join in the launch of this diplomatic maneuver, which met with the head-on opposition of the British.[79] Given the apprehension that this type of initiative generated in the Foreign Office, it is perhaps for this reason that London opted for the middle path of promoting understanding between José María Gil Robles and Indalecio Prieto, which we shall now address.

In effect, the most notable feature of this dubitative British strategy (which we believe was intended to contain the Department of State) was the quest for understanding between Indalecio Prieto, as the equivocal Republican leader, and the monarchists of José María Gil Robles, with Don Juan de Borbón as an active party to the agreement. Our thesis is that this swansong of autonomous British foreign policy with respect to Spain was fundamentally reactive and sought to find a viable, moderate response in place of the approach the Department of State had taken in April. It was, furthermore, a way for the Labour government to express its natural hostility to the Franco regime.

As Xavier Hualde once again indicates, between 15 and 18 October 1947, José María Gil Robles and Indalecio Prieto held four meetings in London, an initiative promoted by the Foreign Office, which was to open the door to the orderly removal of Franco from power. General Aranda, the senior conspirator within the regime, worked behind the scenes as the supposed representative of the interests of Don Juan in Spain.

The contacts bore fruit in a joint memorandum delivered personally by Gil Robles to the Foreign Office.[80] The conclusions had been merely an expression

---

[78] See *Franco Aislado…*, 237 & ff. Also, *El Cerco Aliado…*, 177–178.

[79] Ibid.

[80] Foreign Office to Lord Inverchapel (Archibald Clark Kerr, British Ambassador to the United States), 12 November 1947, NAUK, CAB 21–4859.

of the vacuous good will of both parties in which, according to Gil Robles, the best option to bring down Franco was a joint petition to the signatory powers of the tripartite declaration of March 1946, with the crucial support of the Vatican and, at all events, of the Latin American states.[81] All of this was without having reached an agreement regarding the form of the regime or the steps that must be taken to constitute it after the fall of the Caudillo. At least from Aranda's perspective, a key point of friction made it impossible to create a true front uniting monarchists and socialists. A memorandum sent to London some weeks before the commencement of the contacts, commenting on a meeting with Aranda, noted the trembling precautions of the general, and that he was an unreliable spokesman for the sentiments of the military, and also noted the political sensitivities of the pretender, observing that these sectors would never look approvingly on the replacement of Franco by a provisional government that would shortly hold a referendum on the type of government to be established in Spain. The risk, said Aranda, was for the government to fall into the hands of a radical left-wing coalition by a fixed date.[82] A ceremony of confusion.

On 22 November 1947, a disappointed Bevin informed the *chargé d'affaires* in Madrid of the inconclusive results of the talks, which he defined as confused, and that prevented the United Kingdom from firmly giving determined backing to the opposition. It was necessary to wait, he said, for a complete, viable plan drawn up by the opposition, covering both the means necessary to bring down Franco and the process by which a new regime was to be constituted.[83] It should be added that, a few days later, Bevin met Don Juan de Borbón himself at Buckingham Palace. Despite the requests made to the pretender for discretion about the meeting and its nature, on 2 December George VI's private secretary, Allan Lascelles (an interesting figure who has today become famous as a protagonist in the early seasons of the series *The Crown*), sent a note to the Foreign Office in which he mentioned the open indiscretion of Don Juan regarding the content of the meeting. Lascelles reported that he had told the pretender in no uncertain terms that he should "bite his tongue."[84] It is fairly certain that the indiscretion involved, at least, the Peruvian ambassador in London. Apparently, Don Juan, as well as acknowledging that the meeting had taken place, also declared that he had been favorably impressed with Bevin, who informed him of the contacts between Prieto and Gil Robles. However, said the count of Barcelona, his impression was that the British were underestimating

---

[81] Memorandum from Gil Robles to Bevin, 18 October 1947, NAUK, FO 371–7337.

[82] Memorandum of the British Embassy on the talks between Bd. Malley and Gen. Aranda, 9 September 1946, NAUK, FO 371–7337.

[83] Bevin to Howard (Madrid), 22 September 1947, NAUK, FO 371–7337.

[84] Lascelles to Dixon, 2 December 1947, NAUK, FO 371–7337.

GREAT BRITAIN, SPAIN, AND THE NEW WORLD ORDER   295

Franco's intelligence.[85] In that, Don Juan was not wrong, but the British were not, in the end, overly impressed with the reliability of the pretender.

The Foreign Office failed to find a middle way between inaction and the maximalism of the Department of State. But by now, with George Marshall and his team in Washington bringing a new focus to relations with Spain, which saw understanding with Franco and his regime as necessary, the reforms that Marshall introduced were already clearly being implemented. In effect, in October 1947, a new agency (the Policy Planning Staff) within a reformed Department of State radically vitalized by Marshall submitted the draft of a new policy towards Spain that would receive the support of the secretary of state. President Truman, though loath to do so, approved it and it became doctrine of U.S. foreign policy.[86]

A year later, on 14 November 1949, Ernest Bevin sent the first, very paternal, instructions to the new *chargé d'affaires* in Spain, Robert Hankey. In them, a very sincere Bevin acknowledged that the decision by the General Assembly to recall its ambassadors from Spain had been counter-productive just as, he claimed, he himself had foreseen from the beginning. It had strengthened Franco's position and, noted Bevin, it was difficult to reverse that resolution without seeming to give the impression of backing the Caudillo. In short, the years of international isolation had hardly achieved any significant changes or improvements in the situation in Spain with respect to the Allied powers. In one of the more revealing paragraphs, the foreign secretary encouraged Hankey to explore any path that might possibly lead to peaceful regime change:

> General Franco's regime is oppressive, reactionary and totalitarian. If there were means of bringing about peacefully its replacement by a more acceptable regime His Majesty's Government would be glad to grasp, then; and you should report to me any evidence you may see of such a possibility. At present the prospects of a change appear particularly remote, and the best we can reasonably look for is some gradual improvement in the character of the exiting regime.[87]

Once again, nothing came of this. The static panorama described by Bevin was not, though, entirely accurate. The United States had been pressuring Britain since 1948 to accept a revocation, even though it was only partial, of the 1946 resolution, and allow the ambassadors to return to Madrid.[88] In the 1948 annual review, drawn up by Douglas F. Howard, Hankey's predecessor in Madrid, Howard had not only made that reality patently clear, but also the

---

[85] Cristhwaite to Douglas, 1 December 1947, NAUK, FO 371–7337.

[86] See *El Cerco Aliado...*, 196–204.

[87] Bevin to Hankney, 14 November 1949, NAUK, FO 361–79698.

[88] See, for example, Hoyer-Millar to I. Mallet, 13 July 1949, NAUK, FO 361–79697.

improvement in relations between Spain and France, which contrasted with the deterioration in Hispano-British relations:

> The end of the year left him [Franco] hoping, not without some excuse, that the discovery of Spain by the American Chiefs of Staff (like Columbus in reverse) would produce dollars just in time to save the Spanish economy [...] in other words, that the fabulous luck of the Caudillo would play its best turn yet. [...]

> 3. As far as her relations with the Western democracies were concerned, the most important factor from Spain's point of view was the growing desire in the United States to bring her into the defence system of Western Europe. [...]

> From France, too, came many signs if not of a swing in favour of Spain, at least of a realisation in official quarters that a policy of active hostility towards this country was not in the best interest of France herself. The Pyrenean frontier was officially reopened in February, while a commercial and payments agreement was signed on the 8th of May. [...]

> 5. Their success in so doing was the more conspicuous by contrast with the tenor of Anglo –Spanish relations, with continued to deteriorate through the year.[89]

The United States had, definitively, changed the script, and the United Kingdom found itself out of step with respect to Spain.

***

In August 1949, a Foreign Office memorandum rated the policy implemented towards Spain since 1946 as a failure, with not only political but also economic effects on the United Kingdom. The report considered one last possible attempt to remove Franco from power. It is not easy to understand how this proposal would fit in with the new international scenario, which was increasingly favorable to reaching an understanding with the Caudillo. A glimpse of the ideological heritage of Labourism? Another swansong, this time of the strategic autonomy of the Foreign Office? In this case, the plan was to use the general who, since the Second World War, had been the official backstage conspirator against Franco within the regime, the aforementioned General Antonio Aranda. The memorandum proposed to let the general know that the Allied powers would be willing to accept a post-Franco transition regime led by Aranda himself and other conservative

---

[89] Howard to Bevin, 14 February 1949, NAUK, DEFE 11–379.

GREAT BRITAIN, SPAIN, AND THE NEW WORLD ORDER 297

generals. France, Great Britain, and the United States would rein in the Republican and monarchists forces opposed to the regime outside Spain in order to avoid a bloodbath.[90] In short, the memorandum proposed, desperately, in our opinion, to accept a military solution in Spain, far from the parameters of regime evolution considered the only acceptable path in 1946 and 1947, with a commitment to contain the frustration and hostility of the monarchists and republican forces towards that new military order. It was, undoubtedly, a risky proposal ... and again, doomed to fail. A few days later, Aranda passed from active duty to the reserve. This was communicated to him personally by the former commander-in-chief of the Blue Division, Agustín Muñoz Grandes. It was clear that faint-hearted soldiers in lukewarm opposition to Franco were not about to solve the question of his removal from the Pardo Palace. Aranda, Kindelán and Varela were professional procrastinators, and the fact that the desperate option of some Foreign Office officials in 1949 was to give them a blank cheque simply demonstrates the scale of their lack of perspective.[91]

Topple Franco? The Caudillo Saved by Armageddon

Topple Franco? The option was perhaps never seriously enough considered in London or Washington for it to be a viable, effective possibility. But it should be asked up to what point the United Kingdom embarked on a given policy with respect to Spain through conviction – the fruit of the ideological heritage of the Labour government – or because it was forced to by a new dynamic in international relations, in which its interests were not only subsidiary to those of the United States, but were also fundamentally the result of the weakening of British political power at all levels. Our thesis is that – beyond the hostility of the labor movement to Franco's regime – British diplomacy in 1947 embarked on a strategy that was not entirely its own and that it had to abandon hastily in view of changes in American geostrategic priorities in Europe. British documentation of the time denotes a clear lack of faith in their own policy towards Spain.

It is paradoxical. In our view, the United Kingdom was compelled to adopt a more hardline policy than it would have desired towards the Franco regime – sacrificing at least part of its own economic and geostrategic interests in order to satisfy the United States. And before that policy, which if not imposed, then had in a way been forced by circumstances, could bear any fruit, the United Kingdom was obliged to abandon it for the same reasons: the needs of the United States. In fact, throughout 1948, the military factor became

---

[90] Policy towards Spain, 13 August 1949, NAUK, FO 361–79697.

[91] See G. Cardona, *Franco y sus Generales. La Manicura del Tigre*, Madrid, Temas de Hoy, 2001.

298 EMILIO SÁENZ-FRANCÉS

more significant in relations with Spain, and the tide turned in favour of the occupant of the Pardo Palace, culminating in 1951 with the normalization of diplomatic relations.

On 9 January 1951, *The Times* in London published news of the appointment of Sir John Balfour as ambassador plenary and plenipotentiary in Madrid. Thus ended five years of provisionality in Hispano-British relations. *The Times* article also mentioned what had led to this decision: the failure of the first attempt to normalize the situation in Spain in the General Assembly, unsuccessful as a result of British, French, and American opposition and, finally, the reversal of the 1946 resolution against Spain on 25 November, in the course of the Assembly meetings in 1950. The vote had been favorable to Spain, with thirty-eight votes in favour, ten against and twelve abstentions. Among them was the British vote, "but that was, it is thought, for tactical reasons within the Labour Party."[92]

The Attlee government had been pressured by the grassroots of the party up to the last minute to avoid the normalization of relations with Franco's Spain. On 14 February that year, Miguel Primo de Rivera, the brother of José Antonio, received the placet as ambassador in London. On 18 May, a memorandum of the first lord of the Admiralty suggested that the Royal Navy could once again make courtesy visits to Spanish ports.[93] Clement Attlee was dissatisfied with the change of stance with respect to Spain, which put him in a difficult position with Labour voters in an election year, and asked the embassy in Washington to express its regret at such a radical change of course. But he was also aware, we believe, that little could be expected of the fall or removal of Franco at that time. As he laconically commented regarding this question: "I think that we have done all we can."[94]

Ernest Bevin, ill and exhausted, as fond of excess as his Conservative alter ego, Winston Churchill, left the post of foreign secretary in March 1951. He remained in the government as minister without portfolio. He died in April.

On 25 October 1951, general elections were held in the United Kingdom. Churchill, who since the end of the Second World War had been skeptical of any active attempt to bring down or promote the fall of Franco, returned to Downing Street, further clarifying the panorama of Hispano-British relations. Before the elections, an extensive Foreign Office memorandum to the British cabinet (that is, the entire government), clearly stated the strategic need to move towards closer relations with Spain – for political, military and economic reasons – hand-in-hand with the United States. It was, therefore, a comprehensive renunciation of the policy followed by the United Kingdom since the Labour victory in 1945. The report concluded:

92 *The Times*, 9 January 1951.
93 Memorandum of the First Lord of the Admiralty, 18 May 1951, NAUK, CAB 4859.
94 Downing Street, Note to the Foreign Office, 13 July 1951, NAUK, FO 371–89571.

GREAT BRITAIN, SPAIN, AND THE NEW WORLD ORDER 299

1. It is strategically desirable that Spain should be more closely associated with the west.

2. It is strategically desirable that we should be associated with any bilateral United States–Spanish agreement.

3. It is economically and politically undesirable that Spain should become an exclusive client of the United States.

4. It is economically and politically desirable that we should be free to offer credits and that the ban on supplies of arms equipment should be reviewed.

5. It is politically undesirable that British and American policies should openly diverge, or that the Americans should pursue a policy without due regard to us.

6. It is politically and strategically undesirable that Western morale should be made to suffer a strain which would cancel any strategic advantages.

7. It is politically desirable that some degree of liberalisation should be achieved in Spain.[95]

And, as we have already commented, military considerations were crucial, and the United States thought of Spain purely in geopolitical terms, with the implications of the Cold War, which in Korea was becoming ever more torrid, and was threatening to set Europe and the Mediterranean ablaze. The priorities were exclusively military, the pre-eminence was American and the hour, an hour of need.

***

As we mentioned at the beginning of this chapter, in 1949 Spain's possible role in a nuclear confrontation between the Western powers and the Soviet Union had appeared in a report by the British Ministry of Defence. In it, the scenario of a nuclear war in Europe in 1951 was laid out in cold, thorough detail. On D-Day+90, Soviet forces would have crushed continental Europe as far as the Pyrenees. The use of atomic weapons would have been authorized. In a devastated planet, the West counted on being able to launch a counter-offensive from the peninsula on D-Day+24 months. To be able to defend

---

[95] Cabinet, Memorandum of the Secretary of State for Foreign Affairs, 29 June 1951, NAUK, PREM 8/1531.

the line of the Pyrenees, it was essential to count on Spain as an ally of the Western powers at the outbreak of the conflict. Even so, the defense would be an arduous task, and so the report included the possibility of launching a counter-attack in a scenario in which only the south of Spain remained in Allied hands.[96] A similar report, of 24 April 1951, widened the strategic need for Spanish support to the country's accession to NATO in the medium term.[97]

Great Britain had begun its journey down a path on which it ceased to be the hegemonic global power and became a subsidiary superpower of the United States. Its diplomatic efforts in Spain from 1939 had gone from its effectiveness in the supreme hour of need in 1940 and its masterful handling of wartime divisions in which, at the launch of Operation Torch, Spain was critical to the result of the conflict, to an inevitable feeling of frustration and resignation in the post-war period, when the baton of policy design had irreversibly passed to the other side of the Atlantic. Clement Atlee and Ernest Bevin's hopes of molding American foreign policy, of maintaining strategic autonomy with a view to a certain (backstage) hegemony, was dissolving at the same rate as the British empire.

The signing of the Pact of Madrid in 1953 in a way represented the final certification of the sunset of the golden age of British diplomacy in Spain. The regime, with the determined focus of its foreign policy not now on winning over London, as before, but on winning over the new masters in Washington, played its cards ambitiously in that city, as discussed in other chapters in this book, and opted to establish a true lobby on the banks of the Potomac that would allow it to engineer a position of certain political influence. Great Britain, which had been the cause of many sleepless nights for Franco over the years, became, tellingly and by now radically, a supporting player in the eyes of Spanish foreign policymakers in the Pardo and Santa Cruz palaces. It is also telling that, as soon as diplomatic relations between the Western powers and Spain were normalized, Spain began to toy with the idea of using the UN as a platform to seek the recovery of Gibraltar. No less than this was possible with the United States in command. The powerful new masters. But that is another story ....

[96] Short Term Strategy, A Campaign in Spain, 7 September 1949, NAUK, DEFE-379.

[97] Relationship of Spain to the Defence of Western Europe. 24-4-1951, NAUK, DEFE-379. The contents of this file, focused on essential aspects, are key to understanding the degree of American pressure on Great Britain up to 1951.

Sources

Archives

Archivo del Ministerio de Asuntos Exteriores y Cooperación. Reino de España
National Archives of the United Kingdom

Bibliography

Adonis, A., *Ernest Bevin. The Labour Churchill*, London, Biteback, 2020.
Alpert, M., "Las Relaciones Anglo-Hispanas en el Primer Semestre de la 'Guerra Caliente' La misión diplomática de sir Samuel Hoare," *Revista de Política Internacional*, vol. 160 (1978), 7–31.
Berlin (Potsdam) Conference, 17 July–2 August 1945. (a) Protocol of the Proceedings, 1 August 1945, http://avalon.law.yale.edu/20th_century/decade17. asp.
Bew, J., *Citizen Clem. A Biography of Atlee*, London, Riverrun, 2016.
Bullock, A., *Ernest Bevin. A Biography*, London, Oxford University Press, 2001.
Cardona, G., *Franco y sus Generales. La Manicura del Tigre*, Madrid, Temas de Hoy, 2001.
Carvajal, A., "Encuesta El Mundo Sigma Dos. Menos de la mitad de población aplaude la exhumación de Franco y un tercio se muestra en contra," *El Mundo*, 29 October 2019.
Centro de Investigaciones Sociológicas, "Estudio 2760. Memorias de la guerra civil y del franquismo, CIS, 16–04–2008," http://analisis.cis.es/cisdb. jsp?ESTUDIO=2760.
Collado Seidel, C., *El Telegrama que Salvó a Franco*, Barcelona, Crítica, 2016.
Colville, J. A., *La Sombra de Churchill, Diarios de Downing Street. 1939–1955*, Barcelona, Galaxia Gutenberg, 2007.
Cross, J. A., *Sir Samuel Hoare. A Political Biography*, London, Jonathan Cape, 1977.
Europa Press,"La audiencia media en TV superó los 7 millones de espectadores en la jornada de la exhumación de Franco, casi un 5% más," *Europa Press*, 25 October 2019.
Gómez de Jordana, F., *Milicia y diplomacia: Los diarios del Conde Jordana 1936–1944*, Burgos, Dossoles, 2002.
Hoare, S., *Ambassador on Special Mission*, London, Collins, 1946.
Hualde, X., *El Cerco Aliado. Estados Unidos, Francia y Gran Bretaña ante la Cuestión Española*, Bilbao, Universidad del País Vasco, 2016.
Jarque Iñiguez, A., "Estados Unidos ante el caso español en la ONU, 1945–1950," *REDEN: Revista Española de Estudios Norteamericanos*, vol. 7 (1994), 157–174.
Liddell Hart, B. *The Second World War*, Barcelona, Qaralt, 2006.
Lopez Zapico, M.A., "Against All odds. El diplomático Juan Francisco de Cárdenas durante la Guerra Civil Española y el primer franquismo," en A. C. Moreno Cantano (coord.), *Propagandistas y diplomáticos al servicio de Franco (1936–1945)*, Gijón, Trea, 2012, 303–331.
Lukaks, J., *Cinco días en Londres, mayo de 1940: Churchill solo frente a Hitler*, Madrid, Turner, 2001.

Matson, R. W., "Neutrality and Navicerts: Britain, the United States, and Economic Warfare, 1939–1940," *Journal of American History*, vol. 82, n. 2 (1995), 813–814.

Minder, R., "Plan to Exhume Franco Renews Spain's Wrestle With History," *New York Times*, 7 July 2018, https://www.nytimes.com/2018/07/07/world/europe/spain-franco.html?smid=tw-nytimesworld&smtyp=cur.

Portero, F., *Franco Aislado. La Cuestión Española (1945–1950)*, Madrid, Aguilar, 1989.

Portero, F. "Artajo. Perfil de un Ministro en Tiempos de Aislamiento," *Historia Contemporánea*, vol. 15 (1996), 201–224.

Roberts, A., *The Holy Fox. A Life of Lord Halifax*, London, Phoenix Press, 1999.

Rodao, F., *Franco y el Imperio Japonés*, Barcelona, Plaza & Janes, 2002.

Sáenz-Francés E., *Entre la Antorcha y la Esvástica. Franco en la Encrucijada de la Segunda Guerra Mundial*, Madrid, Actas, 2009.

Saville, J., *The Politics of Continuity. British Foreign Policy and the Labour Government (1945–1946)*, London, Verso Books, 1993.

Smyth, D., "Les Chevaliers de Saint-George; la Grande-Bretagne et la Corruption Des Généraux Espagnols (1940–1942)," *Guerres Mondiales et Conflits Contemporains*, vol. 162 (April 1992), 29–54.

Thomàs, J. M., *La Batalla del Wolframio. Estados Unidos y España de Pearl Harbor a la Guerra Fría (1941–1977)*, Madrid, Cátedra, 2010.

Thomàs, J. M., *Estados Unidos, Alemania, Gran Bretaña, Japón y sus relaciones con España entre la guerra y la postguerra (1939–1953)*, Madrid, Universidad Pontificia Comillas, 2016.

U.S. Department of State, Aide Memoire of the British Embassy in Washington, 18 March 1946, State Department 852.00/3-1846, https://history.state.gov/historicaldocuments/frus1946v05/d721.

U.S. Department of State, *The Spanish Government, and the Axis*, Department of State Publication 2483, European Series 8, Washington D.C., Government Printing Office, 1946, https://avalon.law.yale.edu/subject_menus/spmenu.asp.

Weiler, P. *Ernest Bevin*, London, Routledge Revivals, 2016.

INDEX

Abraham Lincoln Brigade 246, 247
Acció Catalana 280
Acheson, Dean
  Anti-Francoist stance and
    policies 74–76, 81, 118, 129,
    132, 141, 147, 155, 176, 196
  As State Secretary 284
  Change of attitude towards
    Spain 128, 137, 151, 200, 202,
    204, 209, 212, 220, 223–226,
    235
  Economic relations with Spain 62,
    136, 139, 140, 206, 226, 231
  Press release on Spain (1949) 146–149
  Religious liberty in Spain 173, 174,
    176
  Spanish officials' perceptions of 165,
    166
Achilles, Theodore C. 81, 95, 113, 114,
  181
  Attempts to remove Lequerica 157,
    163
  Meeting with Lequerica in
    1946 109–111
Ackerman, Ralph 48
Adams, Eva 183, 195
Aguirre, José Antonio de 128, 246, 247
Alba, Santiago 15
Alcalá Zamora, Niceto 15, 16
Aldrich, Winthrop W. 39, 48, 55, 62, 63,
  64, 102, 106
Alfonso XIII, King of Spain 15, 17
Alianza Catalana 280
Alianza Nacional de Fuerzas
  Democráticas 280
Allied Control Committee (ACC) 54,
  59, 60
Altos Hornos de Vizcaya (AHV) 58
American Chamber of Commerce in
  Spain 179
American Historical Association 103
Amsterdam's Hoppe Bank 14
Anderson, Clayton & Co. 57
Añaza, Manuel 7, 8, 10, 32–34, 37
Ara, Alfonso 24, 26
Aranda, Antonio (Spanish General) 293,
  294, 296, 297
Arburúa, Manuel 42
Areilza, José María de 92, 160, 162

Armour, Norman 80, 81, 87, 97, 101,
  107, 108, 111, 160, 161, 219, 277, 279,
  287, 292
Armstrong Cork 52
Atherton, Ray 134
Attlee, Clement 276, 282, 300
Austin, Warren 113, 132, 210
Aznar, Juan Bautista 14

Balfour, John 298
Banca Commerciale Italiana 14
Banco Hispano-Americano 28, 181
Banco Urquijo 28
Bank of America 14
Bank of France 21, 27
Bank of International Settlements
  (BIS) 13, 14, 18, 21
Bank of Spain 9, 12, 14, 20, 21, 23, 26,
  28, 31, 32, 34, 42 n.12, 43, 46, 62,
  185
Bankers Trust Co. 14
Banque de Paris et des Pays-Bas 14
Baraibar, Germán
  And the O'Konski Amendment 90,
    91
  Attacks by José Félix de
    Lequerica 161
  As chargé d'affaires in
    Washington 79, 98, 99, 101,
    109, 114, 155, 156
  Collaboration with José Félix de
    Lequerica 89, 107, 113, 117,
    137, 184 n.317
  Dismissal 99, 157, 159, 162, 164, 234
  United States change of position
    regarding Spain 116, 129, 154
Barkley, Alben W. 164
Barth, Alfred W. 41, 50, 55–58, 102, 104,
  107, 128
  And US Embassy in Madrid 48
  Arrival to Spain 48, 49
  Economic activities in Spain 53, 61,
    65, 66
  Granted the Order of Isabel la
    Católica 68, 69
  Meeting Francisco Franco 63, 64
  Origins and trajectory at Chase
    National Bank 47, 48, 101
  Relations with Jack Ryan 5, 61, 68

304 INDEX

Relations with José Félix de
Lequerica 181
Vice-presidency of the Chase
Manhattan Bank 68
Wall Street loan to Spain and further
loans 60, 62, 206
Baruch, Bernard 102, 164
Beaulac, William 46, 49
Behn, Sosthenes 26, 29, 31, 34, 101, 102
Berenguer, Dámaso 12
Bermúdez, Alejandro 42
Bevin, Ernest 116
Foreign affairs vision 282, 300
Illness 298
Policy towards Spain 284, 286–288,
294, 295
Style as Foreign Secretary 267, 268,
276, 282
Bigart, Homer 146, 150, 172
Biscailuz, Eugene 242
Bloque Catalán 280
Blue Division 249, 272, 275, 297
Borbón y Battenberg, Juan de 193 n.344,
293, 294
Bowers, Claude G. 7, 23, 26–30, 246
Bowker, Reginald James 275, 276, 278,
279–281
Bowron, Fletcher 243, 255, 257, 262
Bradley, Omar 200, 224, 225
Bretton Woods conference and
institutions 40, 53, 55, 68, 107
Brewster, Ralph Owen 77
And José Félix de Lequerica 102,
105, 115, 136, 137, 156, 208
And religious freedom in Spain 204,
295
Economic aid to Spain 123, 206
Supporting Spain as a lobbyist 84,
233, 106, 122, 127, 128, 138, 139,
142, 143, 148, 166, 179, 199, 233
Visiting Spain 183, 184, 186
Brewster, William Macy 97
Bridges, Styles 127, 167
Brown, Constantine 176–178, 218, 219
Brown, George Rothwell 178
Broz, Josip "Tito" 55, 190, 193
Bullitt, William 101, 118 n.143
Burleson, Omar T. 152
Butler, Sherwel G. 42, 64
Butterworth, Walt 46, 47, 101, 129
Buxton Jr., G. Edward 52
Byington Jr., Homer M. 215, 219, 220

Cacho Zabalza, Antonio 109, 130, 178,
189, 210, 211
Cain Jr., Charles 47, 48, 63, 64, 87, 199,
210
Calderón, Luis 24, 26, 30
Caldwell, Fred 101, 102
Calvo Sotelo, José 11, 21, 31, 93 n.53
CAMPSA 107
Carceller, Demetrio 281
Cárdenas, Juan Francisco de 45, 94, 95,
100, 159, 161, 162, 217, 219, 234, 271
Carr, Wilbur J. 14, 18
Carrero Blanco, Luis 85, 86
Castellane, Georges de 32
Castiella, Fernando María de 96
Central Hanover Bank 52
Central Vasco-Americano 246
Centro Oficial de Contratación de Moneda
(Official Center for Monetary
Transactions) 9
CEPSA 107
Chapaprieta, Joaquín 15, 28, 29, 31, 32
Chase National Bank 14, 43, 69, 101,
102, 104, 107
And Spanish Airports 39, 87
Criticism by José Félix de
Lequerica 62, 181
Freezing Axis assets 48
In relation with US Foreign
Policy 55, 56, 106, 198
Loans to Spain 39, 40, 41, 45, 46, 54,
59, 64, 66, 108, 140, 157, 198,
206
Merging with Equitable 47
Privileged relationships in Spain 65
Relationship with Antonio
Garrigues 60
Chavez, Dennis 79, 191, 221
Churchill, Winston 268, 280, 281
And US in relation to Spain 273, 282
Perceptions on Franco and his
regime 274–276
Relationship with the Duke of
Alba 271
Spain and Operation Torch 272
Clark, Charles Patrick 61, 70, 103,
122–128, 156, 166, 169, 170, 175,
176, 179, 180, 182, 184, 186, 189,
195, 197, 205
CNT (Confederación Nacional del
Trabajo) 280
Cochran, Horace Merle 8, 28, 29, 45
Cohen, Benjamin V. 121

INDEX 305

Columbia University   103, 246, 255
Comisión Nacional de Moneda
   Extranjera   43
Comité de Moneda Extranjera   43
Comité Interventor de los Cambios
   (Committee for Exchange
   Intervention or CIC)   101
Comité Oficial de Contratación de
   Moneda (Official Committee
   for Monetary Transactions -
   COCM)   9, 13, 21–24, 26, 28, 31,
   32–34
Compañía Hispanoamericana de
   Electricidad-CHADE   178
Confederación de Sindicatos Unidos   101
Connally, Tom   123, 133, 137–139, 141,
   191, 198, 200, 206
Connolly, Richard (US Admiral)   170,
   190, 191, 198, 200
Consejo Regulador de Operaciones del
   Cambio (Council for the Regulation
   of Exchange Operations or
   CROC)   21, 21
Consortium of Cotton Textile Industrialists
   (CITA)   66
Cooley, Harold D.   184
Coplon, Judith   125
Credit Suisse   14, 54
Crédito Italiano   14
Culbertson, Paul Trauger
   And military and economic assistance
      to Spain   86, 205
   As chargé d'affaires in Madrid   79,
      81, 82, 87, 95, 98, 99, 107, 108,
      135, 173, 196, 209, 213, 215, 234
   Meetings with Spanish officials   83,
      84, 114, 129, 134, 164, 167, 181
   Misgivings regarding José Félix de
      Lequerica   149, 152, 158,
      159–163, 167–170, 206, 207, 217,
      218, 220, 221
Culbertson, William Smith   102, 126
Cummings, Homer   125
Czechoslovakia   84, 91

Dasher, Charles   87
Degrelle, Léon   249
Del Amo, Jaime   243, 253
Dewey, Thomas E.   78, 103, 106, 107, 114,
   114, 133, 157
Dillon Read & Co.   14
Dollar–Peseta Program   40, 41, 61, 66
Donovan, William   49–51, 57

Dos Passos, John   247
Doussinague, José María   199
Dulles, John Foster   103, 135, 141, 177,
   178, 211, 212
Dunham, William B.   81, 83, 222, 233,
   234
Dunn, James C.   9, 30, 31, 228

Economic Cooperation
   Administration   88, 140, 222
Édouard Herriot   10
Empresa Nacional Torres Quevedo   181
Erice, José Sebastián de   82, 83, 159, 199,
   225
Esquerra Republicana   280
Estat Català Proletari   280
European Recovery Program   55, 82, 89,
   114, 132, 201, 244
Export-Import Bank (EIB)   22, 25, 30,
   44, 45, 51, 53, 59, 61, 62, 66

Falange (Political Party)   110, 132, 136,
   171, 265
   Protects Nazi collaborators hidden in
      Spain   249
   Report by Carlton Hayes   277
   Support by Franco   275
   U.S. demands its elimination   279,
      286, 289
   Women Section of the Falange
      (Sección Femenina)   185, 260
Farley, James A.   104, 128, 153, 167, 172,
   191, 198, 229
Farquhar, Harold   280
Federal Reserve Bank of New York   26
Feis, Herbert   9
Ferguson, Homer   188, 189
Fernández Cuesta, Raimundo   281
Fernandez, Raul (Brazilian Foreign Affairs
      Minister)   116
Fitz-James Stuart y Falcó, Jacobo, Duke
      of Alba   193, 271, 286
Foltz, Charles   19
Ford Co.   23
Forrestal, James V.   85, 87, 115
Fox Film Co.   23
Franco, Francisco   51, 55, 68, 74, 79, 88
   And Cold War   279
   And Luis Carrero Blanco   85, 86
   And US politics   87, 231, 232
   Anticommunism   137, 152
   As a political operator   292
   As viewed by Sir Victor Mallet   285

306 INDEX

Economic Policies 9
Meeting with Charles Clark 179, 180
Perceptions of the United States 113, 115, 117
Positions during the Second World War 271–276
Relations and perceptions regarding José Félix de Lequerica 94, 96, 159, 160, 163, 168, 217
Remains exhumed 265
US supporters, industrialists, and politicians meeting with 190, 191, 193, 194, 195, 227
Francoist dictatorship
Apparent liberalization after the Second World War 82, 92, 111, 112, 151, 142, 153
British approach to after the Second World War 279, 280, 293, 296–300
Condemnation at United Nations General Assembly 288–291
Current perceptions in Spain 266, 267
Economic policies in relation to the United States 41, 42, 44, 52, 56, 84, 90, 121, 136, 138, 141–143, 153, 172, 173, 175
Harry S. Truman and Dean Acheson hostility to 40, 53, 59, 74, 75, 119, 129, 132, 133, 124, 220, 223, 229, 230, 249, 287
Military talks with the USA 223–225
Nazi gold in Spain 107
Opposition to, focalized in several US cities 260, 261
Political nature of the regime 54, 70, 77, 144, 146, 147, 213, 214, 269, 270
Relations with the United States 46, 60, 76, 80, 105, 155, 169, 196, 199, 208, 216, 240, 247, 248, 258
Religious policies 148, 149, 171, 226, 244
Sanctions 38, 43, 56
Supporters in the United States *see* Spanish Lobby; Spanish Bloc
Frente de la Libertad 280
Frente Nacional 280
Front Nacional de Catalunya/Bloque Catalán 280

Galíndez, Jesús 128
Garrigues, Antonio 42, 53, 60, 69, 70
Garzón, Julio 109
Gaston, Herbert E. 222
General Electric 52
General Motors 23
General Petroleum Corporation 257
George, Walter 123
Gibraltar (UK colony and military base) 272, 300
Gil Robles, José María 293, 294
Gilbert, Parker 17
Giral, José 285
Gómez Jordana, Francisco (Count of Jordana) 273, 275, 280
Gordon, Guy 128, 189
Great Depression 10, 12, 28, 34, 55
Greek Civil War 84
Green Jr., William J. 184
Green, Theodore F. 189
Greenup, John C. 23
Gregory, Noel J. 184
Griffis, Stanton G. 48, 215, 216, 220, 221, 223, 224, 226, 228–231, 248
Guaranty Trust Co. 14
Gurney, John Chandler 115, 116, 119

Hammond, Ogden 104
Hankey, Robert 295
Hart, Merwin K. 104
Harvey, Oliver 285
Haselden, E. K. 179
Hayes, Carlton J. 101, 277
And OSS 49–51
As a member of the Spanish Bloc 103, 109, 137
Books on Spain 198, 252
Personal archive 77
Personal policy towards Spain 46
Relations with José Félix de Lequerica 93, 102, 105, 203
Relations with Samuel Hoare 274
Heineman, Dannie 135, 178
Hellman, Lillian 247
Hemingway, Ernest 247
Henderson, George R. (US Admiral) 190
Henderson, Loy W. 101
Hickerson, John L. 24, 81, 87, 95, 110, 113, 114, 132, 157, 163, 164, 218, 219
Hiss, Alger 125, 126
Hitler, Adolf 133, 144, 147, 249, 266, 270, 272, 278, 279

INDEX

307

Hoare, Samuel 269, 270, 272–274, 276, 290
Hoffman, Paul G. 101, 102, 104, 109
Holler-Millar, Frederick 285
Howard, Douglas 292, 295
Huete, Alfonso 9, 23, 24, 26, 32, 42
Hull, Cordell 28, 29
Humelsine, Carlisle 222

Ibáñez, José 191, 199
Ickes, Harold 106, 165, 166, 167, 198
Instituto Español de Moneda Extranjera (Spanish Institute of Foreign Currencies) 9
International Acceptance Bank 14
International Banking Corporation 23, 28
International Brigades 246, 281
International Federation of Women Lawyers (FIDA) 255
International Telephone and Telegraph Corporation (IT&T) 8, 9, 17, 23, 25, 26, 28, 31, 52
Irving Trust Co. 14
Isacson, Leo 90
Italy 17, 38, 84, 90, 91, 113, 133, 139, 142, 144, 150, 192, 193, 240, 242, 243, 245, 272, 273, 277

Jessup, Philip C. 133
Johnston, Eric A. 104, 128
Joint Committee on Foreign Economic Cooperation 170, 183, 191
Juventudes Combatientes 280

Kelly, John Eogan 104
Kennan, George 59, 80
Keogh, Eugene 127, 183, 184, 186, 211
Kiddy, Peabody & Co. 14
Kilgore, Harley M. 188, 189
Kindelan, Alfredo (Spanish General) 297
Kissner, August W. 228
Klein, Arthur J. 184
Klein, Max H. 179, 180, 204
Kluckhohn, Frank L. 15
Knights of Columbus 243, 251, 258
Kuhn, Loeb & Co. 14

Laughlin, Irwin 7, 16, 17
League of Nations 19
Leahy, William D. 118 n.143, 204, 215
Lee Higginson & Co. 14
Leffingwell, Russell C. 14, 18

Lequerica, José Félix de 81
And the United Nations 131, 134, 136, 210–214, 217, 227
Appointed Ambassador in the United States 221–222
Arrival to the United States 59, 232, 78, 79, 89, 92, 98, 101
As Minister of Foreign Affairs 78, 231, 280, 281
Asserting the members of the Spanish Lobby 187–190, 220
Creation of the Spanish Lobby 232, 70, 77, 92, 119, 121–126, 153, 154, 180, 184
Criticism in Spain 197
Negotiating loans to Spain 107, 120, 170, 176, 181, 205, 206–210
Personal profile 93 n.53, 233, 234
Political relations with Spanish authorities 94, 95, 109, 114, 167, 187, 202, 203
Pressures for his withdrawal from the United States 137, 149, 157–160, 162–165, 168, 169
Setting the Plan Otoño ("Fall Plan") see Plan Otoño
Social and political activities in the United States 97, 99, 102, 103, 105, 110, 111, 115, 117, 129, 152, 156, 166, 178
Support to the Republican Party 106 n.100, 198, 218, 231, 232
Team in the United States 100
Lerroux, Alejandro 15
Liberación Nacional Republicana 280
Lippman, Walter 102, 153
Lloyd, Father Robert S. 103
Lodge, Henry Cabot 211
London Economic Conference, 1934 22
Los Angeles Chamber of Commerce 250, 258, 261
Lovett, Robert A. 87, 101
Lufthansa 275

MacArthur, Douglas (US General) 87
MacCormick, Robert R. 88
Madariaga, Salvador de 10, 219, 292
Málaga incident 50
Mallet, Victor
Analysis of the capabilities of the Spanish Army 290, 291
And reaction in Spain to Labour victory in UK 284, 285

308 INDEX

Appointed British representative in
Spain 276
Conversations with Spanish Foreign
Affairs Minister (Martín
Artajo) 287, 292
Presenting his credentials to
Franco 281
Manufacturers Trust Company 40, 63
March, Juan 135, 177
Marshall Plan 3, 38, 40, 55, 58–60, 64,
75, 82, 83, 85, 86, 88–92, 98, 112,
113, 119, 136, 138, 148, 154, 155, 197,
202, 230, 232, 244, 292
And O'Konski Amendment 58, 90,
91
Financial support 64
Spanish aim to benefit from 59, 60,
75, 82, 83, 86, 88, 89, 92, 98,
112, 113, 136, 138, 148, 154, 155,
197, 202, 230, 232
Marshall, George C. 75, 85, 91, 102, 113,
116, 117, 119, 129, 223, 224, 225,
227, 284, 292, 293, 295
Martín Artajo, Alberto
And Franco-Perón Protocol 92
And the Spanish Lobby 109, 121, 137,
182, 187, 196, 203
And the United States 87, 89, 98,
102, 164, 210, 225, 232
Appointed as Foreign Affairs
Minister 280, 281, 285
As a Catholic militant 227, 231
Distrust of José Félix de
Lequerica 94, 96, 160, 162,
163, 168, 206, 209, 217, 220,
221, 234
Stalling tactics as Foreign
Minister 82, 84, 287, 292
Mason, George 172
Maybank, Burnet R. 123, 139
McCarran, Pat 88, 119, 123, 127, 158
As a lobbyist 76, 120, 121 n.152, 128,
136–140, 152, 156, 166, 183, 192,
198, 199, 233
Negotiate loans for Spain 122, 154,
155, 187, 203, 205–208, 222, 227
Personal archive 77
Visits to Spain 170, 182, 184, 191, 193,
195, 196
McCarthy, Joseph 89
McClellan, John L. 188–191
McCormack, John W. 152
McFadden & Bro. 57

McGucken, Joseph 254
McIntyre, Francis 243, 255
McKellar, Kenneth 123, 141, 145, 187,
189
Meière, Hildreth 104
Mendelssohn Bank 32
Mercer, Preston Virginius 85, 86, 170,
187, 191, 196
Merry del Val, Pablo 109, 124, 156, 166,
184, 192, 195
Messersmith, George Strausser 177, 178
Mexican Light & Power Company 178
Millard, Hugh 7
Ministry of Industry and Commerce
(MIC) 43, 66
Miranda y Quartín, Carlos de 115
Moffat, Jay P. 26
Montgomery, Morris 259
Morgenthau, Henry 8, 27–31
Moreno, Andrés 181
Movimiento Libertario 280
Mukden incident 10
Multer, Abraham J. 184
Muñoz Grandes, Agustín (Spanish
General) 297
Murphy, James J. 191
Mussolini, Benito 91, 133, 144, 147, 249,
266, 269, 270, 273, 279

National Association 14
National City Bank 9, 14, 23, 31, 39, 44,
102, 108
National Foreign Trade Council 24, 68
National Institute of Industry (INI) 53,
61, 65, 66, 83, 107, 136, 181
National Security Act 292
NATO 138, 142, 148, 200, 202, 223, 224,
225, 244, 268, 300
Navasqües Ruiz de Velasco, Emilio
de 83, 84
Nazi Germany see Third Reich
Negrín, Juan 251, 285
New York Trust Co. 14
Nixon, Richard 262
Norris, Paulson 257
Nye, Edward V. 189

O'Konski, Alvin 77, 78, 79, 89–92, 119
O'Konski Amendment 58, 79, 88, 92,
107, 112
Office of Strategic Services
(OSS) 47–52, 54, 58, 104

INDEX

Operation Gymnast 272; *see also* Operation Torch
Operation Husky 272
Operation Overlord 275
Operation Torch 48, 272, 273, 300
Oswald, Victor 42

Page, Frank 31
Pan Gómez, Pedro 9, 26, 28–31
Paramount Pictures 48
Partido Republicano Español 280
Pawley, William D. 117, 118, 224, 225
Peñamil, Pedro 256
Pereira, Teotónio 97
Perón, Juan Domingo 54, 59, 92
Pérez del Arco, José 243, 259
  And social life in Los Angeles 255, 256, 260
  Background 253
  Becoming consul in Los Angeles 250, 252
  Lecture series on Spain 257, 258
Peurifoy, John E. 204
Piniés, Jaime de 184, 212 n.407
Plan Otoño "Fall Plan" 186
  Guests in Spain under the scheme 179, 183, 191, 195, 198
  Origins 182, 170
  Outline of objectives 127, 169, 182
  Results 204, 233
  Similar schemes 190
Poage, William R. 184
Pius XII, Pope 192
Portela Valladares, Manuel 32
Porter, Paul B. 222
Portugal 78, 89, 184, 155, 191, 232, 241, 273, 276
POUM (Partido Obrero de Unificación Marxista) 280
Pratt, Jack 50
Price, Francis 259
Prieto, Indalecio 18, 19, 21, 213, 216, 219, 251, 285, 293, 294
Primo de Rivera, José Antonio 265
Primo de Rivera, Miguel 11, 12
  Dictatorship 9, 193 n.344
Primo de Rivera, Miguel (Spanish Ambassador to the UK) 298
PSOE (Partido Socialista Obrero Español) 280

Queuille, Henri 192

Ramsay, Scott 6
Randall 83
Rankin, John E. 152
Reader's Digest 52
Reciprocal Trade Agreements Act (RTAA) 8, 22, 25
Reid, Whitelaw 102
Relations with José Félix de Lequerica 181
Richards, James T. 183, 184, 186, 205
Rieber, Thorkild 101, 102
Rifkind, Simon H. 54
Rivers, Mendel 152
Roberts, Frank 291
Rodríguez, Jesús 45
Roosevelt, Archibald 58 n.232
Roosevelt, Eleanor 132, 133, 137, 211, 250
Roosevelt, Franklin Delano 7, 9, 102, 104
  Administration style 29, 75, 116, 167
  And Harry S. Truman as Vice President 124, 171
  Death 277, 278
  Internationalism and Spanish politics 10, 22, 25, 287
  Relations with Winston Churchill regarding Spain 269, 273, 274, 276, 282
  Sales of arms to Spain 125
  US economic relations with Spain 20, 30, 45
Ruiz Jiménez, Joaquín 100
Russell, Richard B. 188, 189
Ryan, Frank T. 41, 66, 104, 128
  And Marshall Plan 60
  Relations with Alfred Barth 53, 61, 68
  Return to corporate world 52, 58
  Working for the OSS 49–51, 57

S. B. Smith Co. 25
Salazar, Oliveira 89, 117, 276
Sánchez Román, Felipe 15
Sánchez, Pedro (Spanish Prime Minister) 266
Santa Clara University 241
Sanz Briz, Ángel 100
Sanz-Orrio, Fermín 136, 151
Sayre, Francis B. 24
Scott, Joseph (Joe) 256, 167
Second Spanish Republic 6, 9, 244

Exile   91, 93 n.53, 207, 241, 245, 251, 254, 260, 297
Fall   35
Foreign Policy   10
Loans awarded to   44
Monetary System   11
Possible restoration after the Second World War   281, 285, 287
Proclamation   16–18
United States and   7, 131, 142, 148, 150, 246, 247, 253, 256
Segura Pérez del Arco, María Teresa   255
Segura, Pedro (Primate Cardinal of Spain)   172
Senate Tariff Commission   25
Sentís, Carlos   109
Sherman, Forrest (US Admiral)   86, 200, 214, 224, 225, 227, 231
Sicre, Ricardo   58
Singer Sewing Machine Company   278
Smoot–Hawley tariff   13, 19
Sociedad Española de Beneficia Mutua   256
Société de Banque Suisse   54
Société Financière de Transports et Enterprises Industrielles-SOFINA   135, 178
SOFINDUS   108
Soviet Union
    And Korean War   231
    And Spain   197, 249, 251, 289, 291
    And the event of a nuclear war   268, 299
    As a political topic used by Spanish officials   105, 142, 232
    British policy towards   282, 283
    Franco sending the Blue Division to   272
    Growing tension with the United States   59, 74, 79, 125, 249
    Opposing Spain in the United Nations   80, 84, 111, 113, 209, 244, 250
    And O'Konski amendment   90
Spanish Bloc
    As different to the Spanish Lobby   75, 119, 128, 232, 234, 242
    Growing importance   210
    Members of the group   87, 103, 147
    Propagandist activities   198, 199
Spanish Institute of Foreign Currency (IEME)   40, 43, 45–48, 53, 54, 56, 57, 59, 61, 62, 66, 68, 69, 108

Spanish Lobby
    Activities   128, 136, 147, 232, 234, 249, 260, 262, 281
    Defining the concept   74
    Studies on the concept   39, 122, 242
Spanish National Treasury   45
Spanish protectorate of Morocco   56
Spanish Telephone Company (CTNE)   8
Spanish Tobacco Monopoly   25
Spellman, Francis (US Cardinal)   103, 106, 118 n.143, 137, 192, 214
Stalin (Iósif Vissariónovich Dzhugashvili)   245, 249, 275, 276
Standard Oil   52, 107
Stanford University   241
State Department's Division of Western European Affairs (DWEA)   9, 16, 24, 26, 30, 31
Stephenson, William   57
Stettinius, Edward   57, 284
Stockholm's Enskilda Bank   14
Suanzes, Juan Antonio   61, 65, 66, 69, 109, 121, 181, 182, 185, 191, 205, 206, 207, 220, 222, 234
Subversive Activities Control Act   222
Surrey, Walter Sterling   65

Taft, Robert A.   106, 123 n.160, 137, 144, 147, 226 n.456
Talbot, Francis X.   104
TEXACO   97
Third Reich   8, 46, 51, 91, 108, 213, 240, 244, 270–272, 277, 278
Thomas, Elmer   189
Thorning, Father Joseph F.   77, 103, 109, 123–125, 152
Thorp, Willard L.   152
Traction Light & Power "La Canadiense"   135, 177
Trading With the Enemy Act   48
Tripartite Stabilization Agreement   22
Trippe, Juan   123
Trujillo, Rafael Leónidas   120, 127
Truman, Harry S.
    And Marshall Plan   88
    And O'Konski amendment   91
    And the religious freedom in Spain   171, 172, 204, 223, 225, 248
    And United States–United Kingdom possible joint intervention in Spain   245

INDEX 311

And US officials' visits to Spain 170, 176, 177
Changing attitude towards Spain 59, 74, 75, 76, 80, 81, 128, 129, 196, 200, 205, 206, 208, 209–216, 220, 226, 228, 230, 231, 235, 244, 249, 260, 287, 295
Foreign Policy 55, 284
Loans to Spain 61, 106, 136, 147, 198, 207
Reaction to Spanish lobbyists 120, 221, 229
Reelection 60, 78, 105, 114, 118, 134, 136, 148, 178
Relations with Patrick Clark 124, 125, 169, 175, 179
Turkey 84, 225
TWA 52
Tydings, Millard E. 189

U.S. Central Intelligence Agency (CIA) 61, 101, 104
U.S. Commercial Company (USCC) 47–50
U.S. Federal Reserve 11, 14, 27, 43
U.S. Reciprocal Trade Agreements Act (RTAA) 7, 25
U.S. Treasury Department 8, 11, 27, 29, 30, 45, 46, 56, 84, 138
UGT (Unión General de Trabajadores) 280
UNESCO (United Nations Educational, Scientific, and Cultural Organization) 257
Unió Democràtica 280
United Kingdom Commercial Company (UKCC) 47
United Nations (UN) 38, 106, 121, 131, 193 n.344, 194, 197, 202, 256, 257, 284
United Press 52, 101, 102, 109
University of New York 246
Urrutia, Víctor 95

US Defense Department 176, 226, 227, 249
US Senate Agriculture and Forestry Committee 188, 189
US Senate Appropriations Committee 120, 123, 139, 154, 191, 200, 207
US Senate Armed Services Committee 115, 188
US Senate Committee on Agriculture 184
US Senate Committee on Banking and Currency 188
US Senate Finance Committee 123, 187, 188, 189
US Senate Foreign Relations Committee 87, 123, 133, 137, 139, 141, 144, 200, 206

Vacuum Oil Co. 23
Valley of the Fallen 265–267
Vandenberg, Arthur H. 87, 106, 137, 156, 189
Vandenberg, Hoyt S. (US General) 200
Varela, Juan 297
Vaughan, Harry Hawkins (US General) 124, 175, 221, 230
Ventosa, Juan 14–16
Vila, Manuel 42
Villanueva, Miguel 15

Wais, Julio 12–14
Waste Materials Unit 51
Webb, James E. 147, 163, 173
Weintal, Edward 102
Welles, Orson 247
Willoughby, Charles A. (US General) 87, 137 n.204, 199
World Commerce Corporation (WCC) 40, 41, 57, 58, 66, 68, 70

Young, Milton R. 189
Yturralde, Mariano de 83, 205

Printed in the United States
by Baker & Taylor Publisher Services